HEINEMANN MATHEMATICS P7

Teacher's Notes

Heinemann Mathematics P7 is intended for use with children
- working in Key Stage 2 or Key Stage 3, mainly at Levels 4 and 5, of the National Curriculum (England and Wales)
- working in Key Stage 2, mainly at Levels 4 and 5, of the Common Curriculum (Northern Ireland) and
- completing Level D and moving into Level E of Mathematics 5–14 (Scotland).

Heinemann Educational Publishers,
Halley Court, Jordan Hill, Oxford OX2 8EJ
a division of Reed Educational and Professional Publishing Ltd

OXFORD   FLORENCE   PRAGUE   MADRID   ATHENS
MELBOURNE   AUCKLAND   KUALA LUMPUR   SINGAPORE   TOKYO
IBADAN   NAIROBI   KAMPALA   JOHANNESBURG   GABORONE
PORTSMOUTH NH (USA)   CHICAGO   MEXICO CITY   SAO PAULO

Writing team
John T Blair
Ian K Clark
Aileen P Duncan
Percy W Farren
Archie MacCallum
Myra A Pearson
Dorothy S Simpson
John W Thayers
David K Thomson

Designed by Miller, Craig & Cocking
Produced by Gecko Limited, Bicester, Oxon

Printed in the UK by Scotprint Ltd, Edinburgh.

ISBN 0 435 02268 7

Preface

Heinemann Mathematics is a balanced course which provides progression and continuity from nursery through the infant and junior stages to secondary level. It aims to help children to apply mathematics in a variety of situations. The course draws on feedback from practising teachers and experience gained through classroom use of the SPMG materials 'Primary Mathematics – A development through activity'.

A practical approach

The course is based on the belief that mathematics is best learned through practical experience and discussion. The use of materials, diagrams, and pictures is encouraged throughout the Heinemann Mathematics course to help pupils acquire concepts and understand techniques.

Problem solving

There is emphasis on problem solving and investigative activity. Pupils are encouraged to apply their mathematics to solve practical, simulated and real problems. In addition to the problem solving work in the Textbook and Workbook, there are further ideas in the Problem Solving Activities booklet in the Assessment and Resources Pack.

Contexts

Mathematics is presented in a variety of contexts, some related to the world outside the classroom and others to the world of the children's imagination. Such contexts are more likely to stimulate an interest in mathematics and encourage positive attitudes.

Calculation

Heinemann Mathematics encourages mental, paper and pencil, and calculator methods of calculation. All these methods are used in the Textbook, Workbook, Extension Textbook and Reinforcement Sheets.

Approach to learning and teaching

The approach adopted in Heinemann Mathematics fits well with the guidelines provided by the National Curriculum (England and Wales), Mathematics 5–14 (Scotland) and the Northern Ireland Common Curriculum. The course has been designed to provide teachers with resources and a structure to meet the requirements of each curriculum.

Assessment

There is an Assessment booklet in the Assessment and Resources Pack. It contains Check-ups and Round-ups related to the sections of work in the Textbook and Workbook.

Teachers may also wish to select specific questions from the Textbook and Workbook for use in assessment.

Contents

Introduction

Heinemann Mathematics P7 is intended for use with children
- working in Key Stage 2 or Key Stage 3, mainly at levels 4 and 5, of the National Curriculum (England and Wales)
- working in Key Stage 2, mainly at levels 4 and 5 of the Common Curriculum (Northern Ireland) and
- completing level D and moving into level E of Mathematics 5–14 (Scotland).

FORMAT OF THE COURSE

The Heinemann Mathematics P7 materials consist of
- Textbook
- Workbook
- Extension Textbook
- Reinforcement Sheets
- Teacher's Notes
- Answer Book
- Assessment and Resources Pack
- Home Link-Up

The Teacher's Notes suggest activities for introducing mathematical concepts and techniques. Written work for children is then provided in the Textbook and Workbook.

The Teacher's Notes also contain suggestions for further consolidation and additional activities. The Extension Textbook and Reinforcement Sheets supply activities to enrich and consolidate the children's learning. Assessment material related to the content of Heinemann Mathematics P7 is included in the Assessment and Resources Pack. Home Link-Up provides homework activities related to the core material.

TEXTBOOK AND WORKBOOK

The Textbook contains sections of work as outlined below. The Workbook is linked to the Textbook and referenced from it.

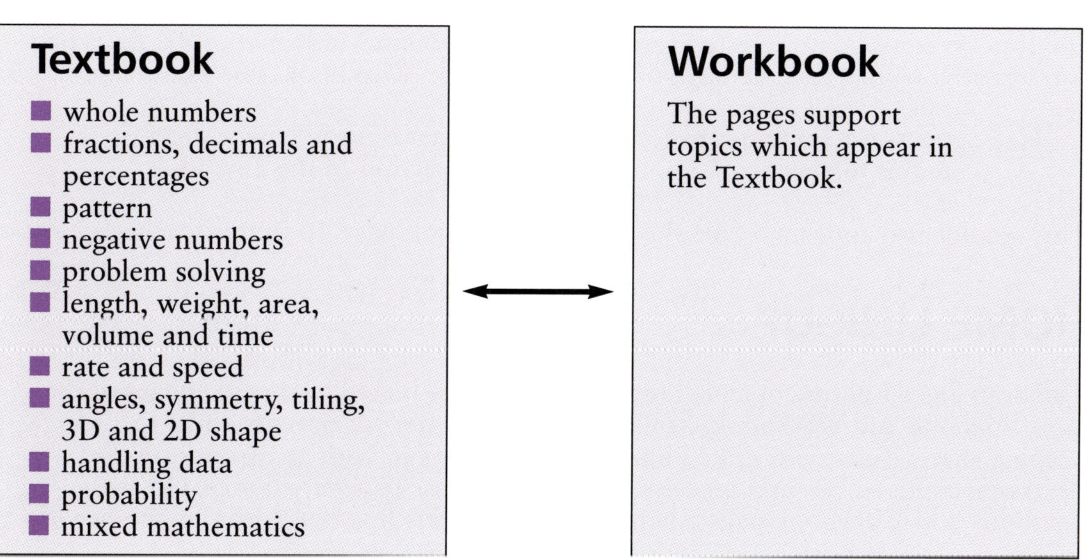

Charts giving details of the mathematical content of Heinemann Mathematics P7 are given on pages 8 to 13.

Number, algebra and money work should be used in more or less the order in which it appears, to provide a continuous development. **Measure, Shape and Handling Data sections should be interspersed with number work** to give balanced coverage of the various aspects of mathematics. The order in which the Measure, Shape and Handling Data sections are used is fairly flexible, and at the teacher's discretion. The end of each section of work is indicated by the instruction

> **Ask your teacher what to do next.**

Some of the pages in the Textbook contain references to a Workbook page where the development of the section is continued. For example on Textbook page 2 there is the instruction

> **Go to Workbook page 1.**

Some of the pages in the Workbook contain references back to the Textbook. For example, the following appears on Workbook page 1.

> **Go to Textbook page 3.**

EXTENSION TEXTBOOK

The Extension Textbook contains work to extend some topics featured in the Textbook and Workbook of Heinemann Mathematics P7. It also provides other activities to enrich the children's experience of mathematics.

References to Extension Textbook pages which are appropriate to particular sections of work are included in the Overviews for those sections in the Teacher's Notes. The Record of Work grids at the back of the Workbook also show how the Extension Textbook relates to the other materials comprising Heinemann Mathematics.

REINFORCEMENT SHEETS

This booklet contains photocopiable sheets designed to provide further practice for children, to consolidate selected topics from Heinemann Mathematics P7. Each page is referenced from a specific page of the Textbook or Workbook. For example,

$\boxed{\text{R4}}$ appears on Textbook page 10 to indicate that reinforcement sheet 4 contains further work appropriate to that section of the Textbook.

This symbol also appears beside the note for Textbook page 10 in the Teacher's Notes.

HOME LINK-UP

This contains 65 photocopiable homework activities linked to specific pages of the core Textbook and Workbook, as well as a model letter for parents and a record-keeping sheet. Pages with linked homework are marked with an asterisk on the Textbook contents list, and on the Overview pages in Teacher's Notes. On the Textbook and Workbook pages themselves, H appears in a box with the number of the activity beside it. For example, $\boxed{\text{H3}}$ on Textbook page 5 (and beside the note for that page in the Teachers Notes) indicates that the work on page 5 is supported by Activity 3 in the Home Link-up book.

SPECIAL FEATURES

Other activity pages

These pages are identified in the Textbook, Workbook and Extension Textbook by a **purple** box containing the teacher's heading and the page number. They are intended to give further opportunities for the children to apply the mathematics they have been learning, or to extend their experience. The Record of Work grids at the back of the Workbook show where these pages are located in the Textbook and Extension Textbook.

These pages can be used in any order as long as the related concepts have been met by the children. The teaching notes for these pages give appropriate advice about this. The teacher should choose when one of the activities is to be used, and the children for whom it is appropriate.

Problem solving

Problem solving

Throughout the Textbook and Workbook, 'flags' have been used to indicate that a page or a question contains this type of work. These flags also appear in the Teacher's Notes. The problem solving flag indicates work of a non-routine nature that will require mathematical thinking if the children are to find a solution. Some of this work may also be described as investigative as the children are involved in finding out about a mathematical situation for themselves.

A short section on problem solving is included in the Heinemann P7 Textbook.

Problem solving flags do not appear on Extension Textbook pages as a great deal of the work is of this nature.

Calculators

This symbol is used to indicate that a calculator is specifically recommended. However calculators may be used throughout to introduce concepts, to extend the work in some aspects and in problem solving.

Contexts

Most of the activities in the Textbook and Workbook are set in a context. For example, the section of work on decimals is related to the theme of 'Orlando', a holiday cruise ship, while the sections on fractions and percentages involve 'Kitbits', a company which manufactures various model and toy kits.

Further details about contexts are given on page 14 in the section 'Using the Course'.

TEACHER'S NOTES

The Teacher's Notes are the central element of the course. They make suggestions about teaching methods, mathematical content and assessment. Ways of introducing and developing contexts are discussed. The notes also include advice about how the Textbook, Workbook and other materials in Heinemann Mathematics P7 might be used to provide a well-balanced course for a school's programme of study.

For each section of work, an 'Overview' describes the purpose and content of the Textbook and/or Workbook pages. 'Resources' for the section are also listed.

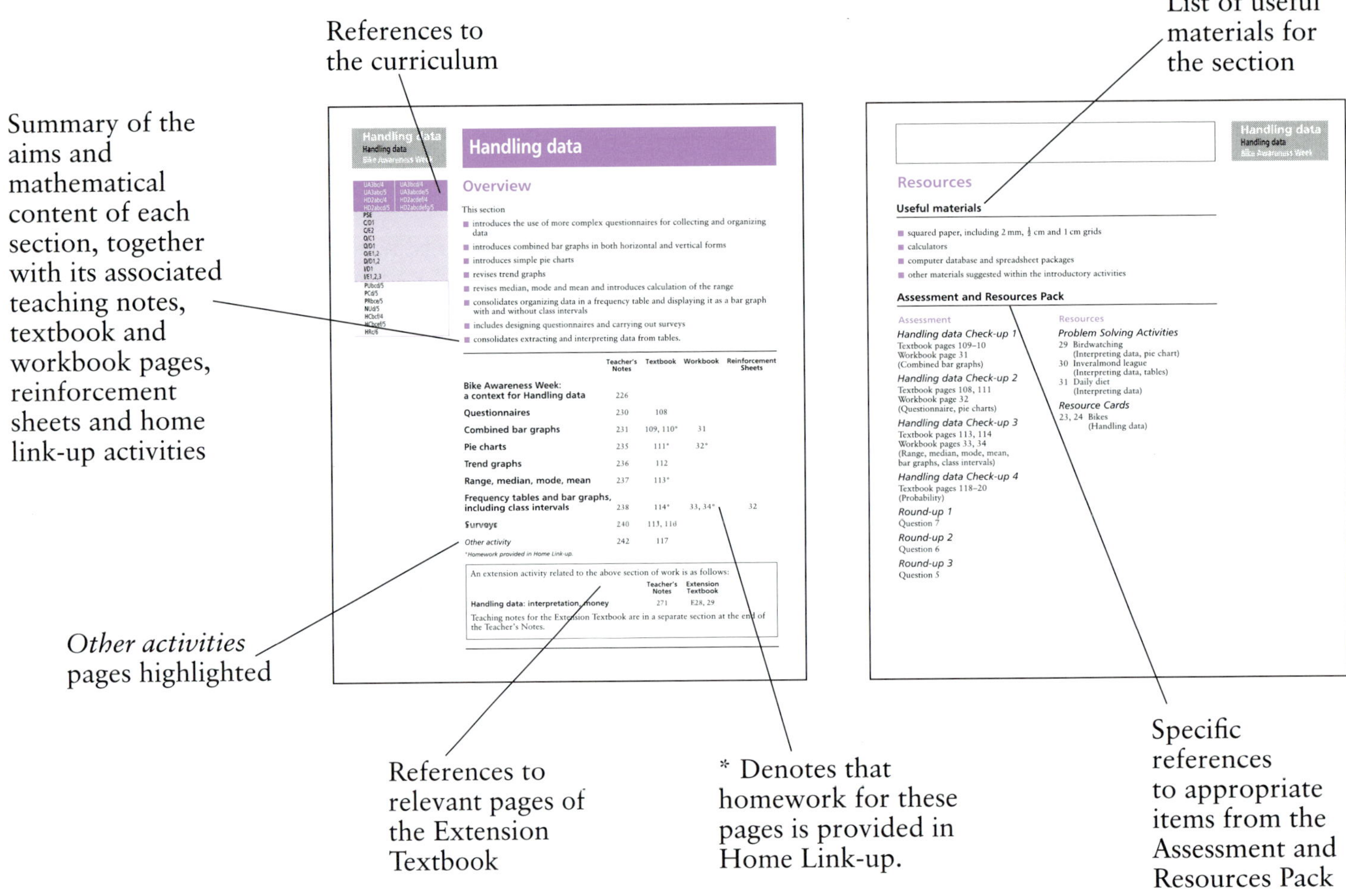

Summary of the aims and mathematical content of each section, together with its associated teaching notes, textbook and workbook pages, reinforcement sheets and home link-up activities

Other activities pages highlighted

References to the curriculum

References to relevant pages of the Extension Textbook

* Denotes that homework for these pages is provided in Home Link-up.

List of useful materials for the section

Specific references to appropriate items from the Assessment and Resources Pack

These pages are supported by teaching notes which provide
- advice about introducing any extended context used in the section of work
- references to the curriculum
- a variety of activities from which the teacher can select to introduce each new section of the work. The activities marked with a (O—) indicate those which are essential to a smooth progression of teaching and learning. There are also activities marked with a which lend themselves to being taught with a class or group. See page 298 for a list of materials needed to resource Heinemann Mathematics P7.
- notes about pages in the Textbook or Workbook which relate to that section of work
- occasional additional activities to give further practice or enrichment
- notes about any 'other activity' pages which appear in this part of the Textbook.
- reference to activities, marked with a , which promote the development of mental skills and techniques.

Teaching notes for the Extension Textbook appear in a separate section at the end of the main Teacher's Notes.

ANSWER BOOK

The Answerbook contains lists of answers for the Textbook and Extension Textbook pages and photo reductions of the Workbook pages with the answers inserted.

ASSESSMENT AND RESOURCES PACK

The pack contains assessment and resource material, including photocopiable record sheets. The teacher should select materials from the pack to suit the needs of particular children.

Assessment

The Assessment booklet contains twenty-five Check-ups. Fourteen are related to number, four to measure, three to shape and four to handling data. There are also three short Round-ups, each containing a number of questions related to the same theme and covering a range of mathematical topics. The work is presented as photocopiable sheets for use with children.

The booklet provides advice to teachers, answers and curriculum references.

Problem Solving Activities

This booklet contains thirty-five activities in the form of photocopiable sheets for children. These are intended to supplement the problem solving activities in the Textbook, Workbook and Extension Textbook. They could be used for assessment purposes. Some of the activities are specifically designed to make use of a calculator. The booklet offers advice to teachers and provides answers.

Resource Cards

The Resource Cards contain games and activities for children. They are linked to the work in the Textbook, Workbook and Teacher's Notes and, in some cases, use the same contexts. A booklet of notes for teachers gives details about preparing and using the cards.

References to the Curriculum

Detailed references to the National Curriculum (England and Wales), Mathematics 5–14 (Scotland) and Common Curriculum (Northern Ireland) are included in the Teacher's Notes in the Overview to each section of work and in the Assessment and Resources Pack. These references are provided as an aid to planning and recording.

National Curriculum (England and Wales)

■ In some cases teachers may find it helpful to record a child's progress against the Key Stage 3 Programme of Study. The Teacher's Notes therefore contain detailed references to the Programme of Study statements within Key Stage 2 and Key Stage 3. The following code is used to identify the sections:

UA Using and Applying Mathematics   **N** Number   **SSM** Shape, Space and Measures   **HD** Handling Data

Key Stage 3 has an additional section: **A** Algebra

Key Stage 2 references are given first. On the Overview pages they look like this:

Key Stage 2 | **Key Stage 3**

This is how they appear on the page notes:

Key Stage 2
Key Stage 3

The referencing shows each section, subsection, part and level.

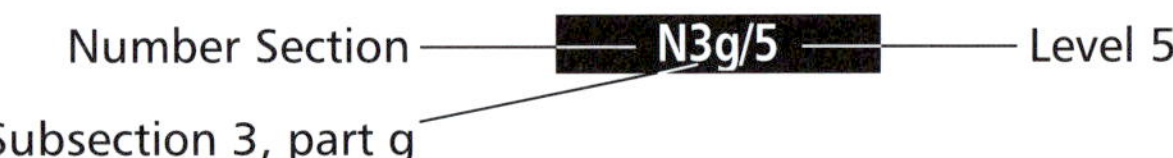

■ Some of the outcomes specified in the Programme of Study statements relate to skills and concepts which children develop over an extended period. In these circumstances the level is sometimes indicated by an arrow. For example,

N3e/4→5

refers to Number work appropriate to children at Level 4 'working towards' a statement which is at Level 5 in the level descriptions.

■ The work in a section of Heinemann Mathematics P7, or even on a single page, frequently relates to more than one subsection or part. On these occasions, for economy of presentation, statements at the same level in a section are combined. For example,

N2a,3e/5

■ Within each section, Subsection 1 overarches all the other subsections. As the Heinemann Mathematics course includes coverage of all the statements in these other sections, no references to Subsection 1 statements are included.

Mathematics 5–14 (Scotland)

In the *Mathematics 5–14 Guidelines*, the following code is used:

Attainment Outcome	Strand	Code
PROBLEM SOLVING AND ENQUIRY		PSE
INFORMATION HANDLING	Collect Organize Display Interpret	C O D I
NUMBER, MONEY AND MEASUREMENT	Range and Type of Numbers Money Add and Subtract Multiply and Divide Round Numbers Fractions, Percentages and Ratio Patterns and Sequences Functions and Equations Measure and Estimate Time Perimeter, Formulae, Scales	RTN M AS MD RN FPR PS FE ME T PFS
SHAPE, POSITION AND MOVEMENT	Range of Shapes Position and Movement Symmetry Angle	RS PM S A

Each reference then consists of the *strand* code followed by the appropriate *level* and the *target*. For example.

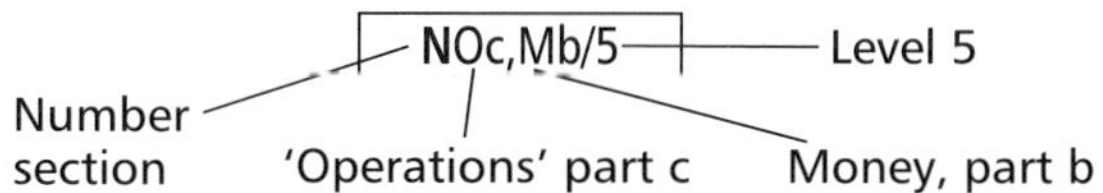

Common Curriculum (Northern Ireland)

For Northern Ireland, references are made to the Key Stage 2 Programme of Study. The five sections and their subsections are coded as follows:

PROCESSES	Using mathematics Communicating Reasoning	PU PC PR
NUMBER	Understanding and notation Patterns, relationships and sequences Operations and their application Money	NU NP NO NM
MEASURES	Measures	M
SHAPE AND SPACE	Exploration of shape Position, movement and direction	SE SP
HANDLING DATA	Collect, interpret and represent data Introduction to probability	HC HP

The reference shows each *section*, *subsection*, *part* and *level*. Sometimes different subsections of the same section may be combined, as follows:

A small amount of work extends into Key Stage 3 and is marked as Level 6.

DEVELOPMENT CHARTS

The following charts outline the mathematical content of Heinemann Mathematics 6 and P7. They relate to Mathematics in the National Curriculum (England and Wales), Mathematics 5–14 (Scotland), and the Common Curriculum of Northern Ireland.

Mathematics in the National

Using and applying mathematics	Number	
	Knowledge and use of numbers	**Algebra**
HEINEMANN MATHEMATICS 6 Practical tasks, mathematical and real-life problems and investigations occur throughout	Mental addition and subtraction Place value to millions Rounding: – two- and three-digit whole numbers to the nearest 10 and 100 – four-digit numbers to the nearest 100 and 1000 Adding and subtracting three- and four-digit whole numbers with/without a calculator Checking addition and subtraction when using a calculator Mental multiplication and division using tables Multiplying mentally two- and three-digit whole numbers by 10 and 100 Multiplying three- and four-digit whole numbers by 2 to 9 with/without a calculator Dividing three- and four-digit whole numbers by 2 to 10 with/without a calculator, checking answers, interpreting answers, rounding a calculator display to the nearest appropriate unit Money: $+$, $-$, $\times$, $\div$, with/without a calculator Multiplying and dividing by a two-digit whole number with/without a calculator Fractions: – simple equivalences – fractions of quantities, eg '$\frac{1}{10}$ of' – fractions of a whole number – mixed numbers One- and two-place decimals: – adding and subtracting with/without a calculator – multiplying mentally by 10 – multiplying and dividing with a calculator Percentages: – concept, 100% is 1 whole – simple percentages of quantities, eg '10% of'	Patterns and relationships in multiplication tables and other topics Recognizing and continuing sequences including square and triangular numbers Use of simple function machines for operations Using and identifying simple word formulae in context
HEINEMANN MATHEMATICS P7 Practical tasks, mathematical and real-life problems and investigations occur throughout	Whole numbers: – mental addition and subtraction – adding and subtracting four-digit numbers – rounding to the nearest 1000 and 100 – mental multiplication and division, table facts, multiples, factors – multiplying: mentally by 10, 100 and 1000; by multiples of 10 and 100; four-digit numbers by 2 to 9 – dividing: mentally by 10, 100 and 1000; multiples of 10 by 2 to 10; four-digit numbers by 2 to 9 – place value to hundreds of millions – using a calculator: rounding answers after division, exact remainders, checking answers, checking by using inverse operations, using the memory Fractions – understanding and using equivalent fractions, mixed numbers and improper fractions; simplification – adding and subtracting fractions, including mixed numbers – multiplying: a whole number times a fraction; fraction of a whole number Decimals: – notation and place value for decimals to 3 places – adding and subtracting one- and two-place decimals – multiplying and dividing: one- and two-place decimals by 2 to 9 and by 10 and 100 – multiplying mentally by 1000 – approximating and estimating – using a calculator, checking and interpreting answers Percentages: – concept, 100% as 1 whole – calculating percentages of quantities, with/without a calculator – fractions as percentages, with/without a calculator – understanding and using interrelationships between fractions, decimals and percentages Negative numbers: concept, 'positive' and 'negative', ordering, adding and subtracting (informally) Problem solving: developing strategies, listing, trial and improvement, simulation/modelling, logical thinking Multiplying and dividing by a two-digit whole number, without a calculator	Exploring number and shape patterns; square numbers, square roots, triangular numbers Continuing sequences and recognizing rules Interpreting and generalising simple relationships Constructing, interpreting and evaluating formulae expressed in words and in symbols coverage at Level 3 coverage at Level 4 coverage at Level 4–5 coverage at Level 5 coverage at Level 5–6

Development Chart

Curriculum (England and Wales)

Shape, Space and Measures		Handling Data
Shape, position and movement	**Measures**	
Using co-ordinates to locate a point Collecting, discussing and making: – 2D shapes including parallelograms, equilateral and isosceles triangles and circles, using side, angle, diagonal, congruent, radius, diameter, circumference – 3D shapes including cubes, cuboids, triangular prisms and pyramids, using face, edge, vertex; recognizing nets of pyramids and prisms Turning through angles given in degrees, eight point compass Creating paths, shapes and rotating patterns using computer turtle graphics Line symmetry – completing shapes and patterns; 4 lines of symmetry; rotational symmetry Comparing angles – right, acute, obtuse Measuring angles accurately within 5 degrees	Choosing and using standard units – length, m, cm – weight, kg, g – area, cm^2, m^2 – volume, litre, ml, cm^3 Relationship between units – 1km = 1000m – 1l = 1000ml = $1000cm^3$ Choosing and using appropriate units and instruments, interpreting numbers on a range of measuring instruments with appropriate accuracy Calculating perimeters of simple shapes in m and cm Using simple scales to calculate true lengths Areas of irregular shapes, rectangles and composite shapes in cm^2 by counting squares Volumes of cuboids and prisms in cm^3 by counting cubes Time: reading and writing times to the nearest minute, am/pm, durations including counting on and back in hours and minutes, 24-hour notation including simple durations, timing in seconds	Constructing and interpreting pictograms, bar, bar-line and trend graphs Interpreting data – by identifying the mode and median – by calculating the mean Constructing and interpreting bar graphs for grouped data Organizing and interpreting data using a computer database or spreadsheet Conducting a survey Probability: – understanding and using ideas of 'likelihood' – distinguishing between 'fair' and 'unfair' – listing possible outcomes of an event
Angles: – acute, right, straight, obtuse, reflex – measuring and drawing angles to the nearest 5° and 1° – calculating angle sizes where angles total 90° or 180° or 360° – bearings Line and rotational symmetry Regular shapes Translating a shape to make a tiling 3D shape: – recognizing nets of pyramids and prisms – finding relationships between the number of faces, vertices and edges of pyramids and prisms 2D shape: – consolidating side, angle and symmetry properties of triangles and quadrilaterals – exploring diagonal properties of squares and rectangles – constructing rigid frameworks by forming triangles – parallel lines, co-ordinate grids	Choosing and using standard units – length, mm, cm – weight, g, kg, tonne – area, cm^2, m^2, km^2 – volume, litre, ml, cm^3 – speed, metres per second, kilometres per hour Understanding relationships between units – 1 cm = 10 mm – 1 kg = 1000 g – 1 tonne = 1000 kg Imperial units in daily use and their approximate metric equivalents Length: – finding perimeter of shapes – using the formulae $P = 4 \times L$ and $P = 2 \times L + 2 \times B$ – using simple scales to calculate true lengths and scaled lengths; drawing to scale Area: – finding areas of irregular shapes, right-angled triangles and composite shapes – finding areas of rectangles using the formula $A = L \times B$ – areas in m^2 and km^2 Finding volumes of cuboids using the formula $V = L \times B \times H$ Understanding and using compound measures of rate and speed Time: 12- and 24-hour notation, finding durations in hours and in minutes, counting on and back Relating circumference and diameter	Constructing and interpreting – combined bar graphs – pie charts – trend graphs Organizing data in a frequency table and displaying it as a bar graph, with/without class intervals. Finding the median, mode, mean and range of a set of data Designing and using data collection sheets and questionnaires, conducting surveys Extracting and interpreting data from tables Probability: – understanding and using ideas of 'likelihood' – understanding and using a probability scale with markings 0, $\frac{1}{2}$, 1 – listing possible outcomes of events, estimating probabilities – distinguishing between 'fair' and 'unfair'

	Problem Solving and Enquiry	Information Handling	Range and Type of Numbers	Money	Add and Subtract	Multiply and Divide	Round Numbers	Fractions Percentages and Ratio
					Number, Money			
HEINEMANN MATHEMATICS 6	Problem solving and investigations occur throughout	Constructing and interpreting pictograms, bar, bar-line and trend graphs Interpreting data – by identifying the mode (most frequent) and median (middle) – by calculating the average or 'mean' Constructing and interpreting bar graphs for grouped data Organizing and interpreting data using a database and spreadsheet Conducting a survey	Whole numbers: – to 100 000 (count, order, read/write) – to millions (read/write) Fractions: – to hundredths – simple equivalences – mixed numbers with halves and quarters Decimals: working with one- and two-place decimals Percentages: – concept – 100% is 1 whole Negative numbers (temperature)	+, −, ×, ÷ of money with / without a calculator	Mental addition and subtraction Adding and subtracting three- and four-digit whole numbers with/without a calculator Checking addition and subtraction when using a calculator Adding and subtracting one- and two-place decimals with/without a calculator	Mental multiplication and division using all tables to 10 Multiplying mentally two- and three-digit numbers by 10 and 100 Multiplying three- and four-digit whole numbers by 2 to 9 with/without a calculator Mutliplying and dividing by a two-digit whole number with/ without a calculator Dividing three- and four-digit whole numbers by 2 to 10 with/without a calculator; checking and interpreting answers Multiplying mentally one- and two-place decimals by 10 Multiplying and dividing one- and two-place decimals with a calculator	Rounding: – two- and three-digit numbers to the nearest 10 and 100 – four-digit numbers to the nearest 100 and 1000 Checking addition and subtraction calculations Rounding a calculator display to the nearest appropriate unit	Finding simple fractions of quantities involving two- and three-digit numbers Finding simple percentages of quantities
HEINEMANN MATHEMATICS P7	Problem solving and Investigation occurs throughout. Additionally, a specific section in the Text-book deals with developing strategies: – produce an organized list – guess, check and improve – simulate, 'act it out' – reason logically	Collecting and organizing data using a questionnaire, frequency table, diagrams Constructing and interpreting – bar graphs – bar-line graphs – trend graphs – compound bar graphs – pie charts Interpreting data – by identifying the mode and median – by calculating the mean and range Constructing and interpreting bar graphs for grouped data Organizing and interpreting data using a database and spreadsheet Conducting a survey	Whole numbers: Place value to hundreds of millions Fractions: – all widely used fractions and equivalences among these – mixed numbers and improper fractions, simplification Decimals: – notation and place value to three places Percentages: – concept – 100% is 1 whole – relationships with fractions, decimals Negative numbers: – concept, 'positive and negative' – ordering	+, −, ×, ÷ of money with/without a calculator Mental calculation, approximate costs	Whole numbers: Mental addition and subtraction Adding and subtracting four-digit numbers Decimals: – adding and subtracting one- and two-place decimals – approximating and estimating answers Calculator: – checking using inverse operations – using the memory Negative numbers: – informal addition and subtraction	Whole numbers: Mental multiplication and division, table facts, multiples, factors Multiplying and dividing mentally by 10, 100 and 1000 Mental multiplication by multiples of 10 and 100 Mental division of multiples of 10 by 2 to 10 Multiplication and division of four-digit numbers by 2 to 9 Multiplication and division by a two-digit number, without a calculator Multiplication and division using a calculator – rounding answers after division – exact remainders – checking answers – checking using inverse operations – using the memory Decimals: multiplying and dividing one- and two-place decimals – by 2 to 9 – mentally, by 10 and 100 Mental multiplication by 1000 Using a calculator, interpreting answers	Rounding to the nearest 100, 1000 Rounding answers after division by calculator	Adding and subtracting fractions, mixed numbers Multiplying a whole number times a fraction Finding fractions of whole numbers, with/without a calculator Finding percentages of quantities, with/ without a calculator Fractions as percentages, with/ without a calculator

Development Chart

(Scotland)

	and Measurement					Shape, Position and Movement			
Patterns and Sequences	**Functions and Equations**	**Measure and Estimate**	**Time**	**Perimeter Formulae Scales**	**Range of Shapes**	**Position and Movement**	**Symmetry**	**Angle**	
Patterns and relationships in multiplication tables and other topics Recognizing and continuing sequences including square and triangular numbers	Use of simple 'function machines' for operations Using and identifying simple word formulae in context	Measuring in standard units: – length, m, cm – weight, kg, g – area, cm², m² – volume, litres, ml, cm³ Relationships between units: – 1 kilometre = 1000m – 1 litre = 1000ml = 1000cm³ – Imperial units in common use Estimating lengths, weights, volumes in standard units Reading scales to the nearest mark on measuring devices in weight and volume Areas of irregular shapes, rectangles and composite shapes by counting squares Volumes of cuboids and prisms in cm³ by counting cubes	Reading and writing times to the nearest minute, am/pm Durations including counting on and back in hours and minutes 24-hour notation including simple durations Timing in seconds	Calculating perimeters of simple shapes in m and cm Using simple scales to calculate true lengths	Collecting, discussing and making: – 2D shapes including parallelograms, equilateral and isosceles triangles and circles, using side, angle, diagonal, congruent, radius, diameter, circumference – 3D shapes including cubes, cuboids, triangular prisms and pyramids, using face, edge, vertex	Using co-ordinates to locate a point Turning through angles given in degrees, eight point compass Creating paths, shapes and rotating patterns using computer turtle graphics	Completing the missing half of a symmetrical shape or pattern Recognizing and drawing up to 4 lines of symmetry in a shape Creating symmetrical shapes Recognizing rotational symmetry in shapes and patterns	Comparing angles – right, acute, obtuse Measuring angles accurately within 5 degrees	
Continuing and describing sequences: – involving square and triangular numbers – finding specified items in sequences	Recognizing and explaining simple relationships between two sets of numbers or objects Using and devising simple rules Constructing, interpreting and evaluating formulae expressed in words and in symbols	Estimating and measuring using standard units: – length: mm, cm – weight: tonne, kg and g – area: cm², m², km² – volume: l, ml, cm³ – speed: metres per second, km per hour Relationships between units 1 cm = 10 mm 1 tonne = 1000 kg Areas of right angled triangles – composite shapes Selecting appropriate units and measuring devices Investigating rate – per minute – per second Developing awareness of common Imperial units: – inches – feet – pounds – pints – gallons	Using 12- and 24-hour notation Calculating durations	Calculating using rules: – perimeters – areas – volumes of common shapes Using scales to interpret or draw maps, plans and diagrams	2D shape: – discussing the side and angle properties of triangles and quadrilaterals – discussing the diagonal properties of squares and rectangles – using the rigidity property of triangles in model-making – recognising and discussing parallel lines – relating circumference and diameter 3D shape: – recognizing and making nets of prisms and pyramids – investigating the relationship between the number of faces, vertices and edges of pyramids and prisms	Using co-ordinates to locate a point Turning through angles given in degrees Using an 8-point compass rose Using bearings and distances to discuss scale drawings of routes Creating tiling patterns by rotating, translating or reflecting a shape	Recognizing and drawing up to 4 lines of symmetry in a shape Recognizing rotational symmetry in shapes and patterns Discussing symmetry properties of triangles and quadrilaterals	Measuring and drawing angles to the nearest 5 degrees, 1 degree Calculating angle sizes where angles total 90°, 180°, 360° Using 'reflex' to describe angles Using standard notation to express bearings	

coverage at Level C coverage at Level D coverage at Level E

Mathematics in the Common

	Processes in Mathematics	Number (including Algebra)
HEINEMANN MATHEMATICS 6	Using mathematics, communicating and reasoning occur throughout	Mental addition and subtraction, estimating to obtain approximate answers Place value to millions Rounding: two- and three-digit numbers to nearest 10 and 100, four-digit numbers to nearest 100 and 1000 Adding and subtracting three- and four-digit whole numbers, with / without a calculator. Mental multiplication and division using tables Multiplying and dividing: – three- and four-digit numbers by 2 to 9 – by a two-digit whole number with / without a calculator Rounding a calculator display to the nearest appropriate unit Money: +, −, ×, ÷ with / without a calculator Fractions: understanding and using simple equivalences, fractions of quantities; fractions of a whole number; mixed numbers Decimals: understanding and using decimals to two places, solving addition and subtraction problems with / without a calculator, multiplying mentally by 10, mutliplying and dividing with a calculator Percentages: recognizing and understanding simple percentages, percentages of quantities Negative numbers: in the context of temperature Generalizing, in words, patterns arising in various situations Understanding and using multiple and factor Understanding and using simple formulae expressed in words Understanding that addition and subtraction are inverse operations and using this to check calculations, with a calculator when necessary Recognizing and continuing sequences including square and triangular numbers
HEINEMANN MATHEMATICS P7	Using mathematics, communicating and reasoning occur throughout	Whole numbers: – mental addition and subtraction – adding and subtracting four-digit numbers – rounding to the nearest 1000 and 100 – mental multiplication and division, table facts, multiples, factors – multiplying: mentally by 10, 100 and 1000; by multiples of 10 and 100; four-digit numbers by 2 to 9 – dividing: mentally by 10, 100 and 1000; multiples of 10 by 2 to 10; four-digit numbers by 2 to 9 – place value to hundreds of millions – using a calculator: rounding answers after division, exact remainders, checking answers, checking by using inverse operations, using the memory Fractions – understanding and using equivalent fractions, mixed numbers and improper fractions; simplification – adding and subtracting fractions, including mixed numbers – multiplying: a whole number times a fraction; fraction of a whole number Decimals: – notation and place value for decimals to 3 places – adding and subtracting one- and two-place decimals – multiplying and dividing: one- and two-place decimals by 2 to 9 and by 10 and 100 – multiplying mentally by 1000 – approximating and estimating – using a calculator, checking and interpreting answers Percentages: – concept, 100% as 1 whole – calculating percentages of quantities, with/without a calculator – fractions as percentages, with/without a calculator – understanding and using interrelationships between fractions, decimals and percentages Negative numbers: concept, 'positive' and 'negative', ordering, adding and subtracting (informally) Problem solving: developing strategies, listing, trial and improvement, simulation/modelling, logical thinking Multiplying and dividing by a two-digit whole number, without a calculator Exploring number and shape patterns; square numbers, square roots, triangular numbers Continuing sequences and recognizing rules Interpreting and generalizing simple relationships Constructing, interpreting and evaluating formulae expressed in words and in symbols Formulae from graphs

Curriculum (Northern Ireland)

Measures	Shape and Space	Handling Data
Understanding the relationship between units – length, m and cm, m and km – weight, kg and g – area, m² and cm² – volume, litres, ml and cm³ – time, h, min, s Making sensible estimates of a range of measures Understanding the concept of perimeter, calculating perimeters of simple shapes in m and cm Finding areas, in cm², by counting squares and volumes, in cm³, by counting cubes Understanding and using the 12-hour and 24-hour clock, durations Understanding the notion of scale Measuring angles to the nearest 5°	Specifying location by means of co-ordinates (in first quadrant) 2D Shape: making shapes such as the parallelogram, isosceles and equilateral triangles, circles, from given information; using associated language such as side, angle, diagonal, congruent, radius and diameter 3D Shape: making shapes such as triangular prisms and pyramids from given information; using associated language such as face, edge and vertex; recognizing nets of pyramids and prisms Understanding the eight points of the compass, using clockwise and anti-clockwise appropriately Understanding and using language associated with angle–right, acute, obtuse Identifying the reflective symmetries in various shapes Recognizing rotational symmetry	Collecting, grouping and ordering data using tallying methods with given equal class intervals and creating frequency tables and diagrams for grouped data Understanding and using range and mode, and calculating the mean of a set of data Organizing and interpreting data in a computer database or spreadsheet Constructing and interpreting – bar, bar-line graphs – trend graphs, knowing that intermediate values may or may not have meaning Conducting a survey Placing events in order of 'likelihood' and using appropriate words to identify the chance Distinguishing between 'fair' and 'unfair' Listing possible outcomes of an event

Choosing and using standard units
– length, mm, cm
– weight, g, kg, tonne
– area, cm², m², km²
– volume, litre, ml, cm³
– speed, metres per second, kilometres per hour
 	
Understanding relationships between units
– 1 cm = 10 mm
– 1 kg = 1000 g
– 1 tonne = 1000 kg
 	
Imperial units in daily use and their approximate metric equivalents
Length:
– finding perimeter of shapes
– using the formulae P = 4 × L and
  P = 2 × L + 2 × B
– using simple scales to calculate true lengths and scaled lengths; drawing to scale
 	
Area:
– finding areas of irregular shapes, right-angled triangles and composite shapes
– finding areas of rectangles using the formula
  A = L × B
– areas in m² and km²
 	
Finding volumes of cuboids using the formula
V = L × B × H
 	
Understanding and using compound measures of rate and speed
 	
Time: 12 and 24-hour notation, finding durations in hours and in minutes, counting on and back
 	
Relating circumference and diameter
	Angles:
	– acute, right, straight, obtuse, reflex
	– measuring and drawing angles to the nearest 5° and 1°
	– calculating angle sizes where angles total 90° or 180° or 360°
	– bearings
	
	Line and rotational symmetry
	Regular shapes
	Translating a shape to make a tiling
	
	3D shape:
	– recognising nets of pyramids and prisms
	– finding relationships between the number of faces, vertices and edges of pyramids and prisms
	
	2D shape:
	– consolidating side, angle and symmetry properties of triangles and quadrilaterals
	– exploring diagonal properties of squares and rectangles
	– constructing rigid frameworks by forming triangles
	– parallel lines, co-ordinate grids
		Constructing and interpreting
		– combined bar graphs
		– pie charts
		– trend graphs
		
		Organizing data in a frequency table and displaying it as a bar graph, with/without class intervals.
		
		Finding the median, mode, mean and range of a set of data
		
		Designing and using data collection sheets and questionnaires, conducting surveys
		
		Extracting and interpreting data from tables
		
		Probability:
		– understanding and using ideas of 'likelihood'
		– understanding and using a probability scale with markings 0, ½, 1
		– listing possible outcomes of events, estimating probabilities
		– distinguishing between 'fair' and 'unfair'

☐ coverage at Level 4	▢ coverage at Level 5
☐ coverage at Level 4–5	▣ coverage at Level 5–6

APPROACHES TO LEARNING AND TEACHING

■ The teaching approach on which the course is based is one where new ideas are introduced through the involvement of the teacher and the children in activities and discussion. This is usually followed by further activities for the children to do by themselves. Written work involving the use of the Textbook and Workbook is only attempted after sufficient practical work and discussion have taken place.

■ Given this approach, the Teacher's Notes are a crucial component of Heinemann Mathematics P7, as they provide suggestions for teaching activities and guidance on the use of other resources.

■ Teaching by the teacher is essential and cannot be replaced by the use of the Textbook, Workbook or other course materials. The function of such materials is to check on what has already been taught, to provide a record of work completed and to set new challenges where the children can apply the mathematics they have learned. The course materials are not designed to teach new concepts to children working through them on their own, without prior teaching and discussion.

■ Heinemann Mathematics P7 provides more ideas for pupil activities, more Textbook and Workbook pages, and more assessment material than should be attempted by any one child. The teacher should *select* the most appropriate activities from the materials to suit the programme of work for particular groups or individual children.

■ Teaching suggestions for each section of mathematics are found in the Teacher's Notes. Some of the activities are structured with initial teacher direction and follow-up tasks for the children. Other tasks are designed to be investigative and to encourage the children to explore new mathematical ideas through a problem solving approach. It is likely that children will complete these tasks in a variety of ways and so follow-up discussion between teacher and children will be required to ensure meaningful learning. The children should also have opportunities to discuss their work among themselves and to report on work completed.

PLANNING

Starting points

■ It is likely that the teacher will identify the mathematical content by referring to national curricular guidelines and the school's programme of study for mathematics. The charts at the end of the book summarize the curriculum coverage provided by Heinemann Mathematics.

■ Information about the children's previous experiences in mathematics can be found by consulting
  - the children's records of achievement in mathematics
  - the development charts on pages 8–13.

■ Information about the work contained in Heinemann Mathematics P7 is found by consulting
  - the contents list in the Textbook
  - the record grids at the back of the Workbook
    or in the Assessment and Resources Pack 'Overview' booklet
  - the overview at the beginning of each new section in the Teacher's Notes.

- The introductory pages at the beginning of each section of mathematics in the Teacher's Notes give
  - the aims for the section of work
  - a list of the relevant pages in the Teacher's Notes, the Textbook, Workbook, Reinforcement Sheets and Home Link-Up
  - a note of any resources the teacher may wish to collect and have available
  - references to the Extension Textbook and to the assessment, problem solving and other resource materials in the Assessment and Resources Pack.

- The teacher should read the Teacher's Notes for the chosen section of work, *selecting* the introductory activities, the Textbook and/or Workbook pages, and additional activities which are the most appropriate to the children's needs. These activities can be supplemented, where desired, by ideas from other sources.

Routes through the material

- Heinemann Mathematics P7 has been designed to be used in a flexible manner. There are many routes through the material. The important principle is to use sections on Number mostly in the given order and to 'slot in' sections from Measure, Shape and Handling data, thus providing a balanced programme of study to meet the needs of the children.

- All the work of a particular section, for example, Decimals, need not necessarily be tackled through *one* sequence of work. Where sections are quite long, the teacher may find it profitable to break these up at a suitable point with other work.

- The sections on Measure, Shape and Handling data, as well as the 'Other activity' pages, need not be tackled in the order given.

- The notes for Extension Textbook and 'Other activity' pages give details, where appropriate, of units of work from the Textbook or Workbook which should be completed before these are attempted.

- The Record of Work grids at the back of the Workbook and in the Assessment and Resources Pack 'Overview' booklet are useful in planning routes through the material.

Differentiation

- There will be times when the teacher will wish to work with the whole class or with individual children. For most activities, however, working with groups of children will be appropriate to allow the teacher to teach and to differentiate work. The teaching suggestions in the Teacher's Notes contain activities for group teaching which might be adapted for use with the whole class or individuals.

- The following features of Heinemann Mathematics P7 can help the teacher to plan differentiated programmes:
  - suggestions in the Teacher's Notes for introductory activities and additional activities
  - the Extension Textbook
  - Reinforcement Sheets
  - 'Other activity' pages in the Textbook and Extension Textbook
  - additional Problem Solving Activities including calculator activities, and Resource Cards in the Assessment and Resources Pack.

- The teacher should omit pages, parts of pages or questions in the Textbook and the Workbook which are not appropriate for specific children. However, all the children should experience some problem solving work.

- Reinforcement sheets should be used to provide consolidation work for those children thought to require it. While the Extension Textbook contains some activities which are designed to challenge the more able children, others should be accessible to most children and can be used for enrichment purposes.

■ The children's progress through the materials is determined by their understanding of the mathematical ideas and should *not* be planned on the basis of a 'page a day'. Children should have suitable experience of activities such as those suggested in the sections on introductory activities in the Teacher's Notes, before attempting to complete the Textbook or Workbook pages.

■ Home Link-Up activities are intended for all pupils. However, they provide consolidation which is particularly appropriate for the middle range of children who need more practice to establish techniques. They also contain some questions which provide challenges for more able pupils.

Contexts

■ An important consideration when planning any piece of mathematics teaching is the context or setting through which the relevant mathematical concepts, knowledge and skills can be developed. This is true whether the mathematics is to be taught through a single lesson, a block of work, or a more extended mathematical theme or topic. These contexts, real, imaginary, simulated or purely mathematical, can be used to
  – present mathematics in an interesting and motivating way
  – encourage the children to draw on and talk about experiences relevant to the context
  – help to develop a positive attitude towards mathematics
  – provide opportunities for other related mathematics
  – provide opportunities for cross-curricular work
  – provide a stimulus for year or stage collaboration.

■ Heinemann Mathematics P7 contains a range of contexts through which various sections of mathematics are developed. The more extended contexts used are as follows:

  ■ Space Station Delta 7
  ■ Kitbits Company
  ■ *Orlando*
  ■ Global Research Technology
  ■ Avonside Country Park
  ■ Creative Studio
  ■ Eurotravel
  ■ Bike Awareness Week
  ■ Arnley

■ 'Space Station Delta 7' provides a context for work on Whole Numbers, including Addition and Subtraction, Rounding and Estimation, Square and Triangular Numbers, Multiplication and Division, Place Value to hundreds of millions and Calculator Work. The context involves an orbiting space station which serves as a base for space exploration and expeditions to other planets.

■ 'Kitbits Company' is the context used to develop work on Fractions and Percentages. Kitbits manufacture various kits, models, games and puzzles.

■ '*Orlando*' is a large, holiday cruise ship which provides the setting for work on Decimals.

■ 'Global Research Technology', an international scientific foundation which tests and produces new inventions, is the context used for work on Pattern and Rate and Speed.

■ 'Avonside Country Park' is the context for work on Length and Angles. Avonside is an area with attractive scenery which provides a range of leisure and recreational activities.

■ 'Creative Studio' is a design company which produces materials such as labels, brochures, signs, banners and stickers. It provides the context for the work on Area and Volume.

- 'Eurotravel', a busy, city-centre travel agent and tour operator, is the context used to develop work on Time.

- 'Bike Awareness Week' involves children in a campaign to promote bicycle care and safety standards. This context is used for the work on Handling Data.

- 'Arnley', a small market town, provides the context for a range of mixed mathematical activities.

- Contexts in Heinemann Mathematics P7 are used primarily to support the learning and teaching of mathematics. They are not meant to dominate or be restrictive. Suggestions on how each context might be used are included in the appropriate section in these Teacher's Notes. Introductory and additional activities are often contextualized – sometimes in the same context as the Textbook and Workbook pages.

ORGANIZING AND IMPLEMENTING

Organizing the materials

- At the beginning of each section of work in the Teacher's Notes, the materials required for the Textbook and/or Workbook pages are listed under the heading 'Resources'. Materials from this list, for a particular page or group of pages, should be easily accessible to the children. Materials required for an introductory or additional activity are detailed in the notes for the activity.

- A complete listing of the materials needed to resource Heinemann Mathematics P7 is given at the back of the book.

- Teachers should take particular note of the calculator symbol which appears on certain Textbook and Workbook pages. The symbol indicates that a calculator is necessary for particular questions.

- Exercise books should be available to the children for the work of the Textbook pages. Sometimes plain, grid or dotty paper is also required. This will usually be listed under 'Resources' for the section.

- Some Textbook and Workbook pages contain a symbol such as $\boxed{\text{R6}}$. This indicates that a Reinforcement Sheet is available to provide extra practice in the work of the section from which it is referenced. Sheets should only be photocopied for those children who require additional practice.

- Some Textbook and Workbook pages contain an $\boxed{\text{H}}$ symbol to indicate related homework activities, which can be photocopied to provide individual work to complement these core pages.

- The Teacher's Notes also contain the notes for the Extension Textbook. In general this work is for more able children, but pages which will be of value and interest to most children are also included.

- The Teacher's Notes contain references to Resource Cards from the Assessment and Resources Pack which are relevant to the section. These cards should be prepared in advance. They mainly provide supplementary activities for individuals or small groups. The notes which accompany these cards describe how they relate to the section of work and how they could be used.

Using the materials

- Introductory teaching, including related practical work, should be carried out before asking the children to attempt the Textbook and Workbook pages. Suggestions for teaching activities are given in the Teacher's Notes. Teachers should select which ones to use or, where appropriate, replace them by activities of their own choosing.

- The activities in the Teacher's Notes have, in most instances, been designed for group teaching and should be adapted for whole class teaching where this is thought to be more appropriate for a particular activity or a specific class. Activities suggested in the Teacher's Notes for children to attempt by themselves, individually or in small groups, should also precede written work.

- Having undertaken appropriate activities, when the children are about to attempt a Textbook or a Workbook page, it may be necessary for the teacher to discuss some of the following:
  - what they have to do, focusing on any difficulties with vocabulary or interpretation of instructions
  - where to find any materials they may need
  - the meaning of any symbols, for example, for the calculator
  - whether they are to use an exercise book
  - how to set out their work and record their answers
  - which questions they should do or omit. For example, some more testing questions, highlighted in the Teacher's Notes, should be omitted by certain children.

- Teachers may wish, on occasions, to ask the children to
  - do questions from a Textbook or a Workbook page with no written record being kept by the children
  - read a question aloud and then express what they have to do in their own words
  - work in pairs or small groups with only one child recording the answers.

- Problem solving questions in the Textbook and Workbook are intended for most children. Such work might be tackled by small groups where the children discuss ways of *starting* the problem. When the children are *doing* the problem, the teacher's role is to observe their progress and offer help if this is requested or the children have misunderstood or cannot progress. Such help should be limited so that the children are left to do their own 'mathematical thinking'. *Reporting* by a group of what they did and found out can often be done orally to the other groups or to the whole class. The reporting might be delayed until several groups have attempted the same problem solving question and discussion can focus on their different methods and, possibly, answers.

- The Problem Solving Activities booklet in the Assessment and Resources Pack provides 'stand alone' problems for use with individuals or small groups. These problems can be attempted at any time as long as the children have met the mathematics involved. The problems are intended to give the children experience in developing simple strategies and mathematical thinking skills. Some of these problems are designed to involve the use of a calculator.

- Calculator activities are an integral part of the course. The children are expected to use a calculator whenever the symbol appears on a page. There will be other occasions when it is sensible to use a calculator, for example, in problem solving.

- The Reinforcement Sheets should be used selectively with those children who need extra practice in specific topics. They should not be used with children who have already mastered a topic. Also, they will not help children whose understanding of the topic is so poor that they require further teaching rather than extra written work. Answers are provided at the back of the Reinforcement Sheets booklet.

- The Home Link-Up activities are intended for children who can benefit from spending some time at home consolidating current or recently completed school work. They are **not** suitable for children who require further teaching of a topic before they attempt related homework activities. Answers are provided at the back of the Home Link-Up booklet.

■ The Extension Textbook provides extra material to enrich and extend the children's experience. Some of the pages are related to topics in the Textbook and Workbook. Information about this is given:
   – in the Overview for these topics in the Teacher's Notes
   – in the notes for the Extension Textbook pages
   – in the Record of Work grids at the back of the Workbook.

These pages can be attempted when the related work in the Textbook and Workbook has been completed.

■ The remaining pages in the Extension Textbook contain 'Other activities' which can be attempted at any time, provided that the children have sufficient understanding of the mathematics involved.

Teachers should choose the pages which are appropriate to particular children. It is important that the completed work is discussed with the children as much of it is of a problem solving or investigative nature.

■ 'Other activity' pages can be attempted by individuals, pairs or groups. The teacher should choose which ones are appropriate for particular children. Some of these pages can be tackled by the children without introductory activities or preceding teacher discussion. The teacher should, however, discuss the work with the children when they have completed the activities.

ASSESSING AND RECORDING

Day-to-day assessment

■ Much of the assessment of children's learning in the primary classroom is informal and continuous. Many everyday tasks that the children are involved in, such as practical work, Textbook and Workbook activities, problem solving and investigations, games, and using a calculator and computer, provide evidence which helps the teacher make informal judgements on a number of important learning and teaching issues. These include establishing the level or stage at which a particular child is working. This evidence may be gathered over a period of time and in different ways. For example, by
   – studying the children's written work
   – talking with them, posing questions and noting responses
   – listening to their explanations and reports on work carried out
   – observing them working, noting individual strengths and weaknesses (including personal qualities such as perseverance and the ability to work co-operatively)
   – pupil self-assessment.

However, some more formal assessment, related to set objectives or targets is also required. The Assessment booklet, containing Check-ups and Round-ups in the Assessment and Resources Pack helps to meet this need.

Assessment booklet

■ When the teacher wishes to use a more objective specific task to check on an individual's or group's understanding of a particular target in mathematics, one of the twenty-five Check-ups provided in the Assessment booklet in the Assessment and Resources Pack could be used. A Check-up might be used after a unit of work has been completed. Each Check-up is linked to a section of the Textbook and/or Workbook of Heinemann Mathematics P7.

■ The notes for the teacher in the Assessment booklet give details of the mathematical topics and relevant Textbook and Workbook pages for each Check-up.

- Three Round-ups, each based on a single theme, are included in the Assessment booklet. Each covers several aspects of mathematics and a range of assessment targets.

- The Check-ups provide a valuable record of achievement that can be
  - discussed with individuals or groups of children
  - shared with parents
  - transferred along with other information to the next class teacher.

- Each Check-up is referenced to the curriculum. The evidence gathered from the Check-ups, combined with information from other sources, including continuous assessment, can help establish an accurate picture of pupil performance. The evidence can also assist in the planning of future programmes of work.

- A class record guide is included with the notes in the Assessment booklet in the Assessment and Resources Pack.

Problem Solving Activities

- The Problem Solving Activities booklet in the Assessment and Resources Pack may be used to assess the children's problem solving skills with particular reference to Using and Applying Mathematics in the National Curriculum (England and Wales), the Processes Attainment Target (Northern Ireland) and the Problem Solving and Enquiry Outcome in Mathematics 5–14 (Scotland).

Record keeping

- There are record keeping grids at the back of the Workbook. A more detailed version of these, which also includes boxes for the Problem Solving Activities and Resource Cards, appears in the Overview booklet in the Assessment and Resources Pack.

  The grids could be used to show when work has been completed or, in a more qualitative way, to show how well a child has performed, for example, by using a code.

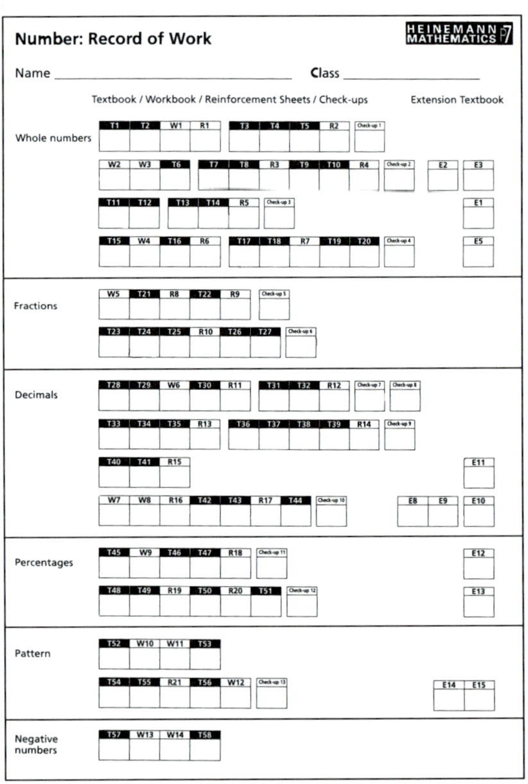

- The Assessment and Resources Pack 'Overview' booklet contains simple check lists for the Key Stage 2 and 3 programmes of study for England and Wales as well as Key Stage 2 for Northern Ireland and Levels D and E for Scotland. Space is provided to note work which has been attempted or the quality of the performance of the individual or group.

- The Assessment and Problem Solving Activities booklets each contain their own charts and record grids.

The Number part of Heinemann Mathematics P7 has eight sections, each with an Overview and accompanying notes.

Space Station Delta 7

A context for Whole Numbers

The work on Textbook pages 1–20 and Workbook pages 1–4 is set in the context of Space Station Delta 7, which is in orbit around Earth. There are many scientific laboratories on Delta 7, which serves as a base for space exploration and expeditions to other planets.

The context involves the arrival of freight from Earth, visits to the food research laboratories and the control room on Delta 7, training of crew members and the collection of supplies in preparation for the exploration of Planet Stobal. There is contact with other interplanetary transporters and a look at life on Planet Zoid, where the miners are assisted by robots called droids. Finally, the transporter *Zarco* is loaded with supplies for the return to Delta 7 and to Earth.

Introducing the context
The context could be introduced by collecting information from newspapers, magazines and perhaps the Internet about Space Station Mir, and discussing the plans.

The activities which follow can be used both to introduce the context and in an ongoing way as the children progress through the work.

1 Delta 7

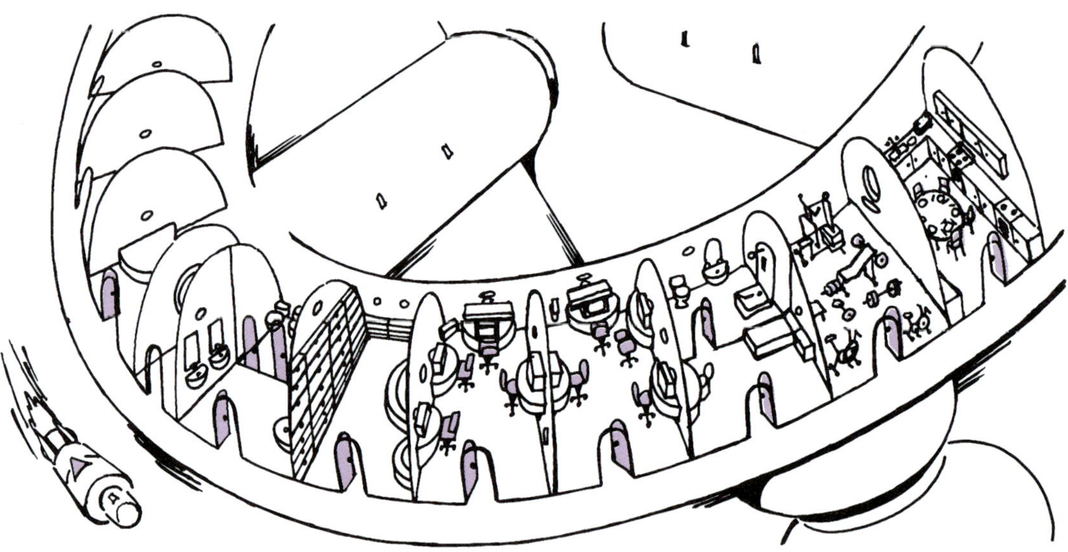

Sketches or plans of the various rooms within the space station could be made and displayed.

Datafiles of the different functions of the space station could also be created, including information about the personnel who work there, details of stock, cargo, experiments, etc.

2 *Delta News*

The children could write newspaper articles and reports of the different places: for example, a group could write about their exploration of Planet Stobal or about their journey from Earth to the space station.

3 Space station archives

The children could create a set of materials for the Delta 7 archives which would chart the planning and building of the space station and record the work undertaken there.

4 Transporters

Each group in the class could plan and sketch their version of a transporter to undertake certain tasks: for example, a transporter to carry foodstuffs or minerals from Planet Stobal.

5 Earthwatch

One of the tasks on the space station could be to monitor life on Earth. The children could explore issues such as

— animal migration and its effects on the land

— disappearing forests

— human migration

— population statistics

— weather.

The information gathered could be used

— to create a database for other members of the class or school to access

— for simple spreadsheet activities

— to create reports for a Delta 7 newsdisc.

Whole numbers

Overview

This section

■ revises and extends work on mental addition and subtraction, including examples, such as 76 + 160, 180 + 54 and 500 − 63

■ revises addition and subtraction of thousands, hundreds, tens and units

■ revises rounding of numbers greater than 999 to the nearest 1000 or 100

■ consolidates table facts and revises multiples, factors, square numbers and triangular numbers

■ revises multiplying by 10 and 100 and introduces a rule for multiplying by 1000

■ introduces mental multiplication by multiples of 10

■ revises a rule for dividing by 10 and introduces rules for dividing by 100 and 1000

■ introduces mental division of certain multiples of 10 by 2 to 10

■ consolidates multiplication and division of ThHTU by 2 to 9

■ revises division using a calculator, interpreting and rounding answers, and exact answers

■ introduces calculation of exact remainders following division, using a calculator

■ introduces checking of multiplication by division and vice versa

■ reintroduces and develops the use of the calculator's memory.

	Teacher's Notes	Textbook	Workbook	Reinforcement Sheets
Space Station Delta 7: a context for whole numbers	22			
Mental addition and subtraction	26	1, 2*	1*	1
Addition and subtraction of ThHTU	29	3, 4*		
Place value: rounding to the nearest 1000 and to the nearest 100, estimation	31	5*		2
Table facts, products, multiples, factors, mental multiplication and division, triangular and square numbers	34	6	2*, 3	
Multiplication by 10, 100, 1000, and by multiples of 10 and 100	36	7, 8*		3
Division by 10, 100, 1000, and multiples of 10 divided by 2 to 10	39	9, 10*		4
Multiplication: ThHTU by 2 to 9	41	11*		
Division: ThHTU by 2 to 9	42	12*		
Place value: hundreds of millions	43	13, 14*		5

	Teacher's Notes	Textbook	Workbook	Reinforcement Sheets
Division by calculator: exact answers, rounding, interpretation of answers, exact remainders	46	15*, 16*	4*	6
Checking answers, the four operations by calculator	50	17, 18*		7
Using a calculator's memory	52	19, 20		

Homework provided in Home Link-up.

Extension activities are as follows:	Teacher's Notes	Extension Textbook
Whole numbers: a million	256	1
Whole numbers: multiples, factors	257	2
Calculator, M+, M−	258	5

Resources

Useful materials

- calculators
- other materials suggested within the introductory activities

Assessment and Resources Pack

Assessment

Number Check-up 1
Textbook pages 1, 2, 5
Workbook page 1
(mental + and −,
rounding to nearest 1000, 100)

Number Check-up 2
Textbook pages 6–10
Workbook pages 2–3
(table facts, mental × and ÷)

Number Check-up 3
Textbook pages 13–14
(place value to hundreds of millions)

Number Check-up 4
Textbook pages 15–20
Workbook page 4
(calculator, +, −, ×, ÷, memory)

Round-up 1
Questions 1(a)(b), 2(a)(b)

Resources

Problem Solving Activities
1 Colour links (mental addition)
2 Carnival (money)
3 Countermove (addition)
4 One hundred (+ and −)
5 Follow a path (place value, rounding)
6 Find the numbers (division)
7 Page numbers (place value)
10 United (number, money)

Resource Cards
1, 2 Rockets and meteorites
     (mental + and −)
3–5 Earth cargo (rounding)

Teaching notes

MENTAL ADDITION AND SUBTRACTION

Heinemann Mathematics 6 included mental methods for adding and subtracting

— single-digit numbers to/from two- and three-digit numbers: for example,
59 + 4   135 + 9   66 – 8   401 – 6

— multiples of ten to/from two-digit numbers: for example,
37 + 40   99 – 80

— two-digit numbers including 'bridging a ten': for example,
18 + 31   48 – 22   27 + 46   91 – 66

The work involving two-digit numbers is revised and extended to include adding and subtracting

— two-digit numbers to/from three-digit numbers, with bridging a ten: for example,
76 + 160   180 + 54   500 – 63

The Space Station Delta 7 context begins with droids on Delta 7 unloading freight from Earth.

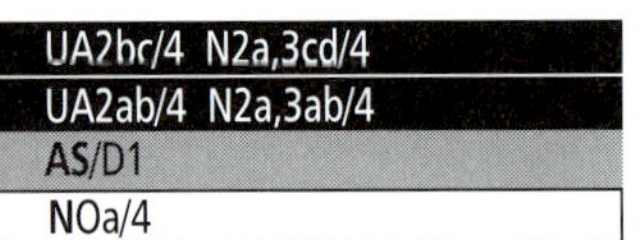

AS/D1

NOa/4

Introductory activities

1   Fuel rods   *(revision of mental addition of two-digit numbers involving 'bridging a ten')*

■ Discuss an example such as

'A droid unloads 57 fuel rods from Hold A and 29 fuel rods from Hold B. How many fuel rods are unloaded altogether?'

One method the children have used previously involves adding the **tens** of the second number to the first number, then adding the units.
For example,

57 + 29   thought of as 57 + 20 + 9

leading to   77 + 9 = 86

■ An alternative method involves adding the units of the second number to the first number, and then adding its **tens**. For example,

57 + 29   thought of as   57 + 9 + 20

leading to   66 + 20 = 86

2 Unloading supplies *(revision of mental subtraction of two-digit numbers involving 'bridging a ten')*

■ Discuss an example such as

'The store contains 74 cylinders of oxygen. A droid removes 28 cylinders. How many cylinders of oxygen are left?'

Two methods the children are familiar with are:

Method 1

   $74 - 28$ thought of as $74 - 20 - 8$

                 leading to $54 - 8 = 46$

Method 2

   $74 - 28$ thought of as $74 - 8 - 20$

                 leading to $66 - 20 = 46$

3 Freight *(mental addition/subtraction of a two-digit number to/from a three-digit number, involving 'bridging a ten')*

■ Discuss an addition example such as

'A droid loads 160 crates of supplies into Hold M. It then adds a further 54 crates. How many crates altogether did the droid load?'

Two possible methods that build on the strategies given in Heinemann Mathematics 6 are as follows:

Method 1

   $160 + 54$ thought of as $160 + 50 + 4$

                  leading to $210 + 4 = 214$

Method 2

   $160 + 54$ thought of as $160 + 40 + 14$

                  leading to $200 + 14 = 214$

■ A suitable example for subtraction might be

'There are 250 boxes to be loaded on to a starfreighter. A droid loaded 27 boxes. How many more boxes are still to be loaded?'

Two possible methods are as follows:

Method 1

   $250 - 27$
$= 250 - 20 - 7$
$= 230 - 7$
$= 223$

Method 2

   $250 - 27$
$= 200 + 50 - 27$
$= 200 + 23$
$= 223$

■ The children may use their own strategies when adding or subtracting. These should be discussed and may be used in preference to the methods suggested above.

4 Droid numbers *(mental addition of three single-digit or two-digit numbers)*

■ Draw a droid number panel on the chalkboard.

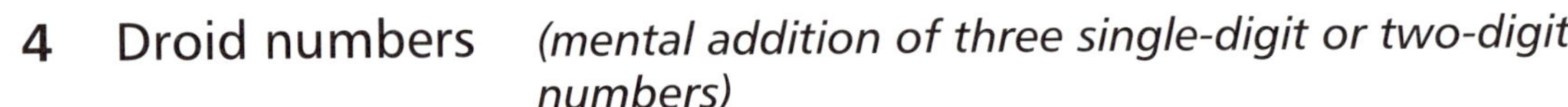

Ask the children to find the total of the three numbers.

Show and discuss the different ways in which the numbers can be added.

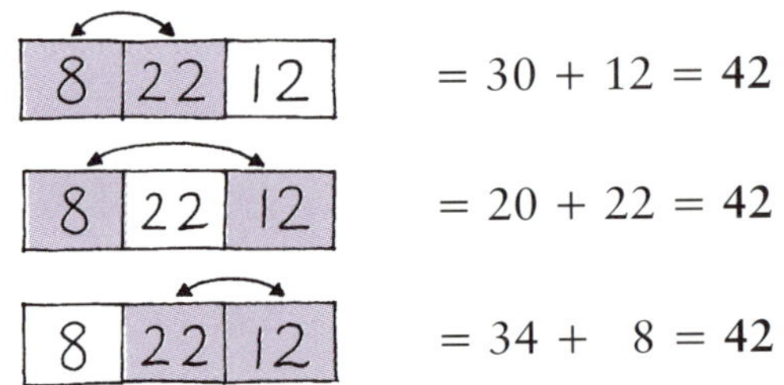

$= 30 + 12 = 42$

$= 20 + 22 = 42$

$= 34 + 8 = 42$

■ Repeat for other examples, such as

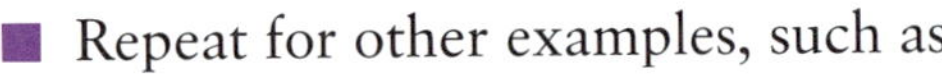

Discuss the order the children find easiest to use when adding three numbers.

Textbook pages 1 and 2   *Mental addition and subtraction*
Workbook page 1

The work on Textbook page 1 involves revision of mental addition and subtraction of two-digit numbers, first introduced in Heinemann Mathematics 6.

Children should be aware that they can choose which pair of numbers to add first when adding mentally.

In question 1(b), the children find the names of the fuel rods by working out which of the answers from 1(a), when added to the unknown rod number, produces a total of 90. For example, the type of fuel in the first container must be Boros, since

$73 + \boxed{17} = 90$

The work on Textbook page 2 and Workbook page 1 is new and mostly involves mental addition and subtraction of two-digit numbers to/from three-digit numbers. Examples include 'bridging a ten'. The three-digit numbers are restricted to multiples of ten.

On Textbook page 2, in question 4, the children have to find two numbers to complete the subtraction. They should write the **letter** and the **number** for each button. For example,

140		40	
N	−	O	= 100

In question 6, in each example the children should decide the order in which it is easiest to add the three numbers. It would be worth discussing which pairs the children found easiest to add first.

On Workbook page 1, in question 2, it is important that the children find and record words to match the answers in question 1 taken row by row across the page.

H₁ R₁

ADDITION AND SUBTRACTION OF THOUSANDS, HUNDREDS, TENS AND UNITS

In Heinemann Mathematics 6, addition and subtraction of thousands, hundreds, tens and units was extended to include totals greater than 10 000.

This work is now consolidated.

The Space Station Delta 7 context continues with the introduction of Dr Martha Thomas, who runs the food research laboratories on Delta 7.

Introductory activities

The following activities revise the written algorithms and associated language previously introduced for addition and subtraction.

1   Ecolabs   *(addition of ThHTU)*

■ Discuss an example such as

'There are 7907 cocopears in Ecolab 1 and 4518 in Ecolab 2. How many cocopears are there altogether?'

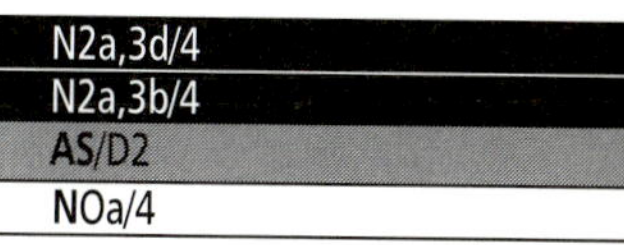

■ Discuss a written algorithm and its associated language. For example,

Recording	Language
7907 + 4518 —— 5 — 1	'Add the units. 8 and 7 is 15. Exchange 10 units for 1 ten.' Write the 5 in the units column and carry 1 ten.'

Using similar language, add in turn the tens, hundreds and thousands to obtain the answer **12 425 cocopears**.

■ Throughout Heinemann Mathematics the 'carrying' figure is placed below the answer line, as shown above. Depending on school policy, the 'carrying' figure may be placed in another position.

■ Repeat for other examples, including some in a horizontal format to give children practice in aligning the digits correctly. For example,

$$3615 + 46 + 802 + 4007 \longrightarrow \quad \begin{array}{r} 3615 \\ 46 \\ 802 \\ +4007 \\ \hline 8470 \\ \hline {\scriptstyle 1 \quad 2} \end{array}$$

2 Plants *(subtraction of ThHTU)*

■ Subtraction can be revised using an example such as

'There are 6005 plants in Ecolab 1 and 2896 in Ecolab 2. How many more plants are there in Ecolab 1?'

■ Discuss a written algorithm and its associated language.

The language and recording shown below relates to the decomposition method.

Recording

$$
\begin{array}{r}
6\,2\overset{0\ 1}{\cancel{1}}5 \\
-\,2\,8\,9\,6 \\
\hline
9
\end{array}
$$

Language

'Subtract the units. 5 take away 6, I cannot.
Exchange 1 ten for 10 units giving 0 tens and 15 units.
15 take away 6 leaves 9.'

Using similar language, subtract in turn the tens, hundreds and thousands to obtain the answer **3319 plants**.

■ Repeat for other examples which involve several exchanges and/or zero digits. For example,

$$
\begin{array}{r}
4\,2\,5\,3 \\
-\,2\,8\,4\,7 \\
\hline
\end{array}
\qquad
\begin{array}{r}
7\,0\,6\,0 \\
-\,3\,7\,8\,9 \\
\hline
\end{array}
\qquad
\begin{array}{r}
8\,0\,0\,0 \\
-\,3\,4\,2\,5 \\
\hline
\end{array}
$$

UA2cb/5 N2a,3df,4a/4
UA2b/5 N2a,3b,4a/4
PSE AS/D2
PUbdf/4 NOa/4

Problem solving

Textbook pages 3 and 4   *Addition and subtraction of ThHTU*

Discuss the context of Textbook pages 3 and 4. Dr Martha Thomas grows a range of hybrid fruits and vegetables in the food research laboratories on Delta 7. The children could be asked to identify which combinations of fruits and vegetables were used to produce the hybrids used in the context.

On Textbook page 3, in question 3, a possible strategy would be to

— find the number of

banapples:
$$
\begin{array}{r}
2\,1\,8\,7 \\
+\,2\,1\,8\,7 \\
\hline
4\,3\,7\,4 \\
{\scriptstyle 1\ 1}
\end{array}
$$

lemoranges:
$$
\begin{array}{r}
6\,5\,7 \\
+\,3\,5\,0 \\
\hline
1\,0\,0\,7 \\
{\scriptstyle 1}
\end{array}
$$

peacherries:
$$
\begin{array}{r}
\overset{2\ 17\ 1}{3\,0\,8\,1} \\
-\quad 9\,4\,5 \\
\hline
2\,1\,3\,6
\end{array}
$$

— find the total number of these fruits:

$$
\begin{array}{r}
4\,3\,7\,4 \\
1\,0\,0\,7 \\
+\,2\,1\,3\,6 \\
\hline
7\,5\,1\,7 \\
{\scriptstyle 1\ 1}
\end{array}
$$

— find the number of other types of fruit remaining in Ecolab 3 by subtracting 7517 from the total.

$$
\begin{array}{r}
7\,9\,9\,7 \\
+\,7\,5\,1\,7 \\
\hline
4\,8\,0
\end{array}
$$

The number 480 can be halved mentally to give the number of kiwiberries and plumpears, 240 of each.

The answers to question 3 should be checked before the children try question 4, which is dependent on them.

In question 4, the children should realize that they first must find the total number of each of the three types of fruit in Ecolabs 1, 2 and 3, and subtract from the given totals for all four Ecolabs to find the number of each in Ecolab 4.

On Textbook page 4, in question 1, the children are introduced to a **fictitious** unit of measure, the galactogram (gg). The children should take care to align the digits correctly in columns when setting down their calculations.

In question 4, a possible strategy is to

— allocate an equal weight
  to all three oniotts

$$3\,200\,\text{gg}$$
$$3\,\overline{)9\,600}$$

3200 gg   3200 gg   3200 gg

— transfer 425 gg from one to another

  3200   3200 gg   3200
– 425   + 425
2775 gg   3625 gg

The oniotts weigh **2775 gg, 3200 gg and 3625 gg.**

Another approach would be to use a guess, check and improve method.

H2

PLACE VALUE: ROUNDING TO THE NEAREST THOUSAND AND TO THE NEAREST HUNDRED, ESTIMATION

In Heinemann Mathematics 6, rounding of three-digit numbers to the nearest ten was revised and rounding numbers greater than 9999 to the nearest thousand or to the nearest hundred was introduced.

The children also rounded two- and three-digit numbers to the nearest ten and three-digit numbers to the nearest hundred to obtain estimated answers to additions and subtractions.

This work is now consolidated and extended to include obtaining estimated answers to addition and subtraction calculations by rounding four-digit numbers to the nearest thousand. For example,

4345 + 2938 is about 4000 + 3000 (7000)

The Space Station Delta 7 context continues with supplies being sent from Delta 7 to miners on Planet Stobal.

Introductory activities

N2a,3d,4c/4
N2a,3bf/4
AS/D1 RN/D1
NUc/4

1 Mining supplies *(rounding to the nearest 1000)*

■ Explain that mining supplies are being sent to Planet Stobal.

Draw a table showing the numbers of some items sent to the planet.

shovels	4872
sacks	6133
lamps	3555
helmets	5340

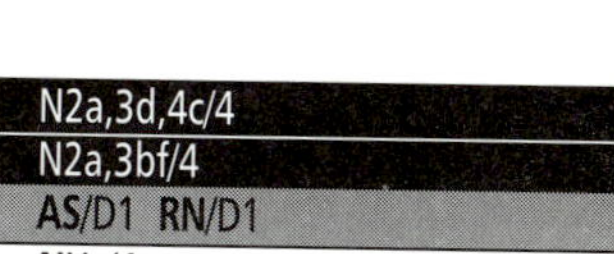

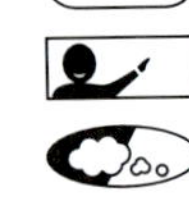

■ Draw a scale on the chalkboard and ask children to indicate the approximate position of each number on the scale.

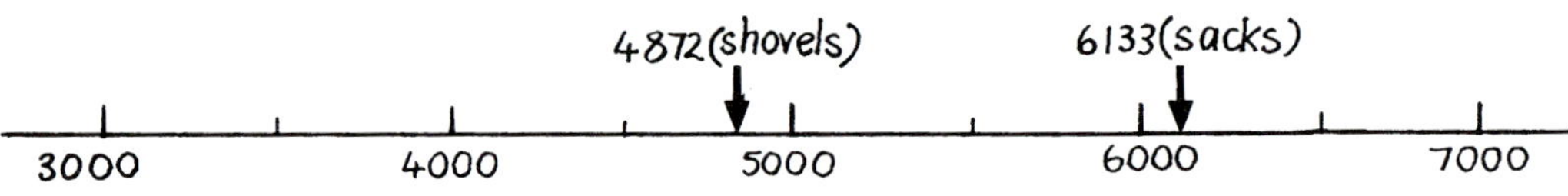

Discuss each number. For example,

4872 shovels — is between 4000 and 5000

— is greater than 4500,

so, 4872 is **5000 to the nearest thousand.**

■ Add another column to the table to show the rounded numbers.

		to the nearest thousand
shovels	4872	5000
sacks	6133	6000
lamps	3555	4000
helmets	5340	5000

■ Extend this idea to numbers greater than 9999. For example,

goggles   18 319

It may help some children to think in this way:

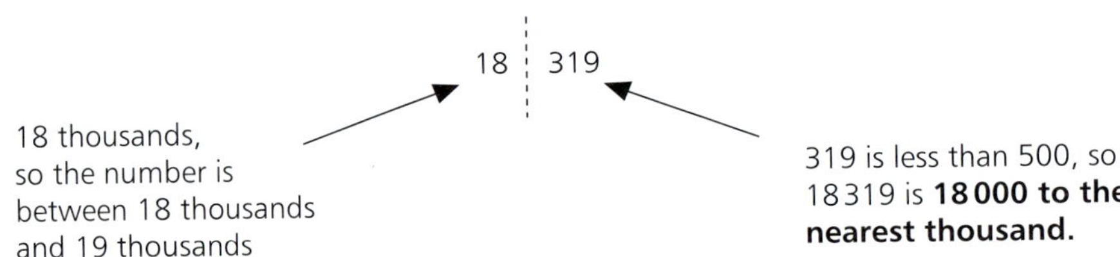

At this point the children could try Textbook page 5, questions 1 and 2.

2   Crystals   *(rounding to the nearest hundred)*

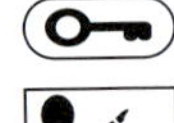

■ Draw a scale like this on the chalkboard and ask a child to indicate the number of shovels on Stobal.

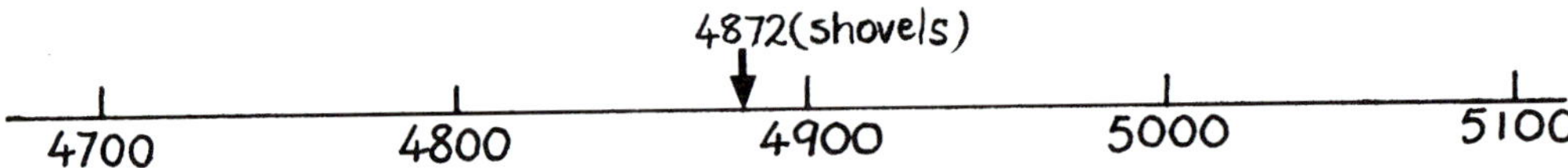

Discuss rounding 4872 **to the nearest hundred.**

It is nearer to 4900 than to 4800, so

4872 is **4900 to the nearest hundred.**

■ The table introduced in activity 1 can be altered to show the numbers of items rounded to the nearest hundred.

		to the nearest hundred
shovels	4872	4900
sacks	6133	6100
lamps	3555	3600
helmets	5340	5300

■ Extend this idea to numbers greater than 9999. For example,

$$31\,362 \longrightarrow 31\,400 \text{ to the nearest hundred}$$

It may help some children to think in this way:

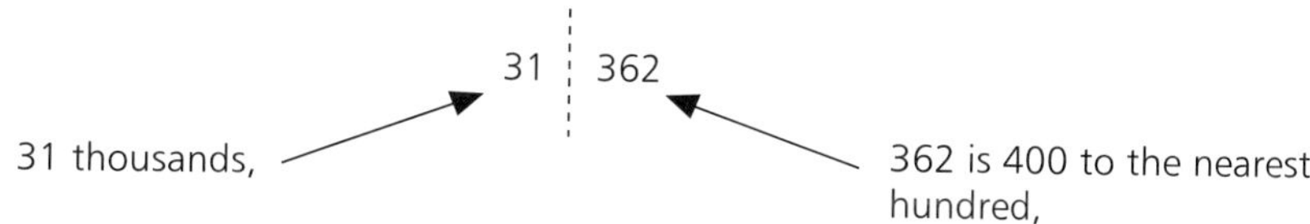

So, 31 362 is 31 400 to the nearest hundred.

At this point the children could try Textbook page 5, questions 3 and 4.

3 Food supplies *(estimating after rounding to the nearest 1000)*

■ Tell the children that the holds of transporters *Zarco* and *Nina* are being loaded with food supplies. Their weights in galactograms are

Discuss the **mental** process of estimating the total weight of the food supplies by

— rounding each weight to the nearest 1000 gg

6213 gg is about 6000 gg

2845 gg is about 3000 gg

— then adding 6000 and 3000 mentally to give a total of **about 9000 gg**.

■ In a similar way, find the approximate difference between the weights of food supplies in the two transporters.

6000 − 3000 is 3000

The difference between the weights is **about 3000 gg**.

■ Repeat for other examples, such as

8215 + 13 762 and 23 670 − 7604

H3   R2

Textbook page 5   *rounding to the nearest 1000, 100*

Discuss the context of supplies being sent from Delta 7 to Planet Stobal.

In question 2(q), some discussion may be required as 33500 lies exactly half way between 33000 and 34000. In the absence of any context which might suggest whether 'rounding up' or 'rounding down' is more appropriate, both 33000 and 34000 are acceptable answers. However, at this stage, the children might adopt 'round up' as a general rule.

In question 4, part (j) may cause some difficulty as 40 040 is 40 000 when rounded to the nearest hundred. Part (l) is another example where rounding to the nearest hundred can be either up or down.

Discuss the worked example above question 5 to ensure the children understand that they should round to the nearest thousand **before** adding or subtracting to find an estimated answer.

TABLE FACTS, PRODUCTS, MULTIPLES, FACTORS, MENTAL MULTIPLICATION AND DIVISION, TRIANGULAR AND SQUARE NUMBERS

In Heinemann Mathematics 6, the children were introduced to several types of numbers – multiples, factors, triangular and square numbers – when consolidating their multiplication tables and exploring number patterns.

Further consolidation of the multiplication tables in Heinemann Mathematics P7 provides an opportunity to remind the children of various types of numbers met previously.

The context continues with areas of exploration on Planet Stobal being surveyed from the orbiting transporter, *Zarco*.

Introductory activity

Training the crew for a visit to Stobal   *(product, multiple, factor)*

- Suggest to the children that they are crew members of *Zarco* and are about to be beamed down to begin the exploration of the new areas on Planet Stobal.

- Revise table facts by asking the children to give the product of various pairs of numbers, such as

    3 and 8   7 and 5   9 and 8

- Discuss the terms 'multiple' and 'factor' by asking the children to list

    — multiples of 3, 7, 10 and so on:
      for example, multiples of 7 are 7, 14, 21, 28. . . 70, 77, 84. . .

    — factors of 24, 36, 45 and so on:
      for example, factors of 36 are 1, 2, 3, 4, 6, 9, 12, 18, 36.

Workbook page 2 *Table facts, multiples, factors*

Discuss the context of the transporter *Zarco* orbiting the Planet Stobal, monitoring the search for minerals.

In question 1(a), some children may be uncertain about where to write the product. Their attention should be drawn to the worked example,

Some children may need to be reminded of the meaning of the word 'product'.

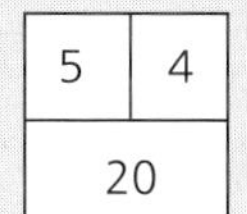

In question 1(c), some children may have difficulty in finding a number which is a multiple of 2 **and** 3 **and** 7. One method is simply to multiply $2 \times 3 \times 7$ and look for 42 on the grid. Another way is to check by finding a number which divides exactly by 2 and 3 and 7.

In question 2(a), it may be necessary to explain to some children that in the first row of the 'portable monitor', one number is already given for each product, whereas in the other rows they are to supply **both** numbers. Their pairs of numbers and the order in which they are written may vary. For example,

4	5
20	

or

5	4
20	

or

10	2
20	

or

2	10
20	

Workbook page 3 *Mental multiplication and division*

Discuss the worked example at the top of the page with the children.

In question 1, the children must realize that for Work Zone 18, each of the four men and women should have a **different factor** of 18 so that each will have a different identity number.

In question 2, the children have to find the work zone numbers by using a multiple of each factor given in the second row.

In the last example, the children have the further challenge of working backwards to find the factor first, **dividing** 36 by 9 because the crew member is male.

Textbook page 6 *Triangular and square numbers*

In question 1(c), it is worthwhile discussing the children's answers. Ask them why they think the numbers 1, 3, 6, 10, 15, 21 . . . are called triangular numbers. It should be obvious from the diagrams that each can be displayed as a triangular stack.

Discuss ways suggested by the children for finding the ninth triangular number. These might include

— finding $1 + 2 + 3 + 4 + 5 + 6 + 7 + 8 + 9$

— adding 9 to the eighth triangular number.

In question 2, discuss the children's answers to part (c). Most children should realize that the panel number is multiplied by itself. For example,

   'The ninth square number is 9 times 9 or 81.'

Encourage children having difficulty with question 3 to look at the diagrams in question 2, where the **colouring** shows that two consecutive triangular numbers add to give a square number.

UA3a/5 N3c/5
UA3a/5 N3a/5
PS/E1
PCa/5 NPb/5

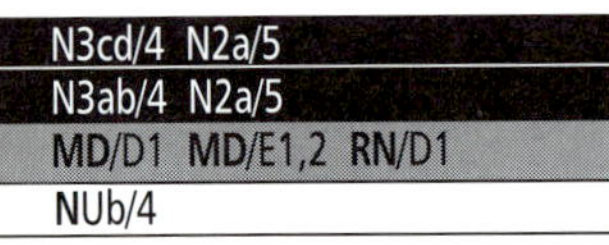

To answer question 3(b), the children should extend the list of triangular numbers they found in question 2. They should find that the triangular numbers 45 and 55 give the tenth square number, 100.

In question 4, the children should realize that they have to find the difference between the two given triangular numbers (105 – 91 = **14**), so that they can add **15** to 105 to get the next triangular number, 120. Some children however, may return to their list of triangular numbers and continue the sequence until they reach 120.

Additional activity

Square roots

■ Ask the children to suggest pairs of factors for some square numbers. List these on the chalkboard. For example:

$$16 \rightarrow \quad 1 \times 16 \quad\quad 2 \times 8 \quad\quad 4 \times 4$$

$$36 \rightarrow \quad 1 \times 36 \quad\quad 2 \times 18 \quad\quad 3 \times 12 \quad\quad 4 \times 9 \quad\quad 6 \times 6$$

$$49 \rightarrow \quad 1 \times 49 \quad\quad 7 \times 7$$

Through questioning establish that for each square number the factors in **one** of the pairs are the same. Discuss the following language:

— 36 is a square number

— because 6×6 is 36, **6** is called the **square root** of 36.

■ Ask the children to find the square roots of the other square numbers from 1 to 100.

■ Some children, using a calculator, could

— try to find square roots of larger numbers such as 144 or 225. They might guess a root and multiply to check

— find square numbers given their square root, for example,

35 is the square root of ☐.

MULTIPLICATION: BY 10, 100, 1000, AND BY MULTIPLES OF 10 AND 100

In Heinemann Mathematics 6, the children multiplied three-digit numbers by 10 and 100 mentally.

This work is now revised and extended to include multiplying four-digit numbers by 10, 100 and 1000. Multiplication by multiples of 10 is revised and extended to include multiplication by multiples of 100.

The scenario of exploring Stobal continues and the work zones are introduced.

N3cd/4 N2a/5
N3ab/4 N2a/5
MD/D1 MD/E1,2 RN/D1
NUb/4

Introductory activities

1 Batteries *(multiplying TU by U)*

■ Consider the following example:

'A storage container holds 7 boxes of 14 batteries. How many batteries are there altogether?'

Discuss a mental method of finding the product. For example,

7 boxes of 14 batteries

There are **98 batteries** altogether.

■ Repeat for other examples.

2   Constructa supplies   *(multiplying by 1000)*

■ Tell the children that Squad 1 is loading space buggies for a trip to Constructa.
They are loading

    53 boxes of floodlights

    175 boxes of light tubes

    326 boxes of energy blocks.

The total number of floodlights can be found by

   — using a calculator

   — using a mental method like this:

■ Repeat for the light tubes and energy blocks.

■ Establish a rule for multiplying by 1000 which emphasizes the digit shift.
For example,

'To multiply by 1000, move each digit three places to the left. Put zeros in the
units, tens and hundreds places.'

At this point the children could try Textbook page 7.

3 Stock control *(multiplying by multiples of 10, 100)*

■ This loading list can be used to discuss a mental method for multiplying a multiple of 10 or 100 by a single-digit number.

■ Discuss how to find the number of Vitapacks loaded by each squad. For example,

Squad 1: 9 boxes of 30 packs

Squad 2: 3 boxes of 200 packs

4 Crystals *(multiplying multiples of ten, estimation)*

■ Consider the following example:

'Miners at the Lineum Mine packed 60 boxes of 40 crystals to send to Delta 7. How many crystals did they send to Delta 7?'

Discuss a mental method for finding the number of crystals sent.

Repeat for other examples, such as 90×70 and 40×20.

■ Write an example like this on the chalkboard.

'There are 28 boxes of 14 light cells.'

Discuss the following method to **estimate** the total number of light cells.

28 boxes of 14 light cells

28 is about 30.

14 is about 10.

$30 \times 10 = 300$

There are about 300 light cells.

Repeat for other examples, such as 18×23 and 17×32.

Textbook pages 7 and 8
Multiplication: by 10, 100, 1000, and by multiples of 10, 100

On Textbook page 7, children who have not completed the introductory activities may need to be reminded of the rules for multiplying by 10 and 100.

In question 8, some children may find the answer to the problem by working out how many sets of 100 magno-pipes were laid ($400\,000 \div 100 = 4000$) then multiplying the answer (4000) by 1000, giving $4\,000\,000$.

Others may work out that 10 credits are earned for every pipe laid ($1000 \div 100$), so the total number of credits is $400\,000 \times 10 = 4\,000\,000$ credits.

On Textbook page 8, in question 1, children who have difficulty working mentally could be allowed to record an intermediate step.

In questions 1, 2 and 3, it would be helpful to remind the children of the fact that 16×4 is the same as 4×16.

In question 5, the children may have to be reminded of the approximate nature of the answers and record as such: for example, by writing for 5(a) 'about 600'.

In questions 5(e) and (f), one of the numbers in each example can be rounded **up** or **down**. As the other number in each rounds up, it is sensible to round 45 and 35 **down** to produce estimates closer to the exact answers.

5(e) 45×16 is about $40 \times 20 = 800$

5(f) 19×35 is about $20 \times 30 = 600$

| R3 | H5 |

DIVISION: BY 10, 100, 1000, AND MULTIPLES OF 10 DIVIDED BY 2 TO 10

In Heinemann Mathematics 6, the rule for dividing by 10 was consolidated.

This work is now extended to include rules for dividing by 100 and 1000, and for dividing multiples of 10 by 2 to 10.

The context continues at the Lineum Mine.

Introductory activities

1   Lineum records   *(dividing by 10, 100, 1000)*

- Tell the children that the amounts mined are used to work out each miner's earnings.

- On the chalkboard, draw or display part of Team D's record for last year.

LINEUM MINE	TEAM D's RECORD	MONTH 4	
Member	Ore	Crystals	Minerals
Andy	900 gg	8 700	456 000 gg
Karen	840 gg	12 300	9 000 gg
Edwin	570 gg	59 200	87 000 gg
Savia	1240 gg	40 000	302 000 gg

■ Tell the children that each 10 gg of ore mined earns 1 credit, and ask them to work out how many credits each worker would receive. For example,

Andy → 900 ÷ 10 = 90 credits

Karen → 840 ÷ 10 = 84 credits

Discuss the answers to remind the children of a rule for dividing by 10 which emphasizes the digit shift. For example,

'To divide by 10, move each digit one place to the right.'

■ Repeat for dividing by 100 and 1000 using other data from the table.

Dividing by 100

For each 100 crystals mined, 1 credit is earned.

— Ask the children to work out by calculator how many credits each worker would receive for their crystals.

Andy   8 700 ÷ 100 =   87 credits

Karen   12 300 ÷ 100 = 123 credits

Edwin   59 200 ÷ 100 = 592 credits

Sobia   40 000 ÷ 100 = 400 credits

— Through discussion establish the rule for dividing by 100 which emphasizes the digit shift. For example,

'To divide by 100, move each digit two places to the right.'

Dividing by 1000

For each 1000 gg of minerals mined, 1 credit is earned.

— Through discussion of the children's answers, from working out the number of credits each worker would receive for their minerals, establish the rule for dividing by 1000 which emphasizes the digit shift. For example,

'To divide by 1000, move each digit three places to the right.'

2   Rations   *(dividing multiples of 10 by 2 to 10)*

■ Squad 4 is issued with enough rations for a seven-day exploration trip. Ask the children to find mentally how many of each item Squad 4 can use, on average, each day.

For example,

Food packs

There are **40 food packs** for each day.

■ Repeat for the energy cells and the light cubes.

Textbook pages 9 and 10
Division: by 10, 100, 1000, and multiples of 10 by 2 to 10

On Textbook page 9, children who have not completed the introductory activities may need to discuss the rules for dividing by 10, 100 and 1000.

On both pages, the children should be encouraged to work out the answers mentally and record only the answers. However, some teachers may prefer a fuller recording. For example,

     1(a)   70 ÷ 10 = 7

On Textbook page 10, some children may need to be reminded of the meaning of 'multiple' and 'factor'.

In question 2(c), the 'safe' route home is shown by the unshaded squares.

	140			
150	420			
210				
490	110	700	250	
			430	300

N3d/4 N2a/5
N3b/4 N2a/5
MD/E1,2
NUb,Ob/5

R4 H6

MULTIPLICATION: THOUSANDS, HUNDREDS, TENS AND UNITS BY 2 TO 9

In Heinemann Mathematics 6, multiplication of thousands, hundreds, tens and units was extended to include products greater than 10 000. This work is now revised.

N3cd/4
N3ab/4
MD/D3
NOb/4

The context is the Space Station Delta 7 control room, where contact is maintained with the interplanetary transporters.

Introductory activity

Delta 7 control   *(multiplication of ThHTU by 2 to 9)*

This activity is intended to revise the algorithm for multiplication of thousands, hundreds, tens and units, and to introduce the context of Textbook pages 11 and 12.

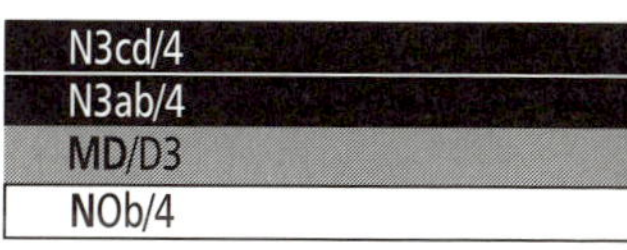

- Refer the children to the planet viewing screen on Textbook page 11 and discuss how to find a planet's number.

  For example, the number for Planet Miros is 7 × 2145.

- Discuss a written algorithm and its associated language.

Recording	Language
2145	'Multiply the units.
× 7	7 times 5 is 35.
5	Write the 5 in the units column and
3	carry 3 tens.'

Using similar language, multiply in turn the tens, the hundreds and the thousands by 7 to obtain the number is 15 015 for Planet Miros.

- For some children it may be appropriate to work initially with products less than 10 000.

UA2ab,3a/4 N3c/4
UA2bc,3a/4 N3ab/4
PSE MD/D3
PUbdef/4 NOb/4

Problem solving

Problem solving

Textbook page 11   *Multiplication: ThHTU by 2 to 9*

The written technique for multiplying a four-digit number by a single-digit number is revised.

In question 1, the multiplications can be carried out in any order. However, to help to avoid omissions, suggest that alphabetical order is followed, starting with planets Ag, By, Cob and so on.

In question 2, 'invisible' is stressed in order to suggest that the planet occupies a position on the viewing screen. The children could systematically multiply each four-digit number on the screen by 1, 2, 3 . . . 9 in turn to find that the multiplication is 7×1089. However, they should be encouraged to apply their knowledge of multiplication to reduce the number of calculations to a minimum. Therefore:

— the single digit cannot be 2, 4, 6 or 8 as 7623 is an odd number

— the single digit cannot be 5 as 7623 does not end in 0 or 5

— the single digit cannot be 1 as none of the screen numbers is 7623

— using an 'end digit' multiplication check, the single digit cannot be 3 or 9 (none of the units digits of 1063, 1089, 2145 and 3274 can be multiplied by 3 or 9 to produce a units digit of 3 as in 7623)

— try 7×1089.

The problem in question 3(c) can be tackled systematically by multiplying each return distance by 5, then adding the other return distances in turn to the product.

Alternatively, if the return distance for each planet is multiplied in turn by 5, this will eliminate By (11565), Cob (7130) and Ef (7740) as these products are greater than 6961.

The five return journeys must be to Dal (5535) **or** to Ag (5410).

Subtracting the totals for Dal and Ag from 6961 gives **1426** and **1551** respectively. This leads to identifying planets Dal (5 return journeys) and Cob (1 return journey).

DIVISION: THOUSANDS, HUNDREDS, TENS AND UNITS BY 2 TO 9

N3cd/4
N3ab/4
MD/D3
NOb/5

In Heinemann Mathematics 6, division of hundreds, tens and units by 2 to 9 was extended to include thousands, hundreds, tens and units. This work is now revised.

The Delta 7 control room scenario continues.

Introductory activity

Message from *Zarco*   *(division of ThHTU by 2 to 9)*

This activity is intended to revise the algorithm for division of thousands, hundreds, tens and units, and to develop the context on Textbook pages 11 and 12.

- Discuss the scenario on Textbook page 12, in which Delta 7 and the transporter *Zarco* exchange messages in code as *Zarco* makes its way to Delta 7.

- Discuss how to use the Galactic Code for a single letter in the message: for example, $7911 \div 3$.

  Revise a written algorithm and its associated language for the division.

Recording	Language
$\frac{2}{3\,\overline{)\,7^{1}911}}$	'Share the thousands. 3 times what is 7? 3 times 2 is 6 and 1 left over.'

Using similar language, divide in turn the hundreds, the tens and the units by 3 to obtain 2637.

Refer to the Galactic Code keypad to convert this number to the letter T.

Textbook page 12   *Division: ThHTU by 2 to 9*

The written technique for dividing a four-digit number by a single-digit number is revised.

In question 1, the divisions may be carried out in any order. However, it may be necessary to explain the structure of the coded message. Each vertical **block of divisions** represents a single word, and each individual division represents a single letter of the word. Delta 7's message is WHAT CARGO IS ON BOARD.

In question 2, *Zarco's* reply is IRON ORE FROM RA. Ra is one of the planets on the viewing screen on Textbook page 11.

In question 3, the children should apply their knowledge of the relationship between multiplication and division. After referring to the Galactic Code, they should realize that they need to make up divisions with answers 1061 and 1278 for P and U respectively.

Multiplying, for example, 1061 by 2 gives 2122, so a suitable division for P would be $2122 \div 2$.

Similarly, multiplying 1061 by 3, 4, 5. . . 9 yields other suitable divisions for P. Multiplying 1278 by 2, 3, 4. . . 7 yields suitable divisions for U.

However, multiplying 1278 by 8 or 9 gives products with five digits, which are inappropriate for the context.

UA2ba,3a/4 N3dcf,4a/4	
UA2bc,3a/4 N3ab,4a/4	
PSE MD/D3	
PUdef/4 NOb/5	

Problem solving

H8

PLACE VALUE: HUNDREDS OF MILLIONS

In Heinemann Mathematics 6, the children dealt with recognizing, naming, writing and ordering numbers to ten million. This work is now extended to hundreds of millions.

The Space Station Delta 7 context continues with the introduction of the spaceship, Star Lab X-4, whose crew collects information about planets in the Varda galaxy.

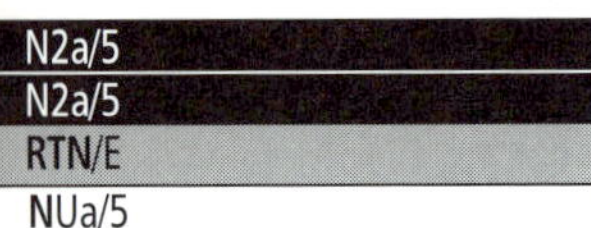

N2a/5
N2a/5
RTN/E
NUa/5

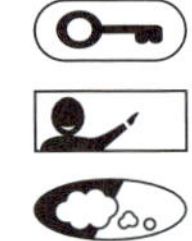

Introductory activities

1 Number names

■ Remind the children of ways of writing

6 million $\longrightarrow$ 6 000 000

$2\frac{1}{2}$ million $\longrightarrow$ 2 500 000

■ Give practice in associating numerals with the corresponding number names, particularly the way the number of millions is said first, then the number of thousands and then the remainder of the number. For example,

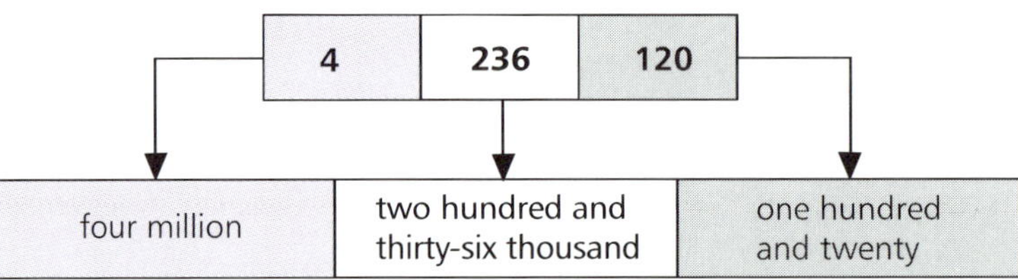

4	236	120
four million	two hundred and thirty-six thousand	one hundred and twenty

In addition, give practice in writing numbers in words as figures, for example:

three million, four hundred thousand, one hundred and six $\rightarrow$ 3 400 106

■ Extend this activity to

— tens of millions

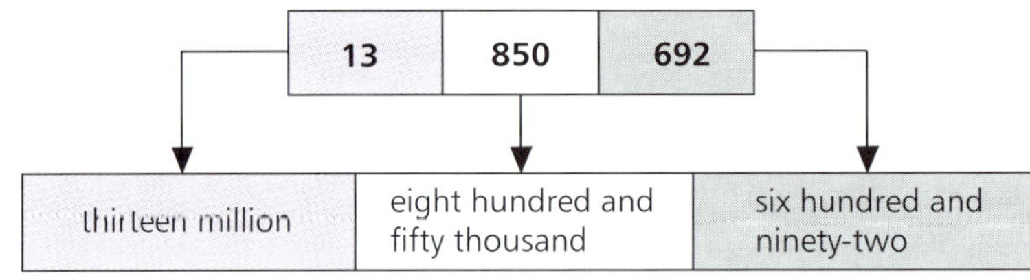

13	850	692
thirteen million	eight hundred and fifty thousand	six hundred and ninety-two

— hundreds of millions

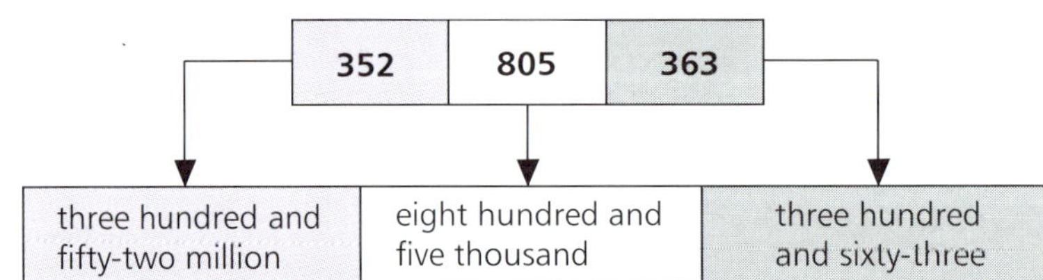

352	805	363
three hundred and fifty-two million	eight hundred and five thousand	three hundred and sixty-three

2 Large numbers in the environment

Ask the children to collect cuttings from magazines or newspapers in which large numbers appear. These could be used to make a wall display.

3   Number cards

Use a set of number cards like these:

| 350 910 | 10 000 542 | 250 000 000 | 999 909 |

| 16 440 728 | 98 445 607 | 123 456 910 |

■ Ask the children to pick cards which show

— the largest number

— the smallest number

— a number greater than thirteen million

— a number which has four hundred and fifty-six thousands as part of it,

and so on.

■ Hold up specific cards and ask the children to read the numbers aloud.

4   Place value

■ The relative values of the digits in different columns should be explored. For example,

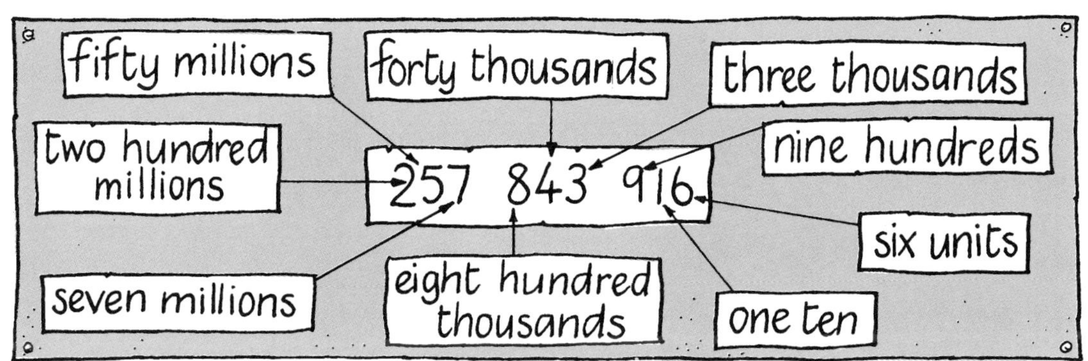

■ Write large numbers on the chalkboard and ask the children about the value of digits in different place-value columns. A table with column headings could be created as the answers are given.

| Millions | Thousands | |
HTU	HTU	HTU
683	794	602

■ Repeat for other examples, including the type where many or all of the digits are the same: for example, 888 888 888.

N2a/5
N2a/5
RTN/E
NUa/5

H9   R5

Textbook pages 13 and 14   *Place value: hundreds of millions*

Discuss Star Lab X-4.

On Textbook page 13, in questions 1 and 2, the children should write large numbers

— in figures grouped in threes, but without commas

— in words, with hyphens and commas where appropriate.

On Textbook page 14, in question 4, children need to realize that there may be more than one number for each condition.

In question 5, it is important that the children look closely at the centre box to note both the value of the number shown **and** the operation to be carried out.

In question 6, examples (d) and (e) are quite challenging as the values of two of the digits change each time.

DIVISION BY CALCULATOR: EXACT ANSWERS, ROUNDING, INTERPRETATION OF ANSWERS, EXACT REMAINDERS

N2b,3fh,4ab/5
N2a,3e,4ab/5
MD/D4 RN/D1
NUc,Ob/5

In Heinemann Mathematics 6, calculator division of hundreds, tens and units by a two-digit whole number was extended to thousands. The work included exact answers and rounding answers both to the nearest unit and to the nearest appropriate unit.

This work is now revised and then extended to include the calculation of exact remainders.

The context of Space Station Delta 7 continues with a look at aspects of life on Planet Zoid.

Introductory activities

1   Revision   *(calculator displays: rounding and interpretation of answers)*

■ Revise rounding of calculator displays showing answers to divisions with more than one decimal place.

Discuss rounding

— to the nearest unit or whole number

— to the nearest **appropriate** unit or whole number, depending on the context.

■ Ask the children to use a calculator to find the answer to a non-contextualized example such as 1234 ÷ 37.

Enter | 1234. | Press ÷ 3 7 = to give | 33.351351 |

Draw a number line on the chalkboard and label it as shown:

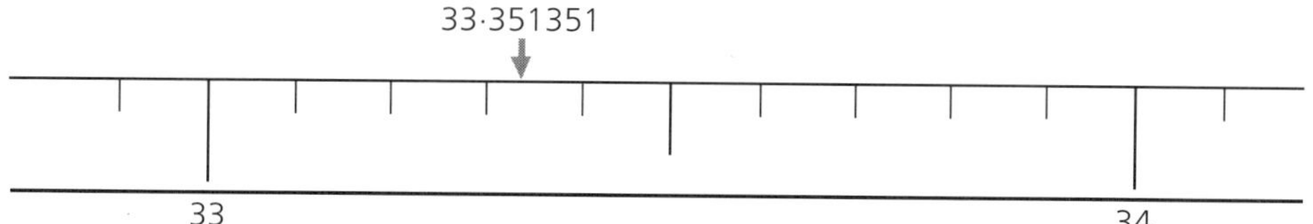

Use an arrow to show the approximate position of the number 33·351351 and discuss different ways of describing it. For example,

— greater than 33 and less than 34

— between 33 and 34

— nearer to 33

— 33 to the nearest unit or whole number

Repeat for other examples, including some where the arrow's position is close to the halfway mark. For example,

$$758 \div 46 = 16.47826 \longrightarrow 16 \text{ to the nearest whole number}$$
$$611 \div 37 = 16.513513 \longrightarrow 17 \text{ to the nearest whole number}$$

■ Discuss a contextualized example such as:

'1050 power packs are shared equally among 83 workers. How many packs are given to each worker?'

$$1050 \div 83 = \boxed{12} . \boxed{650602}$$

number of power packs   and a 'bit'

The display indicates a number between 12 and 13. However, in the context of the problem it does not make sense to share 'bits' of a power pack. The display is 13 to the nearest whole number, but there are not enough packs to give the workers 13 each. So 12·650602 must be **rounded down** to give the **appropriate** whole number, 12 power packs.

If necessary, other examples could be discussed in the same way. The children must realize that they should decide to round the number in the display **up or down by considering the context** in which the question is set.

For example,

— 'A trolley can hold 22 oxygen canisters. How many trolleys are needed for 2035 canisters?' (92·5 **rounded up** to 93)

— 'How many complete ration packs can be made from 3265 lozenges if each pack contains 52 lozenges?' (62·788461 **rounded down** to 62)

At this point the children could try Textbook page 15 and Workbook page 4, question 1.

2   The camps on *Zoid*   *(calculator displays: calculation of exact remainders)*

■ Introduce the following problem.

'Each table in the camp's breakfast room seats 6 workers. How many tables are filled by 26 workers? How many workers are left over?'

Discuss the mental division 26 ÷ 6.

multiply 6 × 4 = 24

subtract 26 − 24 = 2

There are **4 full tables** and **2 workers** left over.

■ Ask the children to use a calculator to find 26 ÷ 6.

Enter  Press ÷ 6 = to give 

Discuss how to find the exact remainder:

— **multiply the whole number part of the display, 4, by 6**

Enter  Press × 6 = to give 

— **subtract** 24 from 26 to find the remainder, 2.

■ Repeat for examples with larger numbers. For example,

'Each buggy which takes the workers to the work zones on Planet Zoid can carry 18 workers. How many buggies are filled by 205 workers? How many workers are left over?'

— Enter  Press ÷ 1 8 − to give 

— Enter Press × 1 8 = to give 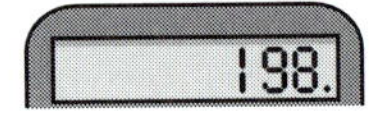

— Find the difference between 205 and 198 (7).

11 buggies are filled and **7 workers** are left over.

3 Transporting the ore *(finding the difference by calculator)*

■ In more difficult division examples, the use of a calculator might be extended to the **subtraction** involved in finding the remainder.

Discuss examples such as:

'Each transporter has space for 318 crates of minerals. How many transporters can be fully loaded from 2025 crates? How many creates are left over?'

— Enter  Press ÷ 3 1 8 = to give 

— Enter 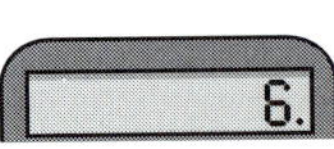 Press × 3 1 8 = to give 

— Enter  Press − 1 9 0 8 = to give 

6 transporters can be filled and **117 crates** are left over.

■ More able children may appreciate this alternative method:

— Leave this product `1905.` in the display.

Press `−` `2` `0` `2` `5` `=` to give `−117.` or `117.−`

— Ignore the negative sign.

The remainder is **117 crates**.

N2b,3fh,4ab/5
N2a,3e,4ab/5
MD/D4 RN/D1
NUc,Ob/5 NPb/4

Textbook page 15 *Division: calculator, rounding answers*
Workbook page 4, question 1 *Division: interpretation of answers*

There should be some discussion of the context to help the children with interpretation of the questions. Planet Zoid is a source of minerals for Delta 7 and Earth. The workers live in camps named Zig, Zag, Zug and so on, although the places where mining is carried out, the work zones, are simply called Zone A, Zone B and so on. The workers are assisted by droids.

All the questions require the use of a calculator to divide a whole number by a whole number. The progression is:

— Textbook page 15, question 1, exact answers

— Workbook page 4, question 1 and Textbook page 15, question 3, rounding answers to the nearest whole number

— Textbook page 15, question 4, rounding answers to the nearest **appropriate** whole number (interpretation of answers).

On Textbook page 15, in question 1, the children should be encouraged to check their answers either by doing the division again or by using *multiplication*.

H10

N3fh,4ab/5
N3e,4ab/5
MD/D4 RN/D1
NOb/5

Textbook page 16 *Division: calculator, exact remainders*
Workbook page 4, question 2

The context should be discussed by referring to the illustrations on Textbook page 16. The workers in Camp Zog can relax in the Diner, which includes on its menu speciality items from a range of sources – Moonjuice, Zogdogs, Milkywafers and so on.

As the work of the page is likely to prove difficult, it is essential that teacher-led discussion along the lines suggested in introductory activity 2 takes place. The worked example on the page should also be discussed to ensure that the children understand both the mathematics and the scenario.

For Workbook page 4, question 2, some help in understanding the layout may be needed.

For Textbook page 16, questions 3 and 4, it may be necessary to point out that the illustration of Zandra contains essential information.

R6 **H**11

CHECKING ANSWERS, THE FOUR OPERATIONS BY CALCULATOR

In Heinemann Mathematics 6, the children used a calculator to add and subtract large numbers up to one million, and were introduced to a method of checking addition by subtraction and vice versa.

This work is now consolidated and extended to introduce methods of checking multiplication by looking at the product of 'end' or unit digits and checking multiplication by division, and vice versa.

The context continues with droids carrying out a range of self-tests before starting work.

Introductory activities

1 Microchips *(end-digit check)*

■ Tell the children that there are

— 318 boxes, each with 134 green microchips

— 617 boxes, each with 153 blue microchips

— 426 boxes, each with 230 red microchips.

Ask

'How would you find the number of green microchips?' (multiply the numbers 318 and 134 together)

If necessary, remind the children that the answer is called the **product**.

■ Display on the chalkboard:

$318 \times 134 = 42\,612$

Underneath, write the unit digits of each of the numbers being multiplied and ask the children to give the product of these digits.

Highlight the unit digit of each pair of **answers**:

$$318 \times 134 = 42\,61\mathbf{2}$$
$$8 \times 4 = 3\mathbf{2}$$

■ Repeat for blue microchips and red microchips.

■ Discuss the relationship between the product of each pair of numbers and the product of their unit digits. Their end digits are the same. This fact can be used to help to check whether or not a product is likely to be correct. However, it should be mentioned that, even if this check appears to work, the product may still be wrong.

This method is sometimes known as an **end-digit check**.

At this point the children could try Textbook page 17, question 1.

2 Faulty chips *(checking answers using inverse operations)*

■ Consider a scenario such as

'There are 36 boxes, each containing 2385 faulty microchips.'

Ask the children to use a calculator to find the total number of faulty microchips, 85 860.

- Discuss how to check the calculation by using the inverse operation, division. For example, multiply 2385 × 36, as follows:

Enter 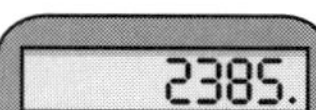 Press   = to give 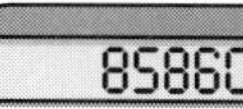

Do not clear the calculator.

To check the answer, 85 860, **divide** by 36.

Press 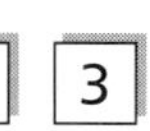  = to give  **again.**

- Repeat for calculations involving the other operations. For example,

  5236 ÷ 187 = 28

  Check by **multiplying**, 28 × 187 = 5236

  2836 + 6098 = 8934

  Check by **subtracting**, 8934 − 6098 = 2836

  9107 − 5387 = 3720

  Check by **adding**, 3720 + 5387 = 9107

UA2cd/4 N3fh,4ac/5
UA2ad/4 N3e,4ac/5
AS/E3 MD/E3
PMf/5 NUc,Ob/5

Textbook pages 17 and 18
Calculator: checking answers, the four operations

Discuss the scenario in which the droids self-test their circuits before they start work.

On Textbook page 17, questions 1 and 2 relate to checking answers in different ways, while on Textbook page 18, questions 3 to 9 relate to the puzzle grid in question 3.

In question 1(b), it is intended that the children notice that the unit digits in each pair of answers are the same. If introductory activity 1 has not been carried out, there should be some discussion to ensure that the children understand the process of checking answers using an **end-digit check**.

In question 1(c), the children should realize that the answer cannot be 233 964, 233 967 or 233 963, since the end-digit check, (3 × 7 = 21), indicates that the answer must end in a 1.

Children who have not carried out introductory activity 2 are likely to need some guidance before attempting question 2. Different ways of checking the calculation which the children should have already met include

— for all four operations, doing the calculation again

— for addition and multiplication, entering the numbers in reverse order.

The grid in question 3 should be carefully copied, with the square shaded as it is used to record the answers to questions 4 to 8.

In question 4, there are six possible products:

148 × 159 = 23 532   148 × 171 = 25 308   148 × 323 = 47 804

159 × 171 = 27 189   159 × 323 = 51 357   171 × 323 = 55 233

In question 4 (a) and (c) respectively, the children should realize that the largest/smallest product is the product of the two largest/smallest numbers. In part (b), a guess and check strategy could be used, although some children may select from a systematically listed set of all six products.

In question 8, the children could round to the nearest thousand and estimate, to see which pair of numbers might give a difference of about 47 681, before using a calculator to check. Alternatively, they could systematically pair the numbers, working out each difference until the appropriate numbers are found.

In question 9, the completed grid should be shown, with the coloured squares showing the message 'OK', confirming that the self-test of the circuits has been completed successfully.

5	4	2	8	3	9	9	5
5	7	3	6	2	0	3	7
2	8	5	6	5	5	8	0
3	0	3	9	5	0	2	6
3	4	2	0	5	0		3

$\boxed{\text{H}12}$ $\boxed{\text{R}7}$

USING A CALCULATOR'S MEMORY

More able children may already have made some limited use of a calculator's memory:

— in Heinemann Mathematics 5, the $\boxed{\text{M}+}$ key was introduced for some calculations involving money (Extension Textbook page 18)

— in Heinemann Mathematics 6, the Teacher's Notes (page 109) suggested that it might be appropriate to use the $\boxed{\text{M}+}$ key with some children.

Heinemann Mathematics P7 formally introduces the use of a calculator's memory to store the answer to one part of a calculation while another part is being carried out.

Both the $\boxed{\text{M}+}$ and $\boxed{\text{M}-}$ keys are used.

The Space Station Delta 7 context comes to its end with the transporter *Zarco* carrying cargo from the planets to Delta 7 and to Earth.

Introductory activities

1   Trips to Delta 7   *(using the $\boxed{\text{M}+}$ key)*

■ Tell the children that tickets for the trip to Delta 7 are sold in travel agents' shops.

Ask them to find the total cost of tickets for 5 adults, 3 children and 2 senior citizens. They may do this in different ways:

— add by entering each of the 10 prices individually

— multiply to find the total cost for each **type** of ticket, record these totals **on paper**, then add to find the grand total, £6675.

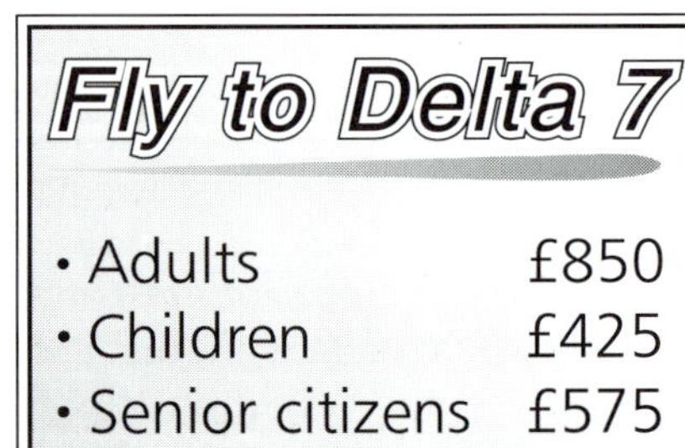

- Discuss how the calculator's memory can be used instead. The steps are
    — clear the display and memory (This initial step should be emphasized.)
    — calculate the total for the adults, 5 × £850
    — use M+ to add this to the memory
    — calculate the total for the children, 3 × £425
    — use M+ to add this to the memory
    — calculate the total for the senior citizens, 2 × £575
    — use M+ to add this to the memory
    — use MR to recall the grand total, £6675, from the memory.

Further examples of the same type should be discussed until the children are confident in using the memory in this way.

- At suitable points the children's awareness of the use of the memory facility can be enhanced by discussing the following:
    — The method of clearing the memory varies from one make of calculator to

    another. It may be necessary to press

    MC or AC or CM or M$_C^R$ M$_C^R$ or . . .

    — The memory is empty only when no small 'M' appears on the display

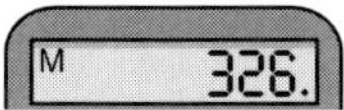

There is something in the memory.

There is nothing in the memory.

    — Switching off does not always clear the memory with some makes of calculator.

    — There are other ways of using the memory for the type of calculation described above. For instance, the last two steps in the above example can be

    replaced by +   MR   = .

At this point the children could try Textbook page 19.

2   Mineral shop   *(using the M− key)*

- Explain that Zimon buys and sells minerals, mined on Planet Zoid, at these prices.

buying price   **selling price**

Give the children the following problem and ask them to try to find the answer using the calculator's memory:

   'Zimon has no money. He sells 7 crates of Lineum crystals and then he buys 4 crates. How much money does he now have?'

■ Discuss how the calculator's memory can be used, building on the children's suggestions. The steps are

— clear the display and memory (again, this initial step should be emphasized)

— calculate the money received by selling, $7 \times £315$

— use $\boxed{M+}$ to add this to the memory

— calculate the money spent by buying, $4 \times £225$

— use $\boxed{M-}$ to **subtract** this from the memory

— use $\boxed{MR}$ to recall the amount of money left, £1305, from the memory.

■ Further examples of the same type should be discussed as necessary.

N3fh,4ab/5
N3e,4ab/5
MD/D4
NOb/5

Textbook page 19   *Calculator* $\boxed{M+}$

The use of the $\boxed{M+}$ key is considered.

Remind the children that *Zarco* transports minerals and other goods from one planet to another. In doing so, *Zarco* travels huge distances measured in galactometres (gm).

In question 1, it is intended that the children find the total distance **without** using the $\boxed{M+}$ key.

The procedure listed in question 2 should be discussed **after** the children have attempted to follow it. Children who have carried out introductory activity 2 should manage without too much difficulty.

In question 4, the children should realize that there are four sets, A, B, C and D.

UA2abc/4→5 N3fh,4ab/5
UA2abc/4→5 N3e,4ab/5
PSE MD/D4
PUab/4→5 NOb/5

Problem solving

Textbook page 20 *Calculator* M–

The use of the M– key is introduced following a similar pattern to that on Textbook page 19.

Discuss the scenario by referring to the illustrations on the page. Controlled by a member of *Zarco*'s crew, droids load crates of minerals bound for Earth. During the journey, the crew transfers some of the minerals into smaller boxes so that they can be unloaded by droids on Delta 7.

Question 1 does not require the use of the M– key.

In question 2, the calculator should be used in the same way as described for the corresponding question on Textbook page 19.

The problem in question 4 can be approached in different ways. For example,

— multiply to build up a table like this:

Number of containers	2	3	4	5	6	7	8	9
Weight of Lineum (gg)	1600	2400	3200	(4000)	4800	5600	6400	too heavy
Weight of Ambal (gg)	1000	1500	2000	2500	(3000)	3500	4000	4500

Search for two numbers, one from each row of weights, which total 7000 and also link with a total of 11 containers: that is, 4000 and 3000. Hence 5 containers hold Lineum and 6 hold Ambal.

— use the memory:

There cannot be more than 8 containers of Lineum as the total weight of 9 or more containers is greater than 7000 gg. Find 8×800 and add this to the memory; find 3×500 and add this to the memory; use MR , giving 6900 gg, which is not the required total.

After clearing the memory, repeat for 7×800 and 4×500 and so on until the correct combination, 5×800 and 6×500, is found.

Kitbits Company

A context for fractions and percentages

The work on Textbook pages 21–7 and Workbook page 5 is set in the context of a
manufacturing company called 'Kitbits', which makes various kits, puzzles and games.

Introducing the context

The context could be introduced by discussing the various departments and people
that may be found in a manufacturing company. For example,

— designers and technicians

— production line

— sales and marketing

— stock control

— managers and directors.

Other possible activities associated with this context are as follows:

1   Favourite toys
Discuss with the children their favourite early childhood toys, perhaps listing those
mentioned. Also discuss those toys owned now by younger brothers and sisters. Have
any changes occurred in the types of toy which are popular?

Focus in particular on construction kit-type toys and ask the children to describe what
they made using these.

2   Kitbits logo
Tell the children that Kitbits is running a competition to design a new logo. Ask them
to draw designs for this. Make a display of logos produced and ask the children to
select the best one. For example,

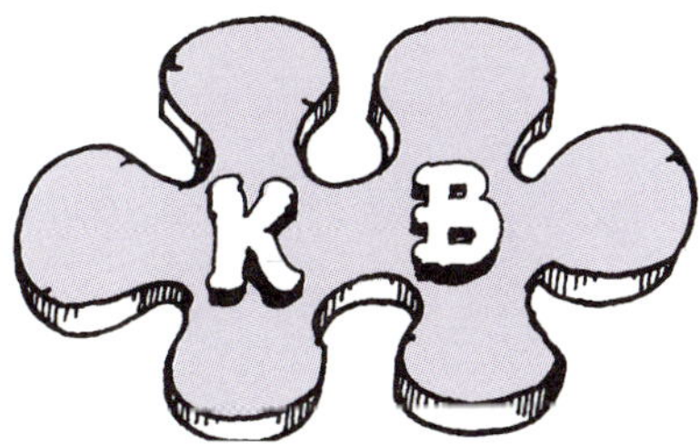
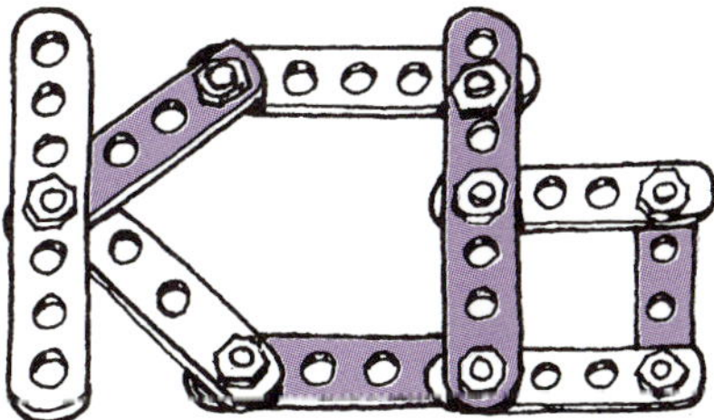

3   Kit boxes
Tell the children that Kitbits is about to launch a new series of kits. Ask them to
produce and display appropriate designs for some of the following kit boxes:

— Delta 7 kit	— Fort kit
— Mosaic kit	— Tower kit
— Technokit	— Dinosaur kit
— Electrokit	— Aeroplane kit.

UA3a/5	UA3a/5
N2c,3g/4	N2b,3d/4
N3gh,4abf/5	N3ce,4ab/5
RTN/E2	
FPR/D1	
FPR/E	
NOb/4→5	
NUd/5	

Fractions

Overview

This section

■ revises and extends work on finding equivalent fractions

■ revises and extends simplification of fractions

■ revises and extends previous work on improper fractions

■ introduces addition and subtraction of fractions

■ introduces addition and subtraction of mixed numbers

■ introduces multiplication of a fraction by a whole number

■ revises and extends work on finding a fraction of a whole number.

	Teacher's Notes	Textbook	Workbook	Reinforcement Sheets
Kitbits Company: a context for fractions and percentages	57			
Fractions: equivalence, simplification	60	21*	5*	8
Mixed numbers, improper fractions	62	22*		9
Fractions: addition and subtraction	64	23		
Addition of a mixed number and a fraction	66	24		
Subtraction of a fraction from a mixed number	67	25*		10
Whole number times a fraction	69	26*		
Fraction of a whole number	71	27*		

Homework provided in Home Link-up.

Extension activities related to the above section of work are as follows:

	Teacher's Notes	Extension Textbook
Fractions to decimals	261	E10
Fractions as percentages	262	E13

Teaching notes for the Extension Textbook are in a separate section at the end of the Teacher's Notes.

Resources

Useful materials

- coloured pencils or pens
- other materials suggested within the introductory activities

Assessment and Resources Pack

Assessment

Number Check-up 5
Textbook pages 21, 22
Workbook page 5
(equivalence, simplification,
mixed fractions)

Number Check-up 6
Textbook pages 23–7
(addition, subtraction, multiplication)

Round-up 1
Questions 3(a), (b)

Resources

Problem Solving Activities
10 United (fractions, percentages)
11 How many fractions?
       (equivalence, improper fractions)
12 Which fraction?

Resource Cards
6–8 Fraction strips
(equivalence, mixed numbers,
improper fractions)

12 and 13 Matching squares
(fractions, decimals, percentages)

Teaching notes

FRACTIONS: EQUIVALENCE, SIMPLIFICATION

N2c/4
N2b/4 N3d/4
RTN/E2
NUd/5

In Heinemann Mathematics 6, rules were established for generating equivalent fractions

— by multiplying $\overset{\times 5}{\underset{\times 5}{\frac{5}{8} = \frac{25}{40}}}$

— by dividing $\overset{\div 7}{\underset{\div 7}{\frac{28}{49} = \frac{4}{7}}}$

This work is now revised and extended to include examples where more than one division may be required to simplify the fraction. For example,

$$\overset{\div 10}{\underset{\div 10}{\frac{60}{80}}} = \overset{\div 2}{\underset{\div 2}{\frac{6}{8}}} = \frac{3}{4}$$

The context is that of the Kitbits Company, a firm which produces a variety of kit toys.

Introductory activities

1   Rectiles   *(equivalence by multiplying)*

■ Display pictures of two rectiles, pieces from a kit for building model houses, that are the same shape and size.

Ask the children to state the fraction of each rectile coloured.

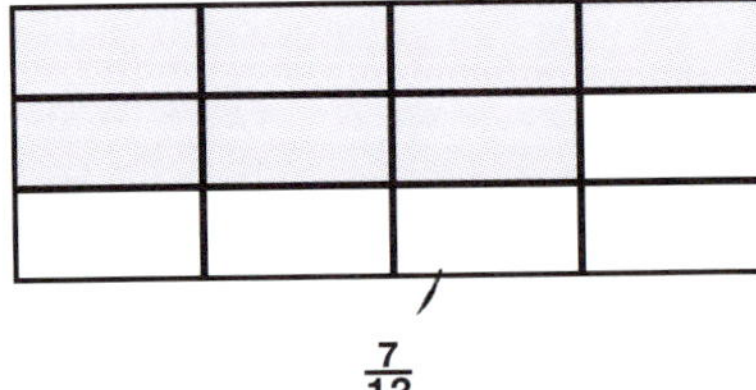
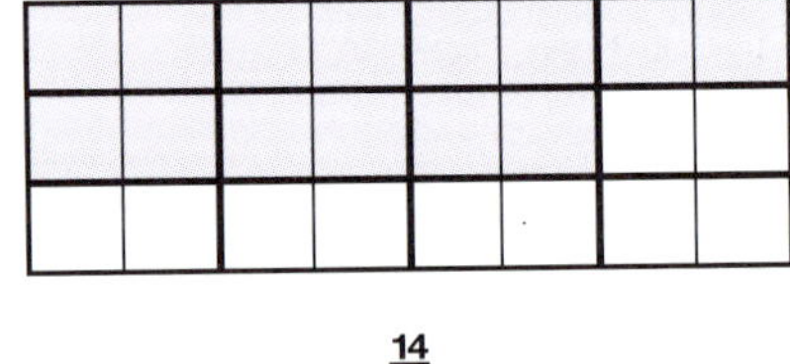

$$\frac{7}{12} \qquad\qquad \frac{14}{24}$$

■ Through discussion, establish that the same amount of each rectile is coloured and hence the fractions are equivalent: that is,

$$\frac{7}{12} = \frac{14}{24}$$

■ Ask the children to change the first fraction to the second one without using a diagram.

'How can you change the top number, 7, to 14?'
(By multiplying by 2.)

'How can you change the bottom number 12, to 24?'
(By multiplying by 2.)

$$\overset{\times 2}{\underset{\times 2}{\frac{7}{12} = \frac{14}{24}}}$$

Through discussion, re-establish the following rule:

'To make an equal fraction, **multiply** the top **and** the bottom by the same number.'

- Use the rule in other examples:

$$\frac{5}{6} = \frac{}{18} \qquad \frac{4}{5} = \frac{20}{} \qquad \frac{1}{3} = \frac{}{15}$$

2 Tritiles *(equivalence by dividing)*

- Draw a pair of tritiles on the chalkboard.

  Ask the children to state the fraction of each tritile coloured.

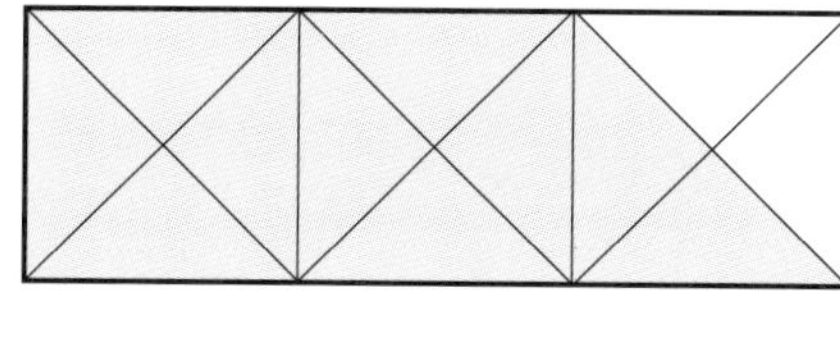
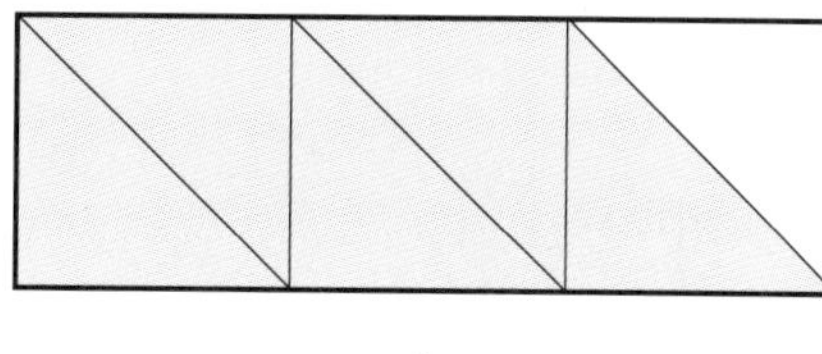

$$\frac{10}{12} \qquad\qquad\qquad \frac{5}{6}$$

Remind them that these fractions are equivalent as they represent the same part of a tritile.

- Ask the children how to change the first fraction to the second without using a diagram.

  'How can you change the top number, 10, to 5?'
  (By dividing by 2.)

  'How can you change the bottom number, 24, to 12?'
  (By dividing by 2.)

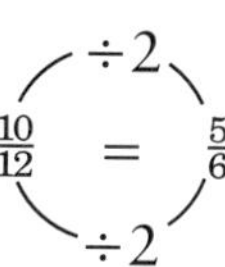

$$\frac{10}{12} \overset{\div 2}{\underset{\div 2}{=}} \frac{5}{6}$$

Through discussion re-establish the following rule:

'To simplify a fraction, divide the top and the bottom by the same number.'

- Use the rule in a number of examples where

  — the numerator of the second fraction is missing. For example, $\frac{20}{30} = \frac{}{3}$

  — the denominator of the second fraction is missing. For example, $\frac{36}{63} = \frac{4}{}$

At this point the children could try Workbook page 5 and Textbook page 21, questions 1–4.

3 Mosaics *(simplifying in more than one step)*

- Introduce a question such as

  'Kitbits sells mosaic tile kits. In the large kit, 60 of the 90 mosaic tiles are white, 15 are red and 15 are blue. What fraction of the tiles are white?'

Through discussion establish that

  — the fraction of tiles that are white is $\frac{60}{90}$

  — the top and bottom numbers can both be divided by 10

$$\frac{60}{90} \overset{\div 10}{\underset{\div 10}{=}} \frac{6}{9}$$

  — the **new** top and bottom numbers can then be divided by 3.

$$\frac{60}{90} \overset{\div 10}{\underset{\div 10}{=}} \frac{6}{9} \overset{\div 3}{\underset{\div 3}{=}} \frac{2}{3}$$

- Repeat for other examples, such as

$$\frac{45}{60} \qquad \frac{50}{75} \qquad \frac{48}{64} \qquad \frac{72}{84}$$

H13 **R**8

Textbook page 21 *Fractions: equivalence, simplification*
Workbook page 5

On Workbook page 5, in questions 1 and 2, the children should colour each pair of drawings to match.

On Textbook page 21, in questions 2 and 4, the children should realize that they need to look at either two numerators or two denominators to identify which multiplier or divisor to use.

In question 6, some children may need to be encouraged to simplify the fraction fully by applying the division procedure for a second time. For example, in question 6,

(a) 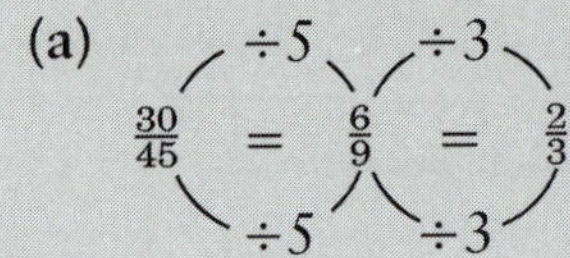
$$\frac{30}{45} \overset{\div 5}{\underset{\div 5}{=}} \frac{6}{9} \overset{\div 3}{\underset{\div 3}{=}} \frac{2}{3}$$

(b) 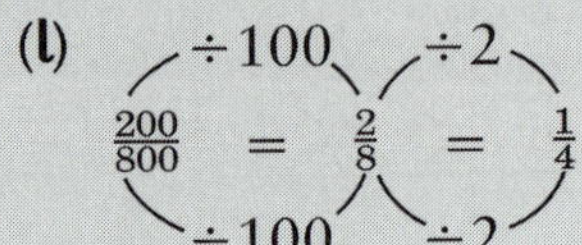
$$\frac{200}{800} \overset{\div 100}{\underset{\div 100}{=}} \frac{2}{8} \overset{\div 2}{\underset{\div 2}{=}} \frac{1}{4}$$

MIXED NUMBERS, IMPROPER FRACTIONS

In Heinemann Mathematics 6, the relationship between mixed numbers and improper fractions was introduced. The examples involved only halves and quarters.

This work is now extended to include other fractions.

The context continues with the introduction of a 'Misfits' kit.

Introductory activities

1 Hexatiles *(fractions of a set)*

Tell the children that hexatiles are roof tiles used when making model houses.

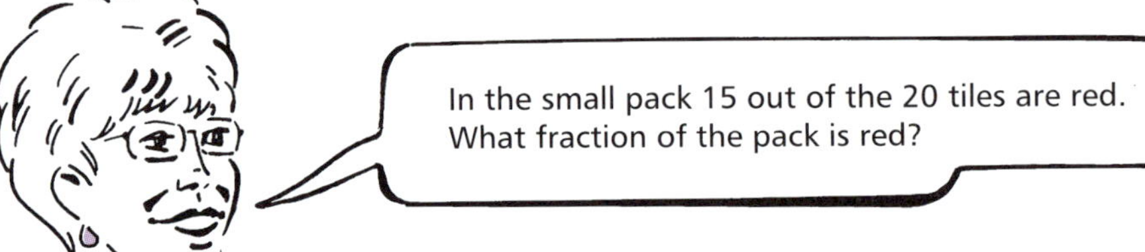

Discuss how the fraction could be recorded and simplified.

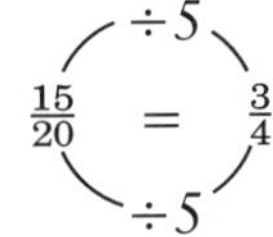
$$\frac{15}{20} \overset{\div 5}{\underset{\div 5}{=}} \frac{3}{4}$$

$\frac{3}{4}$ of the pack is red

Repeat for other examples, including examples where more than one division is necessary to simplify the fraction.

2   Buildakits   *(mixed numbers to improper fractions)*

■ Use drawings of Buildakits, each containing six squares when full.

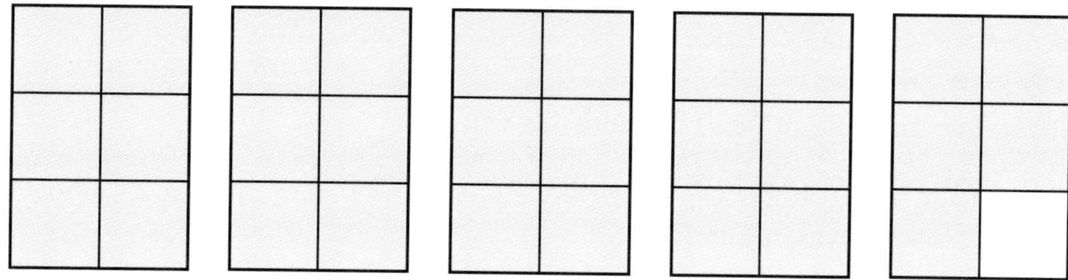

Establish that each square is $\frac{1}{6}$ of a Buildakit.

Tell the children that the drawing shows $4\frac{5}{6}$ kits.

Remind the children $4\frac{5}{6}$ is called a mixed number because it is a mixture of a whole number and a fraction.

■ Through discussion, establish the following:

— in 4 Buildakits there are $4 \times 6 = 24$ sixths

— adding the other 5 sixths gives 29 sixths

— the recording $4\frac{5}{6} = \frac{24}{6} + \frac{5}{6} = \frac{29}{6}$

(Some children may manage without the intermediate step and simply write $4\frac{5}{6} = \frac{29}{6}$.)

— $\frac{29}{6}$ is an **improper fraction**.

Repeat for other examples such as $3\frac{2}{5}$, $5\frac{3}{4}$ and $2\frac{4}{7}$.

3   Patchwork kits   *(improper fractions to mixed numbers)*

Each Patchwork kit contains 8 shapes. Each shape is $\frac{1}{8}$ of a kit.

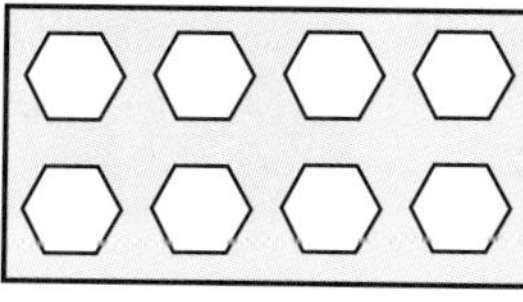
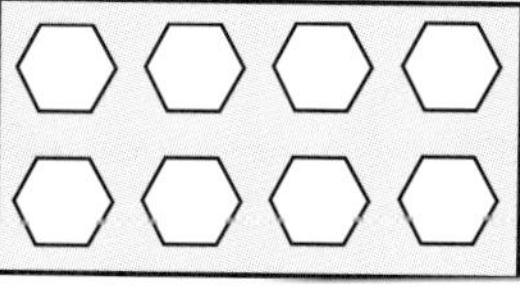
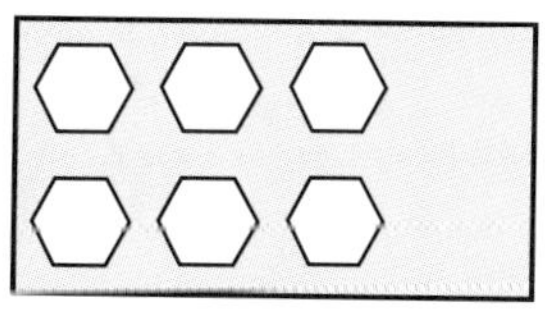

22 eighths make $22 \div 8$ kits, which is 2 whole kits and 6 eighths of a kit.

$$\frac{22}{8} = 2\frac{6}{8} = 2\frac{3}{4}$$

Repeat for other examples such as $\frac{15}{6}$, $\frac{23}{10}$ and $\frac{23}{5}$.

Textbook page 22   *Fractions: mixed, improper*

In questions 1, 2 and 4, some children may need to be reminded to simplify answers where possible. For example, in question 4(c), $\frac{14}{6} = 2\frac{2}{6} = 2\frac{1}{3}$.

N2c/4
N2b/4 N3d/4
RTN/E2
NUd,Ob/5

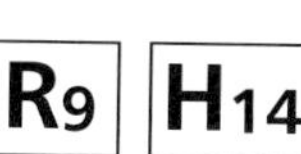

R9   H14

The children are now introduced to methods for

— addition of fractions with the same denominator:

with totals less than 1

with mixed number answers

— subtraction of fractions with the same denominator

— subtraction of a fraction from a whole number.

The work is set in the Kitbits Company's laboratory, where the plastics are prepared for use in the production of parts for construction kits.

Introductory activities

1 Machine displays *(adding fractions; totals less than 1)*

Draw a number line marked in fifths on the chalkboard to represent the display on a machine. Discuss with the children what each interval represents as a fraction of the number line.

Consider the example $\frac{1}{5} + \frac{3}{5}$.

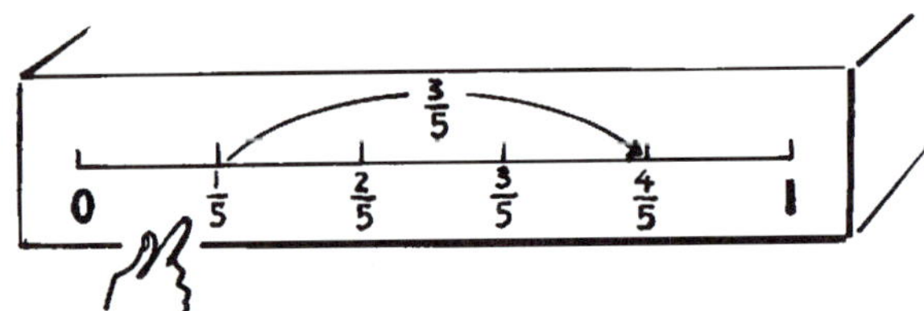

Start at $\frac{1}{5}$. Add $\frac{3}{5}$ by jumping **forwards** $\frac{3}{5}$ to the finishing position $\frac{4}{5}$.

Say aloud the original addition while pointing to the number line. Record the answer simultaneously.

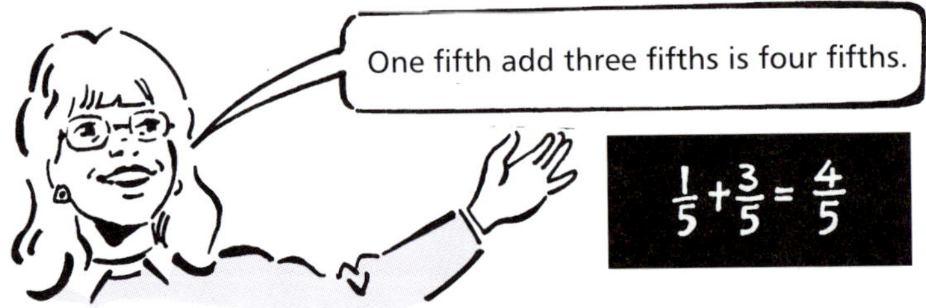

■ Use a number line marked in eighths. In the same way, discuss an addition in which the answer can be simplified: for example, $\frac{1}{8} + \frac{5}{8}$.

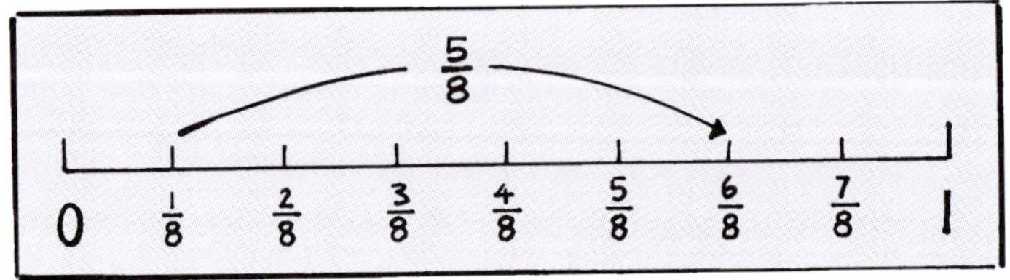

$\frac{1}{8} + \frac{5}{8} = \frac{6}{8}$ 'One eighth add five eighths is six eighths,

$= \frac{3}{4}$ which can be written as three quarters.'

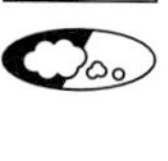

2   Paint dials   *(subtracting fractions)*

Use a number line marked in tenths to represent the dial on a paint machine.
The machine shows how much paint has been used.
Consider the problem,

$$\frac{9}{10} - \frac{6}{10}$$

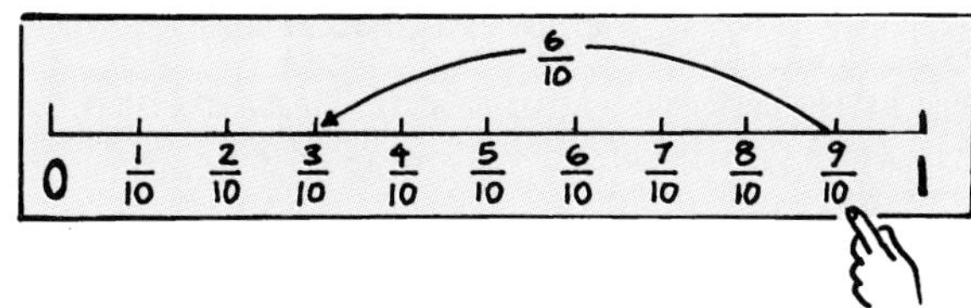

Start at $\frac{9}{10}$ on the dial. Jump back $\frac{6}{10}$ to finish at $\frac{3}{10}$.

$$\frac{9}{10} - \frac{6}{10} = \frac{3}{10}$$ 'Nine tenths take away six tenths is three tenths.'

■ Discuss a subtraction where the answer can be simplified:
for example, $\frac{7}{10} - \frac{3}{10}$

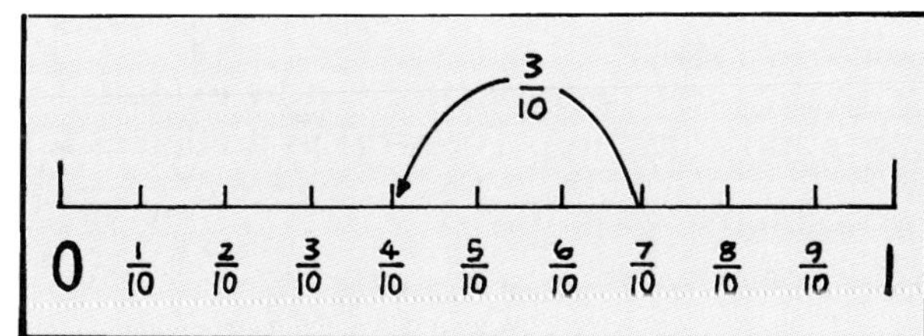

$$\frac{7}{10} - \frac{3}{10} = \frac{4}{10}$$ 'Seven tenths take away three tenths is four tenths.

$$= \frac{2}{5}$$ Four tenths can be written as two fifths.'

3   Paint mixer   *(adding fractions, mixed number totals)*

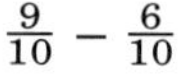

Two containers of paint are put
into the mixer. Draw a number
line marked in sixths to represent
the paint mixer's dial.

Consider the example $\frac{4}{6} + \frac{5}{6}$

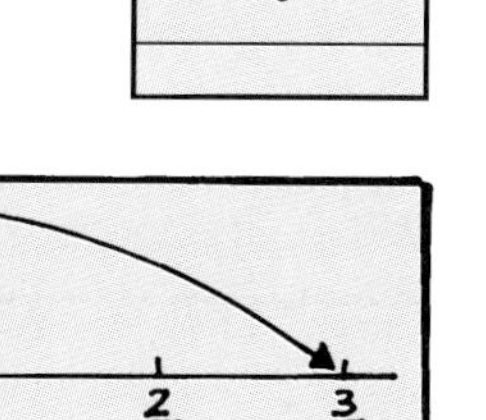

'4 sixths and 5 sixths make 9 sixths.'

Start at $\frac{4}{6}$ and count along one sixth at a time. The children should see that $\frac{9}{6}$ is
equivalent to 1 whole and $\frac{3}{6}$.

$$\frac{4}{6} + \frac{5}{6} = \frac{9}{6}$$
$$= 1\frac{3}{6}$$
$$= 1\frac{1}{2}$$

| UA3a/5 N3g/5 |
| UA3a/5 N3c/5 |
| FPR/E |
| NUd,Ob/5 |

Textbook page 23   *Fractions: addition and subtraction*

The work on fractions continues in the context of Kitbits machines used to mix chemicals for moulding machines.

In question 2, parts (h) and (i) involve subtraction from 1. Part (j) requires the children to apply their knowledge of equivalent fractions and re-write the subtraction as $\frac{2}{4} - \frac{1}{4}$.

In question 3(o), the children should re-write $\frac{1}{2} + \frac{3}{4}$ as $\frac{2}{4} + \frac{3}{4}$ before adding.

ADDITION OF A MIXED NUMBER AND A FRACTION

| UA3a/5 N3g/5 |
| UA3a/5 N3c/5 |
| FPR/E |
| NUd,Ob/5 |

Addition of fractions with the same denominator is now extended to examples involving a mixed number and a fraction. The work is graded as follows:

— total of the fractional parts less than 1

— total of the fractional parts greater than 1.

The Kitbits machines context continues.

Introductory activities

1 Plasti-press   *(mixed number addition)*

Draw a number line marked in sixths to represent the gauge on the Plasti-press. Tins of chemicals are mixed in the machine.

Consider the example $1\frac{1}{6} + \frac{3}{6}$.

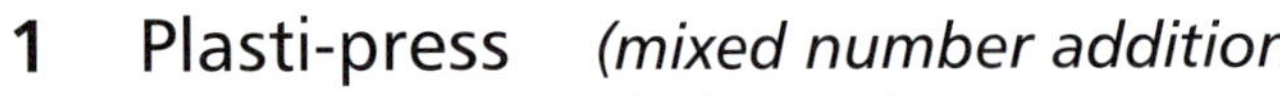

Start at $1\frac{1}{6}$ and count along one sixth at a time. The children should see that $1\frac{1}{6}$ add $\frac{3}{6}$ is $1\frac{4}{6}$.

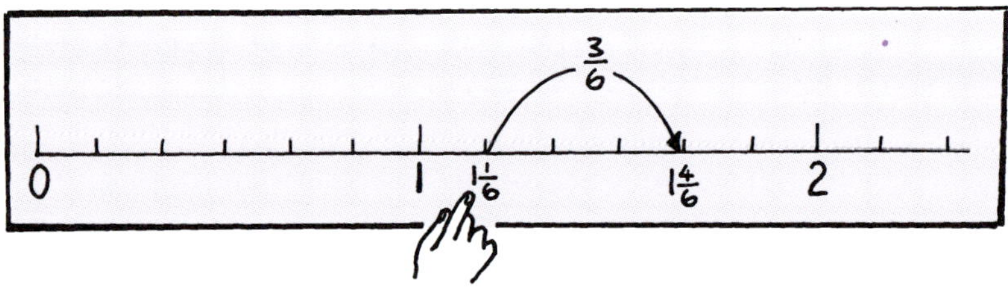

- Repeat for examples where the total of two fractional parts is greater than 1: for example, $1\frac{7}{10} + \frac{5}{10}$.

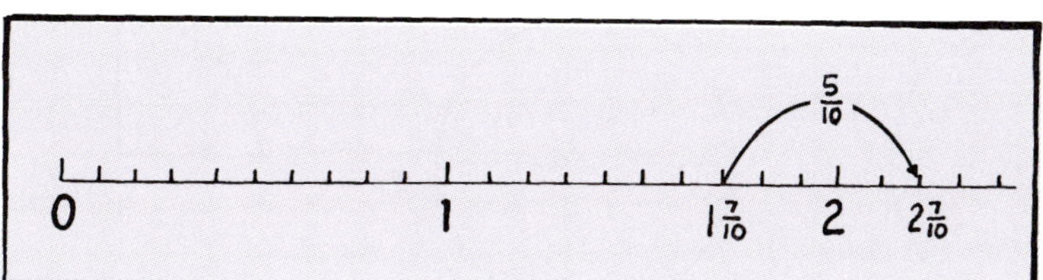

$1\frac{7}{10} + \frac{5}{10} = 1\frac{12}{10}$

$= 1 + 1\frac{2}{10}$

$= 2\frac{2}{10}$

$= 2\frac{1}{5}$

Textbook page 24   *Fractions: mixed number addition*

In questions 1 and 2, the fractional parts, when added, have a total of 1 or less.

In questions 4, 6 and 7 the fractional parts mainly have a total greater than 1. In question 4, parts (k), (n) and (o) the children have to use their knowledge of the equivalent fractions $\frac{1}{2} = \frac{2}{4}$ to enable them to carry out the addition.

UA3a/5 N3g/5
UA3a/5 N3c/5
FPR/E
NUd/5

SUBTRACTION OF A FRACTION FROM A MIXED NUMBER

Subtraction of fractions with the same denominator is now extended to examples involving a mixed number and a fraction. The work is graded as follows:

— no decomposition of one whole required

— decomposition required.

There are computers on the production lines at Kitbits. They display information about machines used at the factory.

UA3a/5 N3g/5
UA3a/5 N3c/5
FPR/E
NUd/5

Introductory activities

1   Colour wedges   *(mixed number subtraction)*

Consider the example $2\frac{3}{4} - \frac{2}{4}$.

Lay out $2\frac{3}{4}$.

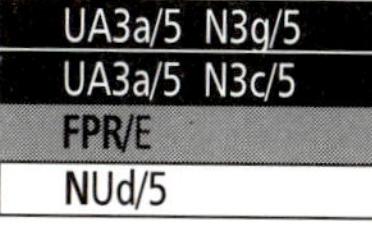

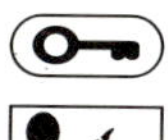

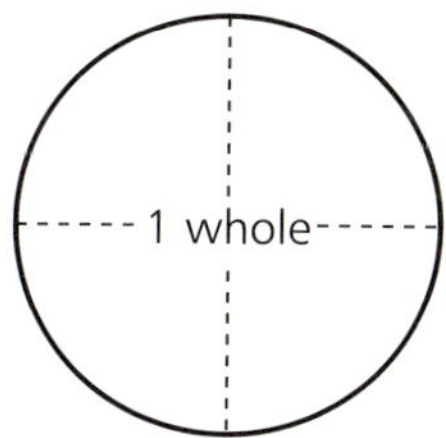
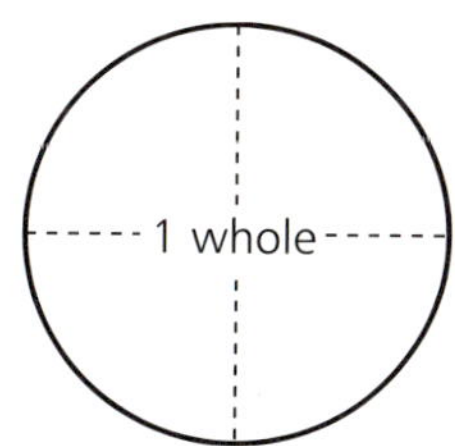
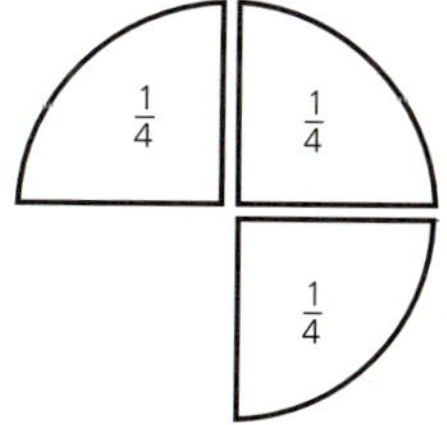

Remove 2 quarters.

Establish that $2\frac{1}{4}$ is left.

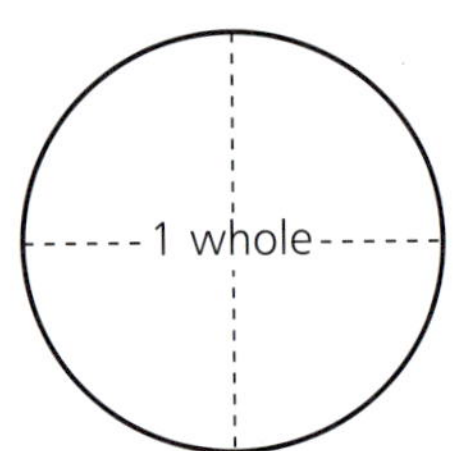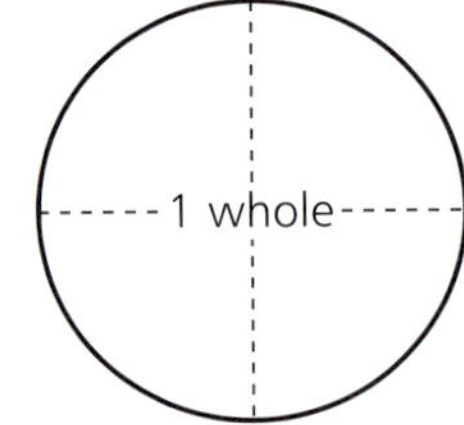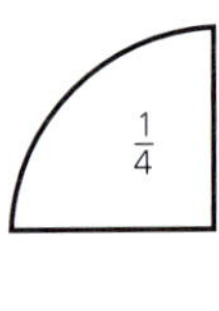

$2\frac{3}{4} - \frac{2}{4} = 2\frac{1}{4}$ 'Two and three quarters take away two quarters is two and one quarter.'

Repeat for other examples, such as $3\frac{4}{5} - \frac{1}{5}$ and $2\frac{7}{8} - \frac{2}{8}$.

■ Use the colour blocks for subtraction with decomposition.

Lay out $1\frac{1}{8}$. 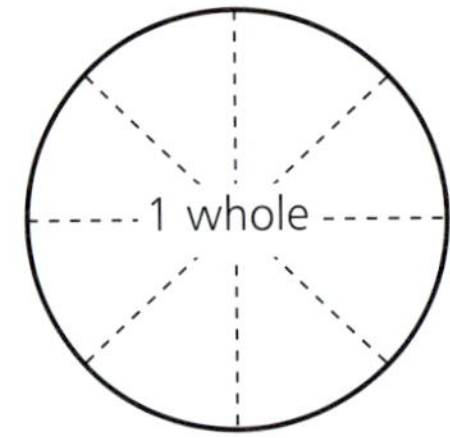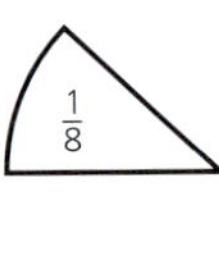

Tell the children that 3 eighths are removed to make paint.

This gives the subtraction $1\frac{1}{8} - \frac{3}{8}$.

Show them how to exchange 1 whole for 8 eighths.

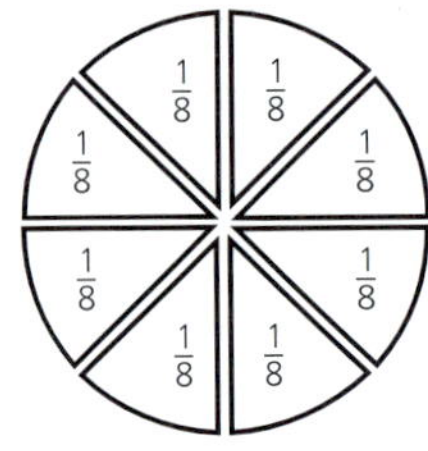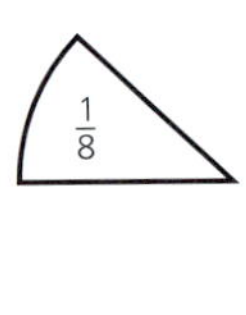

Remove 3 eighths to leave 6 eighths.

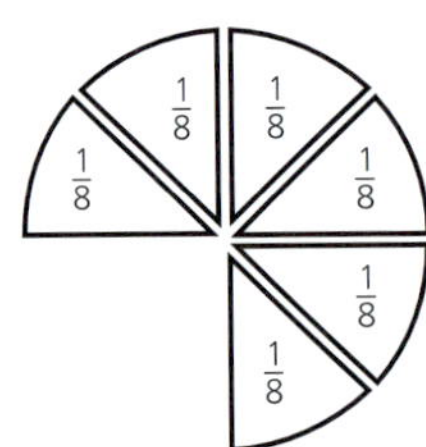

Show the children how to record this subtraction.

$1\frac{1}{8} - \frac{3}{8}$

$= \frac{9}{8} - \frac{3}{8}$ ⟵ exchange 1 whole for 8 eighths

$= \frac{6}{8}$ ⟵ subtract to give 6 eighths

$= \frac{3}{4}$ ⟵ simplify to give 3 quarters

Repeat for other examples.

Textbook page 25   *Mixed number subtraction*

The computers in the Kitbits factory display information about the factory's machines. The drawings of computer displays on this page are **not** intended to illustrate the process of subtraction.

Questions 1 and 2 involve subtraction of a fraction from a mixed number in which no exchange is required.

In question 2(j) the children should apply their knowledge of equivalent fractions and record the subtraction as $4\frac{2}{4} - \frac{1}{4}$, before continuing.

Questions 3 and 4 involve subtracting a fraction from a mixed number where a whole has to be exchanged. Apart from 4(j), none of the **answers** involves mixed numbers.

R10 H15

WHOLE NUMBER TIMES A FRACTION

Simple multiplication involving 'a whole number times a fraction' is now introduced. Examples are at the following three levels:

— product less than 1: for example, $3 \times \frac{1}{4}$

— product a whole number: for example, $6 \times \frac{1}{3}$

— product greater than 1: for example, $4 \times \frac{2}{5}$

Examples in the reverse form, such as $\frac{2}{5} \times 4$, are **not** included.

The work is set within the context of the assembly lines in Kitbits Company's factory.

Introductory activities

1   Assembling kits 1   *(meaning of a whole number times a fraction)*

■ Discuss a board diagram such as the following:

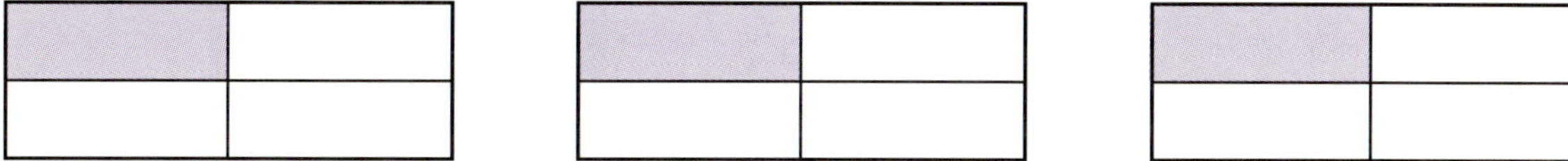

Each rectangle represents a box of plastic construction pieces being filled on the Kitbits factory's assembly line. Each box is one quarter full.

Since there are three boxes, the diagram represents 'three times one quarter', which can be written as '$3 \times \frac{1}{4}$'.

■ Repeat as necessary for diagrams showing different numbers of 'boxes' and filled fractions. The shapes of the boxes should also be varied. For example,

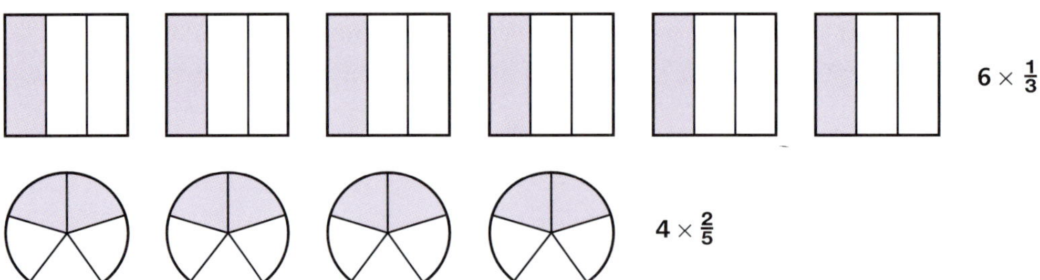

If further practice is required, a worksheet can be prepared containing similar examples.

2   Assembling kits 2
(calculation of a whole number times a fraction)

■ Explain that some of the partly filled boxes of construction pieces are going to be combined to make full boxes.

■ Discuss diagrams at the following three levels of difficulty, emphasizing the associated language and recording:

Product less than 1

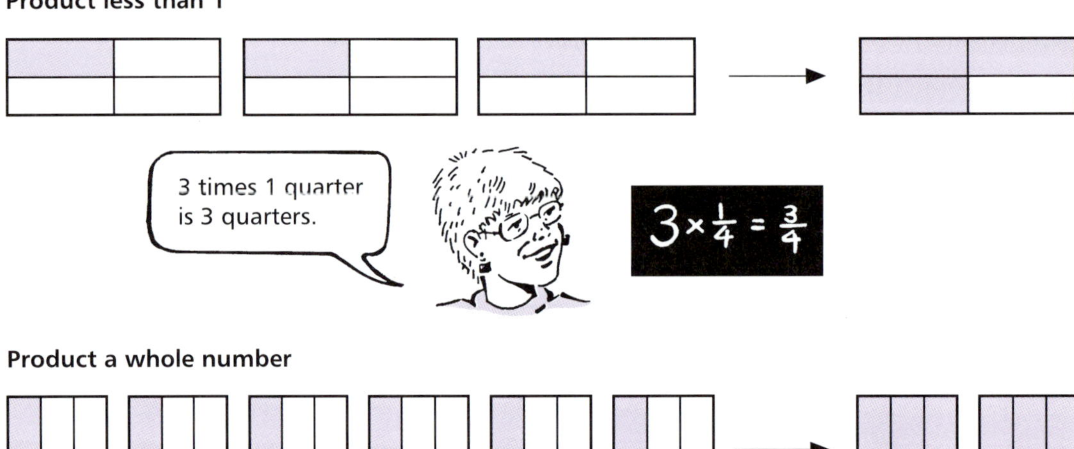

Product a whole number

Product greater than 1

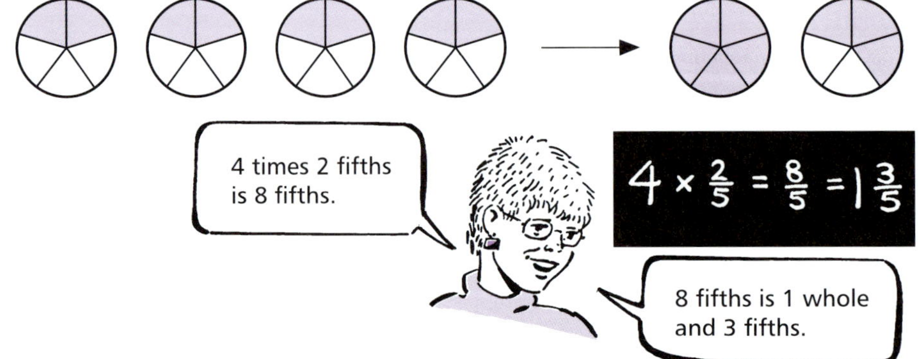

- Include examples which require the use of techniques previously introduced:

$$4 \times \tfrac{5}{8} = \tfrac{20}{8}$$

$$= 2\tfrac{4}{8} \quad \longleftarrow \quad \text{changing an improper fraction to a mixed number (from Textbook page 22)}$$

$$= 2\tfrac{1}{2} \quad \longleftarrow \quad \text{simplification (from Textbook page 21).}$$

N2c/4	N3fg,4a/5
N2b/4	N3c,4a/5
FPR/E	
NUd,Ob/5	

Textbook page 26 *Fractions: whole number times a fraction*

Some discussion may be necessary to explain the context of the assembly lines in the Kitbits Company's factory. As the construction kit boxes move slowly along a conveyor belt, workers insert the pieces appropriately into the boxes.

The grading of examples on the page is by products:

— product less than 1, question 1

— product a whole number, question 2

— product greater than 1, questions 3 and 4.

H16

FRACTION OF A WHOLE NUMBER

In Heinemann Mathematics 6, finding a fraction of a whole number was limited to fractions with numerator 1: for example, $\tfrac{1}{10}$ of 80 (calculated mentally), $\tfrac{1}{8}$ of 816 and $\tfrac{1}{5}$ of 1460 (using the written technique for division).

N3fg,4ab/5	
N3ce,4ab/5	
FPR/E2	
NUd/5	

The work in Heinemann Mathematics P7

— consolidates and extends the above by including examples where the whole number represents a measure or a sum of money: for example, $\tfrac{1}{4}$ of 3 kg, $\tfrac{1}{10}$ of £9

— introduces fractions with numerator greater than 1: for example, $\tfrac{3}{5}$ of 2 hours

— includes the use of a calculator for examples with larger whole numbers, such as $\tfrac{3}{7}$ of 4683.

The context continues with the assembly of construction kits in the Kitbits Company's factory.

Introductory activities

1 Spare parts
(fraction, numerator greater than 1, of a whole number)

- Explain that customers can order packs of spare parts for any kit made by Kitbits Company. Discuss an example such as

'$\tfrac{5}{8}$ of the pieces in a pack of 48 plastic tubes are blue. How many are blue?'

The discussion should emphasize

— dividing by 8 to find **one** eighth of 48

— multiplying that answer by 5 to find **five** eighths of 48.

A recording form such as the one on the right could be used.

<table>
<tr><td colspan="1">Recording</td></tr>
<tr><td>$\frac{1}{8}$ of 48 = 6</td></tr>
<tr><td>$\frac{5}{8}$ of 48 = 5 × 6 = 30</td></tr>
<tr><td>30 tubes are blue.</td></tr>
</table>

■ Include several examples involving the same whole number. For example,

$\frac{2}{10}$ of 140 $\frac{3}{10}$ of 140 $\frac{5}{10}$ of 140

2   Dispatching   *(fraction of a quantity)*

■ The packs of spare parts are weighed in order to find the cost of delivering them to customers. Discuss an example such as

'The pack of rods weighs 3 kilograms. $\frac{3}{5}$ of the rods are red. What is the weight of the red rods?'

The discussion points are similar to those above:

— 3 kilograms is the same weight as 3000 grams

— divide by 5 to find **one** fifth

— multiply that answer by 3 to find **three** fifths.

A recording form such as the one on the right could be used.

<table>
<tr><td colspan="1">Recording</td></tr>
<tr><td>3 kg = 3000 g</td></tr>
<tr><td>$\frac{1}{5}$ of 3000 = 600</td></tr>
<tr><td>$\frac{3}{5}$ of 3000 = 3 × 600 = 1800</td></tr>
<tr><td>The weight of the red rods is 1800 g.</td></tr>
</table>

■ Include examples involving different measures and sums of money. For example,

$\frac{5}{6}$ of 3 hours $\frac{7}{10}$ of 4 metres $\frac{2}{5}$ of £8

3   Stocking up   *(using a calculator)*

■ Use an example such as the following to discuss the use of a calculator when finding a fraction of a whole number.

Each week replacement materials are ordered by Kitbits Company.

'1134 litres of dye are ordered, $\frac{2}{9}$ of it yellow. How many litres of yellow dye are ordered?'

To find $\frac{2}{9}$ of 1134,   Enter   

Divide by 9 $\longrightarrow$ Press ÷ 9 = to give   126.

Multiply by 2 $\longrightarrow$ Press × 2 = to give   252.

252 litres of yellow dye are ordered.

Highlight that only the **final** volume needs to be recorded.

■ Discuss how the calculation need only involve pressing $=$ once:

Enter 

Divide by 9 and multiply by 2 $\longrightarrow$ Press $\div$ 9 $\times$ 2 $=$

to give 252.

Textbook page 27 *Fractions: fraction of a whole number*

Explain that machines on some of the assembly lines in the factory are used to pack construction kits. Sometimes a fault develops in a machine and some wrong pieces are packed in the kits.

In question 1, some children may need to be reminded to change the unit of measurement to that shown in the brackets.

In questions 3(d), (e) and (f), some guidance may be needed about the form of recording expected – see Introductory activity 2.

In question 5(b), simplification of the fraction of the bits which are white might be done in three steps by some children:

$$\frac{450}{1800} = \frac{45}{180} = \frac{5}{20} = \frac{1}{4}$$

A few may realize that halving 1800 gives 900 and halving 900 gives 450, leading to $\frac{450}{1800}$ as $\frac{1}{4}$.

N3fg,4ab/5
N3ce,4ab/5
FPR/D1 FPR/E
NUd,Ob/5

H17

Orlando

A context for decimals

The work on Textbook pages 28–44 and Workbook pages 6–8 is set in the context of the *Orlando*, a large holiday cruise ship.

As the children progress through the Textbook and Workbook pages, they are introduced to the following features and passenger facilities associated with the *Orlando*:

— cargo holds

— air travel between the UK and the *Orlando*'s home port

— embarkation and the ship's speed in knots

— the fitness room

— deck games and activities

— cabin re-fitting

— cabin services

— preparation of meals in the ship's galley

— on-board entertainment and competitions

— emergency and survival equipment.

Activities associated with trips ashore at some of the ports visited by *Orlando* are also met. For example,

— scuba diving

— water skiing

— shopping

— eating out

— sightseeing.

Introducing the context

The context could be introduced by undertaking activities such as the following:

1 Types of ship

Ask the children to suggest various categories of large, non-military ships. Discuss their principal uses and features. For example,

— cruise ships: for holiday cruising between a number of ports, often in different countries.

— cargo ships: for conveying materials from ports in the countries where the materials are produced to ports in countries where they will be used. Some cargo is carried in tankers, such as oil. Other materials are often carried in container ships.

— ferries: for carrying passengers and vehicles between ports which are often relatively short distances apart.

— factory ships: for processing and storing catches of fish landed by several smaller fishing craft, before travelling from the fishing grounds to a home port.

2   Ocean liners

Ask the children to consult reference books and other sources to find out as much as they can about the history of famous Atlantic liners such as the following:

— *Titanic*

— *Mauretania* and *Lusitania*

— *Normandie*

— *Queen Mary*

— *United States*

— *Queen Elizabeth.*

Discuss the significance of these ships in the days before air travel, when European emigration to the USA was at a high level and the Blue Riband was awarded for the fastest crossings. The unfortunate fates of the *Titanic, Lusitania* and *Queen Elizabeth* may be of particular interest and could stimulate various drama- and art-related activities.

3   Modern cruise ships

Discuss the development and role of the modern cruise ship as more of a floating resort than merely a floating hotel or a means of transport. Ships such as the *QE2* and the *Oriana* were designed with this new purpose in mind.

Ask the children to list the kind of features and facilities which they may have experienced or heard about, or would expect to find, on a large cruise ship: for example, arrangements for

— living and sleeping

— eating and drinking

— keeping fit and active

— leisure, recreation and entertainment

— health and safety

— emergencies

— storing cargo

— accommodating the crew

— navigating and steering

— communicating with land and with other ships

— providing power.

Some books and computer software provide interesting cross-sectional pictures of cruise ships which show the various uses of the many decks and levels.

4   Cruise destinations

Holiday brochures are a useful source of information about popular destinations for cruise ships, and also provide details about prices, embarkation ports, on-board facilities and the sort of trips ashore that are available. The children could be asked to use brochures to plan cruising holidays within a given budget. Maps could be drawn to illustrate routes and destinations.

UA2acd/4	UA2abd/4
UA2ad/5	UA2cd,3d/5
N2b,3g,4b/4	N2ab,3c,4bd/4
N2b,3cdfgh, 4ac/5	N2ab,3bcef,4acd/5

PSE
RTN/D3,4
RTN/E2,3
AS/D1,2,3
AS/E3
MD/D1,2,3,4
MD/E2,3,4
RN/D1

PUbdf/4
PUbc/5
NUbd,Mb/4
NUc,Ob/4→5
NPb/5
NUbd/5→6
Me/5

Decimals

Overview

This section

- revises the decimal notation for tenths and hundredths

- introduces decimal notation for thousandths

- revises addition and subtraction of one-place and two-place decimals

- revises multiplication and division of one-place decimals

- introduces written algorithms for multiplication and division of two-place decimals

- deals with multiplication of decimals by 10, 100 and 1000 and division of decimals by 10 and 100

- deals with rounding and approximating decimals in the contexts of money and length

- involves the use of a calculator and includes
  — estimation to check calculator answers
  — interpretation of calculator answers to division problems.

	Teacher's Notes	Textbook	Workbook	Reinforcement Sheets
Orlando: a context for decimals	74			
Notation and place value:				
for one- and two-place decimals	78	28		
for three-place decimals	79	29, 30*	6	11
Addition and subtraction:				
of one- and two-place decimals	83	31, 32*		12
Multiplication:				
of one- and two-place decimals	85	33, 34		
by 10, 100 and 1000	86	35*		13
Division:				
of one-place decimals	88	36		
of two-place decimals	89	37, 38		
by 10 and 100	90	39*		14
Approximation and estimation	92	40, 41*	7, 8*	15, 16
Calculator, checking answers	96	42*, 43*		17
Calculator, interpreting answers	98	44		

Homework provided in Home Link-up.

Extension activities related to the above section of work are as follows:

	Teacher's Notes	Extension Textbook
Decimals: calculator	260	E8, E9
Decimals: fractions to decimals	261	E10
Decimals: money, mental approximation	262	E11

Teaching notes for the Extension Textbook are in a separate section at the end of the Teacher's Notes.

Resources

Useful materials

- calculators
- other materials suggested within the introductory activities

Assessment and Resources Pack

Assessment

Number Check-up 7
Textbook pages 28–30
Workbook page 6
Notation to three decimal places

Number Check-up 8
Textbook pages 31, 32
Addition and subtraction
to two decimal places

Number Check-up 9
Textbook pages 33–39
Multiplication and division
to two decimal places

Number Check-up 10
Textbook pages 40–44
Workbook pages 7, 8
Approximation, estimation, calculator

Round-up 2
Questions 1, 4

Resources

Problem Solving Activities
8 Make the target (Decimals, calculator)
13 Magic grids (Decimals, addition)

Resource Cards
9–11 Souvenirs (Decimals: place value,
addition, subtraction,
multiplication, division
and rounding)

Teaching notes

NOTATION AND PLACE VALUE: FOR ONE- AND TWO-PLACE DECIMALS

The first decimal place was introduced in Heinemann Mathematics 5 and the second decimal place in Heinemann Mathematics 6. This notation is now revised.

The *Orlando* context is introduced through the idea of cargo being stored in the ship's holds.

Introductory activity

Cargo space   *(revision of tenths and hundredths)*

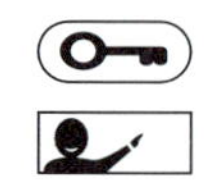

- Introduce the idea of a screen display of 100 squares which shows the **overall** cargo space of the *Orlando*. The 100 square can be drawn on the chalkboard, on squared paper or on an overhead projector transparency.

- Colour 73 squares as shown. Ask the children how many hundredths of the total cargo space are occupied and how this can be written. For example,

$$73 \text{ hundredths} = \frac{73}{100} = 0{\cdot}73$$

- Now ask the children to say and write in the same ways the amount of space **not** occupied by cargo.

- From the same display, show that the space occupied can also be expressed as **7 tenths and 3 hundredths**, and the space unoccupied as **2 tenths and 7 hundredths**.

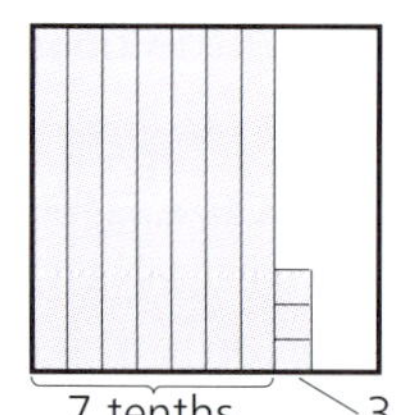

- Repeat the above with different numbers of squares.

N2b/4
N2ab/4
RTN/D3,4
NUb/4

Textbook page 28
Decimals: first and second decimal places, notation

The scenario of the *Orlando* taking on cargo should be discussed if it has not already been encountered in the introductory activity.

In question 1, the children need to realize that there are 100 squares in each of the displays for (a), (b) and (c), and 10 squares for (d).

In questions 1 and 2, the mixture of tenths and hundredths might lead to some children writing, for example, $\frac{1}{10}$ as $0{\cdot}10$ rather than as $0{\cdot}1$, or $0{\cdot}5$ as $\frac{50}{100}$ rather than as $\frac{5}{10}$. Such answers should be discussed to emphasize that $0{\cdot}10$ is $\frac{10}{100}$, which has the same value as $0{\cdot}1$ or $\frac{1}{10}$.

NOTATION AND PLACE VALUE: FOR THREE-PLACE DECIMALS

This section extends notation and place value to three-place decimals.

Computation involving three-place decimals is not included at this stage.

The *Orlando* context continues with passengers flying out to join the ship in its home port and then embarking on a cruise.

Introductory activities

1   Fuel   *(thousandths)*

■ Ask the children if they remember how many millilitres are in 1 litre – a thousand. One millilitre is one thousandth of a litre.

Tell them that only 3457 ml of fuel remain in the fuel tank of the *Orlando*'s launch.

Ask how much this is in litres and millilitres.

Tell the children that 3 litres and 457 millilitres is the same as **3 litres and 457 thousandths of a litre** or $3\frac{457}{1000}$ litres, and that the display on the launch control panel shows this as

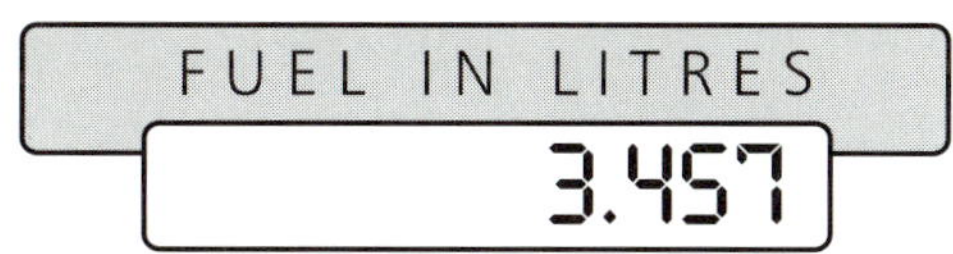

Discuss other examples such as

$$\boxed{2.055}\ \text{litres} \longrightarrow 2\tfrac{55}{1000}\ \text{litres} \longrightarrow 2\ \text{litres}\ 55\ \text{millilitres}$$

■ Produce other control panel displays on the chalkboard or on card and, for each, ask the children to say what volume of fuel is indicated in **millilitres**. For example,

$$\boxed{2.609} \longrightarrow 2609\ \text{millilitres}$$

$$\boxed{10.003} \longrightarrow 10\,003\ \text{millilitres}$$

$$\boxed{0.028} \longrightarrow 28\ \text{millilitres}$$

Include examples with zero digits and also those where the amount of fuel is less than 1 litre.

■ Ask the children to draw displays to show readings for

4320 ml   7000 ml   432 ml   9 ml

At this point the children could try Textbook page 29 and Workbook page 6.

2 Lucky digit *(decimal place-value game for two players)*

■ Two sets of cards are required as follows:

— a set of 6 place-value cards and 1 decimal point card

| H | T | U | t | h | th | • |

— a set of cards with the digits | 0 | to | 9 | .

■ Before commencing the game, familiarize the children with the use of the cards by displaying an arrangement such as

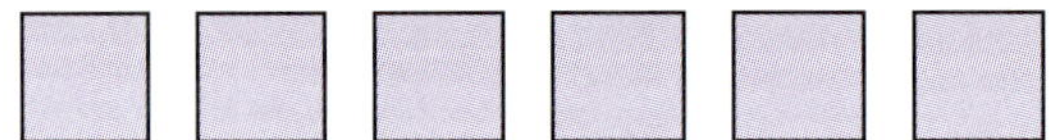

and asking them to say the number shown

'Three hundred and seventy, point six, one, five'

Ask what the value of individual digits is in a given number. For example, in the above number,

'What does the 7 represent?' ⟶ '7 tens or 70'

'What is the value of the 1?' ⟶ '1 hundredth'.

■ To start the game of 'Lucky digit', separate the place-value cards and the digit cards into two piles, shuffle each pile and place them face down on the table.

Players, in turn, use **either** the place-value cards **or** the digit cards. For example,

— player 1 chooses the top 6 digit cards **without looking at them** and lays them in a row, face down.

— player 2 turns over the place-value cards and matches one to each digit card. For example,

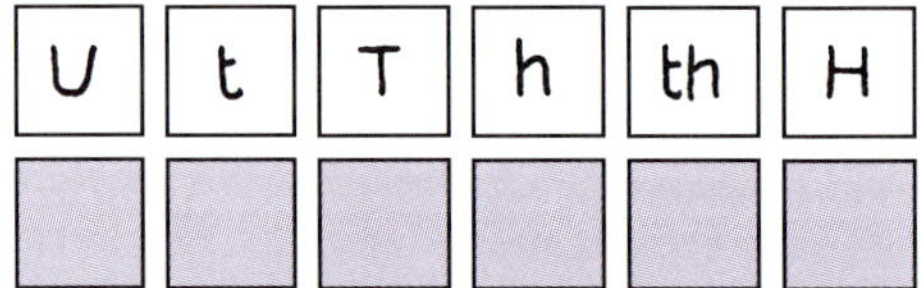

The place-value cards can be laid in **any order**.

— player 1 turns over the digit cards and then re-arranges them, inserting the decimal point card, to show the number which is then recorded.

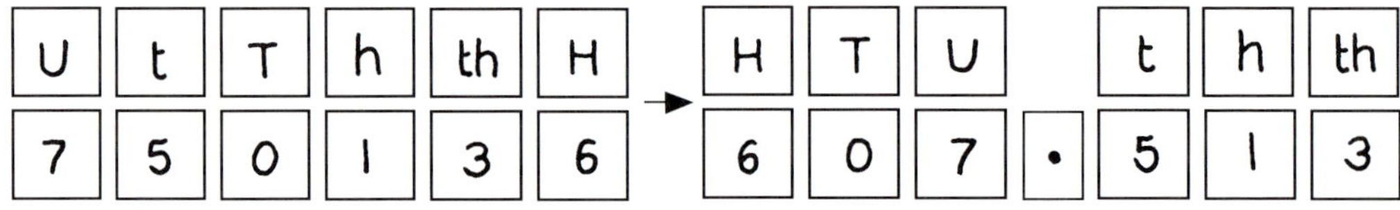

- The sequence is then repeated with player 2 having the digit cards and player 1 the place-value cards.

  The winner is the player who has recorded the larger number. Several turns can be taken and a score kept.

  The game can also be played to win with the **smaller** number.

3   Place the digit   *(decimal place-value game)*

- The following are required:

  — two place-value sheets like this 

  — two sets of ten digit cards numbered 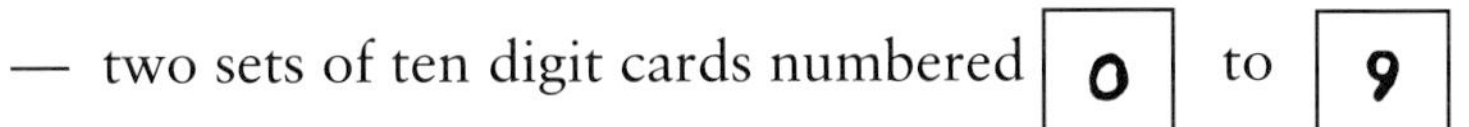 0 to 9 .

- To start the game, the two sets of digit cards are shuffled and one set is placed, face down, in front of each player.

  Each player, in turn, picks the top digit card from their set and places it, face up, on the place-value sheet.

  As the aim of the game is to make the greatest possible number using the cards drawn, each digit should be positioned accordingly. For example,

Player 1   **Player 2**

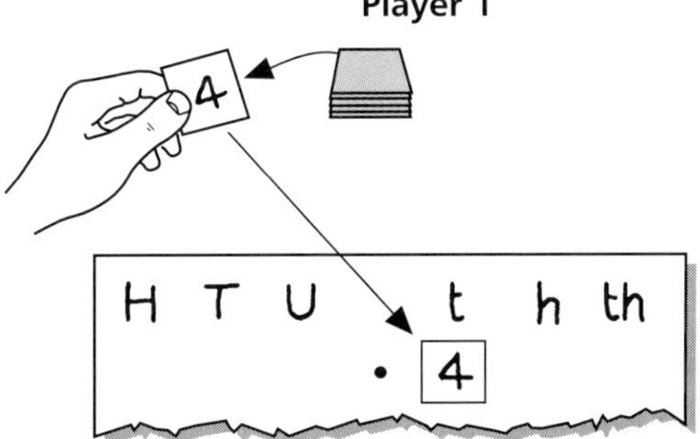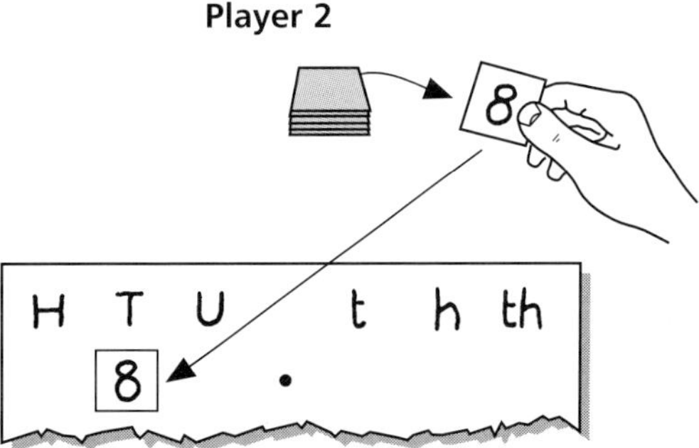

- Subsequent cards are turned over and positioned with the same goal in mind. For example,

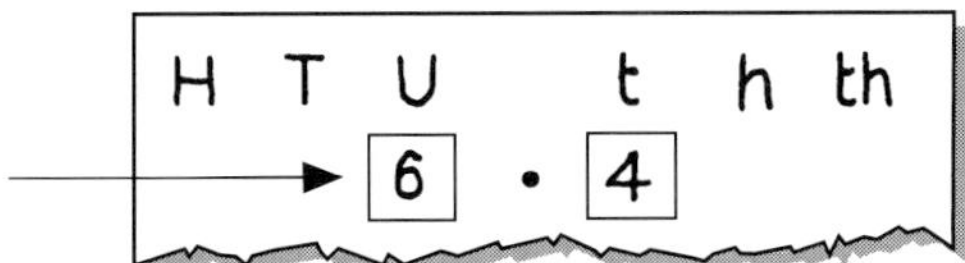

... and so on.

- When all 6 digit cards have been positioned, the winner is the player with the greater number.

  The game can also be played to win with the **smaller** number.

4   Decimal demolition   *(calculator place-value activity)*

■ This is an activity for two players using digit cards $\boxed{1}$ to $\boxed{9}$ and a decimal point card. The first player then

— lays out 4 digit cards, face down, and the decimal point card, face up, as shown.

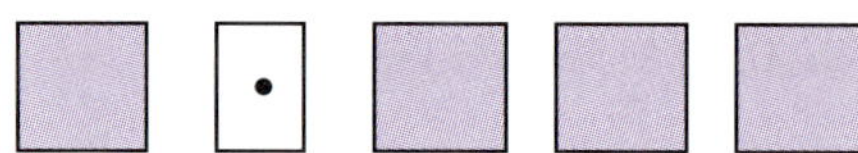

— turns over the digit cards

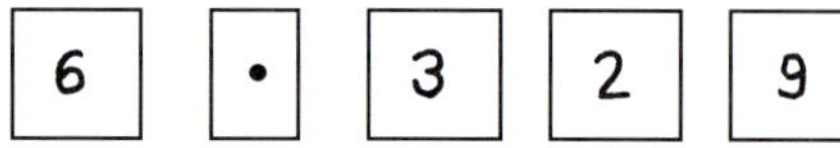

— enters this number into a calculator.

The **other** player now nominates any **one** of the digits in the first player's number, which then has to be 'demolished' (i.e. reduced to zero in a single subtraction).

For example,

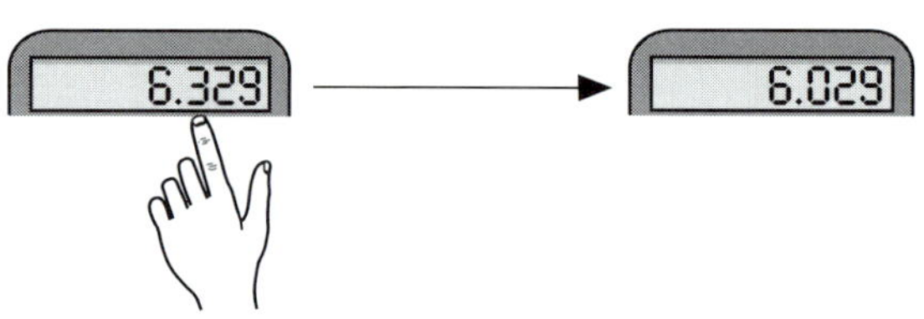

when the 3 is chosen, 0·3 must be subtracted.

■ The game then continues with the second player choosing, in turn, each of the remaining digits to be 'demolished' until the number is zero. The entire process is then repeated with the players' roles reversed.

Textbook page 29   *Decimals: the third decimal place*

Discuss the scenario of flying out to join a holiday cruise. The children should recognize the idea of a display on the aircraft's instrument panel which gives its height or altitude.

In question 2, emphasize that the decimal point separates the kilometres from the metres (or thousandths of kilometres). For example,

0·919 km
919 thousandths of a kilometre
919 metres

In question 3(d), (e) and (h), where the number of metres is less than one thousand, some children may have particular difficulty.

Workbook page 6   *Decimals: first, second and third decimal places*

For the number line in questions 1 and 2, the children have to see the distance between the airport and the *Orlando* as 1 whole, and the points on the lines as indicating fractions of the whole distance.

The number lines in questions 3 and 4 then need to be seen as enlargements of **parts** of the number line in question 2. The colour-tinted panels should help with this.

It may be worthwhile encouraging the children to identify or position numbers by first finding the nearest marked hundredth to the left and then counting on. For example, to position 0·257, find 0·25 and then count 0·251, 0·252 . . . 0·257.

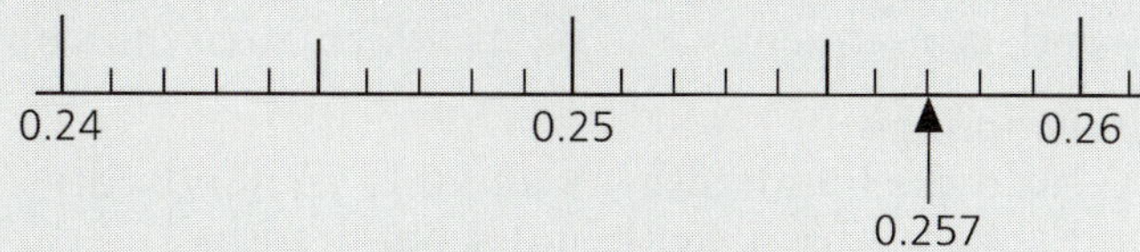

Some children may be able to use the slightly longer 'half-way' marks to speed up the counting on process: for example, going directly from 0·25 to 0·255 and then counting 0·255, 0·256, 0·257.

Textbook page 30   *Decimals: place value, calculator*

Although the place-value idea is introduced through the context of a display showing the *Orlando*'s speed in knots, the displays in question 1 are simply numbers as they would be unrealistic as speeds in knots.

In question 2, some children may just look at the digits and not also at the decimal points when comparing pairs of numbers. This might lead them to conclude, wrongly, that 3·059 is greater than 3·5 in 2(e).

If a calculator activity, such as that described in introductory activity 4 (Decimal demolition), has been undertaken, this will be of benefit to the children when they tackle question 5.

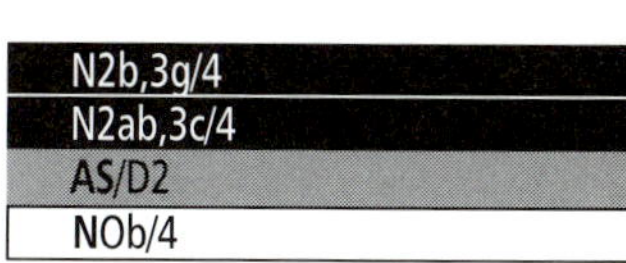

ADDITION AND SUBTRACTION: OF ONE- AND TWO-PLACE DECIMALS

In Heinemann Mathematics 6, addition and subtraction of one-place decimals was revised and addition and subtraction of two-place decimals introduced. This work is now consolidated.

The *Orlando* context continues with some of the passengers taking part in various activities in the fitness room and on deck.

Introductory activities

1   Skating   *(addition)*

■ Discuss an activity for which points are awarded, such as dancing or skating.

Display a set of scores on the chalkboard like this:

Skating score	Sara	John	Lisa	Den
	19·38	23·56	24·6	26

Find the total of Sara and John's scores. Emphasize the need to align the decimal points vertically and, consequently, the digits which have the same place value.

Recording

```
  19·38
+ 23·56
———————
      4
      1
```

Language

'**Add the hundredths.** 8 and 6 is 14 hundredths. Exchange for 1 tenth and 4 hundredths.'

Using similar language, add the tenths, units and tens, in turn, to obtain the answer.

'Sara and John scored **42·94** points.'

■ Discuss other additions where zeros should be inserted to keep digits in the correct columns: for example, 23·56 + 26, written as

```
  23·56
+ 26·00
———————
```

2   Scores   *(subtraction)*

Use the skating scores from introductory activity 1 to revise subtraction of decimals. For example, to find the difference between Den and John's scores:

Recording

```
  5 1
 2⁶·00
−23·56
———————
```

Language

'**Subtract the hundredths.** 0 take away 6, I cannot. There are no tenths to exchange. Exchange 1 unit for 10 tenths, giving 5 units and 10 tenths.'

Recording

```
  5 9 1
 2⁶·⁰0 0
−23·56
———————
      4
```

Language

'Exchange 1 tenth for 10 hundredths, giving 9 tenths and 10 hundredths. Subtract the hundredths. 10 take away 6 leaves 4.'
. . . and so on.
'The difference in scores is **2·44** points.'

Textbook pages 31 and 32
Decimals: first and second decimal places, addition and subtraction

On Textbook page 31, questions 1 and 2 involve one-place decimals only. Some children may need to be reminded to insert zeros where appropriate. For example, 40 should be written as 40·0 in question 2(f).

On Textbook page 32, in question 3, the children should first use the third clue to find Pam's score ($70 - 31·88 = 38·12$). Pam's score can then be used with the second and fourth clues to find Hazel's score ($38·12 - 11·14 = 26·98$). Finally, Marnie's score can be found using the first clue ($88·06 - 26·98 = 61·08$).

| UA2bc/4 N2b,3g,4b/5 |
| UA2ab/4 N2ab,3c,4bd/4 |
| PSE AS/D2 |
| PUbdf/4 NOb/4 |

Problem solving

R12 H19

MULTIPLICATION: OF ONE- AND TWO-PLACE DECIMALS

Multiplication of one-place decimals by 2 to 9 was introduced in Heinemann Mathematics 5 and consolidated in Heinemann Mathematics 6. Multiplication of two-place decimals using a calculator was also included in Heinemann Mathematics 6.

| N2b,3g/5 |
| N2ab,3c/5 |
| MD/D3 |
| NOb/5 |

This section introduces a written algorithm for multiplication of two-place decimals by 2 to 9.

The *Orlando* context continues with the re-fitting of one of the ship's decks while a cruise is in progress.

Introductory activities

1   Electric cable   *(multiplication of one-place decimals)*

■ Revise the recording and language of multiplication using an example such as

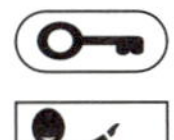

'There are 14·8 metres of electric cable in one roll.
What length of cable is in 7 such rolls?'

Recording	**Language**
14·8 m × 7 ——— ·6 5	'Put the decimal point in the answer space. **Multiply the tenths.** 7 times 8 is 56 tenths. Exchange for 5 units and 6 tenths.'
14·8 m × 7 ——— 103·6 m 3 5	'**Multiply the units.** 7 times 4 is 28 and 5 is 33 units. Exchange for 3 tens and 3 units. **Multiply the tens.** 7 times 1 is 7 and 3 is 10 tens.' 'There are **103·6 metres** of cable in 7 rolls.'

■ Repeat for other examples.

At this point the children could try Textbook page 33.

2 Pipes *(multiplication of two-place decimals)*

■ Introduce multiplication of two-place decimals using an example such as

'A section of copper pipe is 1·85 metres long. What length of pipe is in 5 sections?'

Recording	Language
1·8 5 m × 5 · 5 2	'Put the decimal point in the answer space. **Multiply the hundredths.** 5 times 5 is 25 hundredths. Exchange for 2 tenths and 5 hundredths.'
1·8 5 m × 5 9·2 5 m 4 2	'**Multiply the tenths.** 5 times 8 is 40 and 2 is 42 tenths. Exchange for 4 units and 2 tenths.' . . . and so on. 'There are **9·25 metres** of pipe.'

■ Repeat for other examples. Include those which have zeros or give answers greater than 10. For example,

$$3 \times 4·08 \qquad 0·67 \times 4 \qquad 1·15 \times 8 \qquad 4·87 \times 6$$

N2b,3g/5
N2ab,3c/5
MD/D3
NOb/5

Textbook page 33   *Decimals: first decimal place, multiplication*

On Textbook page 33, the children have to multiply to find each answer and use the **units** digit to decode the message. For example, question 1(a) has an answer of 4·8, which gives **A** as the code letter for **4**.

After decoding, the prize is revealed as

'A VISIT TO THE BRIDGE'

N2b,3g/5
N2ab,3c/5
MD/D3
NOb/5

Textbook page 34   *Decimals: second decimal place, multiplication*

Explain that Deck 2 of the *Orlando* is being re-fitted. Discuss the plan of Deck 2, which shows 8 Regal cabins, 5 Premier cabins, 6 De luxe cabins, 9 Standard cabins and 7 Economy cabins.

Ask the children which type of cabin they think is the most desirable and expensive. (They may suggest Regal, since it is the largest.)

MULTIPLICATION: BY 10, 100 AND 1000

N2b,3dg/5
N2ab,3bc/5
MD/D2 MD/E2
NUb/5

A rule for multiplication of one-place decimals by 10 was introduced in Heinemann Mathematics 5 and consolidated in Heinemann Mathematics 6.

This is now extended to multiplication of two-place decimals by 10. Rules are also introduced for multiplication of one- and two-place decimals by 100 and 1000.

The *Orlando* context continues with the re-stocking of cabins with consumable toiletries.

Introductory activity

Guess the rule

- Ask the children to calculate, mentally, answers to multiplications such as these:

    $24·7 \times 10$ $3·9 \times 10$ $453·6 \times 10$ $0·5 \times 10$

Remind them of the rule,

  'To multiply by **10**, move each digit **one place** to the left.'

- Ask them to suggest answers to the following:

    $3·57 \times 10$ $43·01 \times 10$ $0·91 \times 10$

They should realize that the same rule still applies. A calculator can be used to check.

- Introduce examples such as the following and ask the children to find the answers using a calculator:

    $2·51 \times 100$ $13·09 \times 100$ $0·72 \times 100$

Ask them what they notice about the answer to each multiplication. They should see that the same digits appear, but in different places.

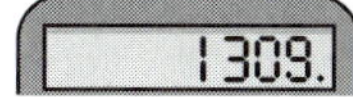

- Ask the children to suggest a rule for multiplying decimals by 100. They should realize that the rule is the same as for whole numbers,

  'To multiply by **100**, move each digit **two** places to the left.'

Discuss, in particular, examples such as $4·3 \times 100$ where as well as shifting the digits, it is necessary to put a zero in the 'empty' units column.

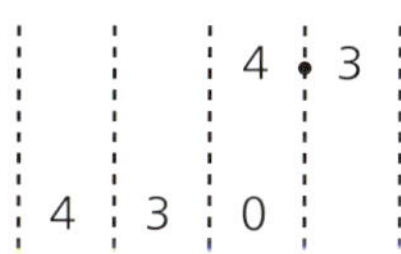

- Based on their knowledge of the rules for multiplying by 10 and 100, ask the children what they **think** a rule might be for multiplying by 1000.

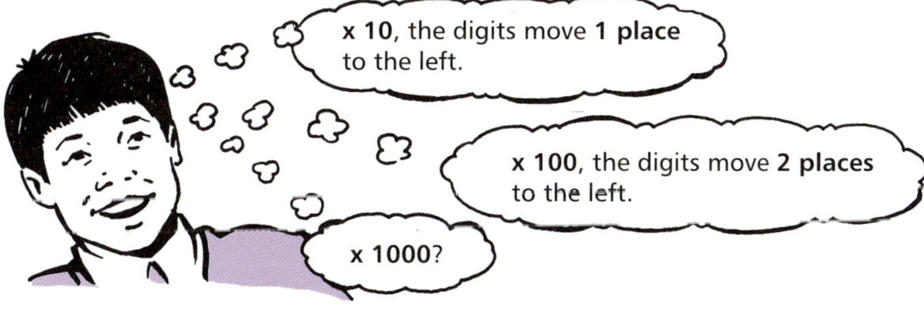

They are likely to suggest,

  'To multiply by **1000**, move each digit **three places** to the left.'

- Ask them to guess the answers to multiplications such as

    $7·43 \times 1000$ $14·08 \times 1000$ $3·1 \times 1000$

and then to check using a calculator to see that their rule applies.

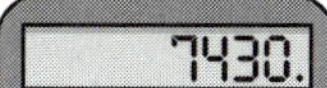

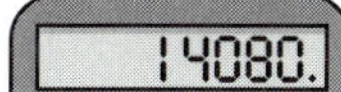

N2b,3dg/5
N2ab,3bc/5
MD/D2 MD/E2
NUb/5

H20 R13

Textbook page 35   *Decimals: multiplication by 10, 100, 1000*

Discuss the context of cabin re-stocking.

Some children may have more difficulty with examples such as $7{\cdot}8 \times 100$, $2{\cdot}61 \times 1000$ and $2{\cdot}7 \times 1000$, where one or more zeros have to be inserted in the answer.

DIVISION: OF ONE-PLACE DECIMALS

N3g/5
N3c/5
MD/D3 MD/E3
NOb/5

In Heinemann Mathematics 6, division of one-place decimals by 2 to 9 was introduced. This is now revised and the numbers extended to include examples like $244 \div 8$ and $806{\cdot}4 \div 9$.

The context continues on the *Orlando* with food being shared among the chefs in the galley.

Introductory activity

Sharing apples   *(division of a one-place decimal)*

■ Talk through an example like the one below to remind the children of a written algorithm and its associated language.

'For cooking, six chefs share equally 112·2 kg of apples.
What weight of apples does each chef cook?'

Recording	Language
$1\,8{\cdot}\,7$ $6\,\overline{)11^{5}2{\cdot}^{4}2}$	**'Share the tens.** 6 times what is 11? 6 times 1 is 6 and 5 tens left over. Exchange the 5 tens for 50 units.

Share the units. 6 times what is 52?
6 times 8 is 48 and 4 units left over.
Exchange 4 units for 40 tenths.

Share the tenths. 6 times what is 42?
6 times 7 is 42.

Each chef cooks **18·7 kg** of apples.'

■ Discuss examples of the type $8\,\overline{)3\,4\,8}$, where the zero has to be inserted in the tenths place,

$$8\,\overline{)348{\cdot}0}$$

so that the answer, which terminates at the first decimal place, can be found.

$$\begin{array}{r} 43{\cdot}5 \\ 8\,\overline{)348{\cdot}0} \end{array}$$

Textbook page 36   *Decimals: first decimal place, division*

Some of the questions involve dividing a whole number by a whole number, giving a decimal answer. All answers terminate at the first decimal place.

Some children may have difficulty with question 6 as it involves working backwards by **multiplying** to find the total amount of punch required. For example, multiply $0 \cdot 3 \times 8$ to give the amount for one table and then multiply by 9 to give the total, $21 \cdot 6$ litres.

DIVISION: OF TWO-PLACE DECIMALS

Division by 2 to 9 of two-place decimals and numbers which give two-place decimal answers is introduced.

The *Orlando* context continues, first by sharing prize money from the Daily Draw and then by finding average scores in competitions.

Introductory activities

1   Prize draw   *(division of a two-place decimal)*

An example like this will illustrate the language extended to hundredths.

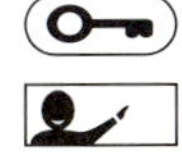

'The first prize of £14·22 is shared equally among three people. How much does each receive?'

Recording

$$4 \cdot 7\ 4$$
$$3\,\overline{)14 \cdot {}^2 2 {}^1 2}$$

Language

'**Share the units.** 3 times what is 14?
3 times 4 is 12 and 2 units left over.
Exchange 2 units for 20 tenths.

Share the tenths. 3 times what is 22?
3 times 7 is 21 and 1 tenth left over.
Exchange 1 tenth for 10 hundredths.

Share the hundredths. 3 times what is 12?
3 times 4 is 12.

Each winner receives £4·74.'

2   Team prizes

'Share £100 equally between the eight team members. How much does each receive?'

For this type of problem the children have to insert the decimal point and two zeros after it.

$100 \div 8$ should be set down as $8\,\overline{)100 \cdot 00}$

Children must appreciate that, when dealing with money, the second decimal place will be involved when answers in pounds and pence are appropriate: for example, £12·50 and not £12·5.

3 Average scores

To find the average score, add to find the total score from the four judges (22·6) and divide (by 4) to find the average.

22·6 ÷ 4 can be set down as

$$4\,\overline{)2^22·{}^26^20}\quad 5·6\,5$$

The average score is **5·65**.

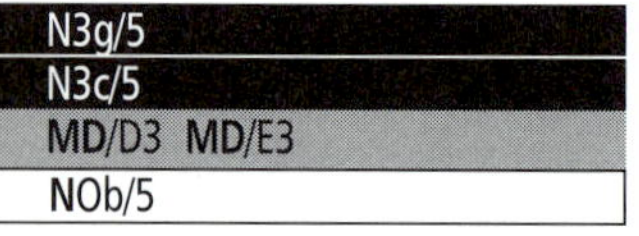
N3g/5
N3c/5
MD/D3 MD/E3
NOb/5

Textbook pages 37 and 38
Decimals: second decimal place, division

On page 37, in question 3, where a whole number of pounds is divided, the answers should be given to two decimal places as they are amounts of money.

In question 4(k), the answer may be given as 14·6 rather than 14·60 as it does not involve money.

On page 38, question 2 involves numbers only, so some answers may be given to one decimal place. Question 3 involves money and therefore answers should be given to two decimal places.

DIVISION: BY 10 AND 100

N2b,3g/5
N2a,3c/5
MD/D2 MD/E2
NUb/5

Mental division of a whole number by 10 was introduced in the 'Whole numbers' section of Heinemann Mathematics P7. This is now revised and the method extended to include division of a decimal by 10: for cxample, 37·4 ÷ 10 to give 3·74. A rule for division by 100 is introduced.

The *Orlando* context continues, with the survival equipment stored in the life rafts.

Introductory activities

1 Life raft   *(division by 10)*

Discuss the life rafts on board the *Orlando* and how the occupants would have a limited supply of food and water which would need to be shared. Consider several worked examples like the one below and derive a rule from them.

'Share 1·5 kg of dried fruit equally among 10 people.

How much does each receive?'

$$10\,\overline{)1·{}^15^50}\quad 0·1\,5$$

Each person receives **0·15 kg** of dried fruit.

State a rule similar to the one for whole numbers:

'To divide by 10, move each digit **one** place to the right.'

2 Dividing by 100

- Use a calculator to divide by 100. For example,

$$35 \div 100 = 0{\cdot}35$$
$$129 \div 100 = 1{\cdot}29$$
$$41{\cdot}6 \div 100 = 0{\cdot}416$$
$$8{\cdot}5 \div 100 = 0{\cdot}085 \quad \text{and so on.}$$

Discuss the patterns shown in the answers – each digit has moved **two** places to the right.

- Remind the children that $100 = 10 \times 10$, so to divide by 100 they can divide by 10 and then by 10 again.

$$35 \div 100 \longrightarrow 35 \div 10 = 3{\cdot}5$$
$$3{\cdot}5 \div 10 = 0{\cdot}35$$

Dividing by 10 moves the digits **one** place to the right, so dividing by 10 twice (i.e. by 100) moves them **two** places to the right.

Confirm a rule for dividing by 100, similar to the one for whole numbers:

'Move each digit **two** places to the right.'

3 Moving digits

Digit cards can be used to demonstrate the rule for dividing by 10 and 100. For example,

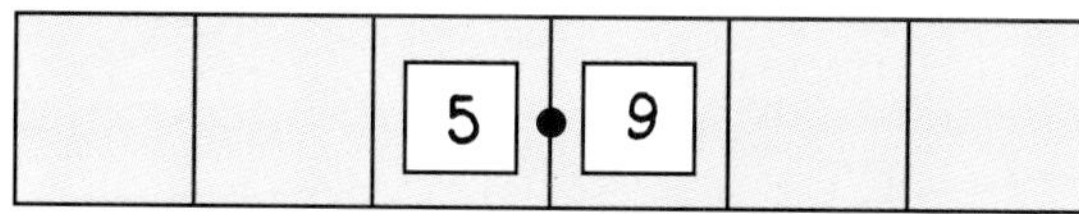

Moving the cards two places to the right gives

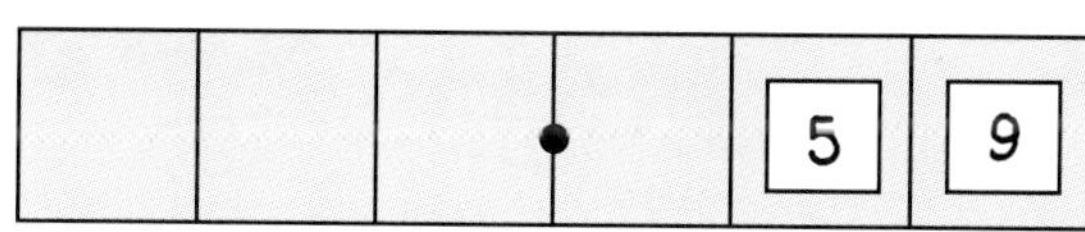

Zeros should then be inserted as follows:

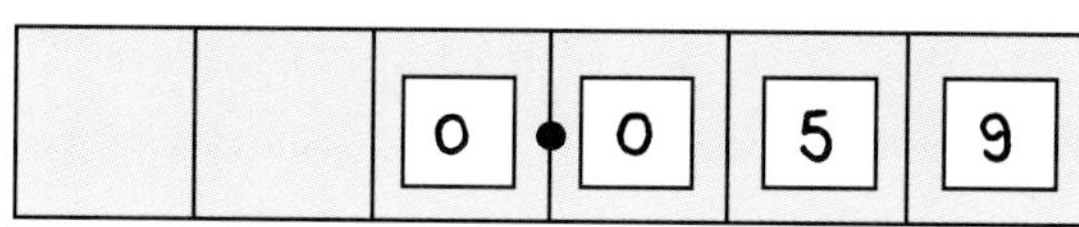

N2b,3g/5
N2a,3c/5
MD/D2 MD/E2
NUb/5 Me/5

Textbook page 39 *Decimals: division by 10 and 100*

In question 1, the children are expected to divide 1 kg by 10 to give 0·1 kg rather than change kilograms to grams first of all. Answers should be found by pencil and paper methods or by using a calculator in question 1. The rule can be applied in question 2.

In question 4, some of the answers have three decimal places.

Question 5(b) involves division by 10 and not 100, which some children may overlook.

R14 H21

APPROXIMATION AND ESTIMATION

N2b,3g,4c/5
N2a,3cf,4c/5
AS/D1,3 MD/D1,4 RN/D1
NUc/4→5 NOb/5

In Heinemann Mathematics 6, the children rounded decimals to the nearest unit. They also found approximate answers to calculations involving addition and subtraction of whole numbers.

This work is now revised and extended to include

— rounding of decimals to the nearest unit and nearest ten, involving sums of money, lengths and times

— mental calculation of approximate answers, involving addition, subtraction, multiplication and division

— the use of a calculator to find exact answers.

The *Orlando* context continues with day trips ashore for the passengers.

Introductory activities

1   Day trips

■ Discuss the idea of the *Orlando* anchoring at a port where passengers can take day trips ashore. Involve the children in suggesting real or imaginary trips.
Adapt and record some of them on a chalkboard. Invent prices for the trips.
For example,

Each of these prices is close to an exact number of pounds.

■ Talk about why prices such as £9·99 are common in shops. Point out that, as each price is nearly a whole number of pounds, it is easy to find approximate costs **mentally**. For example

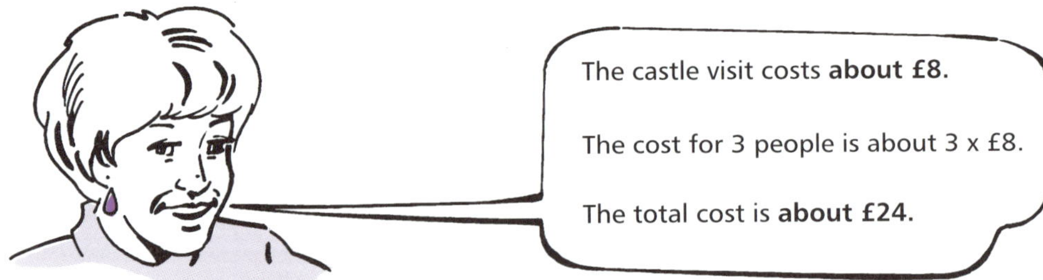

Provide further oral/mental practice involving multiplication, addition and subtraction. For example

— Funland for 3 people costs **about** $3 \times £30 \to £90$

— Pony Trekking **and** Dracula's Castle together cost **about** $£15 + £8 \to £23$

— change from £20 after paying for entry to the Animal Park is **about** $£20 - £10 \to £10$.

■ Introduce new trips and/or change the prices so that they are not of the £7·99 type. For example,

Discuss rounding each price to the nearest pound. For example,

'£19·80 is between £19 and £20. It is more than £19·50, nearer to £20. **£19·80 is £20 to the nearest pound.**'

■ Provide further examples to give the children practice in finding approximate answers mentally. For example,

'The Hang-gliding and the Barbeque together cost about £34 + £18. The total cost is **about £52.**'

At this point the children could try Textbook page 40.

2   Bus trip

■ Discuss a bus trip ashore to visit the places shown on this map.

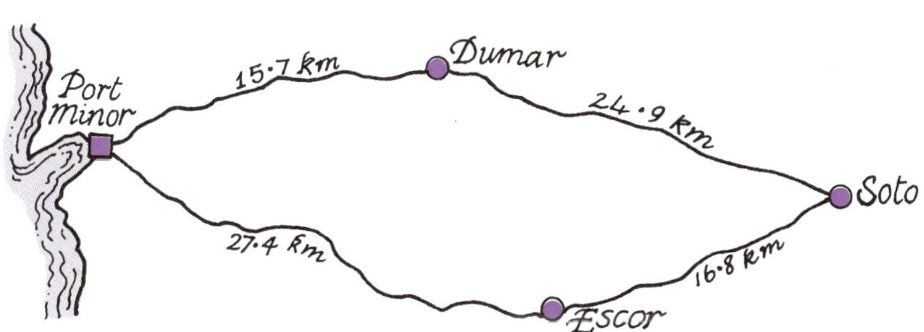

Ask the children to round each distance to the nearest kilometre, using a number line as illustration if required. For example,

'15·7 is between 15 and 16.

It is nearer to 16.

15·7 km is **about 16 km.**

In the same way, 24·9 km is about 25 km, 27·4 km is about 27 km and 16·8 km is about 17 km.

■ Ask the children to use these rounded answers to find, mentally, the **approximate** distances from Port Minor to Soto

— through Dumar → about 41 km   (16 + 25)

— through Escor → about 44 km   (27 + 17).

The children should now find **exact** answers using a calculator:

— through Dumar → 40·6 km

— through Escor → 44·2 km.

Compare the approximate and exact answers. Suggest that calculating mentally is a good way of checking the likely accuracy of a calculator answer.

UA2d/4 N2b,3g,4c/5
UA2d/4 N2a,3cf,4c/5
AS/D1,3 MD/D1,4 RN/D1
NUc/4→5 NOb/5

■ Give further practice in rounding and mental calculation, including subtractions. For example,

$40{\cdot}3 + 17{\cdot}85$ (about $40 + 18 = 58$)

$39{\cdot}7 - 14{\cdot}9$ (about $40 - 15 = 25$)

$52{\cdot}3 - 17{\cdot}5$ (about $52 - 18 = 34$ or $52 - 17 = 35$).

Textbook pages 40 and 41
Decimals: approximation and estimation

On Textbook page 40, questions 1 to 3 deal with prices such as £5·99 and £24·95 which are very nearly whole numbers of pounds, making rounding a simple matter. The remaining questions involve a wider range of prices and more difficult approximations.

On page 41, some examples have approximate answers and exact answers which do not correspond to the nearest whole number. For example, in question 3, for Kate's two dives of 11·6 and 40·2 metres,

approximate difference $= 40 - 12 = 28$

exact difference $= 40{\cdot}2 - 11{\cdot}6 = 28{\cdot}6$ (which is 29 to the nearest whole number).

However, the important point is that the approximate answer, 28, is still a good indicator that the calculator answer 28·6 is likely to be correct.

Question 5(b) may be difficult for some children as they have to realize that 2 minutes is 120 seconds.

In Question 6, the children should subtract **mentally** and discard some skiers until they find that Paul has the greatest difference between his times (about 23 seconds).

H22 R15

3   Gifts

■ Use the scenario of buying gifts ashore to develop the idea that rounding to the nearest **ten** pounds may be more appropriate for some prices, when estimating costs. Produce a set of cards showing possible gifts or use actual objects.

Discuss approximate prices along the following lines:

— using £199 to the nearest pound as the cost of the camera makes mental calculations difficult

— using £200 to the nearest **ten** pounds is more appropriate here.

Ask the children to round each price to the nearest ten pounds.

| about £200 | about £110 | about £80 | about £150 | about £60 |

- Ask the children to estimate the **approximate** total cost of **pairs** of gifts. For example,

> camera and trainers → about £350 (£200 + £150)

Also ask them to find differences in price. For example,

> track suit and jeans → about £50 (£110 − £60)

Subtractions could also involve approximate change from £100 or £200.

Repeat for several examples, done mentally and then by calculator.

- Reinforce the idea of finding an approximate total mentally. For example, after buying a computer game and trainers, find mentally which of these amounts is likely to be the exact cost.

£240·19	£215·19	£230·19

The estimated answer of £80 + £150 = £230 suggests that £230·19 is likely to be the correct cost.

Workbook pages 7 and 8
Decimals: approximation and estimation, calculator

Workbook page 7 involves rounding to the nearest £10 before making mental calculations to find approximate costs. A calculator is used to find exact answers, which are then compared with the approximations.

In question 1, on Workbook page 8, the children should choose to round to the nearest 10 **or** to the nearest whole number, depending on the numbers involved. For example,

> 8·7 + 10·9 → about 9 + 11 → about 20
>
> 37·6 ÷ 2 → about 40 ÷ 2 → about 20.

In question 2, the emphasis shifts to using a calculator first and then checking mentally, where possible, or by repeating the calculation.

Question 3 is challenging as it requires children to look at the four given numbers and mentally assess which pair can be added, subtracted, multiplied or divided to give each given answer.

18·2	102·5	5	37·84

For example, to achieve an answer of 512·5 they should think of

> 102·5 × 5 as about 100 × 5 = 500

and then use a calculator to confirm that 102·5 × 5 is exactly 512·5.

Encourage the children to round each of the four given numbers and write their answers on the page.

18·2	102·5	5	37·84
20	100	5	40

This may help mental calculation of approximate answers in some cases.

UA2bcd/4 N2b,3dfg,4ac/5
UA2abd/4 N2a,3bcf,4ac/5
PSE AS/D1,3 MD/D1,4 RN/D1
PUbdef/5 PRf/4
NUc/4→5 NMb/4 NOb/5

Problem solving

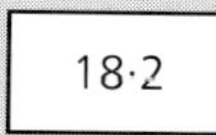

R16 H23

CALCULATOR, CHECKING ANSWERS

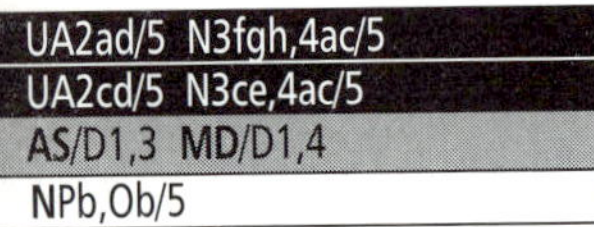

In Heinemann Mathematics 6, the children used calculators for addition, subtraction, multiplication and division involving two-place decimals.

This work is now consolidated. There are further opportunities to use the calculator's memory in suitable examples. Checking of answers by using the inverse operation is included and extended to multiplication and division of decimals.

The *Orlando* context continues with a visit to the Caves of Minor and the bus journey back to the ship.

Introductory activities

1   Using the memory

- A full discussion of ways of using the calculator's memory for calculations involving whole numbers is given in the introductory activities for Textbook pages 19 and 20 (see pages 52–4). The techniques are identical for decimals and, if required, can be revised using suitable decimal examples.

- Remind the children to check their answers by repeating the calculation on the calculator and/or, for those cases where the figures are suitable, by making a mental estimate of the answer.

At this point the children could try Textbook page 42.

2   Checking multiplication by division

- Remind the children that multiplication can be checked by division and vice versa. Use simple examples involving whole numbers to illustrate the idea. For example,

$$72 \div 9 = 8 \text{ can be checked by } 8 \times 9 = 72.$$

- Persuade the children that this method extends to decimals by considering an example such as $197{\cdot}2 \div 29$.

Enter ⟦1⟧⟦9⟧⟦7⟧⟦·⟧⟦2⟧⟦÷⟧⟦2⟧⟦9⟧⟦=⟧   This should give 6.8 .

Without clearing the calculator,

enter ⟦×⟧⟦2⟧⟦9⟧⟦=⟧ which should give the original 197.2 .

This checks that the division has been done correctly.

- Repeat for other examples, including ones where multiplying is checked by dividing.

Textbook pages 42 and 43   *Decimals: calculator*

On Textbook page 42, in some parts of question 1, the calculator's memory can be used to avoid writing intermediate answers on paper. For example, in 1(d), the children can

— calculate adult entrance fees, $6 \times £12·63$, and store the answer in memory using $\boxed{\text{M+}}$

— calculate child entrance fees, $12 \times £6·23$, and add this to the total in memory using $\boxed{\text{M+}}$

— enter the cost of a guide $£9·50$ and add it to the total using

either $\boxed{\text{M+}}$ $\boxed{\text{MR}}$ (where $\boxed{\text{M+}}$ adds the $£9·50$ to the total in memory

and $\boxed{\text{MR}}$ recalls the final answer from memory)

or $\boxed{+}$ $\boxed{\text{MR}}$ $\boxed{=}$ (which adds the total from the memory to the

$£9·50$ in the display)

Methods and keys can vary depending on the type of calculator.

For an example like this, with several steps, encourage the children to record the way in which they tackled the problem as well as the calculator answer. For example,

$$(6 \times £12·63) + (12 \times £6·23) + £9·50 = £160·04$$

Some discussion of the map above question 2 may be necessary so that children understand that all distances are from the Entrance.

In question 4, the children should estimate the position of $193·5$ m on the height scale on the right, and by laying a ruler or paper across the map, discover that Denise is in the Long Gallery. Paul is in the Minor Slope.

$\boxed{\text{H}24}$

On Textbook page 43, questions 1 to 4 deal with checking a calculator answer by using an inverse operation, i.e. addition by subtraction, multiplication by division, and vice versa. For the subtraction $17·7 - 12·85$,

Enter 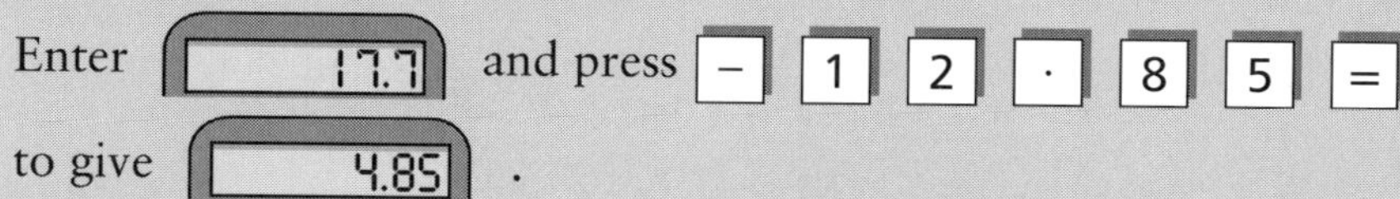 and press $\boxed{-}$ $\boxed{1}$ $\boxed{2}$ $\boxed{·}$ $\boxed{8}$ $\boxed{5}$ $\boxed{=}$

to give $\boxed{4·85}$.

Do not clear the calculator answer, $4·85$. The subtraction can be checked by **adding** $12·85$ to give the original $17·7$ again.

In questions 5 and 6, the checks should be made by the method most appropriate to the child and to the example. In many cases this will be repeating the calculation using a calculator.

In question 5, the children should assume that there is **no** distance between the vehicles. This gives an average length of $3000 \div 625 = 6·4$ m.

In question 6, some children may need help to see that the profit is the total paid in fares less the bus company's total costs.

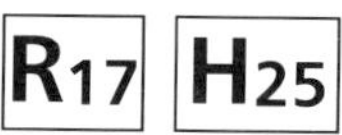

In Heinemann Mathematics 6 and P7, the children have used a calculator for divisions which resulted in decimal answers. They have rounded decimal answers to the nearest whole number and have interpreted decimal displays. This work is now consolidated and extended to include examples such as 211·6 ÷ 8, where the first number is a decimal.

The *Orlando* context finishes with an end of cruise barbeque.

Introductory activity

Interpreting answers

Revise previous work by discussing a problem such as:

'A lifeboat can hold 47 passengers.

How many lifeboats are needed for 354 passengers?'

Enter `354.` Press ÷ 4 7 = to give `7.5319148` .

Discuss the answer. It is **between** 7 and 8. Seven boats would be filled and still leave some passengers, so **8 boats** are required.

Textbook page 44
Decimals: division, interpreting answers, calculator

On this page there is a mixture of rounding up and rounding down depending on the context of each question. In each case the calculator display will show either a two- or a three-place decimal answer before rounding.

UA2d/5	UA2d/5
N2bc/4	N2b/4
N2bc/5	N2b/5
N3gh/5	N3cde/5

PSE
RTN/D4
FPR/D1
FPR/E1,2,3

PUb/5
NUd/4→5
NOb/5
NOc/6

Percentages

Overview

This section

- revises the concept of a percentage, the notation % and the link with common fractions

- revises calculation of 50%, 25% and 10% of a quantity

- introduces calculations based on 10%: for example, 30% and 15% of a quantity

- introduces the link with decimal fractions

- extends work on changing fractions and decimals to percentages and vice versa

- introduces the use of a calculator to find a percentage of a quantity.

	Teacher's Notes	Textbook	Workbook	Reinforcement Sheets
Kitbits Company: a context for fractions and percentages	57			
Percentages: concept, 100% is one whole, link with fractions	102	45, 46*	9	
Percentages based on 10%	104	47*		18
Linking percentages and decimals	105	48*		
Fraction of a set as a percentage	107	49*		19
Fractions, decimals and percentages	109	50*, 51		20

Homework provided in Home Link-up.

Extension activities related to the above section of work are as follows:		
	Teacher's Notes	Extension Textbook
Percentages: increase and decrease	262	E12
Fractions as percentages	262	E13

Teaching notes for the Extension Textbook are in a separate section at the end of the Teacher's Notes.

Resources

Useful materials

- materials suggested within the introductory activities

Assessment and Resources Pack

Assessment

Number Check-up 11
Textbook pages 45–7
Workbook page 9
(concept, link with fractions,
calculations)

Number Check-up 12
Textbook pages 48–51
(decimals, fractions, calculator)

Round-up 3
Questions 6(a), (b), (c), 7(b)

Resources

Problem Solving Activities
10 United (fractions, percentages)

Resource Cards
12 and 13 Matching squares
(fractions, decimals, percentages)

Teaching notes

PERCENTAGES: CONCEPT, 100% IS ONE WHOLE, LINK WITH FRACTIONS

In Heinemann Mathematics 6, the children were introduced to the concept of a percentage, the meaning of 100% as one whole and the relationship between some fractions and percentages: for example, $\frac{1}{2} = 50\%$, $\frac{1}{4} = 25\%$ and $\frac{3}{4} = 75\%$.

The work is now revised and extended to include a wider range of fractions and percentages.

The context of Kitbits Company, first introduced in the Fractions section, continues with the introduction of Centile kits – ceramic tiles used to decorate trays and tables.

Introductory activities

N2c/4 N3g/5
N2b/4 N3c/5
RTN/D4 FPR/E1
NUd/4

1 Centile trays *(fractions and percentages)*

■ Draw a 'tray' which has a design containing 100 small congruent squares. Use the design on the tray to establish that

— there are 100 small squares, all equal in size

— 45 of the 100 squares are red

— $\frac{45}{100}$, forty-five hundredths, of the design is red.

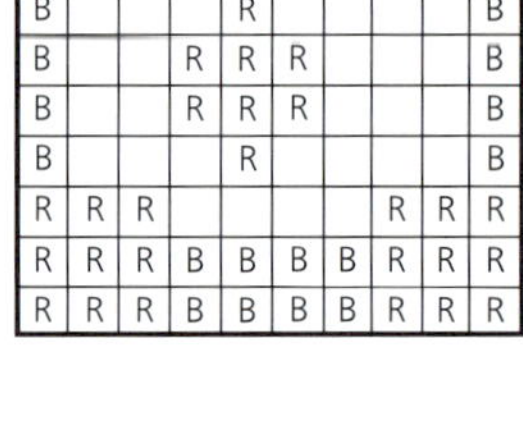

Discuss with the children, the language,

'forty-five per cent' and

'45% of the design is red.'

Repeat for other colours in the design.

■ Draw a 100 square design which could be part of a Mosaic kit made by Kitbits Company.

Establish that 20% of the design is coloured red.

$$20\% = \frac{20}{100} = \frac{1}{5}$$

Repeat for other percentages, such as 25%, 15%, 35% and 5%.

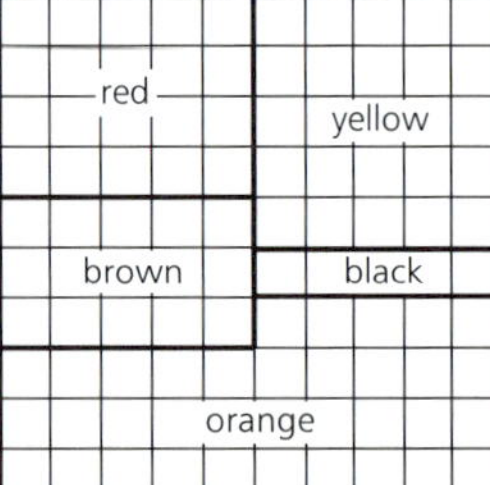

2 Centile designs *(100% is one whole)*

Display some centile designs which have been partially completed: for example, this design is 60% completed.

Ask the children how they can find the percentage of the design which is **not** completed.

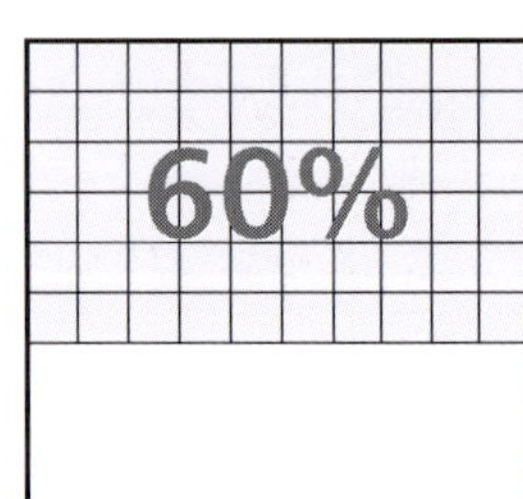

Textbook page 45 *Percentages: concept, 100% is one whole*
Workbook page 9, question 1

Introduce the context of centile designs and ensure that the children are aware that exactly 100 congruent tiles are used to make each design.

On Textbook page 45, in question 1, encourage the children to check that the total for each design is 100%.

On Workbook page 9, in question 1, the children do not need to produce a symmetrical design, although some may do so.

On Textbook page 45, in question 4, the children are expected to count the number of tiles in each design, find the percentage of the design completed, then subtract from 100% to find the percentage of the design not completed.

N2c/4
N2b/4
RTN/D4
NUd/4

3   Pirate kits   *(calculating percentages of a quantity)*

■ Explain that Kitbits Company makes a set of 300 model pirates.

— 1% of the pirates have an eyepatch

— 10% have a dagger

— 25% have a sword.

■ Discuss how to calculate the number of pirates who have an eyepatch.

1% of the pirates have an eyepatch.

1% of 300

$= \frac{1}{100}$ of 300

$= 3$

3 pirates wear an eyepatch.

Repeat for daggers and swords.

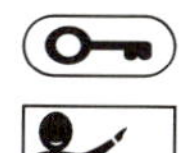

Workbook page 9, questions 2 and 3
Textbook page 46
Percentages: 100% is one whole, link with fractions

On Workbook page 9, in questions 2 and 3, it is expected that some children will know the simplest fractional form for some of the percentages: for example, $50\% = \frac{1}{2}$, $25\% = \frac{1}{4}$ and $10\% = \frac{1}{10}$. For the other percentages, it is likely that the children will simplify in steps to find the equivalent fractions: for example, $20\% = \frac{20}{100} = \frac{2}{10} = \frac{1}{5}$.

On Textbook page 46, the context is based on model soldier kits produced by Kitbits Company. Before starting the work, the children must be familiar with

— the process of simplifying fractions which was dealt with on Textbook page 21

— a method of calculating a fraction of a quantity.

Although some children might be able to do questions 1 to 4 mentally, they should be encouraged to record their answers in a similar way to the worked example above question 2.

N2c/4 N3g/5
N2b/4 N3c/5
RTN/D4 FPR/E1
NUd/4→5

In question 5, some children may need to set down the division. For example, when finding the November sales of Roman kits:

50% of 9420
$= \frac{1}{2}$ of 9420
$= 4710$

$$\begin{array}{r} 4\,710 \\ 2\,\overline{)9^14\,20} \end{array}$$

4710 Roman kits were sold.

In part (b), a possible response is to say that more kits were made in November than in December, so that they would be ready in good time for Christmas.

H26

PERCENTAGES BASED ON 10%

A method of finding percentages such as 30%, 70% and 15% of a quantity by first finding 10% is now introduced.

The Kitbits Company context continues with the introduction of Transport kits.

N3g/5
N3c/5
RTN/D4 FPR/E3
NUd/5

Introductory activity

Bicycle kits   *(percentages based on 10%)*

■ Explain that last week the Kitbits Company made 480 bicycle kits.

40% of them were Racer kits, 30% were Speed kits and 15% were Standard kits.

The number of Racer kits = 40% of 480

Suggest that one way of calculating this is to find 10% first.

10% of 480 = 48

40% of 480 = 4 × 48 = **192**

192 Racer kits were made.

Repeat for Speed kits.

■ Discuss a similar method for finding the number of Standard kits, 15% of 480.

10% of 480 = 48

5% of 480 = 24

15% of 480 = 72

72 Standard kits were made.

Repeat for other examples.

- Some children may be able to suggest other methods for finding 40% of 480. For example,

    — finding 20% (or $\frac{1}{5}$) and doubling it

    — finding 50% (or $\frac{1}{2}$) and subtracting 10%.

UA2d/5 N3g/5
UA2d/5 N3c/5
RTN/D4 FPR/E3 PSE
PUb/5 NUd,Ob/5

Textbook page 47   *Percentages: based on 10%*

Introduce the scenario of Kitbits Company's Transport kits.

In question 2, the children should realize that a total of 90% were sports, racing or classic cars, leaving 10% as vintage cars. Alternatively, the children may find the total number of sports, racing and classic cars and subtract from 4850 to give 485 vintage cars.

In question 5, to find 35% of 9800

    — find 10% of 9800 (980)

    — multiply 980 by 3 to find 30% of 9800 (2940)

    — divide 980 by 2 to find 5% of 9800 (490).

Adding 30% and 5% will then give the required 35% (3430).

    3430 tram-cars were sold.

In question 6, the children should realize that they first need to find the total number of Bus kits made before calculating how many were faulty.

Problem solving

R18 H27

LINKING PERCENTAGES AND DECIMALS

The children are now introduced to writing a percentage as a decimal. They then calculate percentages of quantities using a calculator, by entering the percentage as a decimal.

The context is the stock room at Kitbits.

Introductory activities

1 Stock taking   *(percentages as decimals)*

- Explain that a person who works in the stock room at Kitbits Company needs to know how to write a percentage as a decimal. Ask the children what a percentage such as 17% means: for example, 'seventeen out of a hundred' or 'seventeen hundredths'. Ask what a decimal such as 0·17 means: for example, 'one tenth and seven hundredths' or 'seventeen hundredths'. The children should notice that both 17% and 0·17 have the value of 17 hundredths.

N2c/5 N3gh/5
N2b/5 N3ce/5
RTN/D4 FPR/E2
NUd/5

- Discuss several examples to develop a mental procedure for changing a percentage to a decimal:

    32% $\longrightarrow$ 32 hundredths $\longrightarrow$ 0·32

    28% $\longrightarrow$ 28 hundredths $\longrightarrow$ 0·28

     9% $\longrightarrow$ 9 hundredths $\longrightarrow$ 0·09

2 Kit orders *(percentage of a quantity using a calculator)*

■ Display an order sheet like this:

kits in stock	kits ordered
450 Car kits	18%
680 Aeroplane kits	35%
1275 Farm kits	4%

■ Discuss with the children the use of a calculator. For example,

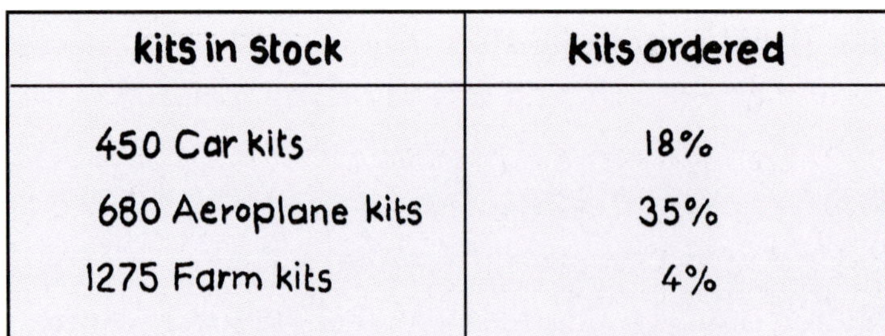

18% $\longrightarrow$ 18 hundredths $\longrightarrow$ | 0.18 |

To find 18% of 450,

enter × 4 5 0 = to give | 81. |

18% of 450 is 81

81 Car kits have been ordered.

Repeat for other examples on the order sheet.

■ Consider another order sheet.

kits in stock	kits ordered
528 Hussar kits	16%
719 Medieval kits	6%
1275 Roman kits	34%

■ Ask the children to find the number of Hussar kits ordered.

16% of 528 $\longrightarrow$ | 84.48 |

Through discussion establish that the answer should be rounded to the nearest whole number, 84 Hussar kits.

Repeat for the other two examples on the order sheet. One answer is rounded down (43) and the other is rounded up (740).

Textbook page 48 *Percentages: percentages as decimals*

The scenario and the worked examples will require discussion if the introductory activities have not been undertaken.

In question 1(g), ensure that 7% is entered as 0·07 and not 0·7.

In question 4(g), the answer 82·5 can be rounded up or down.

In question 5, the context involves a change in the number of kits produced. In part (a), more kits need to be produced, so there is to be an increase. In part (b), fewer need to be produced, so there is to be a decrease.

| N2c/5 N3gh/5 |
| N2b/5 N3ce/5 |
| RTN/D4 FPR/E2 |
| NUd,Ob/5 |

H28

FRACTION OF A SET AS A PERCENTAGE

Identifying a **fraction** of a total and then expressing this fraction as a **percentage** is now dealt with.

The grading of examples is as follows:

— fractions with denominator 100. For example,

$$\frac{32}{100} = 32\%$$

— fractions with denominators 50, 25 and 20, making use of equivalence. For example,

$$\frac{9}{20} = \frac{45}{100} = 45\%$$

— other fractions, including some where the fraction should be simplified first. For example,

$$\frac{21}{28} = \frac{3}{4} = 75\%$$

The questions are set in the context of orders received by the Kitbits Company.

Introductory activities

1 Packing orders

■ Write a list of the kits packed by Melanie on Tuesday. Ask the children what fraction of the kits packed were Technokits.

The children should first find the total number of kits packed (100).

This should establish that $\frac{9}{100}$ of the kits were Technokits.

Expressed as a percentage this gives

$$\frac{9}{100} = 9\%$$

Repeat for other kits.

| N2c,3d/5 |
| N2b3b/5 |
| FPR/D1 FPR/E3 |
| NUd,Ob/5 |

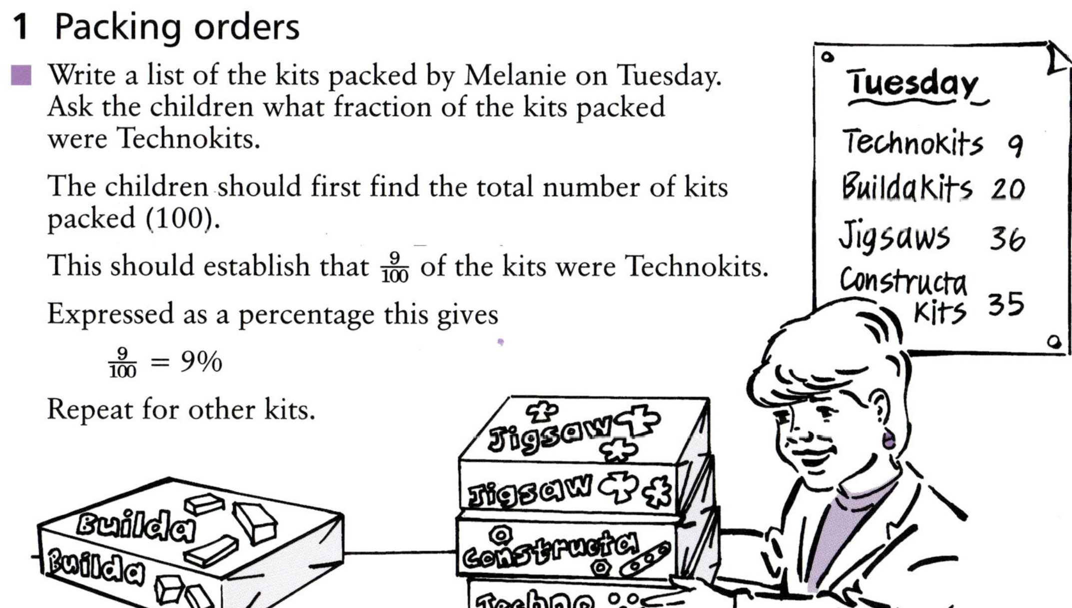

■ Discuss new lists for the other days when Melanie worked only in the morning.

<table>
<tr><td>

Wednesday

Technokits 28

Buildakits 22

</td><td>

Thursday

Constructakits 9

Jigsaws   11

</td><td>

Friday

Constructakits 14

Technokits   11

</td></tr>
</table>

The children should discover that the totals for these days are 50, 20 and 25 respectively.

Discuss the fraction of kits packed which were

— Technokits on Wednesday

$\frac{28}{50}$ ('28 out of 50')

To find the percentage, change the fraction to hundredths

$\frac{28}{50} = \frac{56}{100}$

and then express as a percentage:

$\frac{28}{50} = \frac{56}{100} = 56\%$

— Jigsaws on Thursday

$\frac{11}{20} = \frac{55}{100} = 55\%$

— Technokits on Friday

$\frac{11}{25} = \frac{44}{100} = 44\%$

At this point the children could try Textbook page 49, questions 1, 2 and 3.

2   Kit orders

■ Show the children these orders.

<table>
<tr><td>

Jigsaws order

large   27

small   27

</td><td>

Car kits order

large   18

small   54

</td></tr>
</table>

■ Discuss the totals for each order and the fraction of Jigsaws which were large Jigsaws: $\frac{27}{54}$.

Point out that it is difficult to change 54 to 100 directly.

In this case, it is better to **simplify** the fraction.

$\frac{27}{54} = \frac{3}{6} = \frac{1}{2}$

The percentage can now be found.

$\frac{1}{2} = \frac{50}{100} = 50\%$

50% of the Jigsaws were large.

■ Repeat for small Car kits.

$\frac{54}{72} = \frac{6}{8} = \frac{3}{4}$

$\frac{3}{4} = \frac{75}{100} = 75\%$

75% of the Car kits were small.

■ Ask the children to find the remaining fractions and percentages.

Textbook page 49   *Percentages: fractions as percentages*

In questions 1 to 4, the total number is provided, whereas in question 5, the children have to find the total first.

Question 6 contains a selection of the different types of example given on the page. Some children may be able to take short cuts at this stage. For example, $\frac{5}{10}$ may be recognized as $\frac{1}{2}$, so the children could merely write 50% as the answer.

In question 7, some children could work backwards, beginning with the given percentage. They could reason that if 25% of the order was large Buildakits, then 25% or $\frac{1}{4}$ of the order was 30 kits, so the total order was $4 \times 30 = 120$ kits. The number of small kits is $120 - 30 = 90$ kits. There are other methods of achieving this answer.

FRACTIONS, DECIMALS AND PERCENTAGES

This section concludes by consolidating links between fractions, decimals and percentages.

The context continues with a Kitbits competition.

Introductory activities

1   Quiz book

■ Tell the children that the Kitbits Spykit has a quiz book which shows spies how to change fractions to other forms.

Draw a page from the quiz book on the chalkboard or an overhead projector transparency.

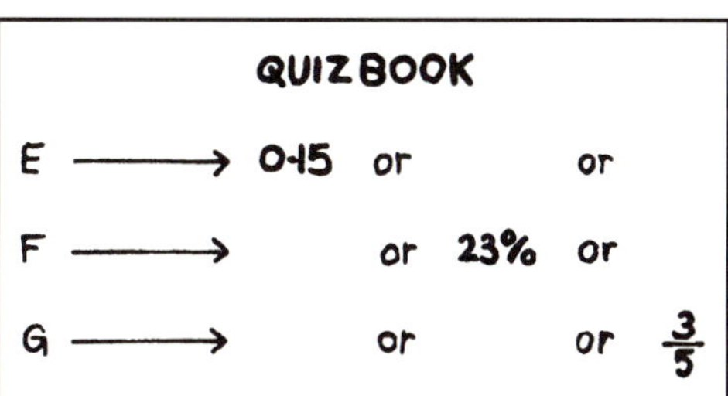

■ Remind the children how to
    — change decimals to fractions and percentages
    — change percentages to decimals and fractions
    — change fractions to percentages and decimals.

Complete this page of the quiz book.

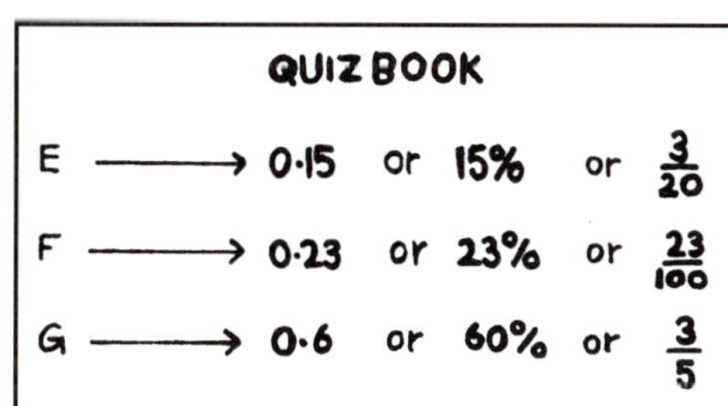

■ Repeat for other examples.

Problem solving

Textbook page 50   *Percentages: fractions, decimals*

In question 1, some children may not realize that each square represents a letter and each block of squares represents a word. Some may also have difficulty initially in finding the equivalent fraction in the code. For example, 6% has to be related to 0·06 in the code to find the first letter of the message, W. The message reads

'WHICH KIT DO YOU WANT TO WIN'

To respond to question 1(b), the children need to look at the flash at the top right of the page.

In question 3(a), the children should copy the table, replace every given entry by a percentage and complete the missing percentages for Mystery kits.

In question 4, the children should find that

1000 winners live in England

200 live in Northern Ireland

200 (one quarter of 800) live in Wales, and

600 live in Scotland.

To find the percentage of winners who live in Wales, the children are likely to follow the procedure of forming a fraction, $\frac{200}{2000}$, simplifying this to $\frac{10}{100}$, and then changing this to the percentage, 10%. As a further challenge, the children could be asked to find the percentage of winners who live in Scotland.

H30 **R**20

2   Surveys   *(interpreting calculator displays)*

■ Using the following survey, discuss how to round to the nearest whole number.

Class 5 has 14 boys out of 29 children.

Class 6 has 17 boys out of 31 children.

Class 7 has 15 boys out of 27 children.

It is difficult to see from this data which class has the largest proportion of boys. The comparison is difficult if we think of fractions such as $\frac{14}{29}$, $\frac{17}{31}$ and $\frac{15}{27}$.

To change each to a decimal using a calculator:

Enter  Press ÷ 2 9 = To give 

To change the decimal in the display to a percentage, the children should first focus on the first two figures after the point – in this case, 48 hundredths.

48 hundredths

As a percentage the figure is 48·27586% or **48% to the nearest whole number**

About 48% of class 5 are boys.

■ Ask the children to repeat this for the boys in Class 6 and Class 7.

Class 6 $\longrightarrow \frac{17}{31} \longrightarrow$ | 0.548387 | $\longrightarrow$ 55% to the nearest whole number.

Class 7 $\longrightarrow \frac{15}{27} \longrightarrow$ | 0.5555555 | $\longrightarrow$ 56% to the nearest whole number.

The classes can now be compared. The largest percentage of boys is in Class 7.

Textbook page 51   *Percentages: fractions as percentages, calculator*

The scenario on this page involves Sam carrying out a survey to find out which kit his classmates would buy, and Leanne finding out how much parents would be prepared to pay for the kit.

Some children may have difficulty interpreting the decimal in the calculator display as a percentage if they have not attempted Introductory activity 2.

Global Research Technology (GRT)

A context for pattern, rate and speed

The work on

> — pattern (Textbook pages 52–6, Workbook pages 10–12)

> — rate and speed (Textbook pages 83–6)

is set within the context of Global Research Technology (GRT), an international scientific foundation.

Introducing the context

The context could be introduced through a general discussion about the work of scientists. The children should be aware that the technological items which are in most homes, and which are often taken for granted, are the results of scientific research.

Other possible activities are as follows.

1   Then and now

In order to emphasize the pace of scientific advancement, the children could be asked to find out about and list changes which have taken place in homes, schools and the wider environment over the period since their parents were at primary school. Discussion could focus on how scientific innovations have affected the quality of people's lives in both positive and negative ways.

A series of 'then' and 'now' illustrations could be produced to show and contrast practices 20 years ago with those of today for aspects such as

> — travelling (both locally and internationally)

> — communicating

> — learning

> — using leisure time.

then ...

... now

2 Famous scientists

Some children may be interested in finding out about famous scientists of the past by researching reference books, computer software and other sources.
Information about the lives and discoveries of scientists such as

— Marie Curie

— Charles Darwin

— Albert Einstein

— Galileo

— Isaac Newton

could be used as the basis for oral reports to other children.

3 My great invention

The idea of a remarkable new discovery which would change the world and make the inventor rich and famous could provide the stimulus for interesting dramatic or imaginative writing activities.

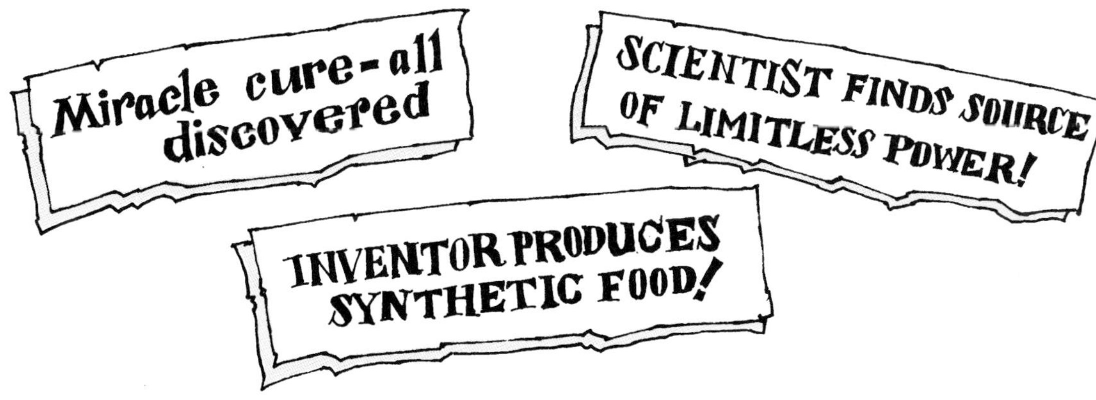

UA2d,3dg/4	UA2d,3bc/4
N3a/4	A2b,3b/4
N3a/5	A2b,3b/5
PS/D1	
PS/E2	
FE/D1	
FE/E4	
PMa/4→5	
NPac/4	
NPcd/5	
AFbe/6	
SPe/4	

Pattern

Overview

This section

- includes work on simple number and shape patterns
- deals with number sequences derived from word descriptions and shape patterns
- revises simple word formulae and introduces symbolic formulae
- includes finding rules describing the relationship between co-ordinates of points.

	Teacher's Notes	Textbook	Workbook	Reinforcement Sheets
Global Research Technology: a context for pattern, rate and speed	112			
Number sequences and shape patterns	116	52*	10*	
Word formulae	118	53*	11*	
Symbolic formulae	119	54, 55		21
Formulae from graphs	122	56	12	

Homework provided in Home Link-up.

Extension activities related to the above section of work are as follows:	Teacher's Notes	Extension Textbook
Formulae, graphs	263	E14
Sequences, formulae	263	E15

Teaching notes for the Extension Textbook are in a separate section at the end of the Teacher's Notes.

Resources

Useful materials

- calculator
- other materials suggested within the introductory activities.

Assessment and Resources Pack

Assessment

Number Check-up 13
Textbook pages 52–3
Workbook page 10–11

Round-up 3
Question 4

Resources

Problem Solving Activities
14 Jump patterns (shape patterns)
15 Checkerboards (formula)

Teaching notes

NUMBER SEQUENCES AND SHAPE PATTERNS

UA2d/4 N3a/4
UA2d/4 A2b/4
PS/D1 PS/E2
PMa/4 NPa/4

In Heinemann Mathematics 6, the children were introduced to square and triangular numbers. Further number sequences were introduced in the Extension Textbook.

This section includes the completion of number sequences which involve recognizing and applying a 'rule'. The work also includes the generation of number sequences from word descriptions and shape patterns.

Introductory activities

1 Cosmic signals *(completion of number sequences)*

 ■ Tell the children that signals from Outer Space are shown on monitors at GRT. On a chalkboard, draw six 'screens' showing this number sequence.

Ask the children to describe the sequence of numbers. They should realize that the numbers increase by 4 each time. Ask for the next two numbers in the sequence and write these on the blank screens.

■ Repeat for other sequences. For example,

20,	17,	14,	11,	——,	——
1,	4,	16,	64,	——,	——
81,	27,	9,	3,	——	

■ Repeat for sequences which have missing numbers in different positions. For example,

90,	80,	70,	——,	50,	——
6,	10,	14,	——,	——,	26
——,	10,	20,	40,	80,	——
——,	——,	21,	28,	35,	42

■ Invite the children to write and describe their own sequences.

2   What's the sequence?

■ Show the children descriptions of sequences, on the chalkboard or on card.

> Start with 28 and subtract 4 each time.

> Start with 7 and add on 3 each time.

> Start with 5 and double the number each time.

> Start with 10. Add 1, then add 2, then add 3, then add 4 and so on.

> Start with 200. Subtract 10, then subtract 20, then subtract 30 then subtract 40 and so on.

■ Read a description aloud and ask the children to write the first six numbers of the sequence. Check their answers: for example,

    28,   24,   20,   16,   12,   8

for the first description.

At this point the children could try Textbook page 52.

3   Satellite signals   *(shape patterns)*

■ Tell the children that GRT investigate signals from satellites. Draw this pattern of signals on a chalkboard or overhead projector transparency.

■ Ask a child to draw the next signal in the pattern. Write the number of lines in each signal underneath it, like this:

  2   4   6   8   10

Ask the children to describe the number pattern in words and to write the next two numbers in the pattern.

Textbook page 52 and Workbook page 10
Pattern: sequences, drawing and continuing

The context of GRT should be discussed if this has not been done as part of the introductory activities.

On Textbook page 52, in question 1(e), some children may have difficulty as they have to find the **first** two numbers in the sequence. It may be helpful for them to consider the consecutive digits within each number.

On Workbook page 10, in question 2, some children may find it helpful to write intermediate values for the 6th, 8th and 9th numbers, when finding the 7th and 10th numbers in each sequence.

UA2d/4	N3a/4
UA2u/4	A2b/4
PS/D1	PS/E2
PRa/4	NPa/4

H31

WORD FORMULAE

UA2d,3bc/4 N3a/4
UA2d,3bc/4 A2b,3b/4
FE/D1 FE/E4
PRa/4 NPc/4

In Heinemann Mathematics 6, the children were introduced to writing word formulae to describe simple shape or number patterns. This work is now consolidated.

The GRT context continues with more satellite signals and molecular models made with beads.

Introductory activities

1 Dots and lines

■ Draw this pattern on a chalkboard or an OHP transparency.

  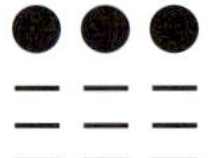  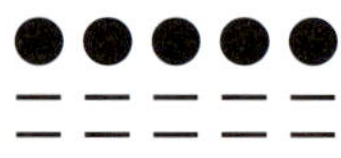

Tell the children they are going to find a link between the number of dots and the number of lines in the signal.

■ Draw a table on the chalkboard. Complete it with the help of the children.

Draw arrows joining corresponding pairs of numbers. Ask for a rule which connects the numbers.

Number of dots	Number of lines
1	3
2	6
3	9
4	12
5	15

Number of dots	Number of lines
1 ⟶	3
2 ⟶	6
3 ⟶	9
4 ⟶	12
5 ⟶	15

Rules such as 'times 3' or 'multiply by 3' may be suggested. Accept these rules, but encourage the children to use a recording method, introduced in Heinemann Mathematics 6 and used on Workbook page 11, which is as follows:

'The number of lines is 3 times the number of dots.'

Ask the children to use the rule to find the number of lines for 8 dots and 10 dots.

■ Repeat for other patterns. For example,

  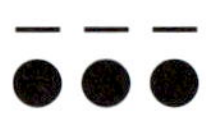 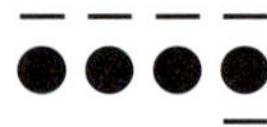 

'The number of lines is one more than the number of dots.'

2 Tables

■ Show the children tables like these.

(a)

Number of dots	Number of lines
2 ⟶	5
4 ⟶	7
6 ⟶	9
8 ⟶	11

(b)

Number of dots	Number of lines
4 ⟶	2
7 ⟶	5
3 ⟶	1
10 ⟶	8

(c)

Number of dots	Number of lines
20 ⟶	4
35 ⟶	7
5 ⟶	1
40 ⟶	8

- Ask for rules connecting the numbers of dots and lines. For example,

   (a) 'The number of lines is 3 more than the number of dots.'

   (b) 'The number of lines is 2 less than the number of dots.'

   (c) 'The number of lines is the number of dots divided by 5.'

UA2d,3bc/4	N3a/4
UA2d,3bc/4	A2b,3b/4
FE/D1 FE/E4	
PRa/4 NPac/4	

Workbook page 11   *Pattern: word formulae*
Textbook page 53

On Workbook page 11, the tables offer progressively less help by omitting arrows and not providing values for the number of lines. Some children may not need to complete the arrows each time.

On Textbook page 53, in question 1, the children should find the number of yellow beads when there are 10 red beads by using their rule, rather than by continuing the table or trying to draw the model.

H32

SYMBOLIC FORMULAE

This section introduces the use of symbols to express word formulae in a more compact form. The children also evaluate symbolic formulae.

| N3a/5 |
| A2b,3b/5 |
| FE/D1 FE/E4 |
| PRa/5 NPc/5 |

The formulae are derived from situations related to GRT's work with plant foods and microchips.

Introductory activities

1   Greenheart

- Introduce the idea of using *Greenheart*, a plant food developed at GRT, to make plants grow better.

  Discuss the instructions on the box:

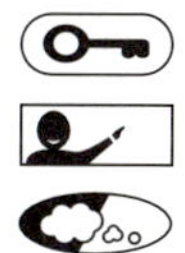

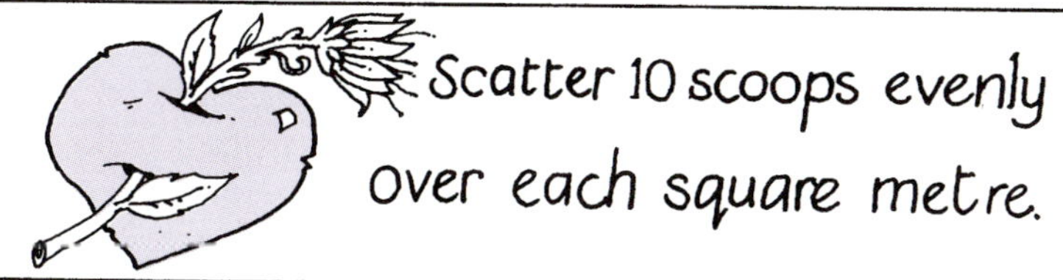

Make a table and, with the help of the children, complete the numbers of scoops for different numbers of square metres.

Number of square metres	Number of scoops
1	10
2	20
3	30
4	40
5	50

- Ask the children to state a rule, in words, for finding the number of scoops to use when they know the number of square metres. For example,

   'The number of scoops is 10 times the number of square metres.'

■ Tell the children that there is a neater and quicker way of writing a rule like this. Insert the symbols

$$M \text{ for square metres}$$

and S for scoops

at the top of the columns of the table.

Repeat the rule in words while writing a formula in symbols.

Number of square metres (M)	Number of scoops (S)
1	10
2	20
3	30
4	40
5	50

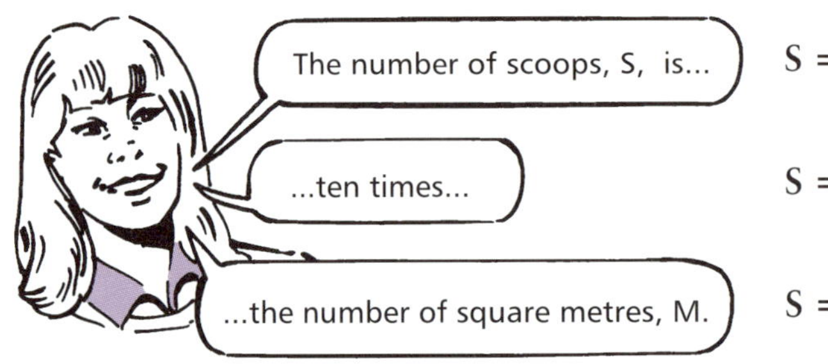

$S =$

$S = 10 \times$

$S = 10 \times M$

Tell the children that $S = 10 \times M$ is a **formula** for finding the number of scoops, S, when they know the number of square metres, M. You may also wish to tell them that another way of writing the formula is to omit the '×' and write $S = 10M$.

■ Ask the children how many scoops of *Greenheart* would be needed for 6 square metres and 10 square metres. They should do the necessary calculations mentally.

2   Spot the formulae

■ Show the children tables like these, either written on a chalkboard or displayed on cards.

Roots	
M	S
1	7
2	8
3	9
4	10
5	11

Greengrow	
M	S
2	1
4	2
6	3
8	4
10	5

Big Bud	
M	S
1	4
2	8
3	12
4	16
5	20

Magic	
M	S
2	1
4	3
6	5
8	7
10	9

Tell them that the tables show the number of scoops, S, of **other** plant foods used for a given number of square metres, M.

■ Choose one of the tables and ask for a rule, **in words**, to find the number of scoops for a given number of square metres. Answers such as 'Add on 6' or '6 more' should be translated into the form

'The number of scoops is the number of square metres, add 6.'

Roots	
M	S
1	7
2	8
3	9
4	10
5	11

■ Display cards with the formulae:

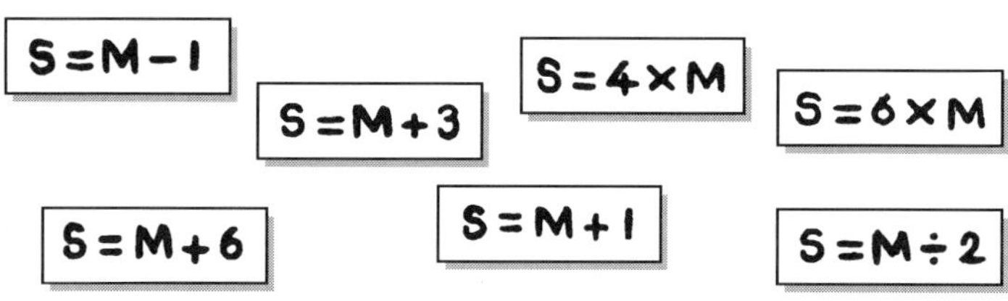

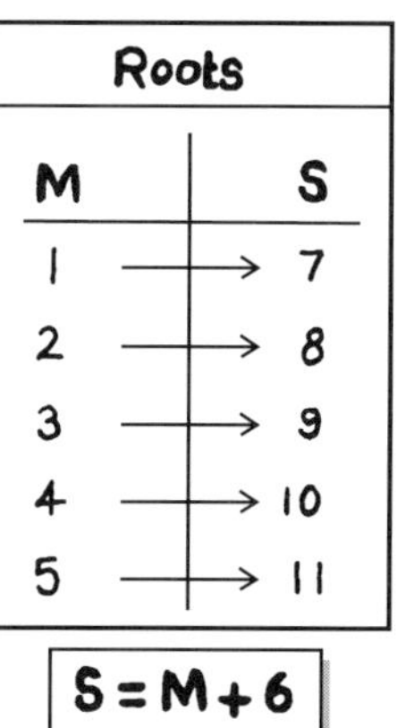

Ask the children to choose one to match this table and the rule.

Display 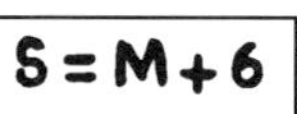 below the table, as shown.

■ Ask the children if they can find a formula for each of the other tables. Tell them to think of a rule, initially in words, and then choose a formula to match.

Greengrow	
M	S
2 →	1
4 →	2
6 →	3
8 →	4
10 →	5

S = M ÷ 2

Big Bud	
M	S
1 →	4
2 →	8
3 →	12
4 →	16
5 →	20

S = 4 × M

Magic	
M	S
2 →	1
4 →	3
6 →	5
8 →	7
10 →	9

S = M − 1

At this point the children could try Textbook page 54.

3   Using a formula

■ Discuss the formula $B = 250 \times H$ where **B** is the number of boxes of *Greenheart* produced in a given number of hours, **H**. Show the children how to use the formula to work out the number of boxes produced in 8 hours.

$$\text{Write the formulae} \longrightarrow B = 250 \times H$$

$$\text{Substitute 8 for } H \longrightarrow = 250 \times 8$$

$$= 2000$$

2000 boxes are produced in 8 hours.

■ Ask the children to calculate the value of **B** for other values of **H**: for example, for $H = 10$ and $H = 6$.

Textbook pages 54 and 55   *Pattern: symbolic formulae*

On page 54, in question 2(b), encourage the children to write each rule in a form that will make it easier to translate into symbols. For example,

Green fingers: 'The number of drops is the number of litres, add 3.'

This rule can be written as the formula $D = L + 3$.

In question 3, the expected formulae are as follows:

(a) $D = L - 1$ (b) $D = L + 3$ (c) $D = L \div 5$

Some discussion of microchips may be required as an introduction to question 4, perhaps by reference to TV programmes showing the internal components of computers. The expected formula is $T = 6 \times M$ or $T = 6M$.

On page 55, encourage the children to set down their working for evaluating formulae in the way shown in the worked example at the top of the page.

In question 2, some children may need help in finding costs. For example, the cost of **one** board with **two** microchips is £2 for the board and £2 for the chips, making £4 altogether. The appropriate formula in 2(b) is $C = M + 2$.

Number of microchips (M)	Cost in £ (C)
1	3
2	4
3	

In question 3(a), the boards are chosen so that the arrangement and number of holes will accommodate an exact number of microchips with 6 tags, with no holes unoccupied. The formula $M = H \div 6$ should be assumed to apply in part (d) also, where the arrangement of the holes is not illustrated.

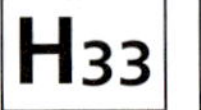

FORMULAE FROM GRAPHS

N3a/5
A2b,3b/5
FE/D1 FE/E4
AFbc/6

This section deals with graphs where the points lie in a straight line. Tables of values taken from the graphs lead to the derivation and use of symbolic formulae.

Written rules describing the relationship between the co-ordinates of points are also considered. Some of these ideas were introduced, in simpler form, in the Extension Textbook of Heinemann Mathematics 6.

The context for part of this section involves Global Research Technology's vitamin pills.

Introductory activity

The children should be able to try Textbook page 56 after some discussion of

— the context underlying the graphs on the page

— the method of representing points in a table.

Otherwise the mathematical ideas are similar to those already introduced for Textbook pages 54 and 55.

What's the point?

■ Prepare a graph like this on a chalkboard or a large sheet of paper.
Graphs like this appear on Workbook page 12.

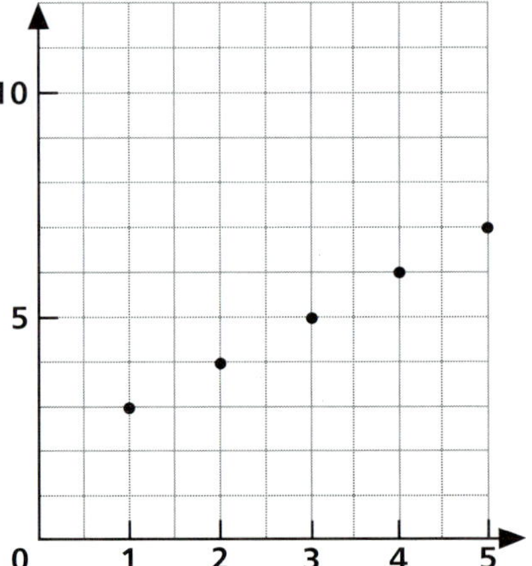

■ Ask the children to list (vertically) the co-ordinates of the marked points.

Discuss a rule, in words, connecting the second co-ordinate to the first one. For example,

   'The second co-ordinate is the first co-ordinate, add 2.'

              (1, 3)
              (2, 4)
              (3, 5)
              (4, 6)
              (5, 7)

■ Ask the children to predict the next two points, (6, 8) and (7, 9). Introduce the idea that the graph could continue, with more points to the right and upwards. Ask which of these points they think would be marked if the graph was continued:

   (15, 13)   (40, 42)   (19, 21)   (32, 54)

Only (40, 42) and (19, 21) satisfy the rule.

Textbook page 56   *Pattern: formulae and graphs*
Workbook page 12

N3a/5
A2b,3b/5
FE/D1 FE/E4
AFbe/6 NPc/5 SPe/4

On Textbook page 56, the context underlying the graphs should be discussed so that the children are clear about what they show. For example, the first graph shows how many real tangerines contain the same amount of vitamins as Global Research Technology's vitamin pills.

On Workbook page 12, the axes of the graphs are not labelled, so the text refers to 'first co-ordinate' and 'second co-ordinate'.

When answering questions 1(c), 1(d), 2(c) and 3(c), the children should keep referring back to the appropriate rule in words.

N2b,3g/4→5	N2b,3c/4→5
RTN/E1 AS/E5	
Mg/5	

Negative numbers

Overview

This section

- consolidates the concept of negative numbers
- uses the language 'positive' and 'negative'
- introduces ordering
- includes informal addition and subtraction using number lines.

	Teacher's Notes	Textbook	Workbook	Reinforcement Sheets
Negative numbers: concept, ordering	125	57	13	
Negative numbers: increase and decrease	128	58*	14	
Other activity	*130*	*59*		

Homework provided in Home Link-up.

Resources

Useful materials

- materials suggested within the introductory activities

Assessment and Resources Pack

Assessment

Round-up 3
Question 2

Resources

Resource Cards
14 Oil rig *Heron* (negative numbers)

NEGATIVE NUMBERS: CONCEPT, ORDERING

Negative numbers were used in Heinemann Mathematics 4, 5 and 6 in the context of temperature. The main ideas included

— extending the sequence 4, 3, 2, 1, 0 using ⁻1, ⁻2, ⁻3, ⁻4 . . .

— ⁻1, ⁻2, ⁻3, ⁻4 . . . are negative numbers, 'negative one, negative two . . .'

— a temperature such as ⁻5°C means negative (or minus) five degrees Celsius or five degrees below zero.

The work in Heinemann Mathematics P7

— consolidates the concept of negative numbers

— uses the language 'positive' and 'negative'

— emphasizes order and relative size, for example, ⁻2 is smaller than ⁺4.

The context for the work is *Heron*, a North Sea oil rig.

N2b,3g/4→5
N2b,3c/4→5
RTN/E1
Mg/5

Introductory activities

1　Oil rig *Heron*　(positive and negative numbers)

■ Discuss oil rigs in general and introduce the *Heron*, which is a **production platform**. Emphasize the huge size of the structure – about 300 metres from top to sea-bed – and compare this to the heights of local buildings such as the school or a block of flats.
The children may have some knowledge about life and equipment on board:

— people who work there, such as drillers, divers, welders and chefs

— equipment for drilling, pumping, storing and lifting

— living accommodation, such as games rooms, restaurants and bedrooms

— helicopter landing pad.

■ Introduce the lifts which are needed to carry people and equipment to the different levels of the oil rig.

Display the level indicator from one of the lifts for the Main Deck and the levels above. The children should be able to suggest suitable numbering for the levels below Main Deck. The level indicator can then be extended appropriately.

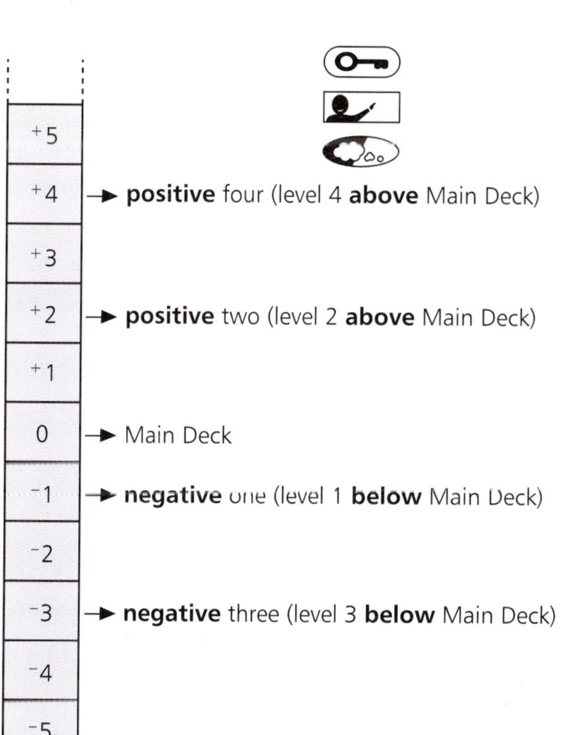

■ Through discussion emphasize

— the numbers decrease from top to bottom

— the sequence is extended using ⁻1, ⁻2, ⁻3, ⁻4, ⁻5 . . .

— the numbers **above** zero are **positive** numbers, 'positive one, positive two . . .'

— the numbers **below** zero are **negative** numbers, 'negative one, negative two . . .' (or sometimes 'minus one, minus two . . .').

The raised position of the positive and negative signs is used throughout Heinemann Mathematics to avoid confusion with the addition and subtraction signs.

2 Weatherwatch on *Heron* *(positive and negative temperature)*

■ Discuss the importance of weather forecasts to the workers on *Heron*.

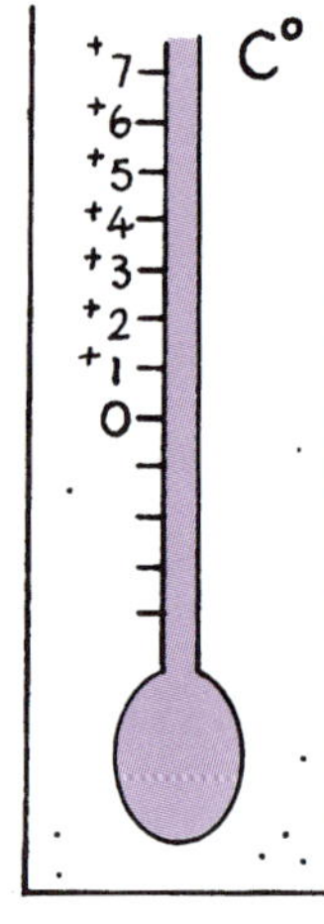

■ Display a large thermometer with the positive markings labelled. Ask the children to label the remaining markings.

Discuss the display, emphasizing

— water freezes at 0°C, zero degrees Celsius

— the temperature ⁺7°C means '7 degrees **above** zero' or **positive** 7 degrees Celsius'

— the temperature ⁻4°C means '4 degrees **below** zero' or **negative** 4 degrees Celsius.

Other language which could be discussed includes

— degrees above/below freezing

— the use of 'minus' as an alternative to negative.

At this point the children could try Textbook page 57.

3 *Heron*'s mini-sub *(ordering)*

■ Introduce the oil rig's mini-sub, used for access to underwater parts of the rig. The flow of oxygen into the pilot's cabin can be controlled. On the chalkboard, display the oxygen gauge as shown.

Ask the children to supply the missing numbers to complete the gauge.

■ Use the gauge as the focus for a discussion which emphasizes

— oxygen flow decreased/increased by sliding the control knob to the left/right

— moving to the left/right, the numbers become smaller/larger.

Discuss examples such as

⁺3 is smaller than ⁺6	and	⁺6 is greater than ⁺3
⁻1 is smaller than ⁺4	and	⁺4 is greater than ⁻1
⁻4 is smaller than ⁺1	and	⁺1 is greater than ⁻4
⁻2 is smaller than 0	and	0 is greater than ⁻2
⁻5 is smaller than ⁻1	and	⁻1 is greater than ⁻5

4 *Heron's* lift   *(positive and negative number patterns)*

- Ask the children to write the level at which the lift on oil rig *Heron* has stopped: for example, $^+10$ (level 10 above Main Deck). Underneath they should create a number pattern by writing, in order, the levels at which the lift stops when it stops at every second level until it reaches a specified level, say $^-10$ (level 10 below Main Deck).

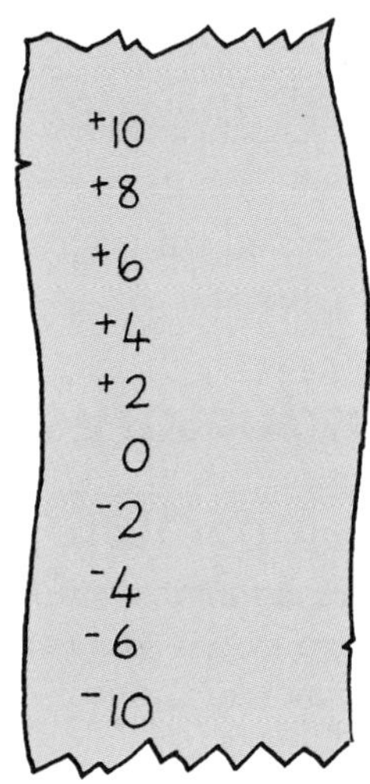

- Repeat the number pattern activity for

  — different starting levels and sequences of stops

  — movements up the shaft: for example, starting at level $^-12$ and stopping at every fourth level.

- A calculator can be used to investigate such number patterns. Note that the negative symbol may be displayed differently from one make of calculator to another. For example,

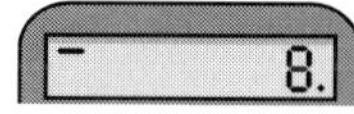

Textbook page 57   *Negative numbers: concept*

Before attempting the work on this page, the children should be introduced to

- the context of oil rig *Heron*

- the language and symbolism of positive and negative temperatures.

In question 4, where there is no dotted line, the children could use a ruler. Acceptable answers should lie in the range of $^-5$ m to $^+5$ m of the 'exact' reading.

| N2b/4→5 |
| N2b/4→5 |
| RTN/E1 |
| Mg/5 |

Workbook page 13   *Negative numbers: ordering*

There should be some discussion of the context, *Heron*'s mini-sub, in order to clarify the meaning of terms such as gauge, stabilizer, cabin pressure, rudder control and depth controls.

The introductory discussion should emphasize that in the sequence

$$^-5, \ ^-4, \ ^-3, \ ^-2, \ ^-1, \ 0, \ ^+1, \ ^+2, \ ^+3, \ ^+4, \ ^+5 \ldots$$

- numbers to the left are smaller than numbers to the right

- numbers to the right are greater than numbers to the left.

| N2b,3g/4→5 |
| N2b,3c/4→5 |
| RTN/E1 |
| Mg/5 |

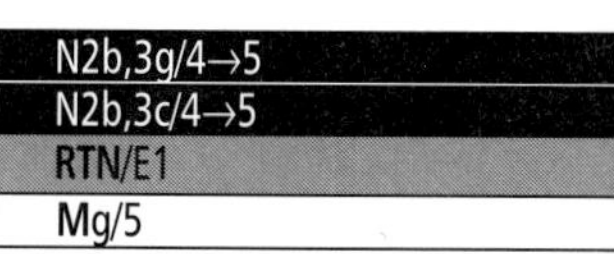

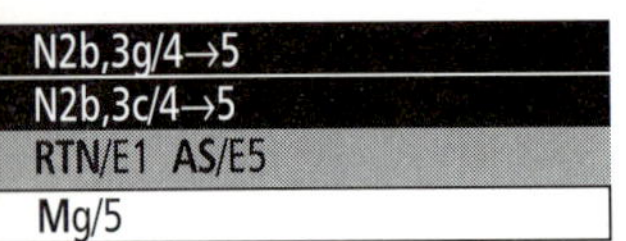

Addition and subtraction are now introduced in an informal way, making use of number lines.

Introductory activities

1 Temperature

- Draw a vertical number line on the chalkboard or on an overhead transparency to represent a thermometer scale. Remind the children that as you move

  — up the scale, the numbers represent warmer temperatures

  — down the scale, the numbers represent colder temperatures.

- Demonstrate how to count along the number line to find, for example,

  — a temperature reading which starts at $^-2°C$ and rises by 5 degrees

  — a temperature reading which starts at $^+3°C$ and falls by 4 degrees

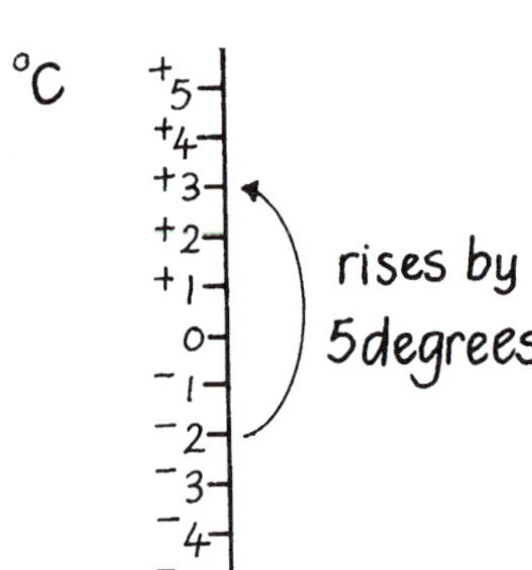

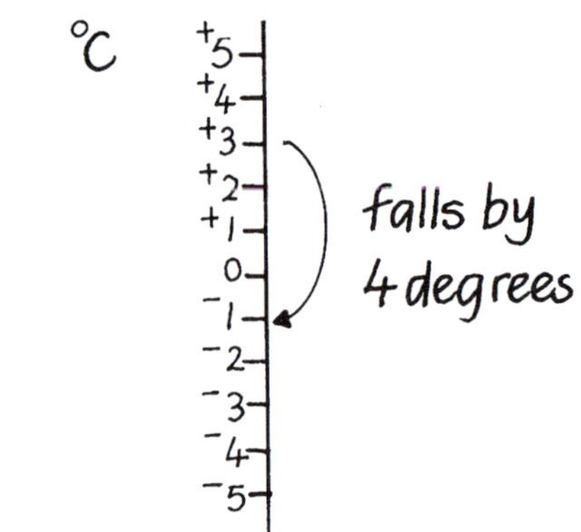

The children should point to the starting temperature and then count up or down to find the finishing temperature.

Introduce the language 'increase' for a rise, and 'decrease' for a fall in temperature. Use this language during discussion, interchanging it with rise and fall.

- Repeat for other examples, such as

  — start at $^-3°C$ and rise by 7 degrees

  — start at $^-5°C$ and rise by 5 degrees

  — start at $^+2°C$ and fall by 2 degrees

  — start at $^-1°C$ and fall by 4 degrees.

- Using the number line, discuss how to find the increase or decrease when a temperature changes. For example, by how many degrees does the temperature

  — increase when it rises from $^-4°C$ to $^+5°C$

  — decrease when it falls from $^+3°C$ to $^-2°C$?

In the first example, a child should place a finger at $^-4°C$ and count up until $^+5°C$ is reached, giving an increase of 9 degrees.

2   The helipad

Tell the children that oil rig *Heron*'s helipad is used by helicopters transporting crew or supplies. The helipad can be heated if it ices up, and there is a thermometer in the control room which is used to monitor its temperature. Display a horizontal number line to represent the thermometer.

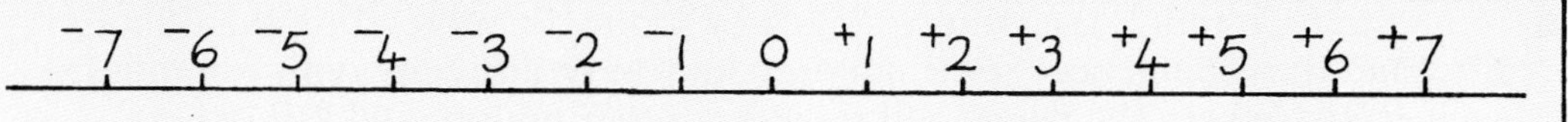

Discuss how to use the number line for examples such as

— 'Find the new reading if the temperature starts at ‾4°C and increases by 9 degrees.'

— 'Find the new reading if the temperature starts at ⁺4°C and decreases by 7 degrees.'

— 'By how many degrees does the temperature increase when it rises from ‾6°C to ‾1°C?'

— 'By how many degrees does the temperature decrease when it falls from ⁺5°C to ‾2°C?'

N2b,3g/4→5
N2b,3c/4→5
RTN/E1 AS/E5
Mg/5

Workbook page 14   *Negative numbers: increase and decrease*
Textbook page 58

On Workbook page 14, in question 1, the children should mark on the gauges each step taken by the pointer as it moves left or right.

In question 3, the meaning of 'increase' and 'decrease' may need to be explained if this language was not discussed as part of an introductory activity.

On Textbook page 58, in questions 1 to 4, some children may find that the drawing of the thermometer helps them to visualize the effects of the temperature changes. Others may need to sketch a scale which they can draw on.

In question 5, the children should read the starting temperatures from the scales given, then use the scale in the panel to help them to visualize the rises in temperature needed to reach ⁺2°C.

In question 7, it may be necessary to emphasize that the children should give the number of degrees and state whether the temperature change is an increase or a decrease. For example, in part (a), the temperature increases by 10 degrees.

H34

Textbook page 59   *Other activity: mental calculation, money*

■ This page involves mental strategies for adding, subtracting and multiplying sums of money. It would be best attempted after Textbook page 40, which deals with approximate costs, has been completed.

■ In questions 1 and 2, the strategy involves adding or subtracting the pounds first, and then the pence. Some children may have difficulty with examples such as 2(k) where the pence add to give another pound, and 2(l), where subtracting the pence gives 0 pence.

■ In question 3, the multiplication examples involve a similar strategy – the pounds are multiplied first and then the pence. The resulting two amounts are then added to give the answer.

■ Question 4 involves multiplication of amounts which are close to a whole number of pounds. For example,

$$4 \times \text{£}3{\cdot}90$$

$$\text{£}3{\cdot}90 = \text{£}4 - 10\text{p}$$

$$4 \times \text{£}4 = \text{£}16, \quad 4 \times 10\text{p} = 40\text{p}$$

$$\text{£}16 - 40\text{p}$$

$$= \text{£}15{\cdot}60$$

Problem solving

UA2abcd,3c/4	UA2abcd,4a/4
PSE	
PCcd/4→5	
PUbcdef/5	

Overview

This section

■ provides problems designed to encourage the use of specific strategies:

— listing

— guess and check

— simulation/modelling

— logical thinking

■ provides mixed problems to develop the children's ability to select appropriate strategies.

	Teacher's Notes	Textbook	Workbook	Reinforcement Sheets
Problem solving strategies:				
listing	132	60		
guess and check	134	61		
simulation	135	62		
mixed strategies	137	63*		

Homework provided in Home Link-up.

Resources

Useful materials

■ coloured counters or cubes

■ squared paper

■ cocktail sticks/toothpicks

■ other materials suggested within the introductory activities

Assessment and Resources Pack

Assessment

Round-up 1
Question 8

Round-up 2
Question 7

Round-up 3
Question 8

Resources

Problem Solving Activities

Resource Cards
22 Triangles puzzle

Teaching notes

Work of a problem solving nature appears in the Textbooks and Workbooks at all stages of Heinemann Mathematics. In addition, there is a booklet of 'Problem Solving Activities' in the Assessment and Resources Pack for each stage. Information about possible strategies is included in the relevant notes for teachers.

This section focuses on particular strategies which the children may have used before – listing, guess and check, simulation ('acting it out', 'making a model', etc.) and logical thinking.

The emphasis is on recognizing certain types of problem where these strategies are appropriate.

The context used is that of a computer adventure game called 'Quest', which involves a journey through a strange, fantasy world, inhabited by weird creatures who provide various tasks and challenges.

PROBLEM SOLVING: LISTING

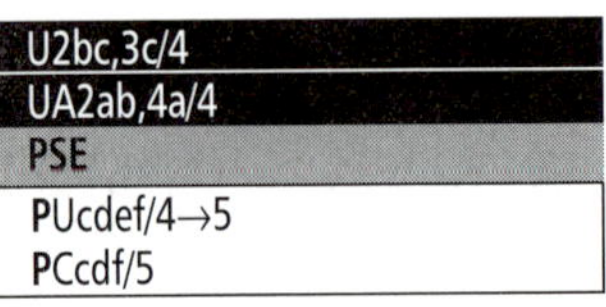

Introductory activity

Postcards

■ Introduce a problem such as the following:

'Five friends, Amy, John, Rob, Leigh and Shona, each send each of the others a postcard, while on holiday. How many postcards are sent altogether?'

Make sure that the children can interpret the problem correctly, perhaps by asking one or two of them to re-state it, in their own words.

Ask the children, in pairs or small groups, to discuss the problem, suggest possible strategies and, using one or more of these, try to find a solution. Provide any materials which are requested.

It is important at this stage not to lead the children towards a particular strategy or to a solution.

■ Bring the groups together and ask each, in turn, to share their solution (if achieved) and to describe the strategy they used. There are several possibilities. For example,

— 'We found the total number of cards by multiplying the number of friends by the number of cards each had to send' (i.e. $5 \times 4 = 20$ cards).

This is essentially **logical reasoning**.

— 'We used counters for cards and "sent" them to each other. Altogether we sent 20 counters.'

This method involves **simulation** with material.

— 'We made a list of the cards sent by each of the friends.' **(listing)**

■ Focus the discussion on listing. Use the children's own descriptions of their methods. Ensure that the following points emerge:

— It is worthwhile simplifying the listing process by using only the first initial in each of the friends' names: for example, A for Amy, J for John, R for Rob, L for Leigh and S for Shona.

— If the postcards are listed in an arbitrary fashion, such as

A to J (a postcard from Amy to John)

J to R

S to L

R to J

and so on . . .

it is quite likely that some cards will be listed more than once or omitted.

— A better way of organizing the list involves a more **systematic** procedure: for example, starting with all of the cards sent by Amy and then moving in turn through each of the friends.

A to J	J to A	R to A	L to A	S to A
A to R	J to R	R to J	L to J	S to J
A to L	J to L	R to L	L to R	S to R
A to S	J to S	R to S	L to S	S to L

This gives a total of **20 postcards** for a group of five friends.

Textbook page 60 *Problem solving: listing*

Discuss the context of a computer fantasy adventure game.

In question 1, if any of the children choose to list the items using initial letters (magic dust – M, scissors – S, etc.), this should be accepted.

In question 2, it is hoped that the children will list the colours of the levers as, for example,

r   b   y   g

In question 3, the children must realize that they are not being asked merely to list the instructions in all possible ways. Only the ways that lead to the goblet being **filled** are valid.

In question 4, it is not necessary for the children to include the unit of length, centimetres, in their lists.

UA2bc,3c/4
UA2ab,4a/4
PSE
PUdef,Cd/4

Introductory activity

Wizards' ages

■ Use a problem such as this:

'The ages of 3 wizards total 307 years. Medwyn's age is three times Grandel's. Wotan is 36 years younger than Medwyn. What are the ages of the 3 wizards?'

Ask the children to work out the solution to the problem, in pairs, using calculators.

■ Discuss the children's solutions and strategies. They are likely to have used guess and check methods to refine and improve their solutions gradually. Some might reason that, since the total is **about** 300 years and there are 3 wizards, a worthwhile starting point could be to investigate the possibilities if Wotan is 100 years old as Medwyn and Grandel are, respectively, older and younger than he. For example,

	Medwyn	Wotan	Grandel
First guess:	↓	↓	↓
	136 years	100 years	about 45 years
	(100 + 36)		(136 ÷ 3)

Checking the total gives 281 years, which is too small. The original guess for Wotan's age needs to be **increased**, therefore, for an improved second guess.

	Medwyn	Wotan	Grandel
Second guess:	↓	↓	↓
	146 years	110 years	about 49 years
	(110 + 36)		(146 ÷ 3)

Checking the total gives 305 years, which is only marginally too small.

A slight increase in Wotan's age gives the solution:

Medwyn	Wotan	Grandel	
↓	↓	↓	(total:
147 years	111 years	49 years	307 years)

■ Alternatively, some children may choose to guess the age of the youngest wizard, Grandel, multiply by 3 to find the age of the oldest wizard, Medwyn, and finally subtract 36 to find Wotan's age.

The guess for Grandel's age can then be adjusted according to whether the total obtained for the three wizards' ages was too small or too large.

| UA2bc,3c/4 |
| UA2ab,4a/4 |
| PSE |
| PUdef/4→5 |

Textbook page 61   *Problem solving: guess and check*

In question 1, the children need to realize that four **consecutive** numbers have to go in the circles. Some may be misled by the fact that the numbers on the joining lines are also partly consecutive.

In questions 3 and 4, if any children have difficulty in getting started, suggest that they 'guess' an appropriate starting number and then apply the given conditions.

For example, in question 3, if the yellow number is 20 then the blue number is 18 and the red number is 36. This gives a total of 74, which is too large. Ask the children to try again, but this time make the yellow number 15.

The children should **not**, however, simply be supplied with one of the numbers.

In question 5, the use of the answers from the previous questions should produce the message

'PUSH HIS BIG TOE'

PROBLEM SOLVING: SIMULATION

Introductory activity

| UA2abcd,3c/4 |
| UA2abcd,4a/4 |
| PSE |
| PUdef/5 |

The glazier's puzzle

- Introduce a problem such as the following:

  'A magician orders a glazier to fit panes of glass into his new window.
  There are 25 panes altogether. The magician tells the glazier that **only 5** panes should be of coloured glass and that these **should appear only once in each row, column and diagonal**. Where should the glazier fit the coloured panes?'

  Discuss the problem with the children to ensure that they understand it. Ask them to suggest ways in which it might be solved and any materials which might be helpful.

- Some children might suggest drawing and colouring on squared paper. It is unlikely that the squares would be correctly coloured at first and this would lead to much rubbing out or re-drawing.

- Whether the children suggest it or not, discuss an approach where coloured counters or cubes are moved around on top of a square grid to find a solution.

- Give out cubes or counters and ask the children to try to solve the puzzle.
  A possible solution is as shown.

UA2abcd,3c/4
UA2abcd,4a/4
PSE
PUdef,Ccd/5

■ Discuss why arrangements such as the following are not correct:

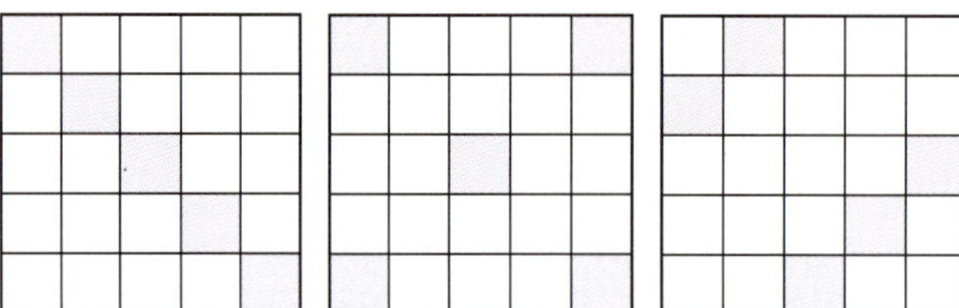

Textbook page 62 *Problem solving: simulation, logical thinking*

In question 1, the children need to realize that, in this context, symmetrical means that the same pattern of colours appears on either side of the line of symmetry. Coloured counters or cubes should be used to give the pattern

Red Blue Green | Green Blue Red

which meets all of the conditions.

In question 2, the children should be encouraged to read the rules carefully. They should draw and colour each grid on squared paper (2 cm grid would be suitable).

Once again, counters or cubes should be used (one colour for the guards and a different colour to represent the player).

Moving counters on the grids should give the minimum number of moves as

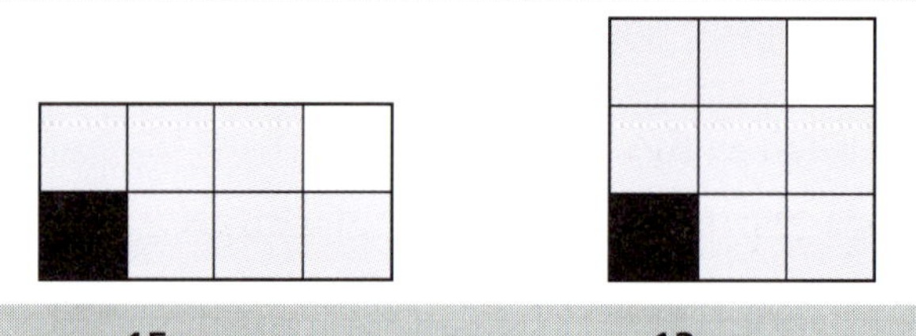

15 moves   **13 moves**

The 3 × 3 grid should therefore be the one chosen.

In question 3, some children may choose to use a listing strategy, possibly in combination with a diagram. For example,

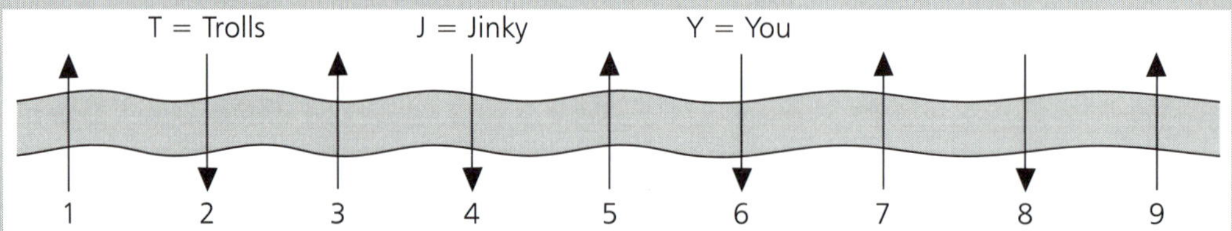

The following key shows a sequence of 9 moves:

1 – J, Y	4 – J	7 – T$_2$
2 – Y	5 – J, Y	8 – J
3 – T$_1$	6 – Y	9 – J, Y

However, it is easier to solve the problem by using counters or cubes to represent the travellers. They can be moved across a table representing the 'moat'. A solution can be reported orally to accompany the moves. This can then be recorded on paper.

UA2abcd,3c/4
UA2abcd,4a/4
PSE
PUbdef,Cd/5

Textbook page 63 — *Problem solving: mixed strategies*

In question 1, some children may be able to deduce from looking at the other pictures that the hidden dice faces show 6 and 3 respectively.

Others will wish to mark numbers on a wooden or plastic cube. Those doing so will need to take care to write the numbers in the correct orientations.

In question 2, cocktail sticks, toothpicks or rods can be used to represent the daggers. Make sure the children realize that **small** squares are required and that, for example, this shows 4 **small** squares:

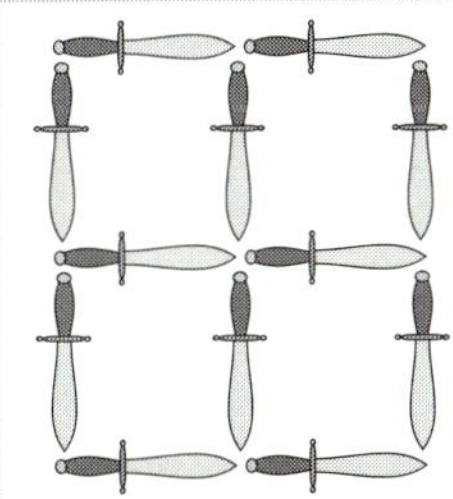

Question 3 can be solved using a guess and check strategy.

In question 4, a listing strategy can be used, with the letters O, I, Y and J representing the four Trolls. Some children might simulate the problem by playing the parts of the Trolls and passing an object from one to the other.

H35,36

N3d/5	N4d/4 N3b/5
MD/E	
NOb/4→5	

Multiplication and division by TU

Overview

This section

■ revises the written technique for multiplication by a two-digit number and extends this to include multiplication of HTU

■ revises division by a two-digit number by repeated subtraction and extends this by reducing the number of subtractions involved.

	Teacher's Notes	Textbook	Workbook	Reinforcement Sheets
Multiplication by a two-digit number	139	64		
Division by a two-digit number	140	65, 66*		
Multiplication and division	143	67*		

Homework provided in Home Link-up.

Resources

Assessment and Resources Pack

Assessment

Number Check-up 4
Textbook pages 64–7
(multiplication and division by TU)

Resources

Teaching notes

In Heinemann Mathematics 6, the children were introduced to a written technique for multiplication by a two-digit number.

This work is now revised and extended to include multiplying HTU by TU.

The activities are set in the context of Brown's Bookshop, a large city centre bookstore.

MULTIPLICATION BY A TWO-DIGIT NUMBER

Introductory activities

N3d/5
N3b/5
MD/E
NOb/4

1 Book deliveries *(multiplication by multiples of 10)*

Revise this technique using an example like this.

> 'The bookshop receives 90 boxes of books, each weighing 17 kg. What is the total weight of the books?'

This can be done by multiplying by 10, indicated by placing a zero in the units space in the answer . . .

$$
\begin{array}{r}
17 \\
\times\,90 \\
\hline
0 \\
\end{array}
$$

. . . and then by multiplying by 9.

$$
\begin{array}{r}
17 \\
\times\,90 \\
\hline
1530 \\
\end{array}
$$

The total weight of the books is **1530 kg.**

2 Book deliveries *(HTU multiplied by TU)*

- Revise language and recording and introduce HTU × TU using an example like this.

> 'The bookstore receives 36 crates of books. Each crate contains 345 books. How many books does the shop receive altogether?'

Discuss the recording.

$$
\begin{array}{r}
345 \\
\times\,36 \\
\hline
\end{array}
$$

$6 \times 345 \;\rightarrow\quad 2070$

$30 \times 345 \;\rightarrow\; +\,10350$

Add to find $\quad 36 \times 345 \;\rightarrow\; \underline{\quad 12420}$

Altogether there are **12 420 books.**

Where schools prefer the children to multiply by the tens first, the recording
would be as shown:

$$
\begin{array}{rcl}
 & & 345 \\
 & & \underline{\times\ 36} \\
30 \times 345 & \to & 10350 \\
6 \times 345 & \to & \underline{+\ 2070} \\
36 \times 345 & \to & \underline{12420}
\end{array}
$$

Altogether there are **12 420 books**.

■ Repeat for other examples if necessary.

N3d/5
N3b/5
MD/E
NOb/4→5

Textbook page 64   *Multiplication by TU*

If you have not done so already, discuss the context of a large bookstore with a
number of branches throughout the country.

In questions 2(c), (e) and 2(g), where the multiplier is a multiple of ten, the
answer should be achieved in a single calculation.

In question 5 the children have to realize that May has 31 days.

DIVISION BY A TWO-DIGIT NUMBER

N3d/5
N4d/4 N3b/5
MD/E
NOb/5

In Heinemann Mathematics 6, a written technique was introduced for division by
two-digit numbers based on repeated subtraction and applied to examples which
arose from sharing or grouping situations.

This work is now revised and extended, and the number of subtractions reduced by
using tables of multiples.

The Brown's Bookshop context continues with books being placed on shelves and
various materials being organized in the stationery department's store room.

Introductory activities

1   Bookshelves   *(revision: subtracting tens and ones)*

Revise the language and recording using an example such as

'828 books are shared equally among 36 shelves.
How many are on each shelf?'

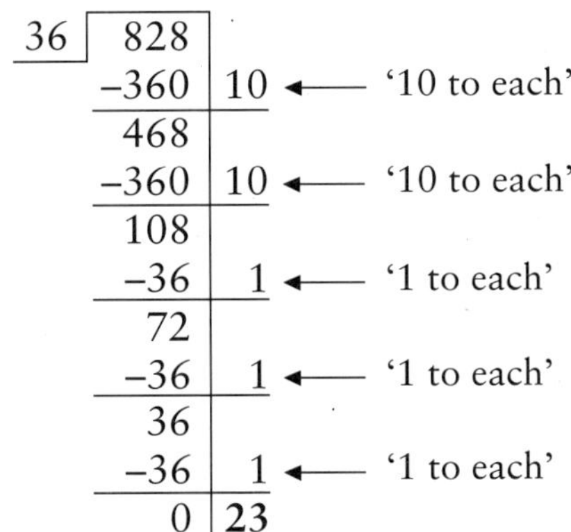

$$828 \div 36 = 23$$ There are **23 books** on each shelf.

2   Paperbacks   *(using a table of multiples)*

In the example above, the last three shares of 1 involved three subtractions. A method
of reducing the number of subtractions is now introduced. Consider the following
example, which is based on a grouping situation.

'Each shelf can hold 32 paperbacks.
How many shelves are needed for 746 paperbacks?'

```
32 | 746
    -320 | 10  ◄——— '10 shelves'
     426
    -320 | 10  ◄——— '10 shelves'
     106 |
```

At this point, where another group of 10 shelves is not possible, show the children
how to build up a table of multiples of 32 (by adding, doubling, etc.). They can then
use **3 shelves**.

```
32 | 746
    -320 | 10          1 × 32 =   32
     426               2 × 32 =   64
    -320 | 10          3 × 32 =   96
     106               4 × 32 = 128
     -96 |  3
      10 | 23
```

$$746 \div 32 = 23 \text{ r } 10$$ **24 shelves** are needed.

3 Maps *(using shares of 5)*

In some divisions, it is appropriate to use shares of 5. For example,

'435 maps are shared equally among 25 boxes. How many are in each box and how many are left over?'

$$
\begin{array}{r|r|l}
25 & 435 & \\
 & -250 & 10 \\ \hline
 & 185 & \\
 & -125 & 5 \\ \hline
 & 60 & \\
 & -50 & 2 \\ \hline
 & 10 & 17
\end{array}
$$

'10 to each' $10 \times 25 = 250$

'5 to each' $5 \times 25 = 125$ ($\frac{1}{2}$ of 10×25)

'2 to each' $1 \times 25 = 25$
 $2 \times 25 = 50$

$435 \div 25 = 17 \text{ r } 10$

There are **17 maps** in each box and **10 maps** are left over.

At this point the children could try Textbook page 65.

4 Comics

The number of subtractions in a division can be reduced still further by using, for example, 1 lot of 40 rather than 4 lots of 10.

Consider the following example:

'There are 18 comics in a bundle.
How many full bundles can be made from 870 comics?'

$$
\begin{array}{r|r|l}
18 & 870 & \\
 & -720 & 40 \\ \hline
 & 150 & \\
 & -90 & 5 \\ \hline
 & 60 & \\
 & -54 & 3 \\ \hline
 & 6 & 48
\end{array}
$$

'40 bundles'

'5 bundles'

'3 bundles'

$10 \times 18 = 180$
$20 \times 18 = 360$
$30 \times 18 = 540$
$40 \times 18 = 720$
$50 \times 18 = 900$

$5 \times 18 = 90$

$1 \times 18 = 18$
$2 \times 18 = 36$
$3 \times 18 = 54$
$4 \times 18 = 72$

$870 \div 18 = 48 \text{ r } 6$

48 full bundles can be made.

N3d/5
N4d/4 N3b/5
MD/E
NOb/5

Textbook pages 65 and 66 *Division: by TU*

The examples on these pages give children the opportunity to use tables of multiples in order to reduce the number of subtractions.

On Textbook page 65, in questions 1 and 2, the examples are such as to require that shares of ten and shares of not more than 4 be made.

In questions 3 and 4, shares of 5 can be made, although some children may still need to be encouraged to do this.

On Textbook page 66, the number of subtractions is further reduced by using multiples of ten.

H37

MULTIPLICATION AND DIVISION

The examples on Textbook page 67 provide a mixture of multiplication and division by two-digit numbers.

The children have to decide which operation to use and to interpret the answers to some of the division examples by considering the context of the question.

Textbook page 67   *Multiplication and division: by TU*

In question 4, the children have to realize that the remainder, 10, gives the number of discs in the last rack and that since each rack can hold 24 discs, another 14 discs would be needed to **fill** this rack.

In question 5(a), Jeremy's prediction means that 920 copies of his book would be sold in 23 days. Jeremy was not correct in question 5(b) as 980 copies were sold in 28 days. He said that 40 copies would be sold each day and $40 \times 28 = 1120$. Some children may divide 980 by 28 to find that the book actually sold at a rate of 35 copies per day.

The Measure part of Heinemann Mathematics P7 has seven sections, each with an Overview and accompanying notes.

Measure

Avonside Country Park

A context for length and angles

The work on

— length (Textbook pages 68–71, Workbook page 15)

— angles (Textbook pages 92–96, Workbook pages 29 and 30)

is set in the context of Avonside Country Park, an area which provides a range of leisure and recreational activities, as well as opportunities to enjoy attractive scenery and observe wildlife.

Introducing the context

The context could be introduced by discussing the need to provide access to areas such as Avonside for people who live and work in towns and cities.

The need to control access to preserve such areas in a relatively unspoiled state could also be discussed. Many children will recognize a similar type of facility in their local area, which they may have visited with the school or their family. Other possible activities are as follows.

1   Extending Avonside

The illustration on Textbook page 68 could be used as the starting point for an activity where the children are told that Avonside has acquired an area roughly equivalent to its present size, immediately to the south of the Boating Lake and Walled Garden (i.e. below these on the Textbook page).

The children can then be asked to discuss, in groups, and sketch out ideas for an expansion of Avonside which would double the size of the park. They should be aware of

— the need to provide access and, possibly, additional car parking

— the desirability of 'screening' such potentially obtrusive features

— any areas where access might justifiably be restricted due to the need to conserve wildlife

— the provision of areas accessible to elderly or disabled people

— the possibility of adding other new features, not included in the existing park.

Groups could report back and ideas could be pooled to produce a single plan.

2   Trees and pondlife

These features of Avonside could provide the stimulus for some children to investigate a local pond or woodland, recording and illustrating the variety of species found. Relevant reference books or materials could be consulted in order to find out more about the habits and/or characteristics of types of trees or pondlife which the children find interesting.

Comparisons could be made with the Avonside wildlife.

3   Orienteering

The Avonside orienteering scenario could be used, with a short course set up in a local park or even, on a smaller scale, in and around the school. Directional or other types of clues could be used with the aim being to complete the course correctly in the shortest time.

N2b/5	N2a/5
N3a/5	A3ab/5
SSM4ac/4	SSM4ad/4
	SSM3d/5

| ME/D1 |
| PFS/D1 |
| PFS/E3 |
| Mde/4 |
| Mehi/5 |

Length

Overview

This section

■ introduces the millimetre and gives practice in measuring in millimetres and in centimetres and millimetres

■ extends the work in scale to involve millimetres, calculation of scaled lengths and simple scale drawing

■ introduces the use of formulae for finding the perimeter of a square and a rectangle.

	Teacher's Notes	Textbook	Workbook	Reinforcement Sheets
Avonside Country Park: a context for length and angles	144			
The millimetre	148	68*		22
Scale	149	69*, 70*	15	23
Perimeter	152	71*		

Homework provided in Home Link-up.

An extension activity related to the above section of work is as follows:

	Teacher's Notes	Extension Textbook
Other activity: historic measures	258	E4

Teaching notes for the Extension Textbook are in a separate section at the end of the Teacher's Notes.

Resources

Useful materials

- rulers calibrated in centimetres and millimetres
- centimetre squared paper
- coloured pencils
- scissors
- other materials suggested within the introductory activities

Assessment and Resources Pack

Assessment

Measure Check-up 1
Textbook pages 68–71
Workbook page 15
(Length: millimetre, scale, perimeter)

Round-up 1
Question 4

Resources

Problem Solving Activities
16 Mini-motors (lengths in cm)
17 Road signs (lengths in km)

Resource Cards
16 and 17 Space Creatures
(lengths in m and cm)

Teaching notes

THE MILLIMETRE

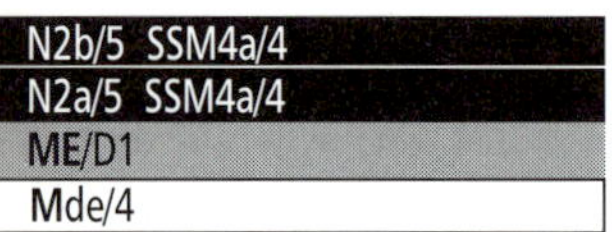

Previously in Heinemann Mathematics, the children have measured lengths to the nearest centimetre or half-centimetre. Measuring to the nearest millimetre is now introduced, using rulers calibrated in millimetres and in centimetres and millimetres.

The work on length is set in the context of Avonside Country Park. The children measure the lengths of drawings of some of the creatures from the wildlife pond.

Introductory activity

How small? *(measurement in millimetres)*

- Produce an overhead projector transparency of a scale marked in centimetres and half-centimetres. This can be done by photocopying and enlarging a ruler and using the photocopy to prepare the transparency.

- Explain that you want to measure the length of a pencil sharpener. Then place it on the scale.

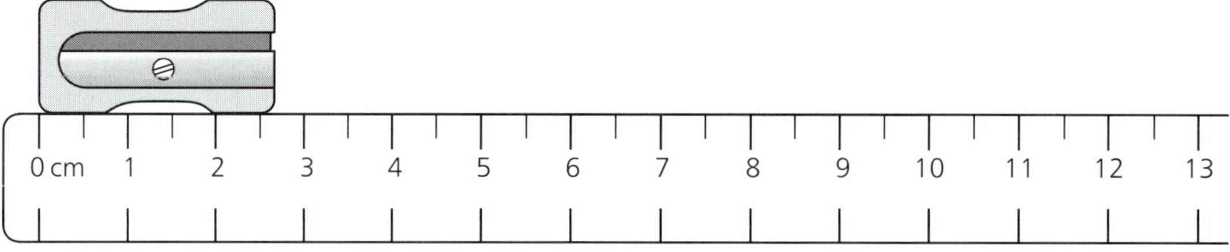

The length is **between $2\frac{1}{2}$ and 3 cm.**

- Tell the children that you want to measure the length more accurately using a smaller unit called a **millimetre**. Overlay a new transparency as shown, and measure the sharpener in **millimetres**.

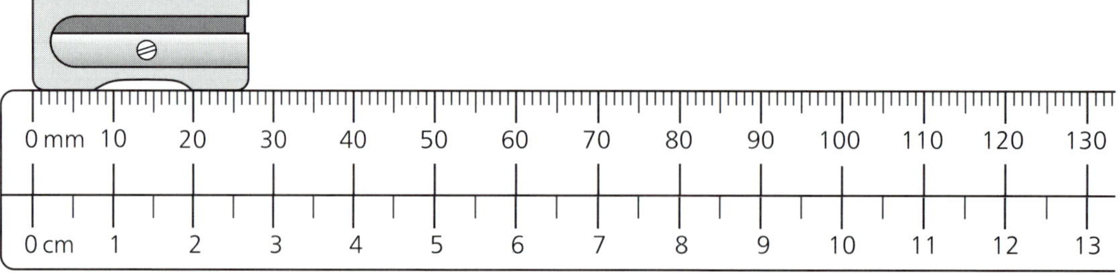

The length is **27 millimetres.**

- Discuss the relationships between centimetres and millimetres.

   10 millimetres = 1 centimetre

Introduce the abbreviation mm for millimetre.

   1 mm = 0·1 cm (a tenth of a centimetre)

■ Replace the previous scales with another showing cm and mm.

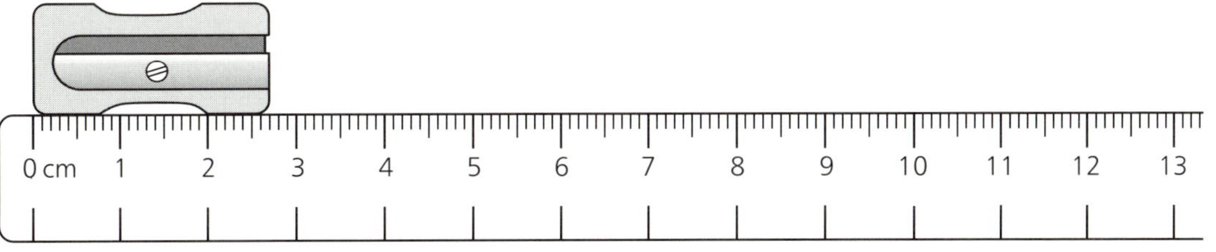

Discuss three ways of recording the length of the sharpener:

27 mm or **2 cm and 7 mm** or **2·7 cm**.

■ Repeat for other lengths. For example,

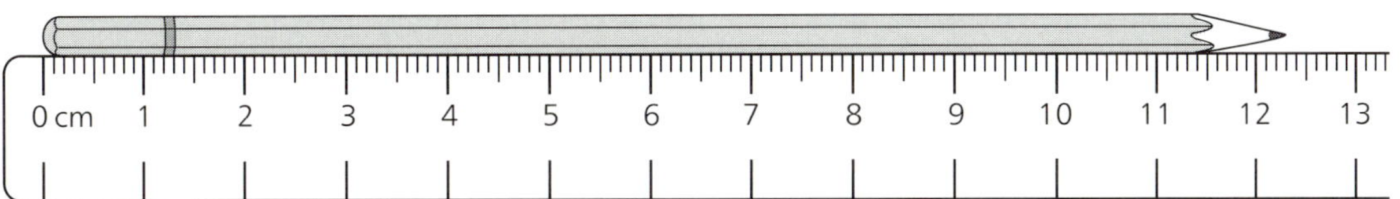

The length of the pencil is **123 mm** or **12 cm and 3 mm** or **12·3 cm**.

■ Give the children practice in measuring objects with a ruler marked in centimetres and millimetres. They should measure lengths

— in millimetres

— in centimetres and millimetres

— in centimetres (in decimal form).

Textbook page 68   *Length: millimetres*

| N2b/5 SSM4a/4 |
| N2a/5 SSM4a/4 |
| ME/D1 |
| Mde/4 |

Discuss the map of Avonside Country Park at the top of the page, especially the Wildlife Pond and the pondlife it contains.

In question 1, the children are expected to measure, accurately, the red lines which indicate the lengths of the creatures. Accept answers which are 1 or 2 mm more or less than the expected length.

In question 4, where the children are asked to draw lines to represent the lengths of some pond creatures, a partner could check these lengths.

R22 H39

SCALE

In Heinemann Mathematics 6, the children were introduced to scale drawings. They measured to the nearest centimetre and calculated true lengths using scales such as 1 cm to 5 cm, 1 cm to 30 cm and 1 cm to 2 m.

| N2b/5 SSM4a/4 |
| N2a/5 SSM3d/5 SSM4a/4 |
| ME/D1 PFS/E3 |
| Mi/5 |

This work is now revised and extended to include measurements to the nearest millimetre. The children are introduced to calculating scaled lengths, given the true lengths. They also create their first scale drawings.

The Avonside Country Park context continues with model boats on the Boating Lake and with the Park's Sports Centre.

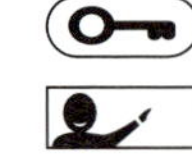

Introductory activities

1 True lengths

■ Produce a drawing of a model boat.

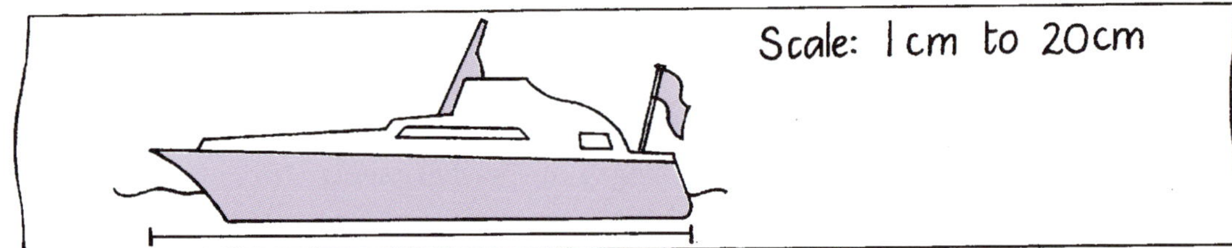

Discuss the scale – 1 cm on the drawing represents 20 cm on the boat. The model boat is

20 times as long   **20 times** as broad   **20 times** as high

■ Ask a child to measure the length of the boat on the drawing: for example 6·2 cm.

Discuss how to find the 'true length' using a calculator.

True length $= 6{\cdot}2\,\text{cm} \times 20$

$= \mathbf{124\,cm}$

■ Repeat for other examples and objects where the scales are of the form

1 cm to 6 cm   1 cm to 80 cm   1 cm to 3 m

At this point the children could try Textbook page 69.

2 Trees   *(scaled lengths)*

■ Talk about a tree near the school and tell the children its 'true height'. A reasonable estimate in metres will suffice.

Make a rough sketch of it on the chalkboard or an overhead projector transparency.

■ Tell them that the height of the tree is to be drawn to scale, using a scale of **1 cm to 2 m**. Discuss how to find its scaled height.

Write the scale in reverse.   2 m $\longrightarrow$ 1 cm

Every 2 metres of the tree will be represented by 1 cm on the scale drawing.

Divide 20 by 2 to find how many 2 m lengths there are in 20 m.   20 m $\longrightarrow$ $20 \div 2 = 10$ cm

This gives the number of **centimetres** in the scaled height.   Scaled height is **10 cm**.

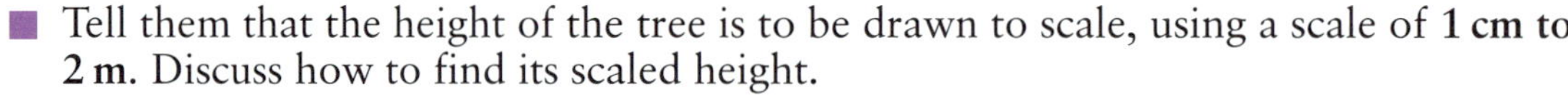

■ Draw a vertical 10 cm line on the chalkboard. You could use a large ruler with 'enlarged' centimetres so that the drawing is of a reasonable size.

Sketch in the rest of the tree.

■ Repeat for another tree with a different height, say 28 m, using a different scale, such as 1 cm to 4 m. Ask the children to:

— make a rough sketch and mark the true height

— use the scale, 1 cm to 4 m, to calculate the scaled height

$$4\,\text{m} \longrightarrow 1\,\text{cm}$$

$$28\,\text{m} \longrightarrow 28 \div 4 = 7\,\textbf{cm}$$

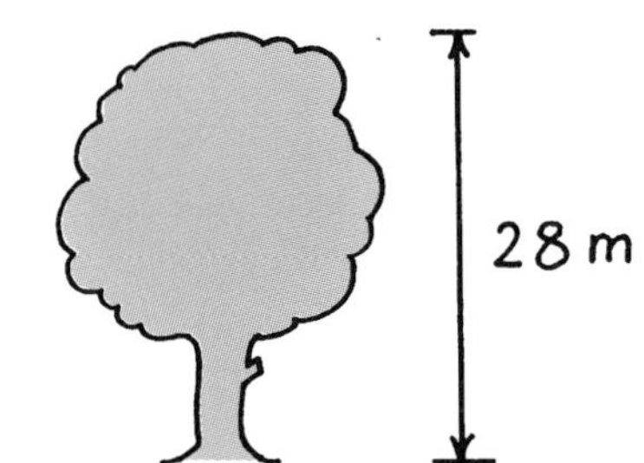

— draw the scale drawing (7 cm line), sketch the rest of the tree and label the drawing with the scale.

3   Plan of a sports field

Discuss a rough sketch of a rectangular sports field, preferably one near the school. Give the scale to be used, 1 cm to 10 m.

Point out that **two** scaled lengths have to be calculated.

Length	**Breadth**
$10\,\text{m} \longrightarrow 1\,\text{cm}$	$10\,\text{m} \longrightarrow 1\,\text{cm}$
$80\,\text{m} \longrightarrow 80 \div 10 = 8\,\textbf{cm}$	$60\,\text{m} \longrightarrow 60 \div 10 = 6\,\textbf{cm}$

The scale drawing should be drawn on squared paper, so that right-angled corners are easily achieved.

Textbook page 69   *Length: scale, true lengths*

Discuss the context of the page. Emphasize that the pond is used for sailing model boats and for canoeing.

Each scaled length on the Textbook page is denoted by a red line for ease of measurement. Accept measurements which are within 1 or 2 mm of the expected lengths.

In question 1(d), both the true length **and** true height of the boat are to be calculated.

In question 2, the children can either calculate the true length of each line and then add to find the length of the course, or they could find the total of the scaled lengths (17·8 cm) and then multiply (by 150) to find the true length (26·7 m).

In question 3, in parts (c) and (d), the scales involve **metres**: for example, 1 cm to 4 m.

N2b/5	SSM4a/4	
N2a/5	SSM3d/5	SSM4a/4
ME/D1	PFS/E3	
Mei/5		

H40

N2b/5 SSM4a/4
N2a/5 SSM3d/5 SSM4a/4
ME/D1 PFS/E3
Mei/5

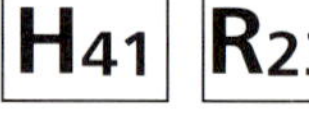

Textbook page 70   *Length: drawing to scale*
Workbook page 15

Ensure the children understand the context of question 1 on Textbook page 70. The park manager is making a poster of the trees to a scale of 1 cm to 5 m. The children are only expected to draw three vertical lines to scale and sketch the shape of the trees around them.

On Workbook page 15, the children should first draw rough sketches of each rectangular area with the given sizes on it, before they calculate scaled lengths and make accurate drawings. Some of the dimensions result in a scaled length involving a half-centimetre (for example, the tennis court drawing will be 7·5 cm by 3 cm). The children should be able to represent this by half a box on their squared paper. There is more than one correct solution to the layout. Accept any reasonable layout which allows a path of, say, about 1 cm (5 m) between the areas.

PERIMETER

N3a/5 SSM4c/4
A3ab/5 SSM4d/4
PFS/D1
Mh/5

Finding the perimeters of shapes was introduced in Heinemann Mathematics 5. In Heinemann Mathematics 6, a simple word formula for calculating the perimeter of a square was introduced.

This work is now extended to using simple formulae for finding the perimeters of squares and rectangles.

Introductory activities

1   The perimeter of a square

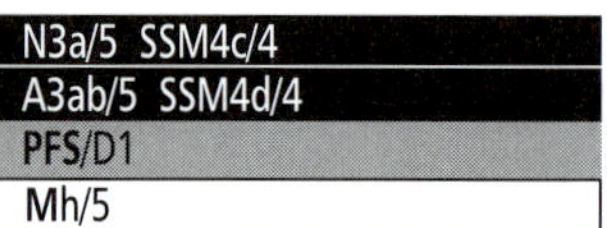

- Sketch a square like this on the chalkboard. Ask the children to find its perimeter. Repeat for squares of side length 2, 3 . . . 6 cm. Ask the children to state a formula in words to find the perimeter of a square.

The perimeter of a square is four times the length of a side.

Introduce a formula for **P**, the perimeter, in terms of the length of a side, **L**.

$$P = 4 \times L$$

- Show the children how to use the formula to find the perimeters of squares of different sizes. For example,

$$P = 4 \times L$$
$$= 4 \times 1·2$$
$$= 4·8 \text{ cm}$$

The perimeter is **4·8 cm**.

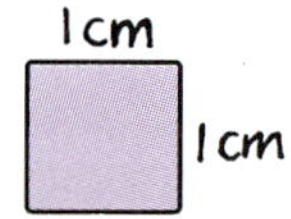

Repeat for other examples.

2   The perimeter of a rectangle

■ Draw a rectangle like this on the chalkboard.

Ask the children how many sides there are of length 5 cm and 7 cm.

Establish that the perimeter of the rectangle can be found **either** by adding all the sides together **or** by multiplying the length and breadth by 2 and adding the answers together.

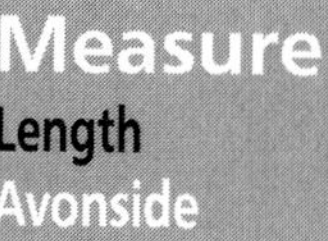

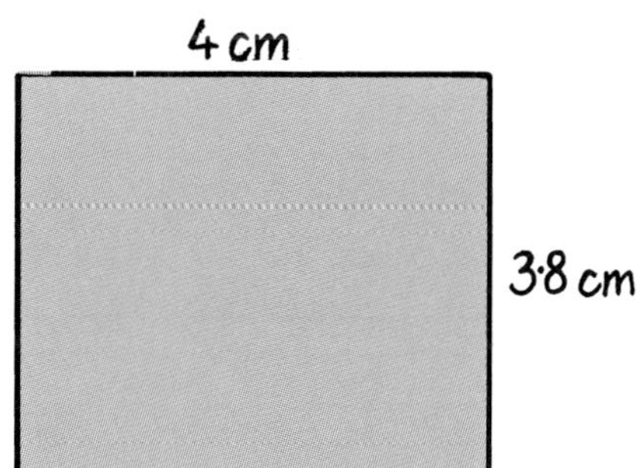

$$P = 5 + 7 + 5 + 7 \quad \textbf{or} \quad P = 2 \times 5 + 2 \times 7$$
$$= 24 \qquad\qquad\qquad = 10 + 14$$
$$= 24$$

The perimeter is **24 cm**.

The perimeter of a rectangle is two times the length plus two times the breadth.

Write the formula:

$$\mathbf{P = 2 \times L + 2 \times B}$$

■ Show the children how to use the formula to find the perimeters of rectangles of different sizes. For example,

$$P = 2 \times L + 2 \times B$$
$$= 2 \times 4 + 2 \times 3{\cdot}8$$
$$= 8 + 7{\cdot}6$$
$$= 15{\cdot}6$$

The perimeter is **15·6 cm**.

Repeat for other examples.

Textbook page 71   *Length: perimeter, formulae*

Encourage the children to set out the calculations as shown in the worked examples on the page. In question 3, the children first measure the length of each side to the nearest millimetre, before calculating the perimeter in centimetres.

H42

UA2c,3c/5	UA2a,4a/5
N2b,3g/4	N2a,3c/4
SSM4a/5	SSM4a/5
PSE	
AS/D3	
MD/D4	
ME/D2,6,8	
ME/E5	
PU/5	
PCc/5	
NOb/5	
Made/5	

Weight

Overview

This section

- revises conversion from grams to kilograms and grams, and vice versa
- includes multiplication of kilograms using a calculator
- introduces the tonne and conversion from kilograms and grams to tonnes, and vice versa
- provides estimating and weighing activities.

	Teacher's Notes	Textbook	Workbook	Reinforcement Sheets
Kilograms and grams	155	72		
Kilograms, tonnes	155	73*		
Estimation, practical work	156	74		

Homework provided in Home Link-up.

Resources

Useful materials

- a calculator
- a set of bathroom scales
- a set of kitchen scales
- a tin of food with the weight of the contents written on the label
- a packet containing a ream of paper
- a box of paper clips
- other materials suggested within the introductory activities

Assessment and Resources Pack

Assessment

Round-up 1
Questions 6(a), (b), (c), (d)

Resources

Resource Cards
16 and 17 Space creatures (weights in tonnes and kilograms)

Teaching notes

In Heinemann Mathematics 6, the children carried out work on conversion from kilograms and grams to grams, and vice versa. They were also involved in addition, subtraction and multiplication of kilograms and grams, and in estimating and weighing activities.

In Heinemann Mathematics P7, the work begins by revising the conversion of kilograms and grams to grams and vice-versa, and introduces the multiplication of kilograms, in decimal form, by a whole number using a calculator.

The context is a builder's yard.

KILOGRAMS AND GRAMS

Textbook page 72   *Weight: kilograms and grams*

N2b,3g/4 SSM4a/5
N2a,3c/4 SSM4a/5
AS/D3 MD/D4 ME/D2
NOb/5 Me/5

Emphasize that there are 3 different types of brick on the page: a brick, a block and a decorative brick.

In question 4, the children should weigh themselves in order to compare their own weight to the weight of 50 bricks (62·5 kg).

In question 6, the children have to use the weights given previously in the worked examples on the page:

brick 1·25 kg   block 2·5 kg   decorative brick 4·55 kg

KILOGRAMS, TONNES

Introductory activities

SSM4a/5
SSM4a/5
ME/E5
Me/5

1   Heavy weights

- Discuss the weight of one brick, 1·25 kg. Ask the children to calculate the weight of 800 bricks (1000 kg). Introduce a new unit of measure, the tonne, and explain that 1000 kg = 1 tonne.

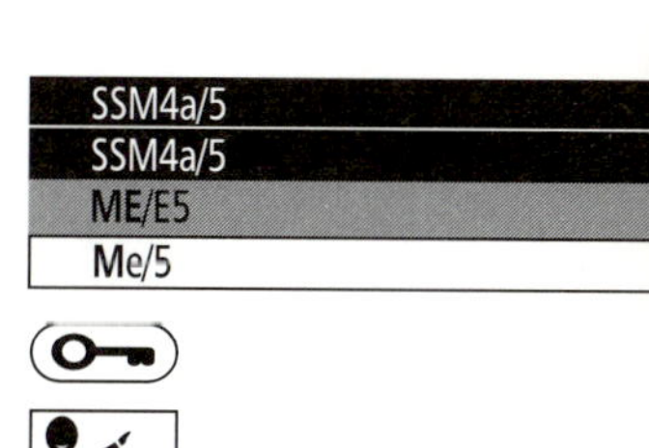

- Ask the children what kinds of object would have their weight measured in tonnes and list them. For example,

■ Sketch pictures of objects with their weights written in kilograms and ask the children to write the weights in tonnes and kilograms. For example,

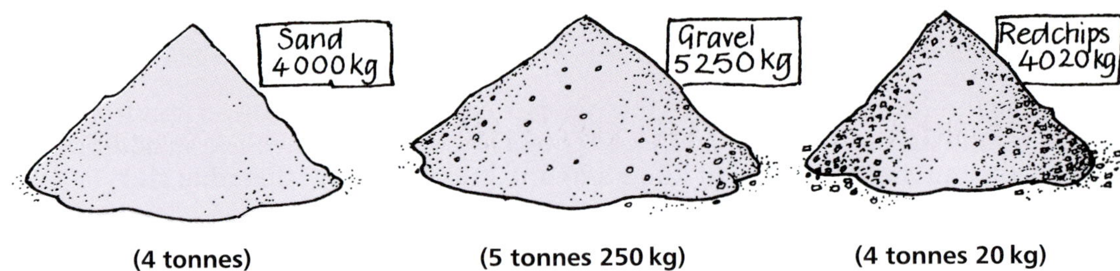

(4 tonnes)   (5 tonnes 250 kg)   (4 tonnes 20 kg)

■ Alter the activity by giving weights expressed in tonnes and kilograms and asking the children to write the weights in kilograms.

N2b,3g/4 SSM4a/5
N2a,3c/4 SSM4a/5
AS/D3 MD/D4 ME/E5
NOb/4→5 Me/5

Textbook page 73   *Weight: kilograms, tonnes*

In question 3, the children should find total weights in kilograms and then express these in tonnes and kilograms.

In question 4, the children should first find the weight of the bricks, 1800 kg, and then convert this to 18 tonnes, giving the total weight of the lorry and bricks as 26·35 tonnes.

In question 6, the children should assume that each 'Wendy' weighs 37 kg, so 27 of them weigh 999 kg – one kilogram less than a tonne.

In question 7, the children may wrongly give the answer as 1000 cubes. However,

$$1 \text{ tonne} = 1000 \text{ kg}$$
$$= 1000 \times 1000$$
$$= 1\,000\,000 \text{ g}$$

A million cubes are needed to weigh 1 tonne.

H43

ESTIMATION, PRACTICAL WORK

UA2c,3c/5 SSM4a/5
UA2a,4a/5 SSM4a/5
PSE ME/D2,6,8 ME/E5
PU,Cc/5 NOb/5 Mad/5

Problem solving

Textbook page 74   *Weight: estimation, practical work*

In question 1, the children may find it helpful to start with the more obvious items and weights. For example, the jumbo jet will be the heaviest weight, so it is matched to 350 tonnes, the letter will be the lightest weight, so it is matched to 60 grams, and so on. The weight which is unmatched is 350 kg.

In question 2, the children should find or draw objects with a range of weights.

In question 4, the children are expected to weigh the tin including contents and then subtract the weight printed on the tin.

In question 5, the children are expected to weigh the packet of paper and then divide the weight by the number of sheets stated on the packet to find the weight of one sheet. A similar technique is expected to find the weight of one paper clip.

Creative Studio

A context for area and volume

The area work on Textbook pages 75–8 and Workbook pages 24–7 is set in the context of Creative Studio, a design company which makes a wide range of products such as stickers, labels, flags, banners, mobiles and brochures.

The volume work on Textbook pages 79 and 80 and Workbook page 28 uses the scenario of Nature First, a client of Creative Studio.

Introducing the context

The context could be introduced by showing the children a range of products which have labels and discussing, for example,

— the purpose of a label

— the materials which can be used

— the information given on the label

— the use of a designer for colour, layout, lettering, etc.

— the production process.

The following activities could be used in an on-going way as the children progress through the work.

1 Collecting stickers, labels, leaflets, tickets

Discuss with the children the range of products which a design company such as Creative Studio might produce. The items could include

— tickets for functions

— information leaflets

— programmes for events

— catalogues for mail order

— brochures for various places, clubs and holidays

Examples of some of these could be collected and the children could comment orally, or in writing, on various features such as artwork, photography, layout, clarity and colour. Any information provided, such as weight, volume, price and date of production/use, could also be investigated. Clients of Creative Studio could be invented and discussed or written about.

2 Lettering

Discuss with the children the different types of lettering used on some of the items they have collected:

— Are the letters capitals, small letters or a mixture of these?

— Are capitals or small letters used when you would not expect them to be?

— Is some of the print bolder than the rest?

— Is the lettering of different types or sizes?

UA2bcd,3a/5	UA2abd,3a/5
N3a/5	A2a,3b/5
SSM4c/5→6	SSM4d/5→6
PSE	
ME/C3	
ME/D4	
PFS/E1	
PUabcd/5	
PCd/5	
PRc/5	
SMj/6	

Area

Overview

This section

- revises finding the area of a rectangle by multiplying the number of rows by the number of squares in each row

- introduces the formula $A = l \times b$ for the area of a rectangle

- involves the use of the formula to find areas of composite shapes made up of rectangles and squares

- revises, and introduces a new technique for finding the area of an irregular shape

- introduces finding the area of a right-angled triangle as half the area of its surrounding rectangle

- applies this technique to finding areas of composite shapes made from rectangles, squares and right-angled triangles

- revises the square metre (m^2) and introduces the square kilometre (km^2).

	Teacher's Notes	Textbook	Workbook	Reinforcement Sheets
Creative Studio: a context for area	157			
Area of a rectangle using $A = l \times b$	160	75, 76*		24
Area of an irregular shape	162		24	
Area of a right-angled triangle	163	77*	25*	25
Area of a composite shape	166		26*	26
Areas in square metres and square kilometres	167	78	27	

Homework provided in Home Link-up.

Extension activities related to the above section of work are as follows:		
	Teacher's Notes	Extension Textbook
Area: enlargement	264	E16
Area: reduction	264	E17

Teaching notes for the Extension Textbook are in a separate section at the end of the Teacher's Notes.

Resources

Useful materials

- metre stick or tape
- large sheets of paper (newspaper or poster size)
- chalk, scissors and sticky tape
- centimetre squared paper
- other materials suggested within the introductory activities

Assessment and Resources Pack

Assessment

Measure Check-up 2
Textbook pages 75–8
Workbook pages 24–7
(Area: rectangles, right-angled triangles, composite and irregular shapes)

Round-up 2
Question 2

Resources

Problem Solving Activities
15 Checkerboards (Investigation involving area and shape patterns)
18 Mike's garden (Area of a composite shape)
22 Tropical fish (Area of a rectangle)

Teaching notes

AREA OF A RECTANGLE USING A = l × b

In Heinemann Mathematics 6, the children were introduced to a method for finding the area of a rectangle drawn on a square grid by multiplying the number of rows by the number of squares in each row. They also applied this method to finding the areas of composite shapes formed by joining together a number of rectangles and/or squares.

This work is revised and then extended through the introduction of the formula A = l × b for finding the area of a rectangle.

The work is set in the context of a design company called Creative Studio, and its designs for labels on CDs, tapes and videos.

Introductory activities

UA2a, 3a/5 N3a/5 SSM4d/5→6
UA2c,3a/5 A2a,3b/5 SSM4d/5→6
ME/C3 PFS/E1
PUab/5 Mh/5

1   Studio designs   *(area of a rectangle – revision)*

■ Draw a rectangular label so that some of the squares in its background grid are obscured and cannot be counted individually. Revise a quick way to find the area of a rectangle by

Area = 15 cm²

— counting the number of squares in one row

— counting the number of rows

— multiplying to find the area.

■ Repeat for other labels.

2   Happy stickers   *(area of a rectangle using l × b)*

■ Draw a 'happy sticker' and let the children find its area as in activity 1.

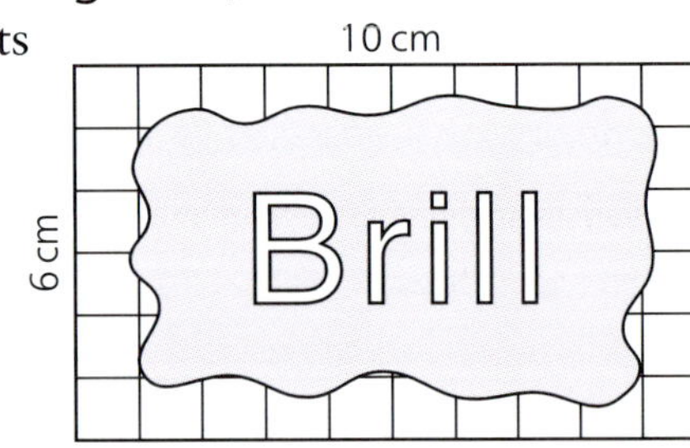

■ Point out that

— the **number of squares in a row** is the same as the number of centimetres in the **length** of the rectangle.

— the **number of rows** is the same as the number of centimetres in the **breadth** of the rectangle.

Give the formula in words:

'The area of a rectangle is its length times its breadth.'

Write the formula in symbols:

A = l × b

■ Draw other 'happy stickers' which have no background grid. Show how to use the formula to find the area of one of them.

$$A = l \times b$$
$$= 8 \times 4$$
$$= 32 \text{ cm}^2$$

Ask the children to find the areas of the other stickers, one of them a square.

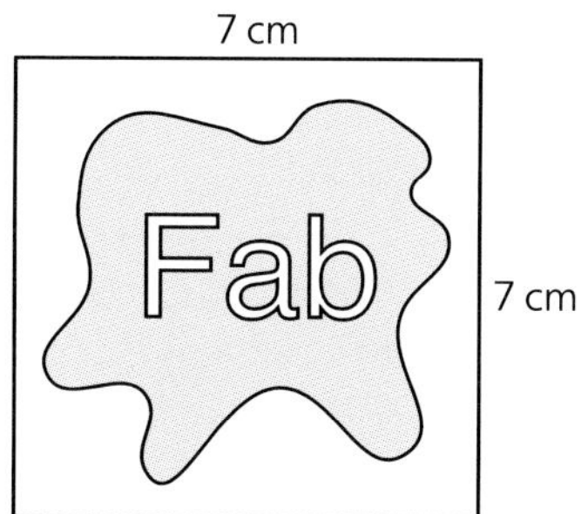

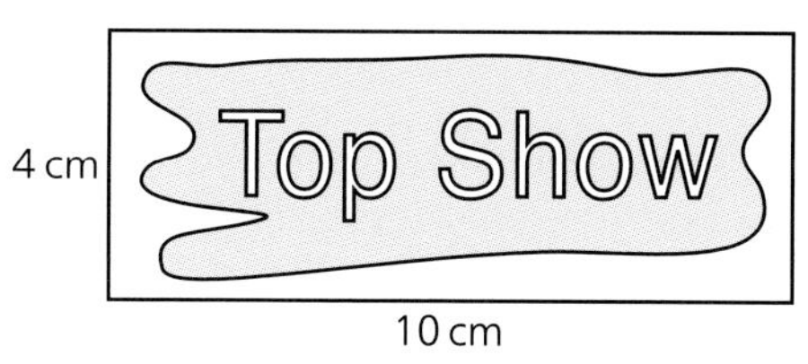

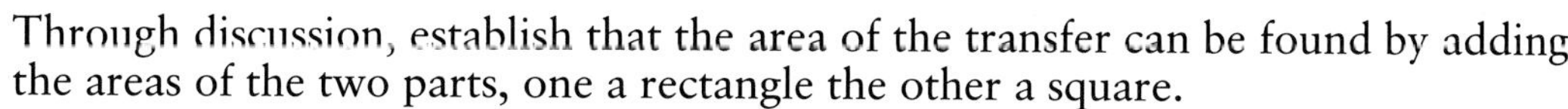

At this point the children could try Textbook page 75.

3 Transfers *(area of a composite shape)*

■ Draw a 'transfer' as shown, by joining together rectangles and squares.

Through discussion, establish that the area of the transfer can be found by adding the areas of the two parts, one a rectangle the other a square.

Calculate the area as follows:

Area of rectangle
$$A = l \times b$$
$$= 10 \times 6$$
$$= 60 \text{ cm}^2$$

Area of square
$$A = l \times b$$
$$= 3 \times 3$$
$$= 9 \text{ cm}^2$$

Area of transfer = 60 + 9 = **69 cm²**

■ Repeat for other transfers, asking the children to show where they would draw lines to divide each transfer into rectangles and/or squares.

This should lead to a discussion about different ways to divide each transfer. For example,

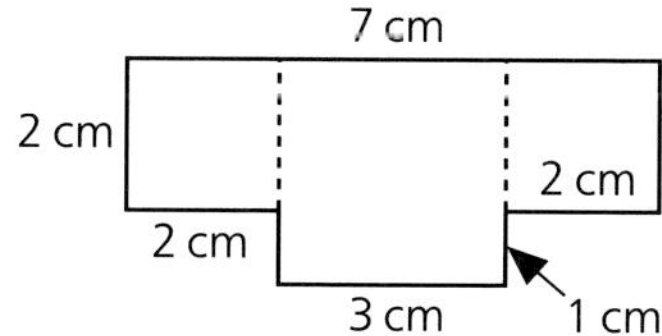

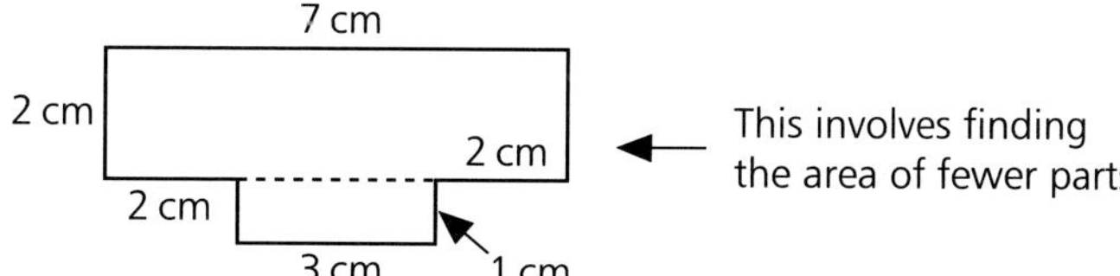

← This involves finding the area of fewer parts.

UA2b,3a/5 N3a/5 SSM4c/5→6
UA2b,3a/5 A2a,3b/5 SSM4d/5→6
ME/C3 PFS/E1
Mh/5

H44 **R**24

Textbook page 75   *Area: A = l × b*
Textbook page 76   *Area: composite shapes*

Discuss the context of Creative Studio if it has not been previously introduced.

On Textbook page 75, in question 2, all the grid squares around the perimeter are visible to enable the pupils to find the length and breadth of each label in centimetres.

In question 3, each label's length and breadth in centimetres is shown and the children use these dimensions in the formula A = l × b to find the area of each rectangle.

On Textbook page 76, in question 1, each of the transfers is drawn to actual size and already divided into parts. The lengths and breadths should be measured so that the areas can be calculated then added to find the area of each transfer.

In question 2, parts (d) to (f), the children should be encouraged to subdivide each diagram into as few parts as possible.

AREA OF AN IRREGULAR SHAPE

In Heinemann Mathematics 6, the children revised finding the areas of irregular shapes by counting squares and half squares.

This method is now made more efficient by combining it with the use of the formula A = l × b for rectangular areas within the irregular shapes.

The Creative Studio context continues and features a set of labels designed for one of its clients, Nature First.

UA2bc/5 N3a/5 SSM4c/5→6
UA2ab/5 A3b/5 SSM4d/5→6
ME/C3 PFS/E1
PUab/5 Mh/5

Introductory activity

Healthy eating   *(area of an irregular shape)*

■ Draw a fruit or vegetable outline on a grid on a chalkboard, squared paper or overhead projector transparency.

Revise a way of finding the area of the shape.

A likely method is to

— count all the whole squares

— count the other squares which are more than half a square as whole squares

— add to find the area.

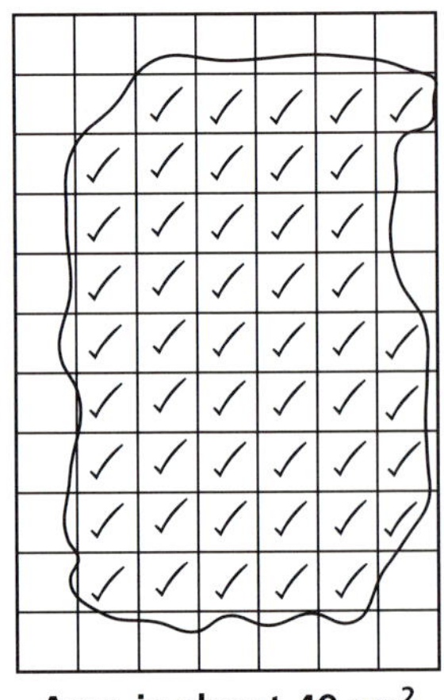

Area is about 49 cm²

■ Ask the children about a quicker way to find the area without counting each square individually.

Focus on the idea of drawing rectangles or squares inside the shape and using the formula to find their areas.

$$A = l \times b$$
$$= 7 \times 4$$
$$= 28 \text{ cm}^2$$

The remaining area, 21 cm², is found by counting as before, giving a total area of $28 + 21 = \textbf{49 cm}^2$.

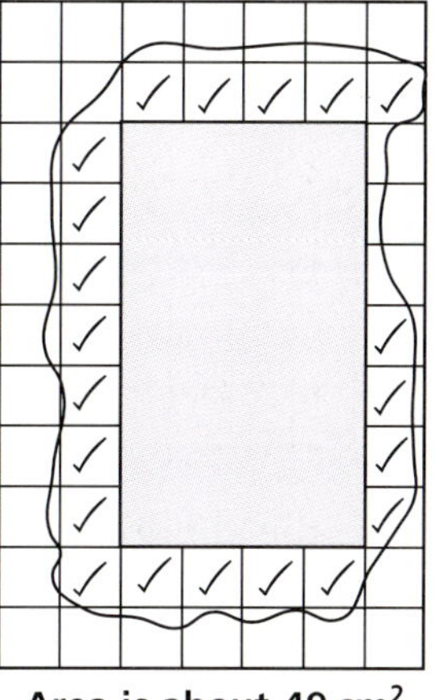

Area is about 49 cm²

Workbook page 24   *Area: irregular shapes*

The scenario of Nature First should be discussed.

In each example, the children should be encouraged to draw the **largest** possible rectangle or square.

AREA OF A RIGHT-ANGLE TRIANGLE

The method of finding the area of a right-angled triangle as half the area of the surrounding rectangle is now introduced.

The scenario is Creative Studio's sticker, flag, banner and mobile designs.

Introductory activities

1   Right-angled triangles

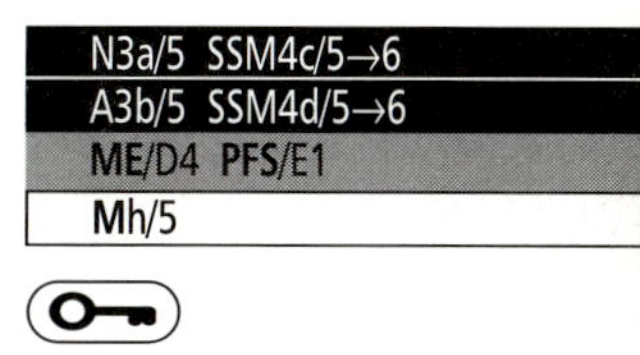

■ Prepare a **large** card rectangle with a 10 by 4 square grid as shown. Cut it along a diagonal to give two right-angled triangles.

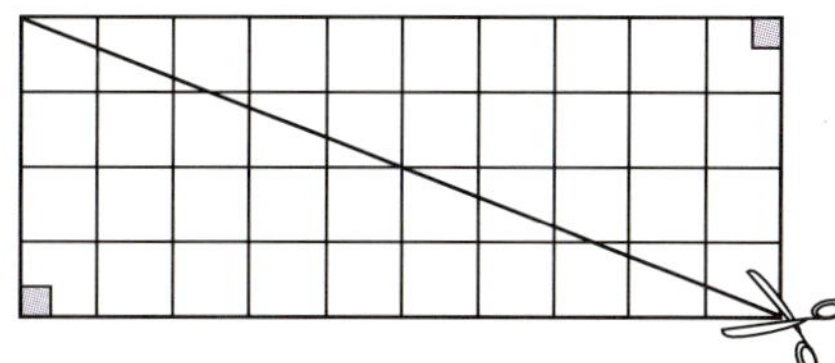

■ Show the children one of the triangles and explain that some of Creative Studio's designs are right-angled triangles. Ask the children how to find its area.

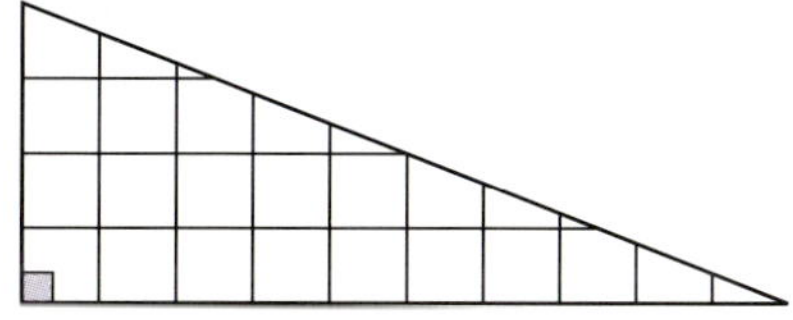

They may suggest a method of counting squares, similar to the one used for irregular shapes.

Tell the children that there is an easier way.

■ Place the other triangle on top of the first one to show that the two right-angled triangles are congruent and have equal areas. Rotate **one** of the triangles to form a rectangle.

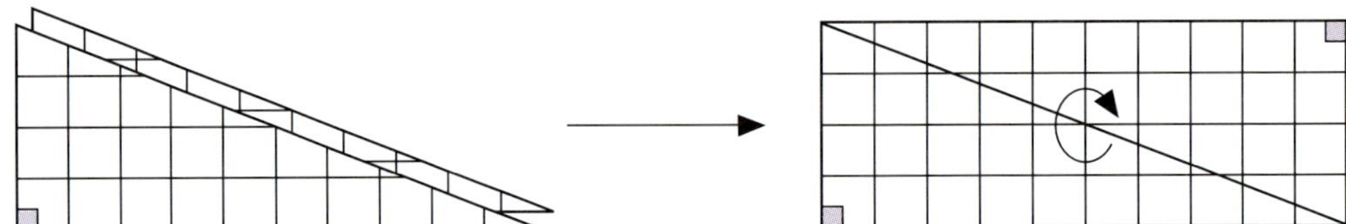

Ask the children to find the area of the rectangle, **40 squares**.

Ask them how to use this to find the area of **one** of the triangles – by halving it to give **20 squares**.

Point out that they found the area of a right-angled triangle by halving the area of a rectangle.

2   Sticker designs   *(area of a right-angled triangle)*

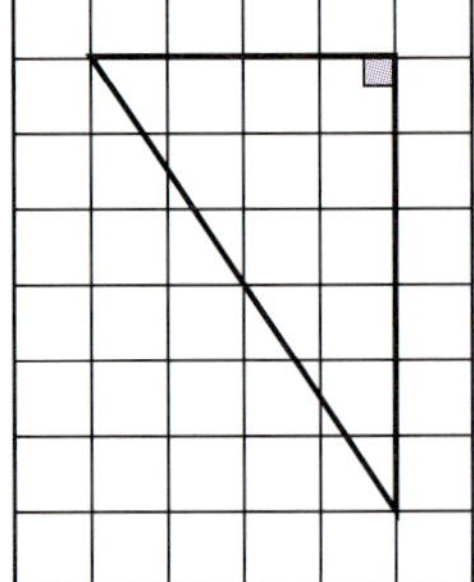

■ Discuss a drawing of a sticker as shown.

It is a right-angled triangle.

Ask the children how they could make it into a rectangle.

■ Draw the other sides of the rectangle as dotted lines. Reinforce the idea that the area of the right-angled triangle is **half the area of the surrounding rectangle.**

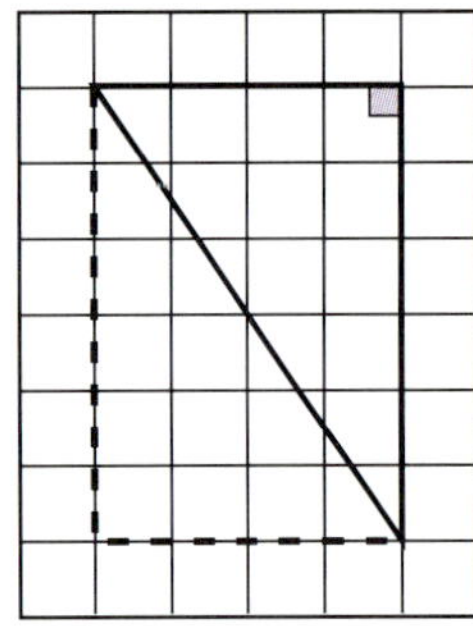

■ Show how the calculation can be recorded.

Area of rectangle $= 6 \times 4 = 24\,\text{cm}^2$

Area of triangle $= \frac{1}{2}$ of 24

$= 12\,\text{cm}^2$

■ Ask the children to find the area of other stickers which are right-angled triangles, some involving $\frac{1}{2}\,\text{cm}^2$.

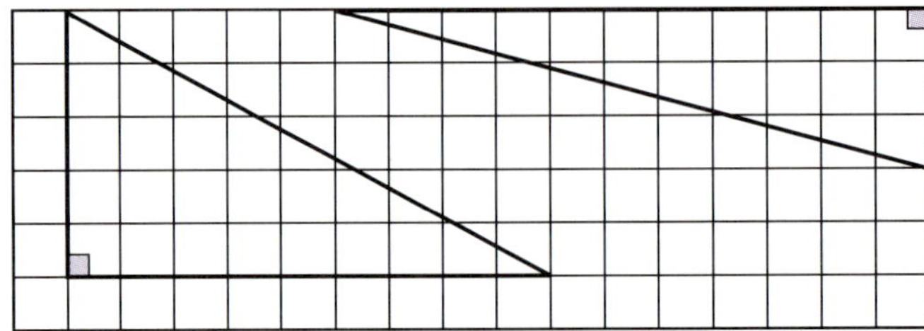

3 Flags *(areas of right-angled triangles not on a grid)*

■ Show the children a paper flag or a drawing
in the shape of a right-angled triangle.

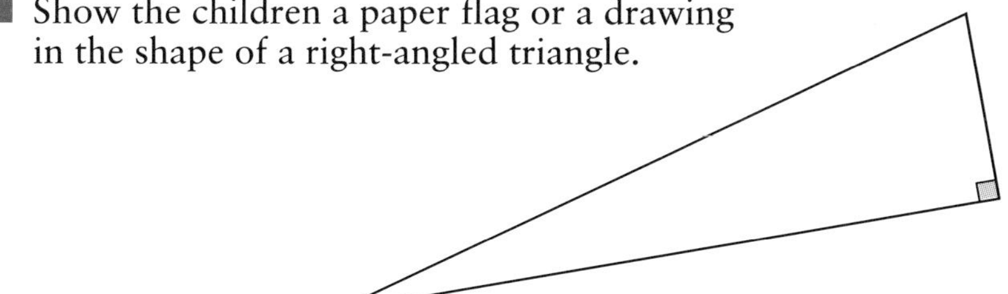

Discuss how the designer at Creative Studio could find its area.

A good procedure is to

— mark the right angle

— **measure** the two sides forming
the right angle

— find the area of the surrounding
rectangle and halve it.

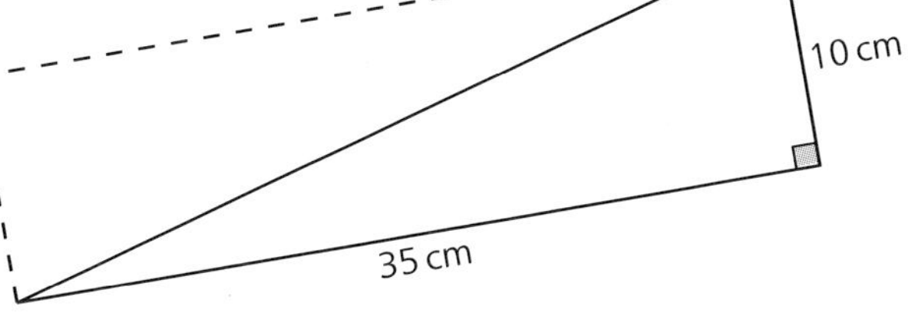

Area of rectangle $= 35 \times 10$

$$= 350 \text{ cm}^2$$

Area of triangle $= \frac{1}{2}$ of 350

$$= 175 \text{ cm}^2$$

■ Repeat for other right-angled triangles.

At this point the children could try Workbook page 25.

4 Banners and mobiles *(calculating the areas of scaled drawings)*

Tell the children that Creative Studio produces very large banners, flags and mobiles.
Show them a drawing of a banner with sizes marked in metres, and calculate its area.

Area of the rectangle $= 12 \times 4 = 48 \text{ m}^2$

Area of the triangle $= \frac{1}{2}$ of 48

$$= 24 \text{ m}^2$$

The area of the banner is **24 m²**.

Workbook page 25   *Area: right-angled triangles*
Textbook page 77

On Workbook page 25, in question 2, the children should draw the
surrounding rectangles.

In question 3, some children will not need to draw the surrounding rectangle,
but space is available for those who do.

In question 4, the children could draw two different rectangles, each with an
area of 24 cm², and insert a diagonal in each to give the required triangles.

On Textbook page 77, the children may find the area of the surrounding
rectangle mentally.

For example, in question 1 (a),   Area of the rectangle $= 32 \text{ cm}^2$

Area of the triangle $= \frac{1}{2}$ of 32

$$= 16 \text{ cm}^2$$

Problem solving

R25   H45

AREA OF A COMPOSITE SHAPE

The children now apply the methods they have learned to finding the areas of composite shapes formed by joining rectangles, squares and right-angled triangles.

The context of Creative Studio continues with the company designing labels for Nature First.

Introductory activity

Nature First   *(area of a composite shape)*

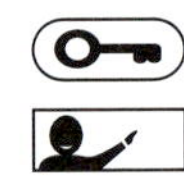

■ Explain to the children that one of Creative Studio's clients is a company called Nature First. Nature First makes jams, juices and beauty products from flowers, plants, fruits and vegetables. The company likes to have labels in unusual shapes for its products. Show the children some composite shapes.

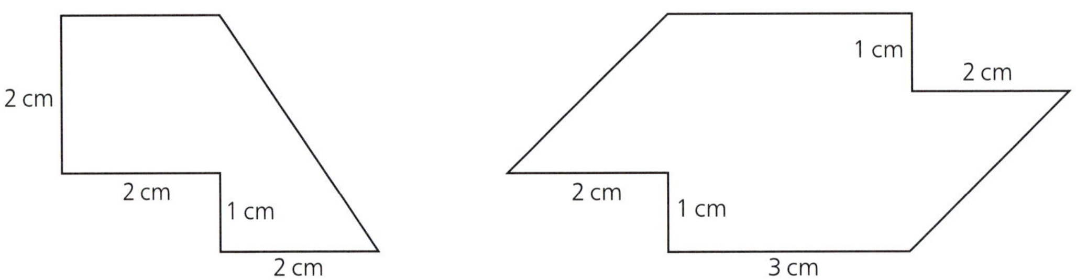

■ Discuss with the children how to find the areas of such shapes by dividing them into rectangles and right-angled triangles, finding the area of each and then calculating the total area.

For example,

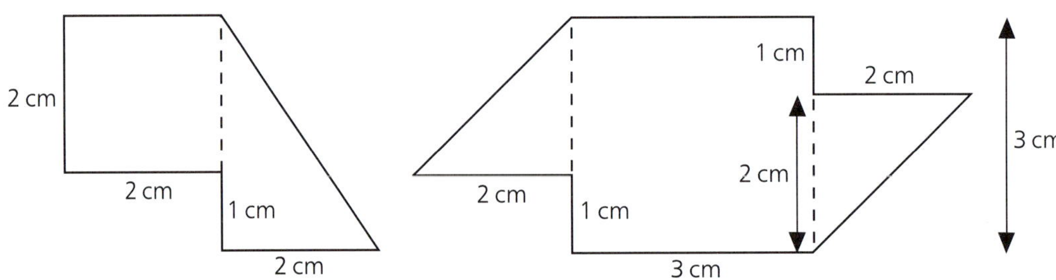

Area of square $= 2 \times 2 = 4 \, cm^2$ Area of square $= 3 \times 3 = 9 \, cm^2$

Area of triangle $= \frac{1}{2}$ of $6 = 3 \, cm^2$ Area of triangle $= \frac{1}{2}$ of $4 = 2 \, cm^2$

Area of shape $= 7 \, cm^2$ Area of triangle $= \frac{1}{2}$ of $4 = 2 \, cm^2$

Area of shape $= 13 \, cm^2$

Workbook page 26   *Area: composite shapes*

On Workbook page 26, the children should

— draw lines to divide each shape into rectangles and right-angled triangles

— write the area on each part

— write the total area on the answer line provided.

In question 1, the third shape is made up of two right-angled triangles and a rectangle. Some children will find the area of each part separately, then add.

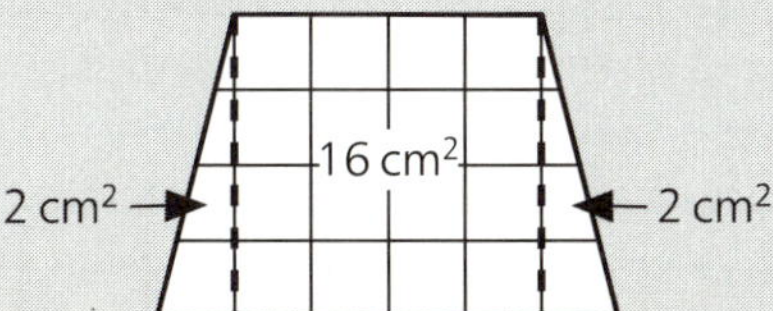

Others may realize that the two triangles are identical, find the area of one triangle and double it to find the area of the two triangles.

When correcting the children's work, discussion about different methods of dividing the shapes would be useful.

UA2d/5 N3a/5 SSM4c/5→6
UA2d/5 A3b/5 SSM4d/5→6
PSE ME/D4 PFS/E1
Mh/5 SMj/6

R26 H46

AREAS IN SQUARE METRES AND SQUARE KILOMETRES

In Heinemann Mathematics 5, the children were introduced to the square metre and the notation m^2.

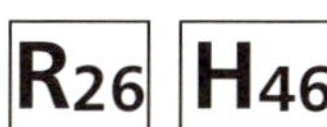

The use of the square metre is now extended and the square kilometre is introduced.

The context of Creative Studio continues with the company planning an extension and designing tourist brochures.

Textbook page 78 *Area: square metres, square kilometres*
Workbook page 27

Before the children attempt Textbook page 78, show them a square metre made from paper and remind them that this unit is suitable for measuring larger areas, such as a room.

The children should work in small groups to carry out the practical work.

In question 4 (b), there is more than one solution. It is important that the children leave clear pathways for cars to manoeuvre in and out of a space. When discussing the area required for a parking space, the children should allow for opening car doors. One possible solution for 20 cars is as follows:

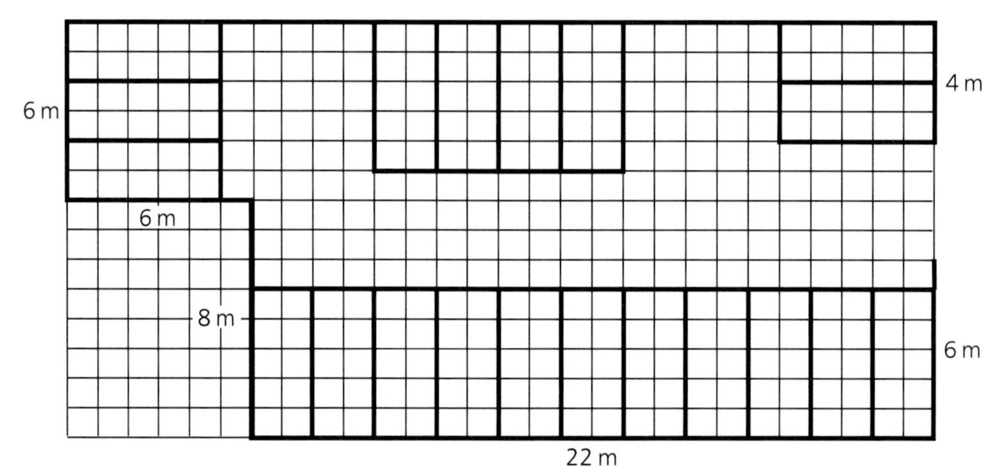

On Workbook page 27, in question 2, the children need to recall the method used for counting squares when finding areas of irregular shapes on Workbook page 24. They also need to remember that each square in these examples represents 1 square kilometre.

Volume

UA2cd/4	UA2ad/4
UA3a/4	UA3a/5
N3a/5	A3ab/5
SSM4ab/4	SSM4ab/4
SSM4c/5→6	SSM4d/5→6
PSE	
ME/D3	
PFS/E2	
PUab/5	
Meh/5	

Overview

This section

- revises finding volumes of cuboids in cubic centimetres (cm^3)
- introduces the formula $V = l \times b \times h$ for the volume of a cuboid
- revises marking and reading scales in millilitres (ml)
- revises 1 litre as $1000 \, cm^3$ and $1 \, ml = 1 \, cm^3$.

	Teacher's Notes	Textbook	Workbook	Reinforcement Sheets
Volumes of cuboids, $V = l \times b \times h$	170	79, 80*		
Millilitres	172		28*	

Homework provided in Home Link-up.

An extension activity related to the above section of work is as follows:

	Teacher's Notes	Extension Textbook
Volume: displacement	266	E19

Teaching notes for the Extension Textbook are in a separate section at the end of the Teacher's Notes.

Resources

Useful materials

- card, sticky tape, scissors
- various cylinders: for example, kitchen roll centres, washing-up liquid bottles
- other materials suggested within the introductory activities

Assessment and Resources Pack

Assessment

Round-up 2
Question 5(a)

Resources

Problem Solving Activities
22 Tropical Fish (volume, area)

Resource Cards
16 and 17 Space creatures (volumes in l, ml and cm^3)

Teaching notes

VOLUMES OF CUBOIDS, $V = l \times b \times h$

In Heinemann Mathematics 6, the children found volumes of cuboids by working out the number of centimetre cubes in a layer and then multiplying by the number of layers.

In Heinemann Mathematics P7, this work is revised and the formula $V = l \times b \times h$ for the volume of a cuboid is introduced.

The Creative Studio context continues with the children being introduced to the products of one of its clients, Nature First.

Introductory activity

1   Layers   *(volumes by counting cubes)*

■ Revise the method used in Heinemann Mathematics 6 to find the volume of a cuboid:

— find the volume of one layer of centimetre cubes

— multiply this volume by the number of layers.

For example,

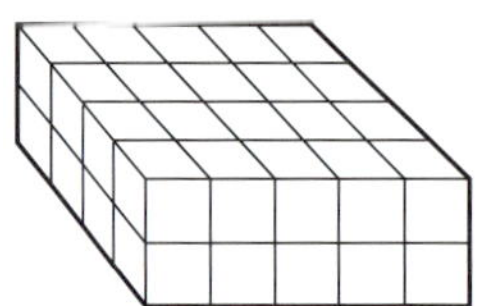

Volume of 1 layer is $5 \times 4 = 20 \,\text{cm}^3$

Volume of 2 layers is $20 \times 2 = \mathbf{40 \,cm^3}$

■ Build cuboids with centimetre cubes and ask the children to use this method to calculate the volumes.

At this point the children could attempt Textbook page 79.

2   Volumes of cuboids   *(the formula $V = l \times b \times h$)*

■ Use cubes to build a cuboid as shown. (Larger cubes, such as Multilink, would be suitable.) Ask the children to find its volume.

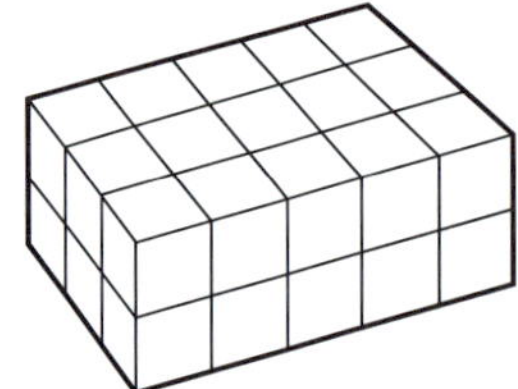

Volume of 1 layer is $5 \times 3 = 15$ cubes

Volume of 2 layers is $15 \times 2 = \mathbf{30\ cubes}$

■ Show the children a table like this on the chalkboard and discuss the results from the first cuboid.

Cuboid	Number of cubes in a row	Number of rows	Number of layers	Volume
1st	5	3	2	30 cubes

■ Alter the cuboid as shown by removing some cubes. Ask the children to find its volume.

Volume of layer is $4 \times 3 = 12$ cubes

Volume of 2 layers is $12 \times 2 = \mathbf{24}$ **cubes**

■ Enter and discuss the results for the second cuboid.

Cuboid	Number of cubes in a row	Number of rows	Number of layers	Volume
1st	5	3	2	30 cubes
2nd	4	3	2	24 cubes

Ask the children if they notice anything about the results in the table.

Some may spot that $5 \times 3 \times 2 = 30$ and that $4 \times 3 \times 2 = 24$.

Tell them that more examples are needed to be sure that this is true for other cuboids.

Ask the children to complete question 1 on Textbook page 80.

■ Discuss their results.

Cuboid	Number of cubes in a row	Number of rows	Number of layers	Volume in cm^3
A	4	3	3	36
B	4	4	2	32
C	6	3	4	72

Demonstrate that the number of centimetres

— **in the length** is the same as the number of cubes in a row

— **in the breadth** is the same as the number of rows

— **in the height** is the same as the number of layers.

Replace the table headings as shown.

Cuboid	Length	Breadth	Height	Volume in cm^3
A	4	3	3	36
B	4	4	2	32
C	6	3	4	72

Discuss the table and introduce the formula $\mathbf{V = l \times b \times h}$ for any cuboid.

■ Use an example like this to show how useful this formula is when the rows and layers are not shown. For this cuboid,

$V = l \times b \times h$

$= 10 \times 5 \times 8$

$= \mathbf{400\ cm^3}$

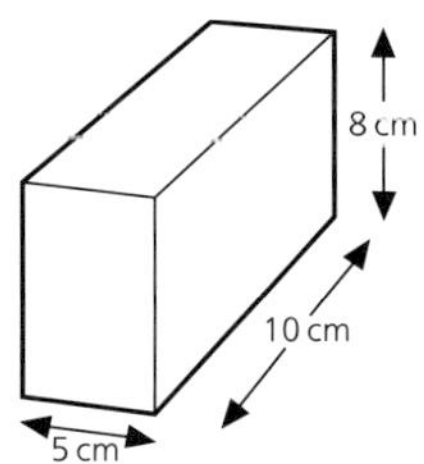

171

UA3a/5 N3a/5 SSM4c/5→6
UA3a/5 A3ab/5 SSM4d/5→6
PFS/E2
Mh/5

H47

Textbook pages 79 and 80
Volume: cubic centimetres, $V = l \times b \times h$

On Textbook page 79, in question 1, the children should multiply the number of cubes in a row by the number of rows, rather than count cubes, to find the volume of each layer.

In question 2, the children should find the volume of one layer and then multiply by the number of layers to find the volume of the whole cuboid.

In question 3, the children should divide the volume of the cuboid by the number of layers to find the volume of each layer. The number of cubes in each row and the number of rows in each layer can then be found. For example, in part (a), the volume of one layer is 15 cm^3. This leads to several possible answers, but it is likely that the children will choose 5 rows of 3 cubes or 3 rows of 5 cubes.

On Textbook page 80, in question 2, the cuboids are not marked to show centimetre cubes, but represent boxes containing products produced by Nature First. The children must use the formula $V = l \times b \times h$ to find the volume of each cuboid.

MILLILITRES

SSM4ab/4
SSM4ab/4
ME/D3
Md/4 Meh/5

The millilitre and the relationship 1 litre = 1000 ml were introduced in Heinemann Mathematics 6. Also introduced were 1 litre as 1000 cm^3 and 1 ml = 1 cm^3.

These ideas are now consolidated with an emphasis on marking and reading scales on measuring cylinders.

Introductory activities

1   Shampoo   *(measuring scales marked in ml)*

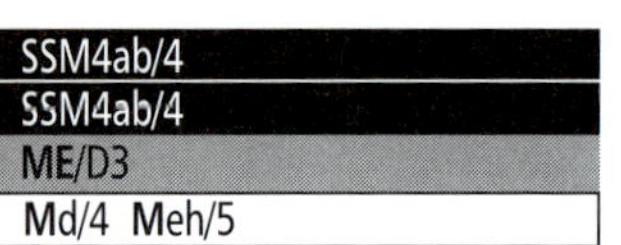

■ Draw these three scales on the chalkboard or on an overhead projector transparency. Ask the children to give the missing values. Complete each scale.

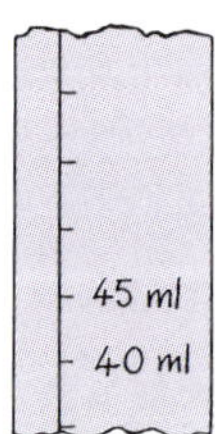

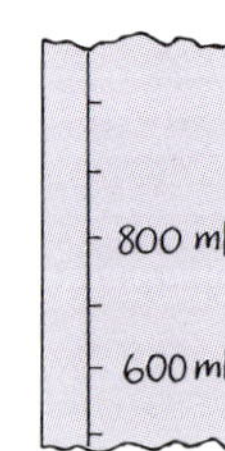

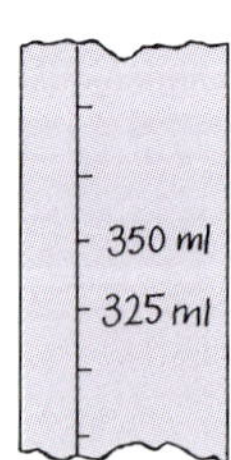

■ Ask which of the scales would be appropriate for indicating a volume of 55 ml.

The children should identify the first of the scales because the volume, 55 ml, falls within the range indicated on the scale, 40 ml to 60 ml. Repeat for volumes of

1 litre

275 ml

2   Containers   *(1 ml = 1 cm³)*

■ Show the children a centimetre cube and record its volume as 1 cm³ on the chalkboard. Ask what the connection is between millilitres and cubic centimetres. From their previous experience they should recall that 1 ml = 1 cm³ and that 1 litre = 1000 cm³.

■ Show them several containers, some labelled in millilitres, others labelled in cubic centimetres. Ask the children to express each volume in another way. For example,

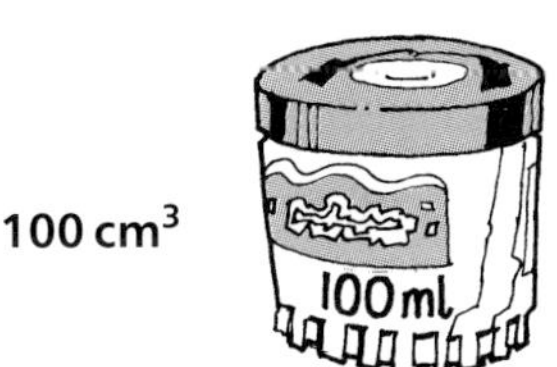

100 cm³

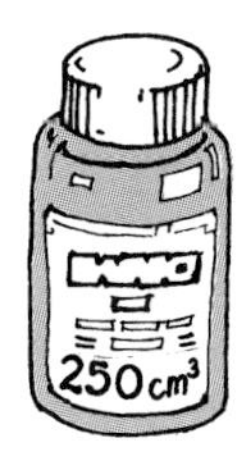

250 ml

Some containers labelled as, for example, 100 cc, might be included and the children told that cc is another abbreviation used for cubic centimetres.

Workbook page 28   *Volume: millilitres*

In question 2, the children should mark the missing values on each scale before considering which scale is the most suitable to indicate the volume of each product. The matching could be indicated by drawing an arrow from each product to the appropriate scale.

Before the children attempt question 3, there should be a discussion of the relationship between ml and cm³, if this has not already taken place as suggested in the introductory activities.

In question 4, some children may attempt to make a cuboid, using their knowledge of the formula $V = l \times b \times h$. For example, they may draw the net of the cuboid with length 10 cm, breadth 5 cm and height 2 cm (since $10 \times 5 \times 2 = 100$) and then build a cuboid from the net.

Others may use a cylindrical object to make a container. This can be done by sealing one end, filling it with 100 ml of sand and then cutting the cylinder at the appropriate height. It would be helpful to have available a supply of easily cut cylindrical objects such as kitchen roll centres and washing-up liquid containers.

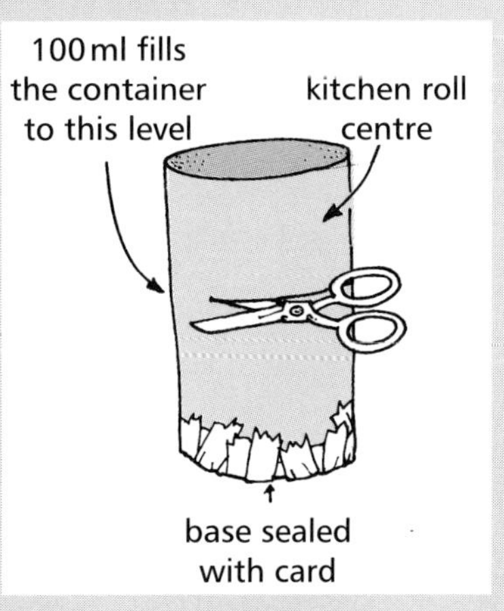

UA2cd/4 SSM4ab/4
UA2ad/4 SSM4ab/4
PSE ME/D3
PUab/5 Meh/5

Problem solving

H48

UA3a/5	UA3a/5
SSM4a/5	SSM4a/5
ME/D9	
NOb/5	
Mf/5	

Imperial measures

Overview

This section

- deals with the Imperial units – inch, foot, pound, pint and gallon
- relates these Imperial units to appropriate metric units.

	Teacher's Notes	Textbook	Workbook	Reinforcement Sheets
Imperial units	175	81, 82		

Resources

Useful materials

- a ruler or tape showing feet and inches
- other materials suggested within the introductory activities

Teaching notes

In Heinemann Mathematics 6, some work on Imperial units was introduced in the Extension Textbook.

This section re-introduces measurements in Imperial units, which are then converted into metric units using the following equivalents:

— one inch is about $2\frac{1}{2}$ cm

— one foot is about 30 cm

— one pound is about $\frac{1}{2}$ kg

— one pint is about $\frac{1}{2}$ litre

— one gallon is about $4\frac{1}{2}$ litres.

The context involves a visit to an old sailing ship, *Seamaiden*.

IMPERIAL UNITS

Introductory activities

| UA3a/5 SSM4a/5 |
| UA3a/5 SSM4a/5 |
| ME/D9 |
| Mf/5 |

1 *Seamaiden*

Discuss the context shown on Textbook page 81. An old sailing ship *Seamaiden*, is preserved as a museum and children can join the crew for a day to experience, at first hand, some of the activities of life aboard such a ship.

There could be discussion of activities which a visit might involve. For example,

— sleeping in a hammock

— eating salted beef and ship's biscuit

— scrubbing decks

— climbing masts and rigging

— pulling ropes to trim sails

— manning guns below deck

— repairing clothes and sails

— cooking for the crew, etc.

2   The new midshipman   *(inches, feet and pounds)*

■ Tell the children that a young lad joining the navy as a junior officer at the end of the 18th century often started as a midshipman.

Write some details about a new midshipman, Jack, joining the *Seamaiden*.

> Length of jacket: 30 inches
>
> Height: 5 feet 2 inches
>
> Weight: 100 pounds

■ Show the children an inch on a ruler or tape and compare it with a scale showing centimetres. Establish that

1 inch is about $2\frac{1}{2}$ cm.

Discuss the abbreviation 'in' for inch.

Involve the children in finding the length of Jack's jacket in centimetres.

> Length of jacket is 30 in.
>
> 30 in is about $30 \times 2\frac{1}{2}$ cm
>
> $= 75$ cm
>
> The length of the jacket is **about 75 cm.**

The calculation could be done mentally by thinking of '30 twos' and '30 halves', or by finding 30×2.5 using a calculator.

■ Match a 12-inch ruler with a scale showing centimetres. Through discussion, establish that the ruler is **1 foot** long and that

1 foot is about 30 cm.

Discuss the abbreviation 'ft' for feet or foot.

With the help of the children, change Jack's height to centimetres.

> Jack's height is 5 ft 2 in.
>
> 5 ft 2 in is about $5 \times 30 + 2 \times 2\frac{1}{2}$ cm
>
> $= 150 + 5$ cm
>
> $= 155$ cm
>
> Jack's height is **about 155 cm.**

■ Discuss his weight and the abbreviation 'lb' (from the Latin *libra*). Tell the children that

1 lb is about $\frac{1}{2}$ kg.

A kitchen scale marked in both units could be used to confirm this, or a 500 g bag of sugar might be weighed on a scale showing pounds – it should weigh slightly more than 1 lb.

Change Jack's weight to kilograms.

> Jack's weight is 100 lb.
>
> 100 lb is about $100 \times \frac{1}{2}$ kg
>
> $= 50$ kg
>
> Jack's weight is **about 50 kg.**

3 Bottles and barrels *(pints and gallons)*

■ Discuss the storage of water and other liquids aboard a sailing ship. Barrels and bottles packed in straw were often used. Capacities were measured in pints and gallons.

■ Allow the children to compare a pint and a litre measure. Establish, preferably by pouring, that

1 pint is about $\frac{1}{2}$ litre.

Find the volume of wine in this bottle from the *Seamaiden*, in litres.

Volume of wine is 4 pints.

4 pints is about $4 \times \frac{1}{2}$ litres

$\qquad = 2$ litres

The volume of wine is **about 2 litres.**

■ Tell the children that

1 gallon is about $4\frac{1}{2}$ litres.

Find the volume of water in this barrel, in litres.

Volume of water is 30 gallons.

30 gallons is about $30 \times 4\cdot5$ litres

$\qquad = 135$ litres

The volume of water in the barrel is **about 135 litres.**

30 gallons

Textbook pages 81 and 82   *Imperial units*

The context of *Seamaiden* should be discussed with the children if this has not been done as part of the introductory activities.

On Textbook page 81, in question 1, the children could calculate $34 \times 2\frac{1}{2}$ in various ways when changing 34 inches to centimetres. They could use a calculator to find $34 \times 2\cdot5$, or they might think of '34 twos' as 68 and '34 halves' as 17. Adding 68 and 17 gives 85.

In question 2(b), the children should think of other hammocks on either side and lying in such a small space all night – very cramped, especially for an adult.

For question 3(c), the children would have to know or measure their heights, preferably in feet and inches.

On Textbook page 82, in question 1, when changing 12 lb to kilograms the children could think of $12 \times \frac{1}{2}$ as '12 halves', giving an answer of about 6 kg.

In question 3(b), one possible approach is to change the volumes of tankard and barrel to litres.

Volume of tankard is 2 pints.   Volume of barrel is 40 gallons.

2 pints is about $2 \times \frac{1}{2}$ litres   40 gallons is about $40 \times 4\cdot5$ litres

$\qquad = 1$ litre $= 180$ litres

The barrel will fill more than 100 tankards.

N3f,4a/5	UA3d/5
SSM4a/5	N4a/5
	SSM4a/5

PSE
RN/D1
MD/D4
FPR/E4
T/D3,4

PUb/5
NOb/5
Mj/5
SMd/6

Rate and speed

Overview

This section introduces

■ rates per minute and per second

■ speeds in metres per second and in kilometres per hour.

	Teacher's Notes	Textbook	Workbook	Reinforcement Sheets
Global Research Technology: a context for pattern, rate and speed	112			
Rate:				
per minute	180	83		
per second	182	84*		
Speed:				
metres per second	183	85		27
kilometres per hour	184	86*		27

Homework provided in Home Link-up.

An extension activity related to the above section of work is as follows:

	Teacher's Notes	Extension Textbook
Rate: mph	266	E20

Teaching notes for the Extension Textbook are in a scparate section at the end of the Teacher's Notes.

Resources

Useful materials

- stopwatch or wristwatch for timing in seconds
- long metric tape (10 m, 20 m or 25 m)
- string and metal nut or key (for pendulum activity on Textbook page 84)
- other materials suggested within the introductory activities

Assessment and Resources Pack

Assessment

Check-up 3
Textbook 83–6

Round-up 3
Question 7(a)

Teaching notes

RATE: PER MINUTE

N3f,4a/5
N4a/5
MD/D4 FPR/E4
NOb/5 Mj/5

This section introduces the idea of a rate per minute through practical activities and examples involving a wide variety of situations.

The context involves Global Research Technology and the activities of its scientists, inventors and technicians. Global Research Technology was introduced in the Pattern section of Heinemann Mathematics P7.

Introductory activities

1 Signatures *(concept of a rate)*

- Remind the children of Global Research Technology (GRT) and its involvement in many activities, from receiving signals from Space to developing better plant foods.

- Tell the children that Dr Zelman at Global Research Technology uses a machine to sign her reports, rather than doing so herself. This saves her time. Write the following on a chalkboard to show how many times the machine can sign in 1 minute:

    48 signatures in 1 minute

Introduce the word 'rate':

    Rate = 48 signatures per minute

- Ask the children to sign their own names while someone times them for 1 minute. When the time is up, ask them to count how many signatures they have completed. Ask them to record their rates. For example,

    Rate = 9 signatures per minute

Discuss possible reasons for different rates – longer/shorter names, faster/slower writers, etc. Ask how many signatures they could do in 10 minutes at this rate (90 for the example above).

2 Printers *(rate per minute)*

- Tell the children that Dr Zelman uses two different printers to print reports from her computer. Show results for the two printers like this:

Printer A	Printer B
20 pages in 5 minutes	15 pages in 3 minutes

Discuss finding a rate in pages per minute to make it easier to see which is the faster printer…
'How many pages in 1 minute?'

Printer A	Printer B
20 pages in 5 minutes	15 pages in 3 minutes
Rate = 20 ÷ 5	Rate = 15 ÷ 3
= 4 pages per minute	= 5 pages per minute

Printer B is faster.

■ Calculate other rates. For example,

— 60 envelopes addressed in 10 minutes (6 envelopes per minute)

— 24 stamps stuck on in 2 minutes (12 stamps per minute).

3   Alarms   *(timing in seconds; finding a rate per minute)*

■ Tell the children that GRT is developing an alarm with a flashing light.

It flashes 14 times in 10 seconds. Write this result as follows:

14 flashes in 10 seconds

■ Ask the children how to find the rate in **flashes per minute.**

If necessary, ask

'How many lots of 10 seconds are in 1 minute?' to help them see that they can multiply by 6 to give the number of flashes in 60 seconds or 1 minute.

14 flashes in 10 seconds

Rate $= 14 \times 6$

$= 84$ **flashes per minute**

■ Give one of the children a torch. Tell the children that they are going to find the fastest rate at which the torch can be flashed. Ask how this rate can be found. The task should be split up: for example, one child flashes the torch, another counts the number of flashes and a third child times for 30 seconds. (Do not allow 1 minute.) Carry out the experiment two or three times with different children and work out the rates. For example,

17 flashes in 30 seconds

Rate $= 17 \times 2$

$= 34$ **flashes per minute**

■ This could be repeated for other rates. For example,

— pencils counted per minute (time for, say, 10 seconds)

— winks per minute (time for, say, 30 seconds)

— toe touches per minute (time for, say, 20 seconds).

Textbook page 83   *Rate: per minute*

In question 2(a), the children may need help to find their pulse. In part (b), they should multiply their result in (a) by 3 to find the number of beats in 1 minute. In part (c), the number of beats in 1 minute should be multiplied by 60 for 1 hour and then by 24 for 24 hours.

In question 3, parts (a) to (d), the children should **divide** by the number of minutes to find rates per minute. In part (e), they should **multiply** by 2 to find how many pills are made in 1 minute. Part (f) could be set out as follows:

£30 in 60 minutes

Rate = 30 ÷ 60

$= $ **£0·50 per minute** or **50p per minute**

Question 4 makes use of some of the rates found in question 3, which should be checked before attempting question 4. For example, in 3(a), Dr Dee's rate is 60 signals per minute. In question 4(a), he will send $60 \times 20 = 1200$ signals in 20 minutes.

N3f,4a/5
N4a/5
MD/D4 FPR/E4
NOb/5 Mj/5

RATE: PER SECOND

This section introduces rate per second and continues the context of activities and experiments at Global Research Technology.

Introductory activity

Code machines   *(rate per second)*

- Tell the children that GRT has been testing three machines that change messages into secret code. Show them the test results:

> **Sphinx:**   codes 65 letters in 13 seconds
>
> **Myst:**   codes 203 letters in 35 seconds
>
> **Enigma:**   codes 262 letters in 1 minute.

Ask which machine is fastest.

- Discuss the difficulty of finding a rate **per minute** – 13 seconds and 35 seconds cannot be easily 'changed' to 60 seconds. Suggest finding rates **per second** instead, using a calculator.

Sphinx 65 letters in 13 seconds	**Myst** 203 letters in 35 seconds
Rate $= 65 \div 13$	Rate $= 203 \div 35$
$= 5$ letters per second	$= 5{\cdot}8$ letters per second

Enigma   262 letters in 60 seconds

Rate $= 262 \div 60$

$= 4{\cdot}3666666$ letters per second

Myst is the fastest machine.

- Discuss the calculator answer for the Enigma machine.

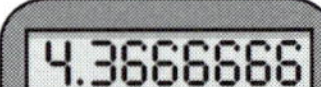

Ask the children to round it to the nearest whole number – **about 4 letters per second.**

Textbook page 84   *Rate: per second*

Point out the need to pay attention to the types of answer required for

- question 2: 'to the nearest whole number' (36, 3, 4)
- question 3: 'as decimals' (2·85, 6·4, 1·25)

In question 4(a), the children should make tally marks, grouped in fives 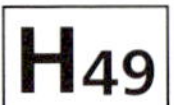, so that the rate is not too high. As they are timing for 10 seconds, the rate is likely to be a first-place decimal.

In question 5, the rate will depend on the length of the string, but it is likely to be around 1 swing per second or less.

Speeds in metres per second are introduced as rates involving distances in metres and times in seconds.

The context involves the testing of 'space vehicles' at Global Research Technology.

| N3f,4a/5 SSM3a/5 |
| UA3d/5 N4a/5 SSM4c/5 |
| RN/D1 MD/D4 FPR/E4 T/D3,4 |
| PUb/5 NOb/5 Mj/5 |

Introductory activities

1 Walking on the Moon *(calculating speeds in metres per second)*

■ Discuss the scenario of GRT experimenting to find out how fast an astronaut could 'walk' on the Moon wearing different space suits. 'Walking' on the Moon can be faster than on Earth, due to its low gravity. Write results for two suits on a chalkboard, as follows:

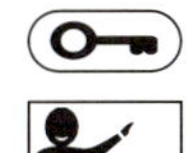

Rainbow suit	**Xtra suit**
105 metres in 15 seconds	96 metres in 12 seconds

■ Lead on to the idea of finding a 'rate per second' to see which suit allows faster walking.

Rainbow suit	**Xtra suit**
105 metres in 15 seconds	96 metres in 12 seconds
Rate = 105 ÷ 15	Rate = 96 ÷ 12
= **7 metres per second**	= **8 metres per second**

Ask the children about another word for a 'rate' which is in metres per second or kilometres per hour or miles per hour. They should suggest 'speed'. Replace 'rate' by 'speed' in the two examples.

■ Ask the children to use a calculator to find the speed achieved with another space suit, in metres per second to the nearest whole number.

Star suit

200 metres in 31 seconds

Speed = 200 ÷ 31

    = **about 6 metres per second**

$$6.4516129$$

Discuss rounding of the calculator display.

2 Walking on Earth
(practical activities to find speeds in metres per second)

■ Astronauts walk very slowly on Earth when wearing a space suit. Discuss this idea and suggest that one of the children could walk 'heel to toe' to simulate walking in a space suit.

Ask the children how they could find the speed for this walk. Lead onto the idea of

— measuring the **distance in metres**

— measuring the **time in seconds.**

■ Measure a whole number of metres across the classroom.
Have one child time another walking slowly for this distance.

Calculate the speed. For example,

5 metres in 15 seconds

Speed $= 5 \div 15$

$= 0.3333333$ metres per second

This speed is **less than 1 metre per second**.

N3f,4a/5 SSM3a/5
UA3d/5 N4a/5 SSM4c/5
PSE RN/D1 T/D3,4
SMd/6

R27

Problem solving

Textbook page 85   *Speed: metres per second*

In question 1, the speeds in metres per second, are either whole numbers or first-place decimals.

In question 3(a), speeds, are to the nearest whole number. In 3(b), it is worthwhile discussing the speeds of *Canaveral* and *Ariel*, both of which are 12 metres per second to the nearest whole number. *Canaveral*'s speed **before** rounding was 12·45 metres per second, making it an Alpha Class vehicle. *Ariel*'s speed was 11·722222 metres per second **before** rounding. It does not travel at more than 12 metres per second and is therefore **not** Alpha class.

In question 4, the children should walk normally, neither too fast nor too slow, for 10 seconds, and then measure the distance in metres.

Question 5 can be tackled in a similar way to question 4, to find a running speed.

SPEED: KILOMETRES PER HOUR

N3f,4a/5 SSM3a/5
UA3d/5 N4a/5 SSM4c/5
PSE RN/D1 FPR/E4 MD/D4 T/D3,4
SMd/6

Speeds in kilometres per hour are now introduced.

The context involves various Global Research Technology vehicles delivering materials to places around the country.

Introductory activity

Deliveries   *(speeds in kilometres per hour)*

■ Discuss a situation where GRT delivers a small computer to Newton Space Industries, 320 kilometres away.

Newton

320 km

Give times, in hours, taken by different vehicles for this journey.

Car: 5 hours   Van: 6 hours   Helicopter: 2 hours

■ With contributions from the children, find the speed for each vehicle. Stress that each speed is in **kilometres per hour.**

$$\text{Speed of car} = 320 \div 5$$
$$= 64 \text{ kilometres per hour}$$

$$\text{Speed of van} = 320 \div 6$$
$$= \textbf{about 53 kilometres per hour}$$ 

$$\text{Speed of helicopter} = 320 \div 2$$
$$= 160 \text{ kilometres per hour}$$

■ Make sure the children realize that, if the speed of the car is 64 kilometres per hour, it travels 64 km in **one** hour. Give the speed for another vehicle doing this journey. For example,

Motor bike   90 kilometres per hour

Ask the children how far the bike would travel, at this speed, in 1 hour, 2 hours, 3 hours ... 10 hours (90, 180, 270 ... 900 km).

Textbook page 86   *Speed: kilometres per hour*

In question 1, make sure the children realize that they should find the distance for each journey from the diagram at the top of the page.

In question 3, the children do not have ready-made techniques for finding the time or distance for a journey. In 3(a), knowing that 35 kilometres per hour implies a distance of 35 km in 1 hour can lead to calculating $2 \times 35 = 70$ km for 2 hours and $5 \times 35 = 175$ km for 5 hours. In 3(b), the children may see that 210 km can be travelled in **6 hours** at 35 kilometres per hour by making a table:

1 h $\longrightarrow$ 35 km

2 h $\longrightarrow$ 70 km

3 h $\longrightarrow$ 105 km

4 h $\longrightarrow$ 140 km

5 h $\longrightarrow$ 175 km

6 h $\longrightarrow$ 210 km

N3f,4a/5 SSM3a/5
UA3d/5 N4a/5 SSM4c/5
PSE RN/D1 T/D3,4
PUb/5 NOb/5 Mj/5 SMd/6

Problem solving

R27 H50

Eurotravel

A context for time

The work on time on Textbook pages 87–91 and Workbook page 16 is set in the context of Eurotravel, a busy city-centre travel agent and tour operator.

Introducing the context

The activities suggested below are intended to encourage the children to draw on their own experiences of visiting a travel agent, looking at holiday brochures or booking a trip.

1 Holiday display

Ask the children to create a holiday/travel display using a collection of posters, brochures and advertisements for a variety of holidays, short breaks or tours. The display could also include posters and other illustrations produced by the children themselves.

2 Holiday destinations

Use a world map and mapping pins. Ask the children to put a pin in a country they have visited or would like to visit. Display the collated information around the map. Information about these countries, their currency, language, population, etc., could also be found and included.

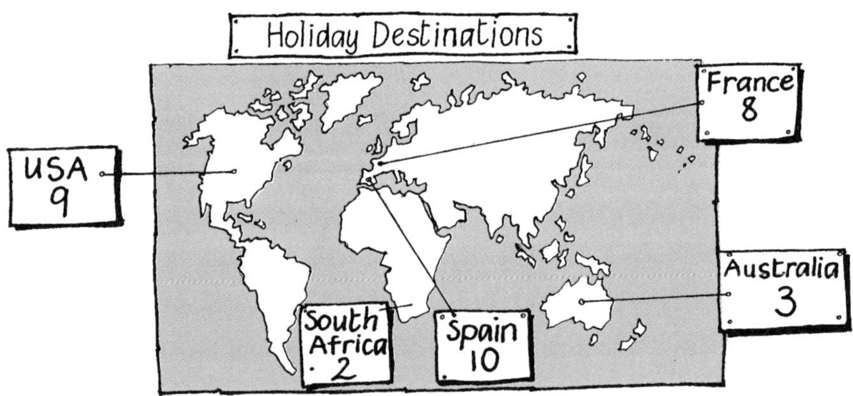

3 Holiday competition

Ask the children to make a holiday quiz sheet. Discuss with them the types of question that could be used. For example,

— What is the capital of. . . ?

— The yen is the currency of which country?

— What language is spoken in Brazil?

— Qantas is the national airline of which country?

— The Leaning Tower of Pisa is in which country?

4   Holiday snaps

The children could be asked to bring in their favourite or most amusing holiday snap. Ask each child to write an appropriate caption for the photograph. Use the photographs to make a wall display.

5   Holiday horrors

Ask the children to describe, write or draw about holiday mishaps they have experienced. For example,

— flight delays

— travel sickness

— unsuitable accommodation

— bad weather

— noisy guests

— lost luggage.

Time

Overview

This section

- revises 12-hour notation and durations in hours and minutes
- revises 24-hour notation and extends it to

  — durations in minutes and in hours and minutes, with bridging of an hour

  — counting on and counting back in hours and in minutes, with bridging of an hour.

	Teacher's Notes	Textbook	Workbook	Reinforcement Sheets
Eurotravel: a context for time	186			
12-hour notation: durations	190	87*		
24-hour notation:				
applications	192	88*		
durations	193	89*		
counting on	194	90*	16	28
counting back	197	91*	16	29

Homework provided in Home Link-up.

An extension activity related to the above section of work is as follows:		
	Teacher's Notes	Extension Textbook
Time: 24-hour clock, durations	267	E21

Teaching notes for the Extension Textbook are in a separate section at the end of the Teacher's Notes.

Resources

Useful materials

- analogue clockfaces
- other material suggested within the introductory activities

Assessment and Resources Pack

Assessment

Measure Check-up 4
Textbook pages 88–91
Workbook page 16
(Time: 24-hour clock, durations,
counting on and back)

Round-up 3
Questions 1(a), (b), (c)

Resources

Problem Solving Activities
19 Confusing clocks (Time)
20 Part-time (Calendar)

Resource Cards
15 Eurotravel rally

Teaching notes

In Heinemann Mathematics 6, work with 12-hour times included

— the notation 'am' and 'pm'

— durations, counting on and counting back in minutes and in hours and minutes, including bridging an hour.

Heinemann Mathematics P7 begins by revising this work with 12-hour notation.

The context introduces Eurotravel, a travel agent and tour operator, and some of the tasks carried out by staff at its city-centre branch.

12-HOUR NOTATION: DURATIONS

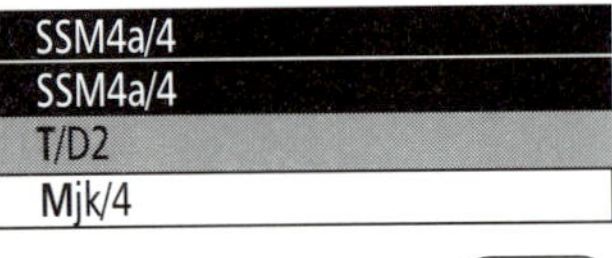

Introductory activities

1   Tour timetable
(durations in hours and minutes, counting on, counting back)
Display a Eurotravel tour timetable.

Eurotravel Historic Tours	
Market Tour	8.30 am — 9.55 pm
Fort Tour	9.15 am — 10.05 am
Old Town Tour	10.20 am — 12 noon
Palace Tour	11.45 am — 1.20 pm
Abbey Tour	1.55 pm — 3.25 pm

Ask questions such as

'How long does each tour last?'

If necessary, use two clockfaces to help the children calculate the time interval.
For example,

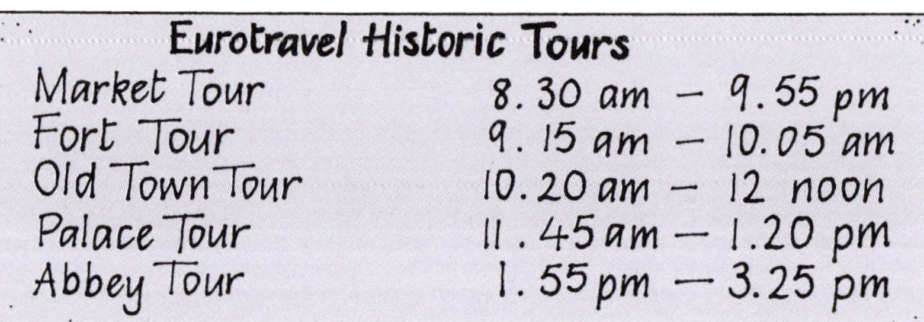

Rotate the hands on the first clock to match the finishing time on the second clock, while discussing a way of finding the duration.

'Nine fifteen to ten o'clock is **45 minutes.**

Ten o'clock to ten five is **5 minutes.**'

The Fort tour lasts for **50 minutes.**

2   Tours   *(counting on to find a finishing time)*

Produce an information sheet like this for another selection of Eurotravel tours.

Ask questions such as,

   'When will the Art Gallery tour finish?'

The children should

   — count on the hours: 9.25, 10.25, 11.25

   — count on the remaining 30 minutes

to give a finishing time of 11.55 am.

The Art Gallery Tour finishes at **11.55 am.**

Some children may need access to a clock to visualize the counting on process.

3   City walks   *(counting back to find a starting time)*

Prepare a set of large cards like these, or write these durations on the chalkboard.

Display a clock showing the finishing time for the City Walk, 4.15 pm.

Ask the children when the walk started.

The children should count back 1 hour, to 3.15 pm. . .

and then a further 50 minutes to give 2.25 pm.

Give further examples to reinforce this quite difficult technique. Some pupils may also benefit from having access to a clock.

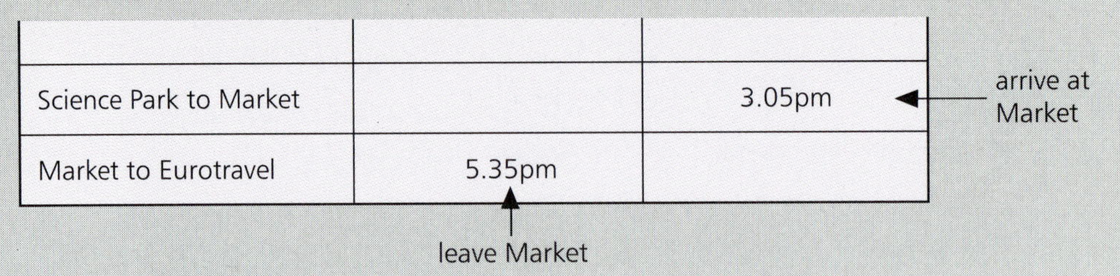

Textbook page 87   *Time: 12-hour clock, durations*

In questions 3 and 4, the children must find the duration between an arrival time and a departure time which are in different rows of the table. For example, they use the times indicated below to find how long is spent at the Market.

Science Park to Market		3.05pm	← arrive at Market
Market to Eurotravel	5.35pm		

leave Market

24-HOUR NOTATION: APPLICATIONS

In Heinemann Mathematics 6, the children were introduced to 24-hour notation in applications such as television schedules and airport timetables. This work is now revised.

The Eurotravel context continues with coach trips, one of them to France.

Introductory activities

1   Tour Guide Planner   *(24-hour notation)*

■ Draw a time line and add labels as shown.

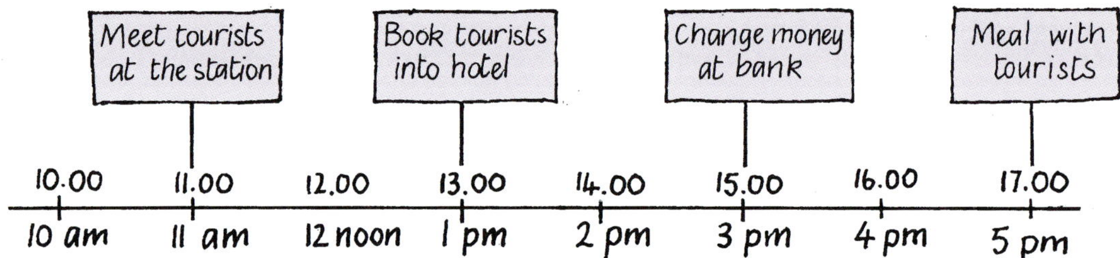

Ask the children to say the time when the guide has to change money at the bank.

They may say,

■ Discuss why 24-hour notation is used in rail, bus and air timetables: that is, to avoid confusion with times such as 9.15 which may be a morning or an evening time.

2 Time cards *(using 24-hour notation)*

Display a set of 12-hour and 24-hour times.

| 6 am | 23.34 | 2.29 pm | 08.08 | 16.15 |

Select a time such as 2.29 pm and ask a child to

— say the time

— change it to the other notation.

For example,

Textbook page 88   *Time: 24-hour clock*

In questions 5 to 7, the children have to interpret the table to decide what happened at times not specified in the driver's log book.

SSM4a/4
SSM4a/4
T/D2
Mjk/4

H52

24-HOUR NOTATION: DURATIONS

In Heinemann Mathematics 6, simple durations expressed in 24-hour notation were introduced. This work is now revised and extended to counting on from a starting time to find the finishing time.

SSM4a/4
SSM4a/4
T/D1,2
Mjk/4

The Eurotravel context continues with activity holidays and customers' travel enquiries.

Introductory activities

1 Holiday activities   *(durations in hours)*

Discuss with the children different holiday activities such as horse riding, cycling and skiing. Display a timetable like this.

	skiing	sledging	lunch	skating
Start	09.15	10.30	12.00	14.45
Finish	10.15	11.30	14.00	16.45

Ask the children how long, in hours, was spent on each activity.

2 Winter sports *(durations in minutes)*

■ Tell the children that Ross went on a Eurotravel Winter holiday. Ross had

— skiing lessons from 09.15 until 09.48

— skating lessons from 15.05 until 15.32.

Ask the children to find how long Ross spent on each lesson. They should explain how each duration was calculated. For example,

skiing lesson: from 09.15 to 09.48

Alternatively, some children may count on in intervals of 5 minutes, 10 minutes, 45 minutes or even 1 hour.

■ Discuss further examples if necessary. For example, the children could find out how long each of these activities lasted:

Time	Activity
12.45	sledging
13.10	skating lesson
13.55	skating
14.25	café
14.50	ski lesson
15.45	skiing
16.20	tea

SSM4a/4
SSM4a/4
T/D1,2
Mjk/4

Textbook page 89 *Time: 24-hour clock, durations*

In question 2, discuss the relay race scenario where the team has only three runners.

In question 3, the children should realize they need to look at all four timetables for information.

In 3(e), the children should use the timetable format illustrated.

H53

24-HOUR NOTATION: COUNTING ON

SSM4a/4
SSM4a/4
T/D1,2
Mjk/4

Finding finishing times by counting on in hours or in minutes, or in hours and minutes, using 24-hour notation is now introduced.

The Eurotravel context continues with staff at the city branch dealing with a number of customer enquiries.

Introductory activities

1   Journeys
(counting on in hours or in minutes to find a finishing time)

■ Use a time line showing whole hours, beginning and ending at midnight, to discuss car journey times.

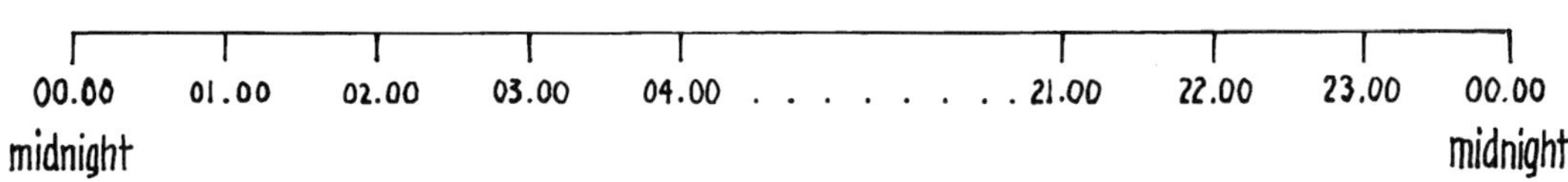

For example, children living in Glasgow would take about

— 1 hour to travel to Edinburgh

— 2 hours to travel to Dundee

— 3 hours to travel to Aberdeen.

■ Ask a question such as

'Mike leaves Glasgow at 07.40. When should he arrive in Dundee?'

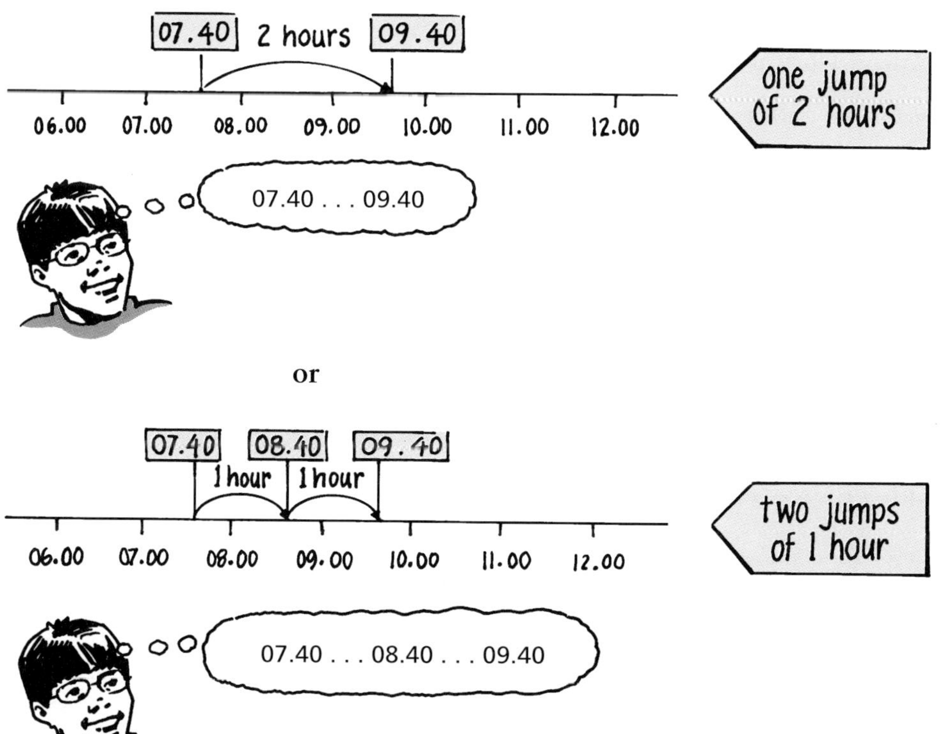

Mike arrives in Dundee at **09.40**.

■ Repeat for other questions, such as

'Zoë leaves Glasgow at 09.25. When should she arrive in Edinburgh?'

'Clive leaves Glasgow at 11.15. When should he arrive in Aberdeen?'

■ Use a time line showing 5-minute intervals.

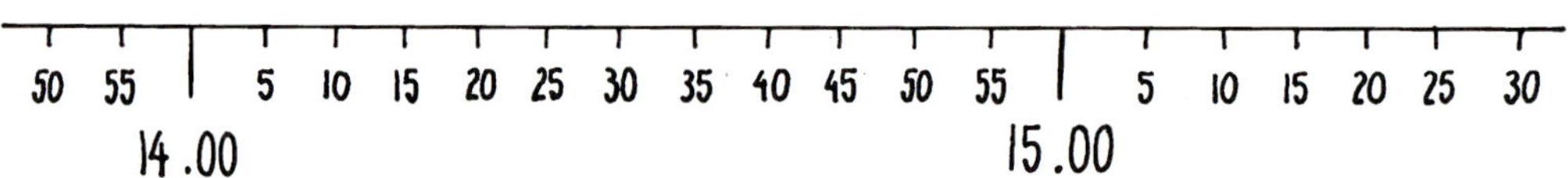

Ask the children a question such as

'Janie leaves home at 14.50. She arrives at the town centre 35 minutes later. When does she arrive?'

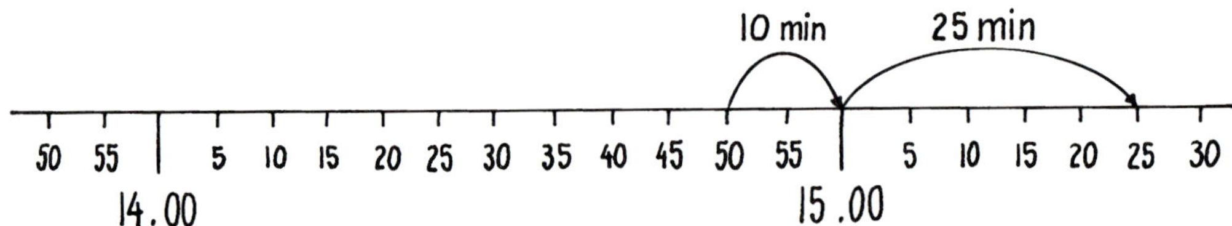

Encourage the children to count on to the next hour and then count on the extra minutes:

14.50 and 10 minutes gives 15.00

15.00 and 25 minutes gives 15.25

Janie arrives at **15.25**.

At this point the children could try Textbook page 90, questions 1–4.

2 Getting there
(counting on in hours and minutes to find a finishing time)

Consider a journey which starts at 15.35 and takes 3 hours 45 minutes.

Start at 15.35. Count on 3 hours 45 minutes.

15.35 and 3 hours is 18.35

18.35 and 25 minutes is 19.00

19.00 and 20 minutes is 19.20

The finishing time is **19.20**.

SSM4a/4
SSM4a/4
T/D2
Mk/4

Textbook page 90 *Time: 24-hour clock, counting on*
Workbook page 16, question 1

On Textbook page 90, some children may benefit from using a time line to help them with the counting on process. The counting on work is graded as follows:

Questions 1 and 2 – in whole hours

Questions 3 and 4 – in minutes which bridge the hour

Question 5 – in hours and minutes with no bridging of the hour

Question 7 – in hours and minutes which bridge the hour.

On Workbook page 16, question 1 allows the children to draw jumps as they count on to find the finishing times. The illustrated example shows the hour jump first, but allow any child, who wishes to do so, to count on the minutes first.

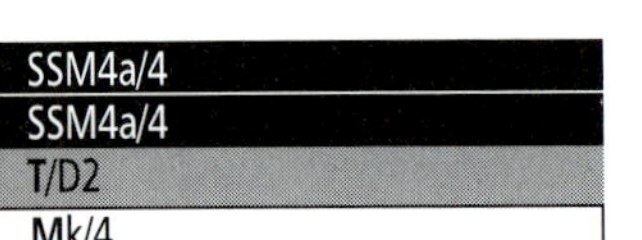

This section deals with counting back to find a finishing time.

The context continues with travel by air.

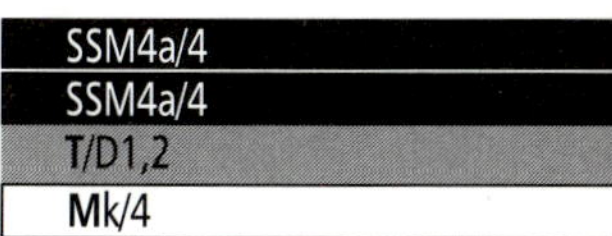

Introductory activities

1   Travelling by air
(counting back in hours or in minutes to find a starting time)

■ Discuss the checking-in procedures at an airport, where passengers check in, say, 2 hours before departure. Ask the children how they would find the check-in time for a flight leaving at 11.10. They may suggest counting back one hour at a time

$$11.10 \ldots 10.10 \ldots 9.10$$

or simply subtract 2 from 11.

■ Boarding times, which are 20 minutes before departure, can also be found. For example

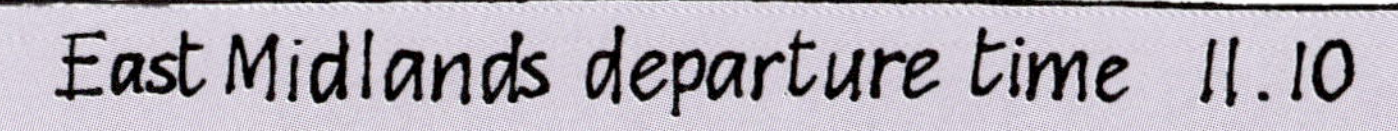

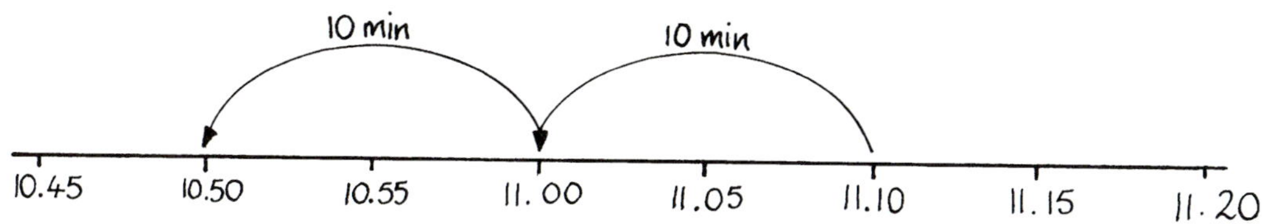

Count back 10 minutes to 11 o'clock, then back another 10 minutes to 10.50.

The boarding time for the East Midlands flight is **10.50**.

2   International journeys
(counting back in hours and minutes to find a starting time)

■ Display timetable like this.

International flights	
Destination	**Departure time**
Amsterdam	10.30
Boston	11.40
Tunis	12.15
Tokyo	13.50
Milan	14.20

Check-in 1 h 45 min before Departure time

Ask the children to find the check-in time for the flight to Milan.

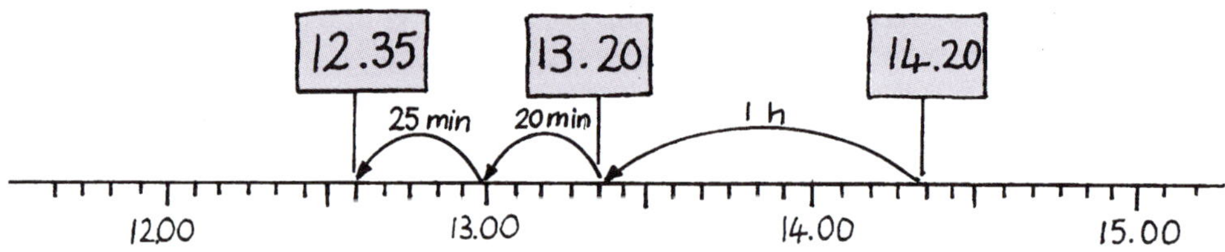

The children should be encouraged to

— count back the hour (14.20, go back 1 hour is 13.20)

— count back the minutes to the previous hour (13.20, go back 20 minutes to 13.00)

— count back the remaining minutes to find the check-in time (13.00, go back 25 minutes to 12.35).

The check-in time for the Milan flight is **12.35**.

■ Repeat for the other destinations.

SSM4a/4
SSM4a/4
T/D1,2
Mjk/4

Textbook page 91   *Time: 24-hour clock, counting back*
Workbook page 16, question 2

Ensure that the children are familiar with check-in procedures at an airport. Information display boards with flight numbers and destination and departure times could be discussed with the children.

On Textbook page 91, in questions 3, 4 and 5, some children may benefit from the use of an analogue clock or time line marked in 5-minute intervals to help them count back.

Questions 4 and 5 require two consecutive durations to be counted back. Some children may find the interpretation of these questions difficult and require discussion about the context.

The Shape part of Heinemann Mathematics P7 has four sections, each with an
Overview and accompanying notes.

Shape

Angles

Overview

This section

- revises acute, right, straight and obtuse angles and introduces the term 'reflex' for angles between 180° and 360°

- revises measuring angles to the nearest 5° and introduces measuring angles to the nearest 1°

- introduces drawing angles to the nearest 5° and 1°

- introduces calculation of angle sizes in situations where angles add up to 90° or 180° or 360°

- introduces bearings.

	Teacher's Notes	Textbook	Workbook	Reinforcement Sheets
Avonside Country Park: a context for length and angles	144			
Angles: measuring and drawing in degrees	200	92*	29, 30*	30
Angles: calculation	203	93*		
Bearings	204	94, 95, 96*		

Homework provided in Home Link-up.

Extension activities:	Teacher's Notes	Extension Textbook
Angles: position fixing	267	E22
Shape: position and movement	268	E23

Resources

- Resource Card 18 in the Assessment and Resources Pack can be photocopied onto acetate to provide six 360° protractors.

Assessment and Resources Pack

Assessment

Check-up 1
Textbook 92–3
Workbook 29–30

Check-up 2
Textbook 94–9

Round-up 1
Question 5

Resources

Resource Cards
18 360° protractors (Angles)
19 and 20 Bearings game (Angles)

Problem Solving Activities
27 LOGO puzzle (Angles)
28 X marks the spot (Bearings, scale)

Teaching notes

The use of degrees to describe right angles (90°), half right angles (45°) and their multiples was introduced in Heinemann Mathematics 5.

In Heinemann Mathematics 6, the terms 'acute', 'right' and 'obtuse' were used to describe angles. Cut-out angles were measured to the nearest 5° by laying them on top of a 360° protractor scale.

This work is now consolidated and extended to include

— the use of the term 'reflex'

— the use of a 360° protractor to measure and draw angles to the nearest 5° and then to the nearest 1°.

This section reintroduces the Avonside Country Park context, first used for the work on Length.

ANGLES: MEASURING AND DRAWING IN DEGREES

SSM3c/5
SSM2d/5
A/D1 A/E1
SPbc/4 SPd/5

Introductory activities

1 Types of angle *(introducing reflex angles)*

■ Draw a mixture of acute, right and obtuse angles on a chalkboard or overhead projector transparency, with the angles labelled and marked as shown.

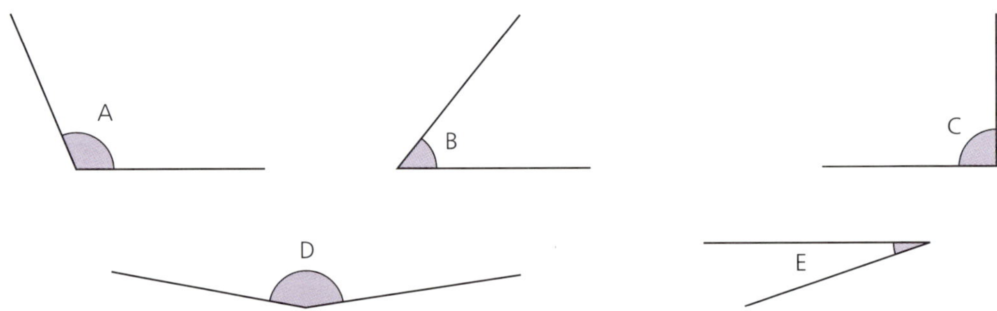

Point to each, in turn, asking the children to name the type of angle (acute, right or obtuse), giving a reason in each case.

For example,

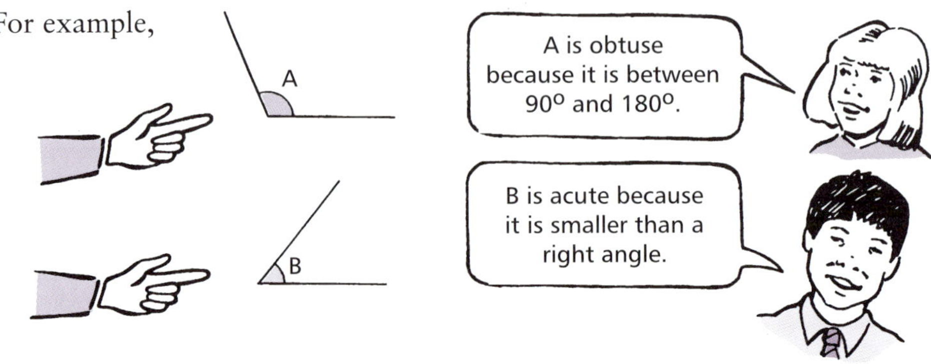

A right-angled corner could be placed on top of each angle to show whether it is greater or smaller than 90°.

■ Mark and label the 'other' angle on each diagram. For example,

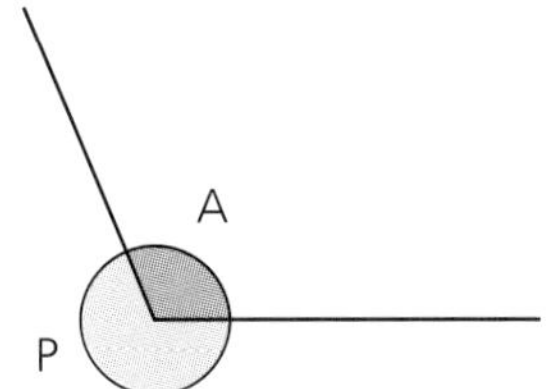
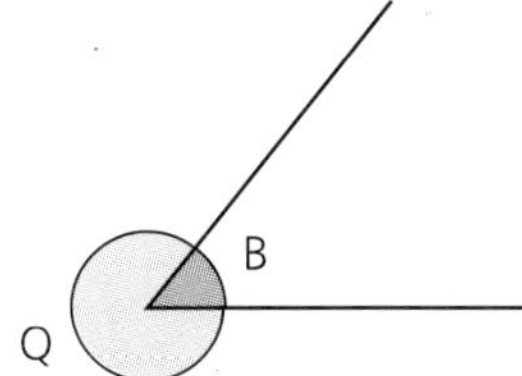
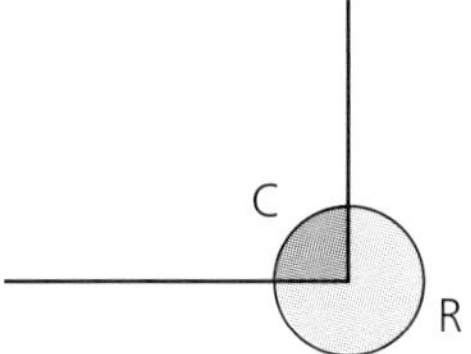

Ask the children what makes angles, P, Q, R. . . different from angles A, B, C. . . What characteristic do they share? Through discussion, lead them to observe that each of these angles is larger than a straight angle. Each measures between 180° and 360°. Tell them that these angles are called **reflex** angles.

2   Measuring and drawing angles   *(using a 360° protractor)*

■ Distribute 360° protractors and discuss their features with the children. Although these may vary according to the type in use, they are likely to include some or all of the following:

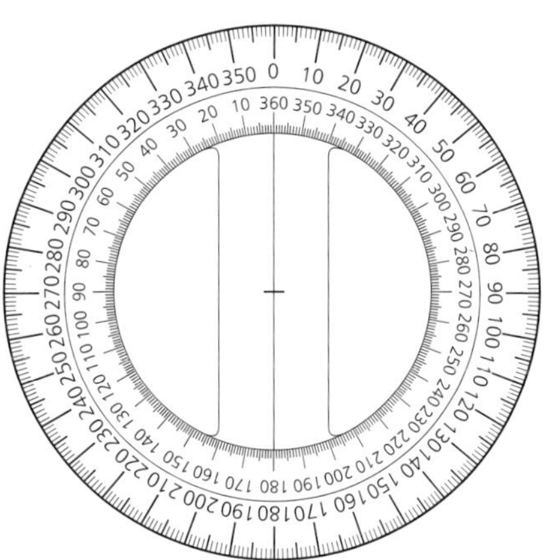

— marks showing every degree

— longer marks showing every 5 degrees

— **labelled** marks every 10° from 0° to 360°, both clockwise **and** anti-clockwise.

■ Demonstrate how to use the protractor to measure a variety of angles drawn on a large sheet of paper and laid on a table. Include acute, right, obtuse and reflex angles in different orientations. Emphasize the following:

— the need to lay the 0° line along one arm of the angle with the centre of the protractor at the angle vertex

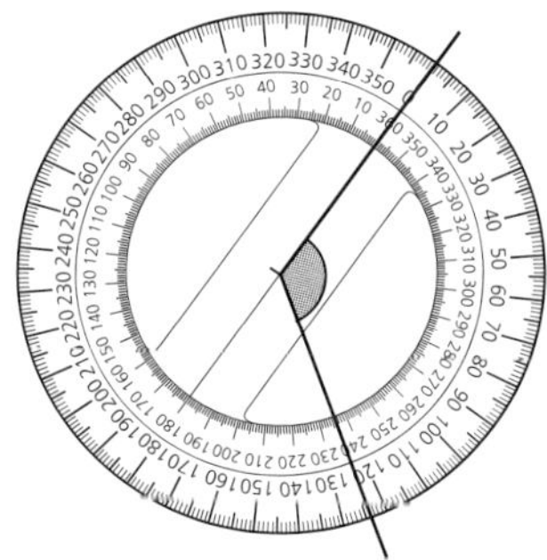

— finding the size of the angle by counting round from zero and then counting on from a labelled mark

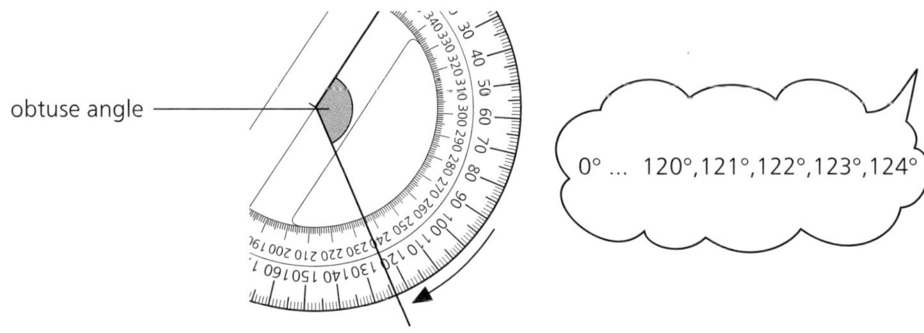

— the possibility of reading clockwise **or** anti-clockwise, depending on the size
and orientation of the angle.

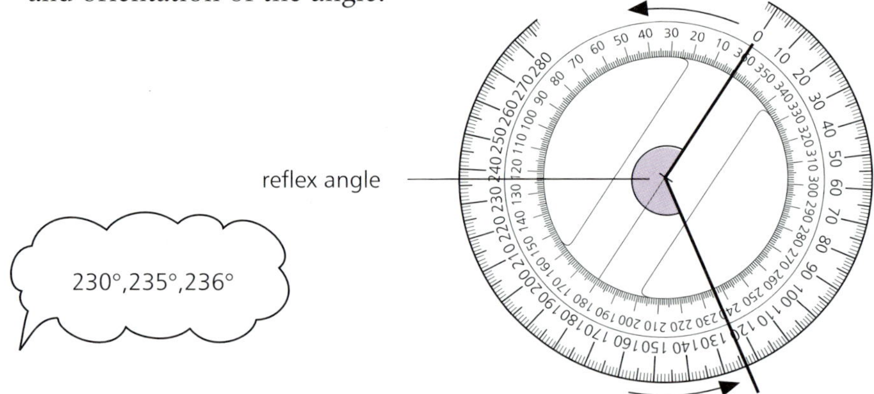

reflex angle

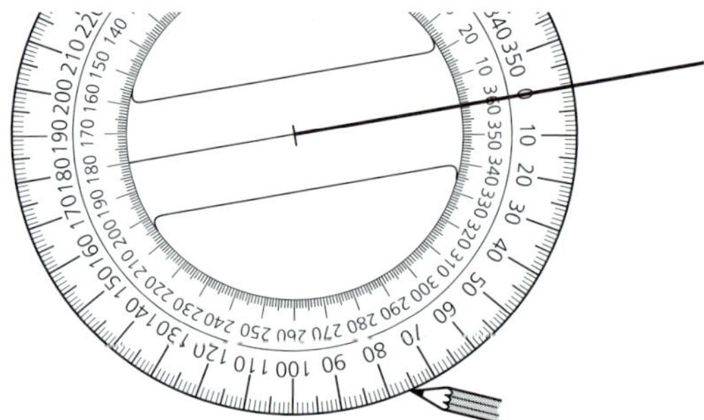

■ Also show the children how to **draw** an angle of a given size, such as 76°, by

— drawing a line to represent one arm of the angle

— placing the 0° line of the protractor along this line with the centre of the
protractor at the end of the line, reading off 76° and marking a dot on the
circumference of the protractor

— drawing a new line through the marked dot and the end of the line

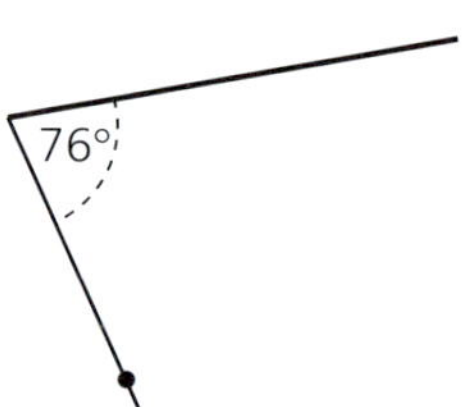

— in some situations, the children could count round **anti-clockwise** using the
inner scale of a protractor like this.

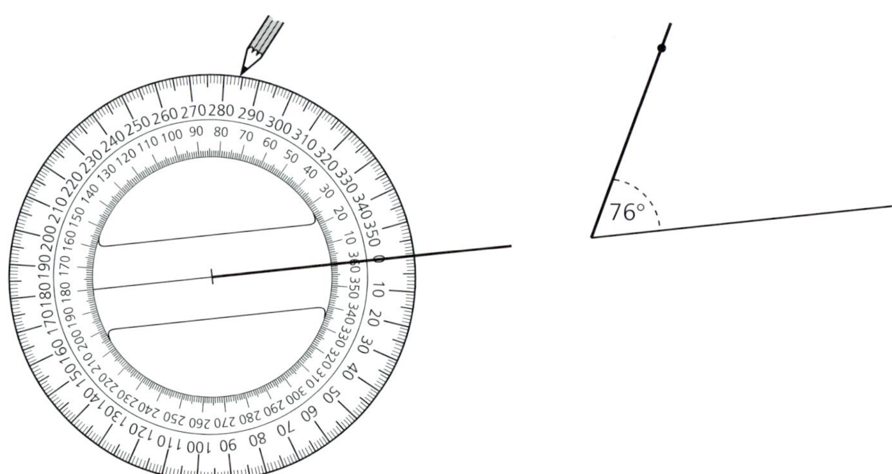

The children should also practise drawing angles whose vertices are at the 'right
hand' end of the original line.

Textbook page 92   *Angles: measuring, drawing*
Workbook pages 29 and 30

It will be necessary for the children to have had practice in using circular, 360° protractors to complete the work on these pages.

On Workbook page 29, all of the angles are measured or drawn to the nearest 5°.

On Workbook page 30, the angles are measured or drawn to the nearest degree.

The drawing questions on each of these pages require the children to read protractors in both clockwise and anti-clockwise directions.

On Textbook page 92, in questions 3 and 4, the children could be asked to find the sum of the three angles in each triangle, giving answers of around 180°. The idea that the sum of the three angles of any triangle is 180° is further developed on Extension Textbook page E26.

SSM3c/5
SSM2d/5
A/D1 A/E1
SPbc/4 SPd/5

R30

ANGLES: CALCULATION

Previous stages of Heinemann Mathematics have introduced the children to the ideas of

— a right angle as 90°

— a straight angle as 180°

— one full turn as 360°.

This knowledge is now used to calculate the sizes of other angles. For example,

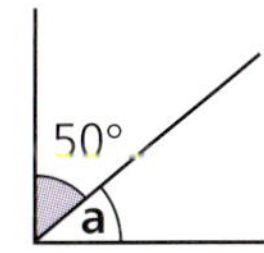

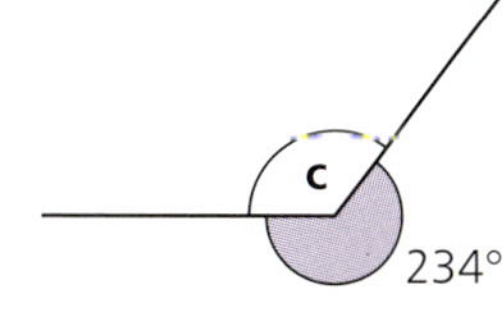

a = 90° – 50°
  = 40°

b = 180° – 57°
  = 123°

c = 360° – 234°
  = 126°

Introductory activity

SSM2d/5

SPbc/5

Calculating angle sizes

- Draw a right angle on the chalkboard or an overhead transparency and establish that it is 90°. Use a ruler, pencil, straw or strip (and blu-tack if required) to create two angles as shown.

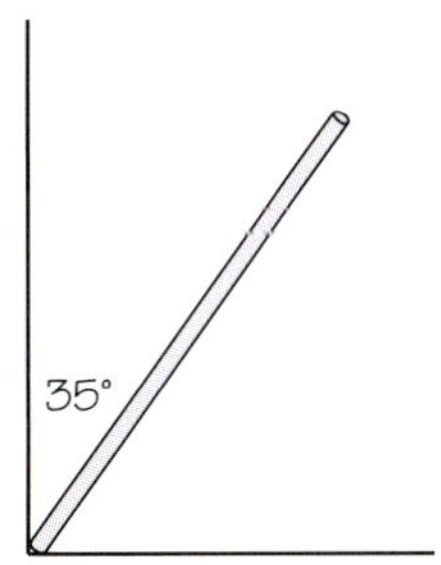

Write the size of one of the angles.

Remind the children that, together, the two angles total 90°. Ask them to calculate, **mentally**, the size of the 'other' angle (90° − 35° = 55°).

Rotate the straw and repeat for a new angle. For example,

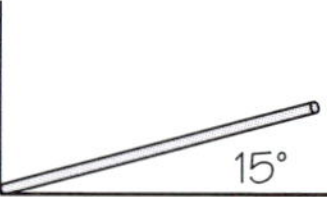

- Start with a straight angle of 180°. Use a similar procedure to that described above and ask the children to calculate the size of the 'other' angle (180° − 100° = 80°).

  Rotate the straw and repeat.

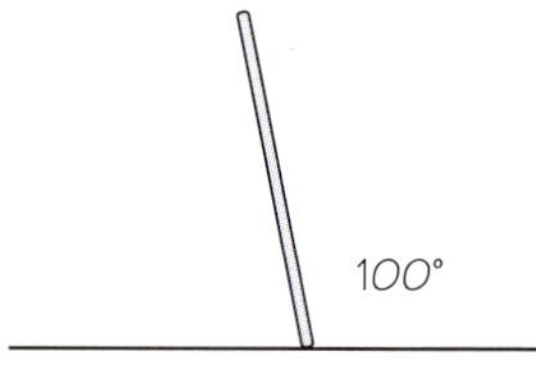

- Start with a diagram like this:

Rotate a straw to give two angles as shown.

Remind the children that the two angles total 360° and ask them to find the 'other' angle (360° − 110° = 250°).

Repeat for other angle.

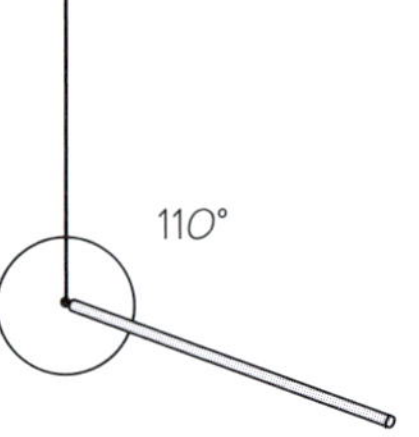

SSM3c/5

SSM2d/5

SPcd/4→5

Textbook page 93   *Angles: calculation*

Discuss the worked examples on the page and how the calculations can be set down on paper.

BEARINGS

The 8-point compass was introduced in Heinemann Mathematics 5. In Heinemann Mathematics 6, compass directions were associated with turns (clockwise and anti-clockwise) of 45°, 90°, 135°, 180°, 225°, 270°, 315° and 360°.

In this section, compass directions are associated with bearings of 045°, 090°, 135° ... 360°. Bearings to the nearest 5° are then measured using a protractor.

The Avonside Country Park context continues.

Introductory activities

1 Compass points and bearings

■ Prepare a large compass marked as shown.

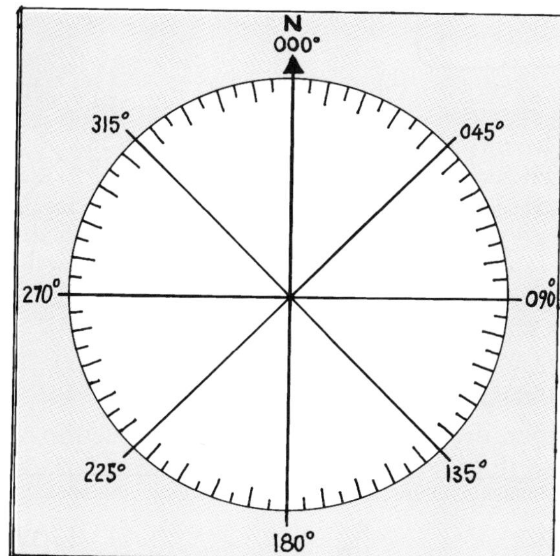

■ Place the compass on a flat surface so that it lines up with magnetic North (which can be found by using a pocket compass).

Tell the children that directions on a compass can also be expressed as bearings. Emphasize that bearings are

— measured **clockwise from North**

— expressed using **3 figures**.

■ Ask the children to give the bearings of compass directions such as South-East, West, North-East, etc.

■ Attach an arrow to the compass using Blu-tack or a paper fastener.

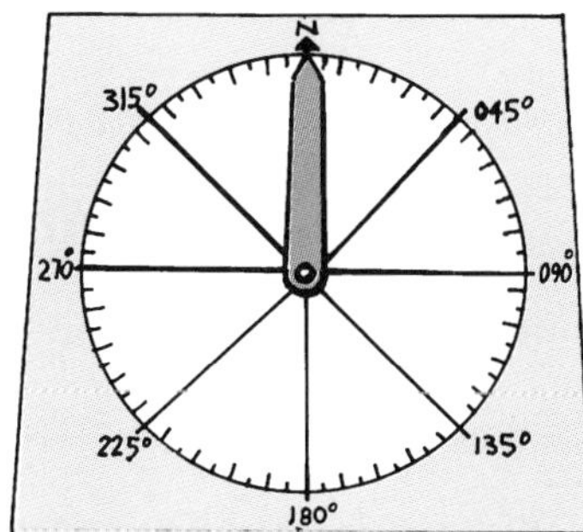

■ Rotate the arrow so that it points to a 10° or 5° mark and ask a child to give the bearing. For example,

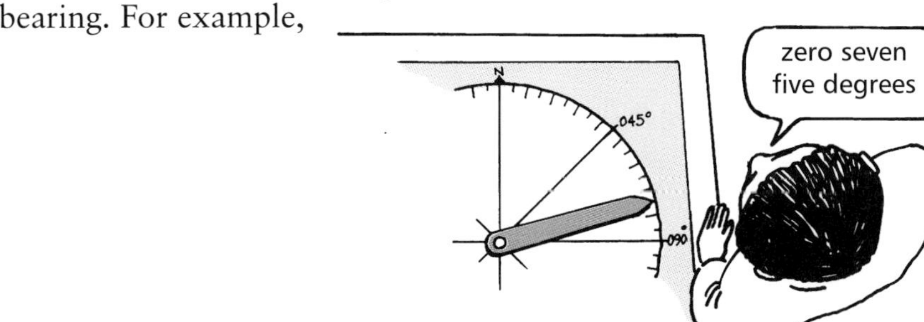

and write it on the chalkboard. 075°

Repeat for other directions/bearings.

■ Give bearings, either verbally or in written form, and ask children to rotate the arrow to show the appropriate direction. For example,

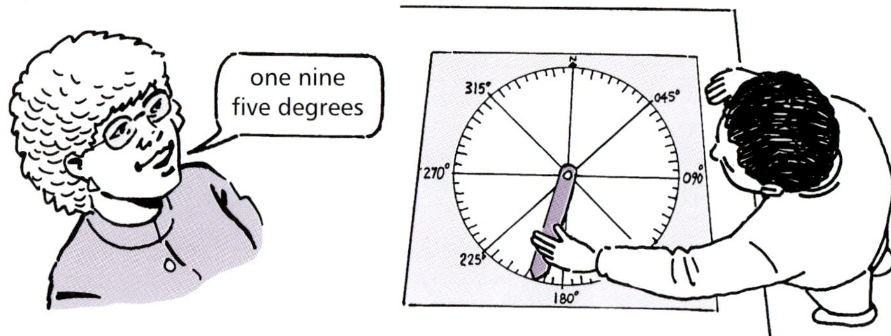

At this point the children could try Textbook page 94.

2   Measuring bearings

■ On a large sheet of paper, draw lines to indicate the directions of various 'towns' from a central city. Also draw a North line at the centre. For example,

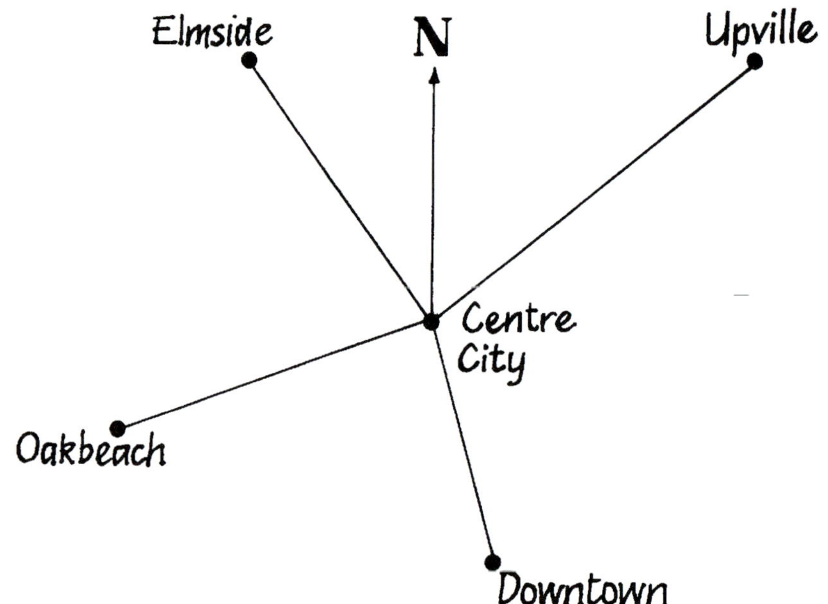

Each angle to be measured should be drawn to a 5° or 10° mark.

■ Demonstrate how a circular protractor is used to measure the bearings of Elmside, Upville, Downtown and Oakbeach from Centre City. Emphasize the need to

— align the 0° line of the protractor with the North line

— read the bearing by counting in a **clockwise** direction from North

— express each bearing **using 3 figures.**

■ An alternative, and more challenging, activity could involve drawing North lines at Elmside, Upville, Downtown and Oakbeach, and finding the bearing of Centre City from each of these towns.

Textbook page 94   *Angles: bearings*

In question 1, the children should be reminded that on an 8-point compass the angle between one bearing and the next is 45° or half a right angle.

They may find it useful to think of the angle in, for example, 1(c) as $1\frac{1}{2}$ right angles and then convert to degrees. Alternatively, they may simply calculate $3 \times 45°$.

In question 4, the bearings can be found by counting on or back from a marked interval. For example, to find the bearing of the Changing Rooms 90° add 10° gives 100°, while to find the bearing of the Wildlife Pond 270° less 10° gives 260°.

SSM3c/5
SSM2d/5
PM/D2 A/D2
SPa/4 SPb/6

Textbook page 95   *Angles: bearings around a point*

SSM3c/5
SSM2d/5
A/D1,2
SPd/5 SPb/6

In question 1, the coloured angles should help the children to remember to measure clockwise from North each time.

In question 2, however, this is likely to prove more difficult, especially for part (b). Some may need help to see that the bearings to be measured are as shown.

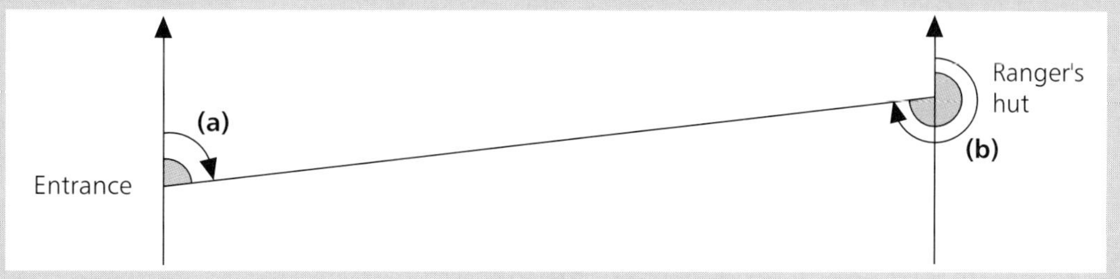

Textbook page 96   *Angles: bearings*

SSM3c/5
SSM2d,3d/5
PFS/E3 A/D1,2
SPb/6 Mi/5

All bearings on this page should be measured to the nearest 5° or 10° interval. Lines should be measured to the nearest centimetre.

In question 1, some difficulty may be caused by the fact that the children are asked to measured the bearings of, for example,

    Start **to** A

       A **to** B, etc.

They may find it useful to think of these also as

    A **from** Start

    B **from** A, etc.

SSM2bc/4	SSM2bc/4
SSM3a/5	SSM3bc/5
RS/D2,3,5	
S/D1	
S/E1	
SEa/4→5	
SEa/5	
SPd/6	

Symmetry and tiling

Overview

This section

- consolidates line symmetry and rotational symmetry
- extends rotational symmetry by considering more complex designs
- introduces the term 'regular'
- introduces translation.

	Teacher's Notes	Textbook	Workbook	Reinforcement Sheets
Line and rotational symmetry	209	97	17, 20	
Tiling: translation	211	98	18, 20	

An extension activity related to the above section of work is as follows:

	Teacher's Notes	Extension Textbook
2D shape: tiling	269	E24

Teaching notes for the Extension Textbook are in a separate section at the end of the Teacher's Notes.

Resources

Useful materials

- paper, card or plastic shapes
- card, coloured pens/pencils, scissors
- plain paper – A4 and poster sizes
- other materials suggested within the introductory activities

Assessment and Resources Pack

Assessment

Round-up 2
Question 3

Round-up 3
Question 3(b)

Resources

Problem Solving Activities
25 Symmetrical shapes
   (Making symmetrical shapes)
26 Designs
   (Bilateral and rotational symmetry)

Teaching notes

Shapes and designs with more than two lines of symmetry were introduced in Heinemann Mathematics 5. This work is now consolidated.

Rotational symmetry was introduced in Heinemann Mathematics 6 by exploring the number of ways a shape or design could fit its own outline in one full turn. This work is now consolidated and extended to include the construction of more complex designs.

The term 'regular' is introduced to describe a 2D shape with all its sides the same length and all its angles the same size.

LINE AND ROTATIONAL SYMMETRY

Introductory activities

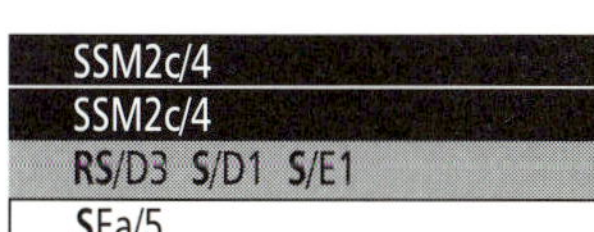

1   Line symmetry   *(revision)*

Use large paper shapes or designs and discuss

— folding to make matching halves

— fold lines as lines of symmetry.

The shapes or designs might include the following:

isosceles triangle	rectangle	equilateral triangle	circle design
1 line of symmetry	2 lines of symmetry	3 lines of symmetry	4 lines of symmetry

2   Rotational symmetry   *(revision)*

■ Use plastic, paper or card shapes, and draw round them on the chalkboard.
Alternatively, draw congruent shapes on two separate overhead projector transparencies. Discuss and demonstrate how a shape can be fitted into its own outline by turning it round, and that a shape which fits its own outline more than once in one full turn has **rotational symmetry**.

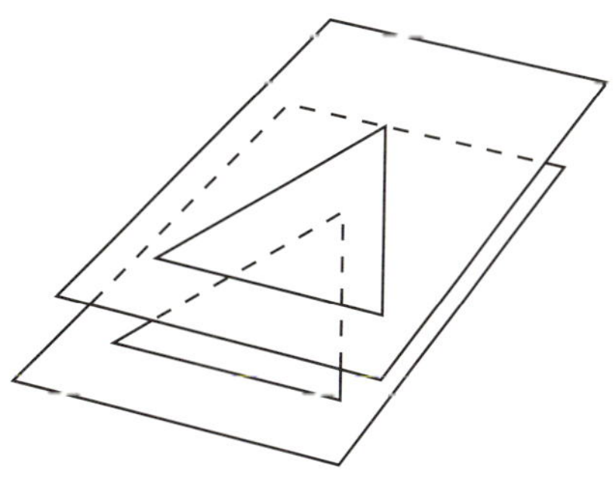

■ For some children it may be appropriate to introduce the term 'order' to describe the number of ways a shape fits its own outline in one full turn. For example, a square fits its own outline 4 ways in one full turn and so has **rotational symmetry of order 4**.

A useful way of keeping track of the number of fittings is to mark the same corner of both the shape and its outline as shown.

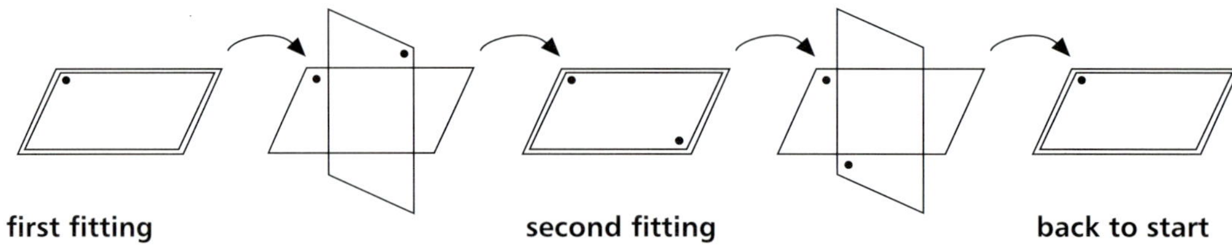

first fitting   **second fitting**   **back to start**

The shapes might include the following:

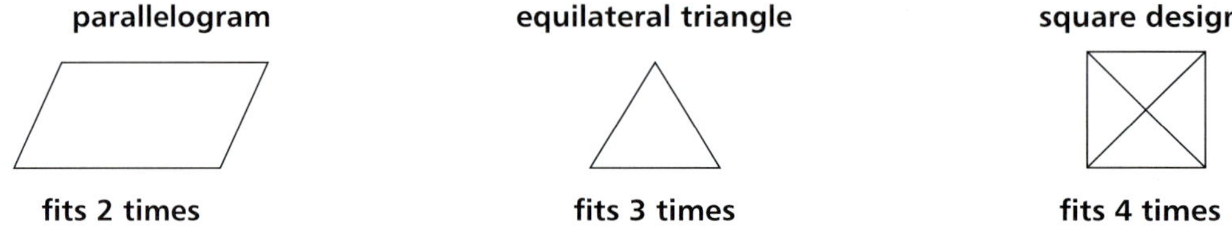

parallelogram   **equilateral triangle**   **square design**

fits 2 times   **fits 3 times**   **fits 4 times**

■ Colour parts of the shapes as shown below and discuss how the number of times the shape or design fits its own outline is affected.

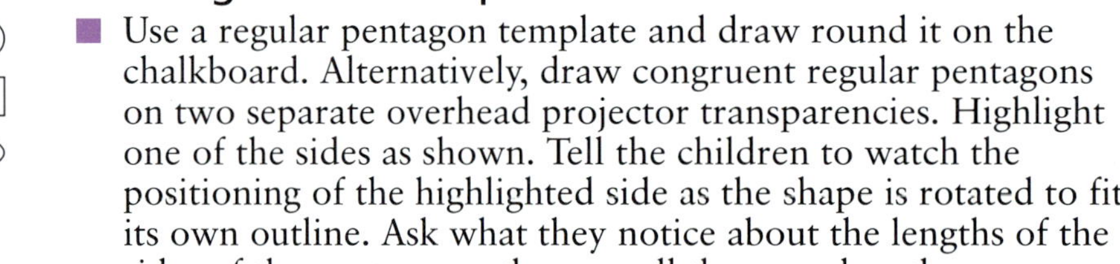

fits only once   **still fits 3 times**   **fits only 2 times**

3   Regular 2D shapes

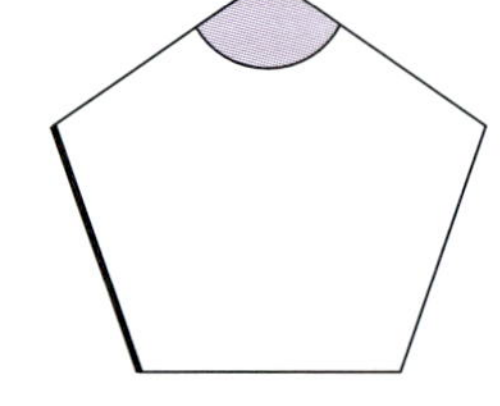

■ Use a regular pentagon template and draw round it on the chalkboard. Alternatively, draw congruent regular pentagons on two separate overhead projector transparencies. Highlight one of the sides as shown. Tell the children to watch the positioning of the highlighted side as the shape is rotated to fit its own outline. Ask what they notice about the lengths of the sides of the pentagon – they are all the same length.

Mark one angle and rotate the pentagon again. Ask the children what they notice about the sizes of the angles of the pentagon – they are all the same size.

Introduce the term 'regular' to describe a shape which has all its sides the same length **and** all its angles the same size. In this case the shape is called a **regular pentagon**.

■ Repeat if necessary for a different regular shape: for example, a **regular hexagon**. Ask the children to name any other regular shapes they know, such as a square and an equilateral triangle.

Workbook page 17 *Rotational and line symmetry*

In question 1, it may be necessary to emphasize the instruction that the
activities should be carried out for each shape **in turn**. For example, once the
name of shape A has been entered in column 1 of the table, the tracing of the
shape should be made and used for finding the entry for column 2. Any lines of
symmetry should be drawn on the given drawing of the shape. Some children
may be able to give the number of fittings in one full turn without the aid of a
tracing. Full names are expected for each triangle – isosceles triangle (shape C)
and equilateral triangle (shape I).

SSM2c/4
SSM2c/4
RS/D2,3 S/D1 S/E1
SEa/4→5

Textbook page 97 *Rotational symmetry*
Workbook page 20

SSM2bc/4
SSM2bc/4
S/E1
SEa/5

The work requires the children to consider how the colours in a design can
affect the number of times the design fits its outline in one full turn.

In questions 2, 3 and 4, it is easier to draw round the shapes from the
Workbook page if they are stuck onto card before being cut out.

In question 4, the children should construct their own shapes on card. Designs
produced by the children could be used to make an attractive wall display. They
should write beside each design the number of times it 'fits' in one full turn.

Additional activity

Rotational symmetry collection

In newspapers, magazines and comics, and in the children's wider environment, there
are many examples of items which display rotational symmetry, such as road signs,
car badges and company logos. The children could collect examples for a wall display
or add them to the wall display suggested above.

TILING: TRANSLATION

The idea of a 'translation' is now introduced. The activities involve the children in

— making a pattern by sliding or translating a shape in a straight line in any
  direction

— creating a design on a square tile and using it to generate a repeating pattern.

Work of this nature may have been met previously by children who have attempted
activities in the Extension Textbook of Heinemann Mathematics 6.

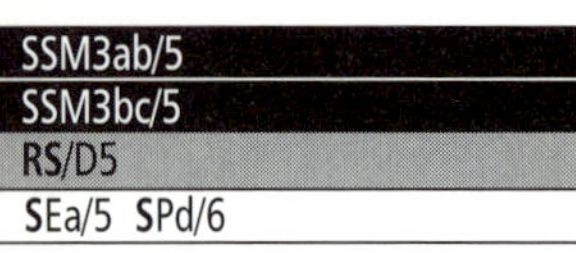

SSM3ab/5
SSM3bc/5
RS/D5
SEa/5   SPd/6

Introductory activity

Slide patterns   *(translating a shape)*

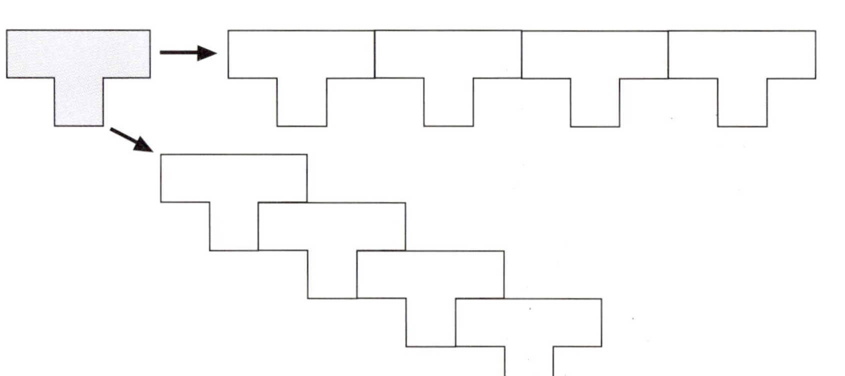

■ Provide card shapes such as these:

Discuss how to slide a card and draw
round it to make patterns. For example,

It is often helpful to draw a faint straight line
and use it as a guide for aligning the card shape
with the existing part of the pattern.

In some patterns the drawn shapes may overlap:

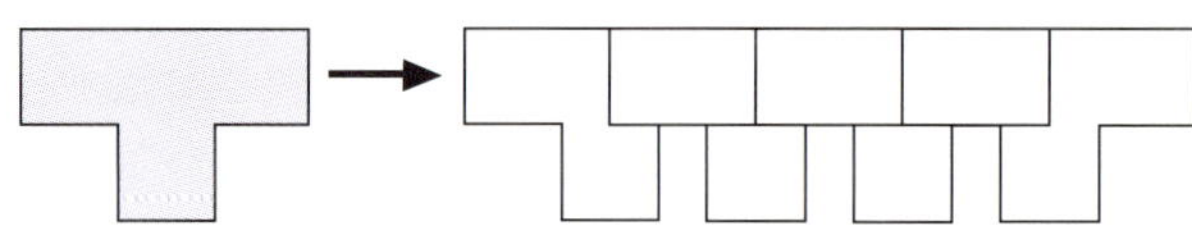

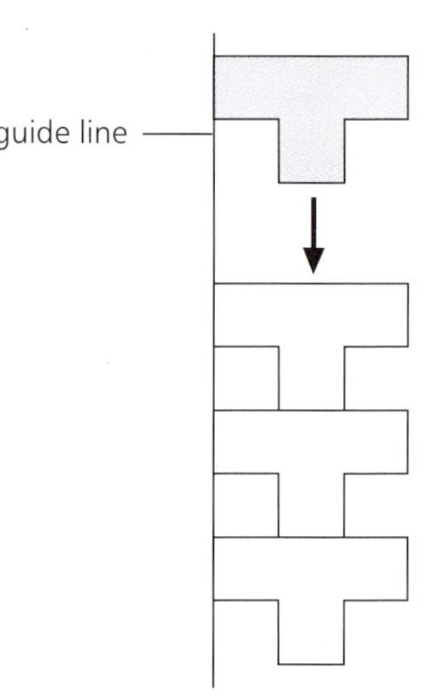

■ Introduce the term 'translate' as a mathematical
word for 'slide', which describes the way in
which the shape is being moved.

SSM3ab/5
SSM3bc/5
RS/D5
SEa/5   SPd/6

Textbook page 98   *Tiling: translation*
Workbook pages 18 and 20

In question 1, the children could trace the shape in the top right-hand corner of
the page on plain paper, or draw it on squared paper before sticking it on card.
It may help to discuss how each of the patterns is made and to remind the
children that the word 'translate' is used to indicate sliding in this way.

In questions 3 and 4, the children, working in groups, use a supply of identical
square or triangular tiles to generate different repeating patterns. It might be
worthwhile sticking Workbook pages 18 and 20 on card before cutting out as
the tiles would then be easier to manipulate when making patterns.

3D shape

Overview

This section

- consolidates and extends work on nets of pyramids and prisms
- looks at relationships between the numbers of faces, vertices and edges of pyramids and prisms.

	Teacher's Notes	Textbook	Workbook	Reinforcement Sheets
Pyramids and prisms	214	99, 100		

Resources

Useful materials

- construction kits with interlocking plastic faces, such as 'Clixi' and 'Polydron'
- other materials suggested within the introductory activities

Assessment and Resources Pack

Assessment

Round-up 2
Questions 5(b), (c)

Resources

Resource Cards
21 Cube puzzle

Teaching notes

In Heinemann Mathematics 6, work on cubes and cuboids was consolidated. Nets and skeleton models of triangular prisms, square pyramids and triangular pyramids were introduced, with some emphasis on their faces, vertices and edges.

This work is now consolidated and the range of pyramids and prisms extended.

PYRAMIDS AND PRISMS

SSM2ab/4
SSM2ab/4
RS/D1,2 RS/E4
SEb/5

Introductory activities

1   Nets   *(revision)*

■ Show the children nets like these made with interlocking shapes or from cartons, cut and opened out.

Invite the children to predict which 3D shape each net will make when folded.

■ Fold the nets. Discuss the name and the numbers of faces, vertices and edges of each 3D shape.

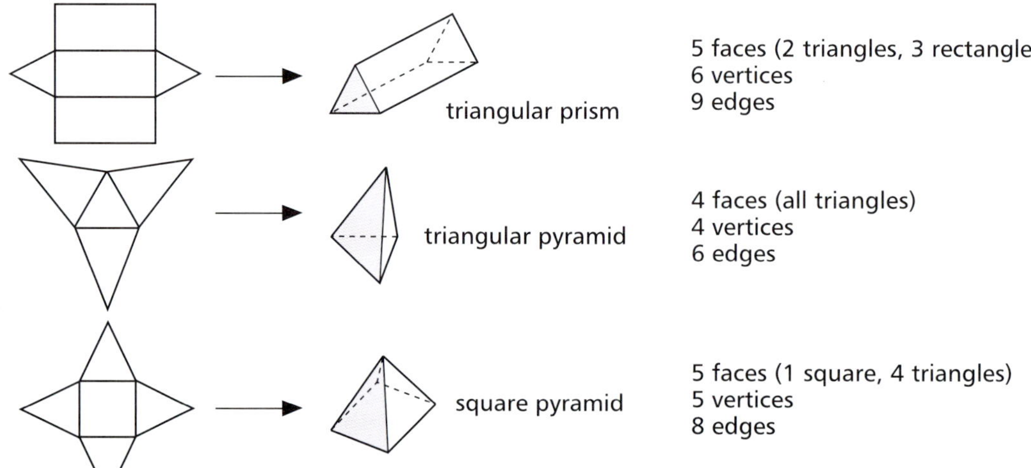

triangular prism

5 faces (2 triangles, 3 rectangles)
6 vertices
9 edges

triangular pyramid

4 faces (all triangles)
4 vertices
6 edges

square pyramid

5 faces (1 square, 4 triangles)
5 vertices
8 edges

2   Pyramids

■ Show the children a set of pyramids like these, perhaps made from interlocking plastic shapes.

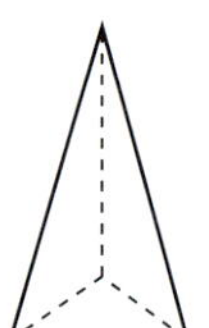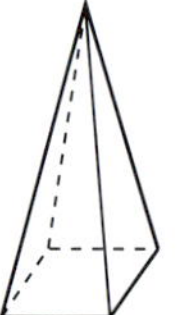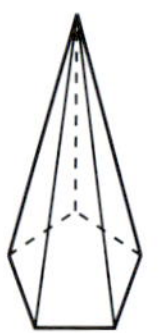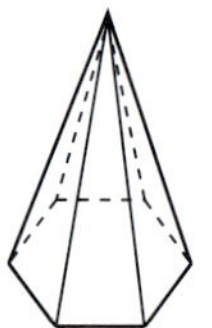

■ Tell the children that each of these shapes is a pyramid. Through discussion, establish that

— each shape comes to a 'point'

— the shape of the 'base' gives each pyramid its name

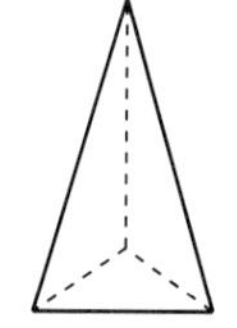  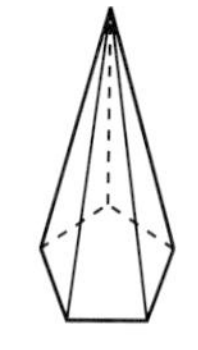 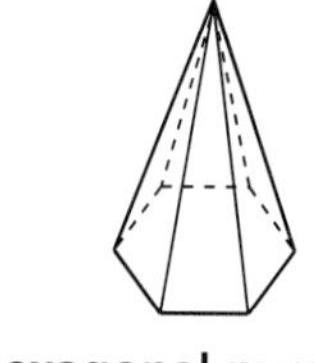

triangular pyramid   **square pyramid**   **pentagonal pyramid**   **hexagonal pyramid**

— all their other faces are triangles.

Some children may ask about a cone – it can be called a 'circular pyramid'.

At this point, the children could try Textbook page 99.

3   Prisms

■ Show the children shapes like these, perhaps made from interlocking plastic shapes.

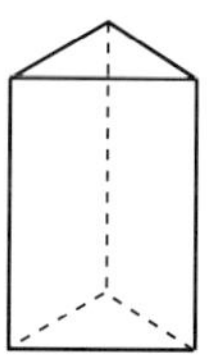 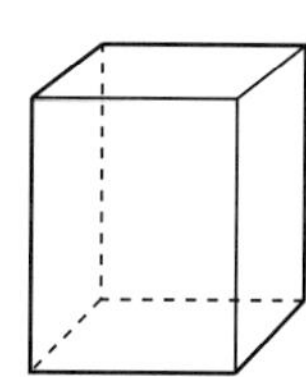 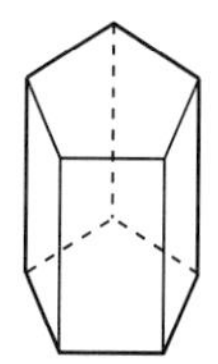 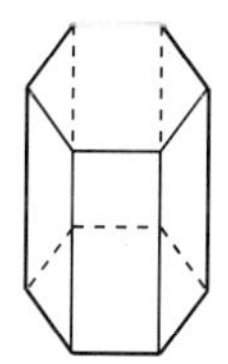

■ Tell the children that each of these shapes is a prism. Establish through discussion that

— the faces at their ends (base and top) are congruent

— these faces give the prisms their names

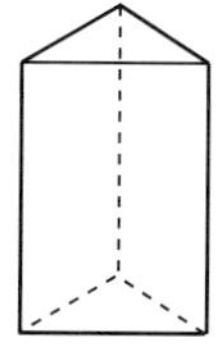 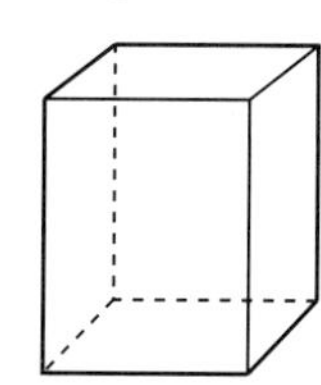 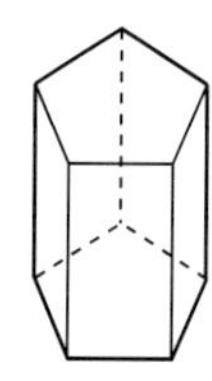 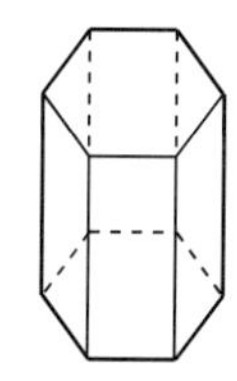

triangular prism   **rectangular prism (cuboid)**   **pentagonal prism**   **hexagonal prism**

— their other faces are rectangles.

A cylinder can be called a 'circular prism'.

Textbook pages 99 and 100
3D shape: nets, faces, vertices and edges

The work of constructing 3D shapes should be shared among a group of children. It is essential that the children use 3D shapes when completing the tables on Textbook pages 99 and 100. Patterns within the tables will be more obvious if the shapes are listed in this order – 'triangular', 'square', 'pentagonal', 'hexagonal'.

On Textbook page 99, in question 2, the children should notice that for each pyramid,

— the numbers of faces and vertices are the same. Each is one more than the number of sides on the 'base' shape

— the number of edges is double the number of sides on the 'base' shape.

Shape	Number of faces	Number of vertices	Number of edges
triangular pyramid	4	4	6
square pyramid	5	5	8
pentagonal pyramid	6	6	10
hexagonal pyramid	7	7	12
heptagonal pyramid	8	8	14
octagonal pyramid	9	9	16

On Textbook page 100, in question 3, the children should notice that the numbers in the 'faces', 'vertices' and 'edges' columns of the table increase by 1, 2 and 3 respectively each time. These patterns should allow them to complete the last two rows.

Shape	Number of faces	Number of vertices	Number of edges
hexagonal prism	8	12	18
heptagonal prism	9	14	21
octagonal prism	10	16	24

Some children may also notice that

— the number of faces is two more than the number of sides on the 'base' shape

— the number of vertices is two times the number of sides on the 'base' shape

— the number of edges is three times the number of sides on the 'base' shape.

In question 4, the children meet a new shape, the **octahedron**, which can be made by sticking two congruent square-based pyramids together.

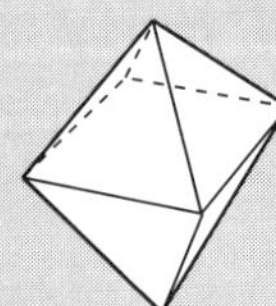

2D shape

Overview

This section

- consolidates knowledge of the side, angle and symmetry properties of isosceles triangles, equilateral triangles and four-sided shapes
- revises the term 'diagonal' and introduces the diagonal properties of squares and rectangles
- introduces the rigidity property of triangles
- introduces parallel lines
- provides further practice in using co-ordinate grids.

	Teacher's Notes	Textbook	Workbook	Reinforcement Sheets
Sides and angles	218	101, 102*	22	31
Diagonals, rigidity	220	103, 104		
Parallel lines	223	105*		
Other activities	225	106, 107		

Homework provided in Home Link-up.

Extension activities:	Teacher's Notes	Extension Textbook
2D shape: curve stitching	269	E25
2D shape: triangle properties, construction	270	E26
Other activity: Celtic designs	272	E30

Resources

Useful materials

- tracing paper
- protractor
- plastic strips and fasteners
- scissors
- centimetre squared paper
- other materials suggested within the introductory activities

Assessment and Resources Pack

Assessment

Check-up 3
Textbook pages 101–5

Round-up 3
Question 3(b)

Resources

Resource Cards
22 Triangle puzzle
(2D shape, problem solving)

Problem Solving Activities
24 Shape sketches (2D shape)

Teaching notes

In Heinemann Mathematics 6, the exploration of side, angle and symmetry properties of 2D shapes was extended to include the parallelogram. The terms 'isosceles' and 'equilateral' were introduced in relation to triangles. These properties are now consolidated by folding, by tracing and turning, and by measuring sides and angles.

SIDES AND ANGLES

SSM2abc,3c/5
SSM2abcd,3c/5 SSM3c/5
S/D1 RS/E1
SEa,Pd/5

Introductory activities

1   Shape properties

■ Make large paper shapes like these.

square   rhombus

■ Ask one of the children to point out a line of symmetry of the square. Fold along the line of symmetry and discuss how the matching parts of the square indicate equal sides and angles.

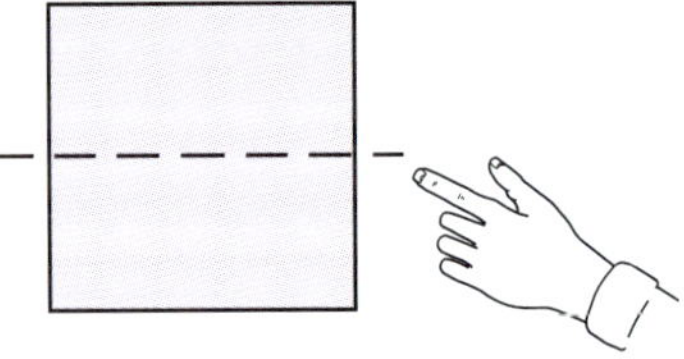

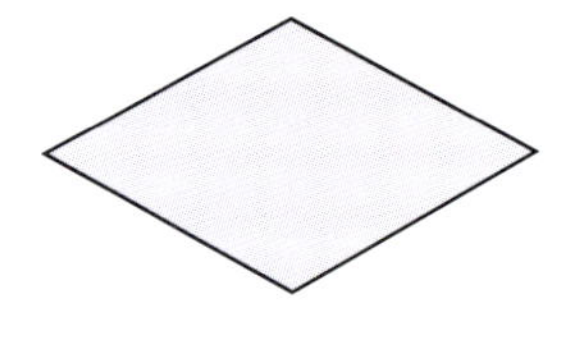

Identify then fold along the other axes of symmetry and confirm that the square has 4 equal sides and 4 equal angles.

Ask one of the children to check these properties by **measuring** the sides and angles of the square.

■ Ask the children to identify the 2 lines of symmetry of the rhombus.

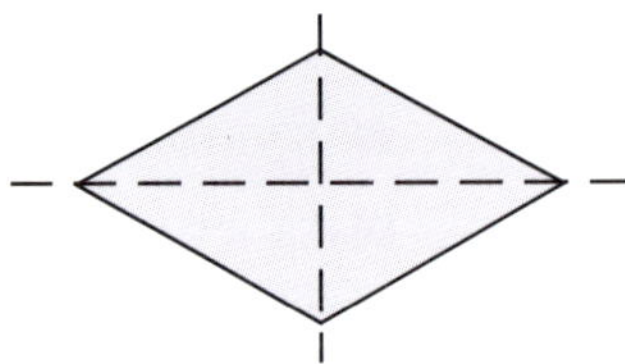

Mark one corner of the rhombus and then make a tracing of the rhombus, marking the same corner.

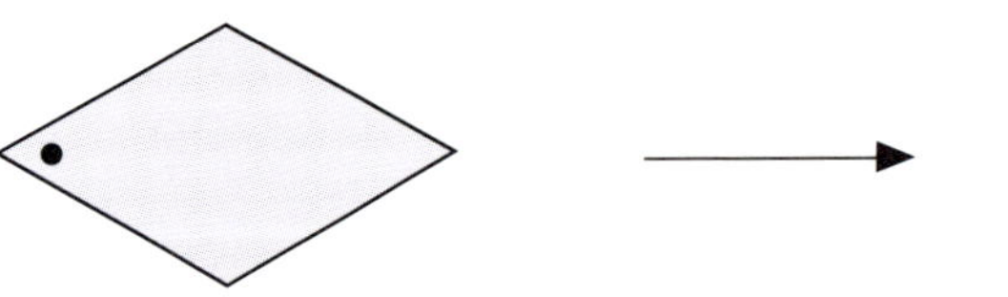
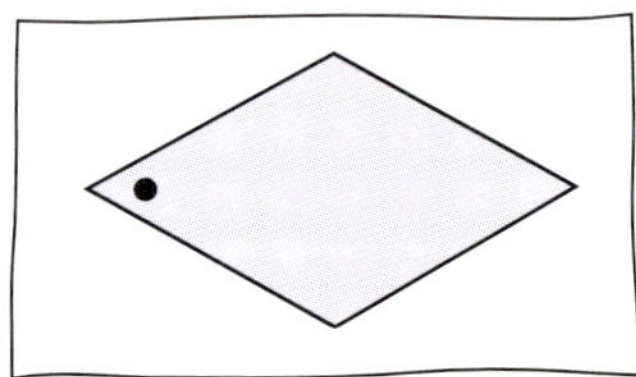

Rotate the tracing until the rhombus fits its own outline again.

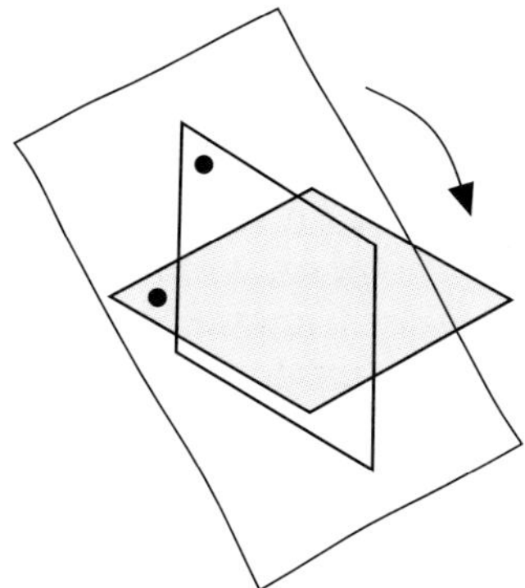

Discuss the matching sides and angles of the rhombus, establishing that its sides are equal and its **opposite** angles are equal.

Ask one of the children to check these properties by **measuring** the sides and angles of the rhombus.

■ Make sure the children realize that they can explore properties of shapes by folding **or** tracing and turning **or** measuring.

2   What shape am I?

■ Display a set of large paper shapes like these.

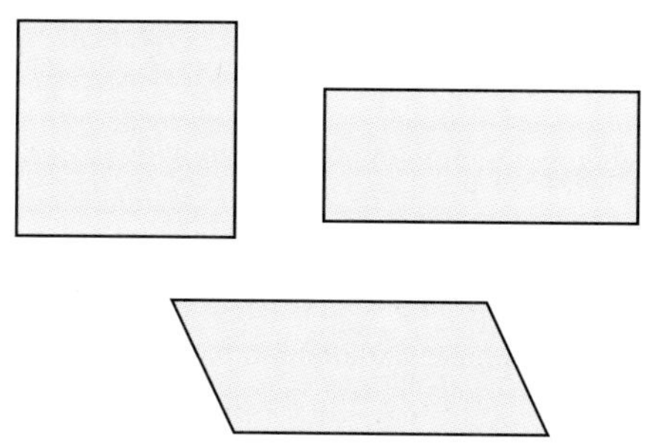

Tell the children that you are **thinking** about one of these shapes and ask them to identify it from a set of clues, read out one at a time. For example,

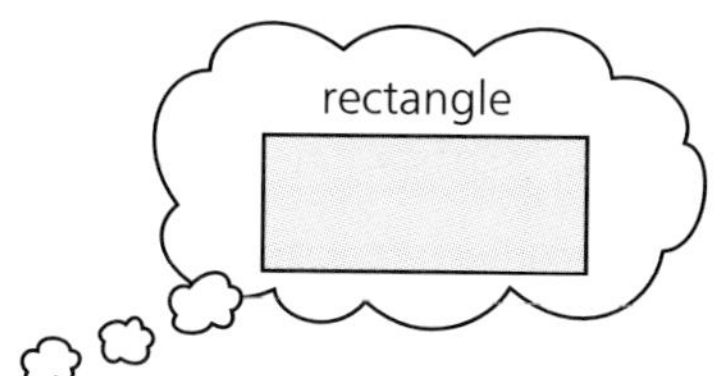

Clues

- It has 4 sides.
- It has 2 different pairs of equal sides.
- It has 2 lines of symmetry.

The children may suggest a number of possible shapes from the first clue: for example, the square, rectangle, rhombus, kite, parallelogram or trapezium. The other clues can then be used to eliminate some of the suggested shapes, leaving only the rectangle.

■ Clues which could be used with other shapes include:

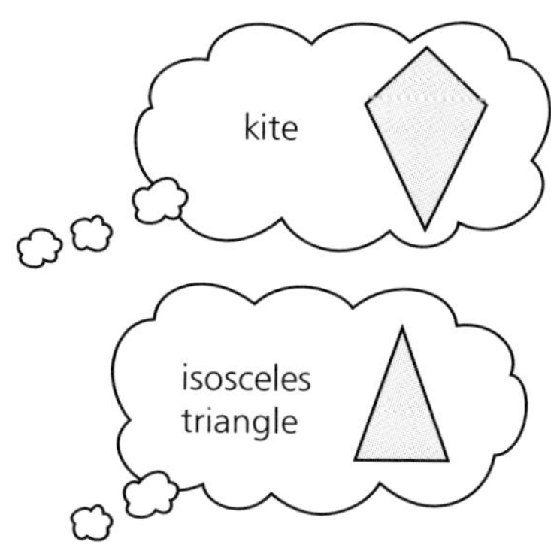

Clues

- It has only 1 axis of symmetry.
- It has 4 sides.
- It has only 1 pair of equal angles.

Clues

- It has 3 sides.
- It has only 1 pair of equal angles.

SSM2abc,3b/5·
SSM2abcd,3c/5
S/D1 RS/E1
PUcf,Ca/5 SEa/5

Problem solving

H59 R31

Textbook pages 101 and 102   *2D shape: sides, angles*
Workbook page 22

On Workbook page 22, it is important that the shapes are accurately cut out as the sides and angles are to be compared.

On Textbook page 101, some children may find it helpful to draw the lines of symmetry first. When the page has been completed, discuss the answers with the children, emphasizing the language that has been used to describe sides and angles. The three techniques of folding, tracing and turning, and measuring should also be discussed as possible ways of finding out about the properties of shapes.

On Textbook page 102, in question 4, the children can choose one or more of the methods used previously to investigate the side and angle properties of each shape.

In question 6(a), various answers are possible. For example,

— red shape: rhombus, parallelogram

— blue shape: square, rhombus, equilateral triangle

— green shape: kite, isosceles triangle

In question 6 (b), the children should decide what each coloured shape is to be and then write a second clue to make the shape unique. For example, to make the red shape a rhombus, the following clue could be used:

> **Clue**
> • Its diagonals are its only lines of symmetry.

DIAGONALS, RIGIDITY

SSM2abc/4
SSM2abcd/4
RS/D1 S/D1
SEa/5

In Heinemann Mathematics 6, the meaning of the term 'diagonal' was first introduced. This work is now consolidated. Through practical investigations which involve constructing 'frameworks' using plastic strips and fasteners, the children

— investigate how to make a framework rigid by adding strips to create triangles

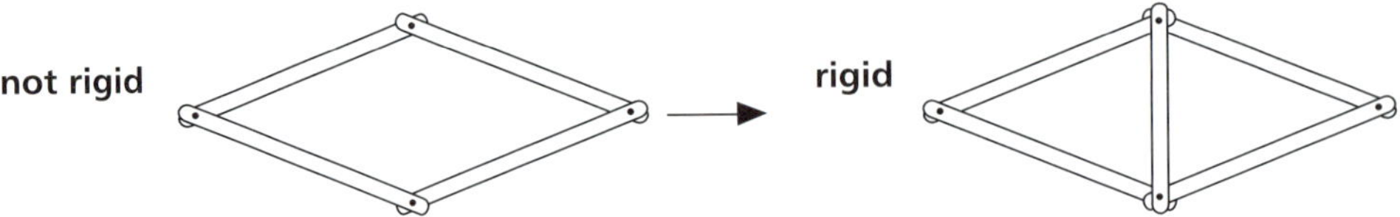

— discover how the form of a 4-sided shape relates to its diagonals

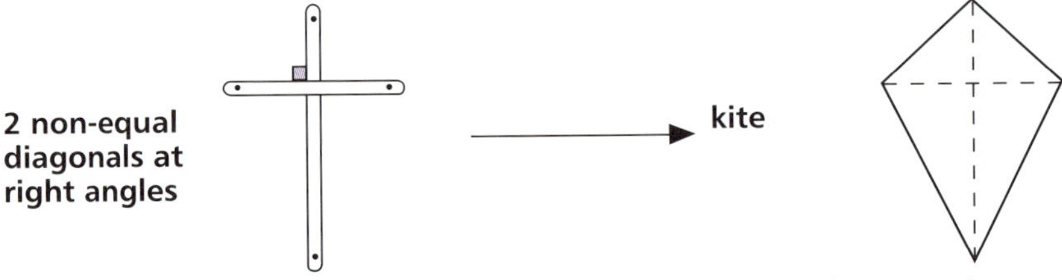

— find that the lengths of the diagonals of squares and rectangles are equal.

Introductory activity

The work in the Textbook is presented as a series of practical investigations which should be self-explanatory. For some children, however, revision of the term 'diagonal' may be necessary.

Diagonals   *(revision)*

Draw – or use plastic strips and elastic to construct – and discuss a variety of shapes, emphasizing that

— a diagonal is a straight line joining two corners of a shape, but it **cannot** be a side

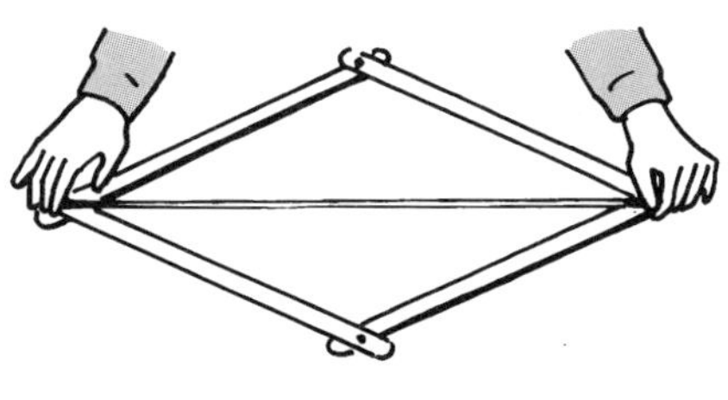

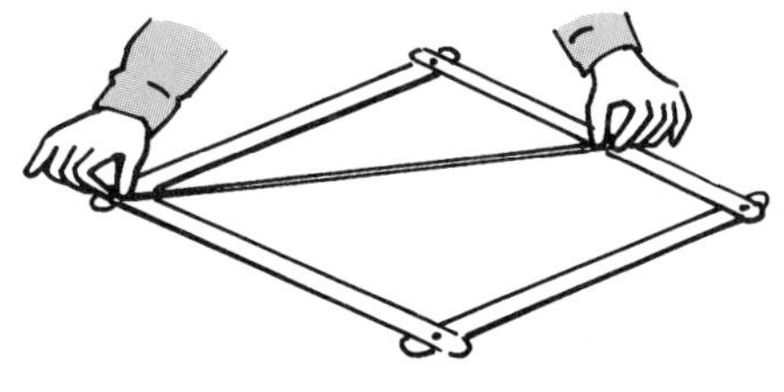

— shapes with four sides have two diagonals

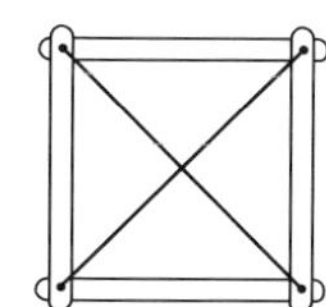

— shapes with more than four sides have more than two diagonals

some of the diagonals of an 8-sided shape (octagon)

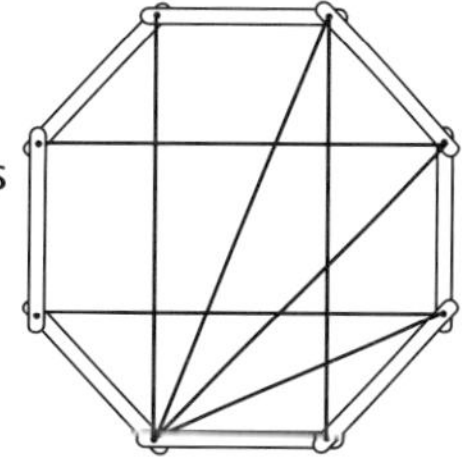

— more than one diagonal can start or finish at the same corner

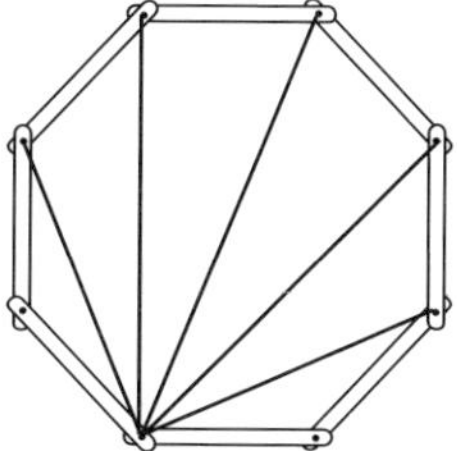

— a diagonal may or may not be a line of symmetry.

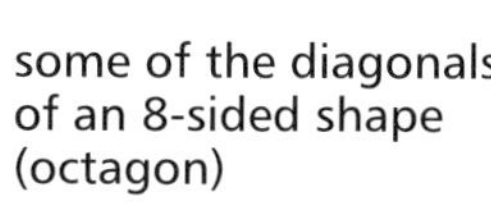

This last point could also be demonstrated by folding a paper hexagon along the diagonal to check whether the two parts on either side of the diagonal match.

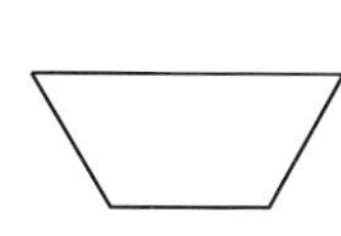

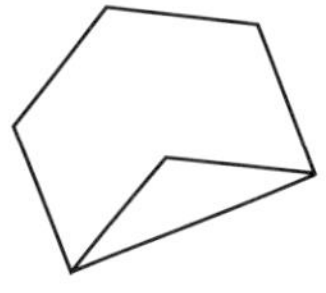

UA2bc/4 UA3ac/5 SSM2ab/4
UA2ab/4 UA3ac/5 SSM2ab/4
PSE RS/D1,7
PCacd/5 SEa/5

Problem solving

Problem solving

SSM2ab/4
SSM2ab/4
RS/D1 RS/E1
PUa,Cd,Re/5 SEa/5

Textbook pages 103   *2D shape: diagonals, rigidity*

The initial work is designed to consolidate the meaning of the term 'diagonal'.

In question 3 (a), suggest to the children that they

— place blank paper on top of the 7-sided shape (heptagon) on the page

— mark each corner of the shape with a dot

— remove the paper and join the dots using a ruler.

In question 3 (c), some children are likely to multiply their answer for the number of diagonals from each corner by 7 to give 28 diagonals. However, this counts each diagonal twice, once in each direction. When the children check by drawing, they should discover that there are only 14 diagonals.

In question 4, the children are likely to use a combination of reasoning and guess and check strategies. Having answered question 3, the children may reason that the shape will have less than 7 sides and they know that a 4-sided shape has only 2 diagonals. They may therefore sketch a pentagon or a hexagon as a first guess and check by drawing all the possible diagonals. The shape with exactly 9 diagonals, a hexagon, need not be regular.

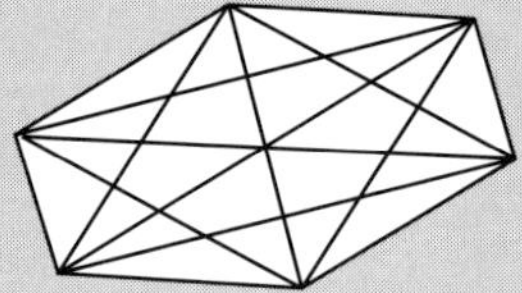

For questions 5 and 6, it is essential that the children have access to strips and fasteners if a proper understanding of what makes a framework rigid is to develop.

In question 8, the children are likely to use a trial and improvement strategy. Some children may be asked to find more than two solutions. Possible solutions are:

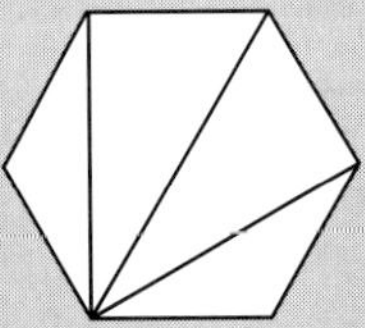 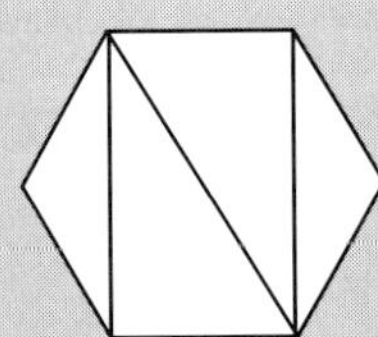 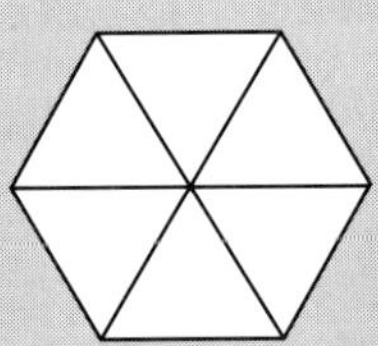

Textbook page 104   *2D shape: diagonals*

It is essential that the children have access to strips and fasteners for this practical investigation. Some children may also benefit from using a right angle tester. In all the questions a ruler should be used when drawing the shapes.

In question 1, some children may need help in interpreting the instructions: for example, by referring them to the illustration.

In question 4 (b), the children could be asked to colour the diagonals of their shapes as this will help them to distinguish between sides and diagonals.

In question 4 (c), the children should notice that the lengths of the diagonals of squares and rectangles are equal. For some children it would be worth examining properties of these diagonals in greater depth:

— the diagonals meet at their mid-points (*or* the diagonals **bisect** each other)

— the diagonals of a square meet at right angles

— the diagonals of a rectangle do not meet at right angles.

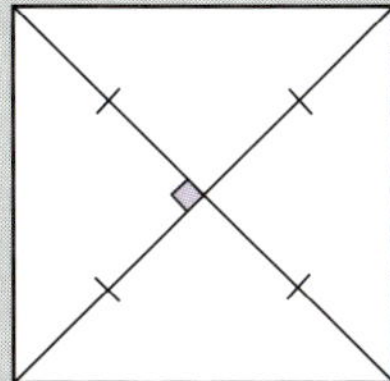
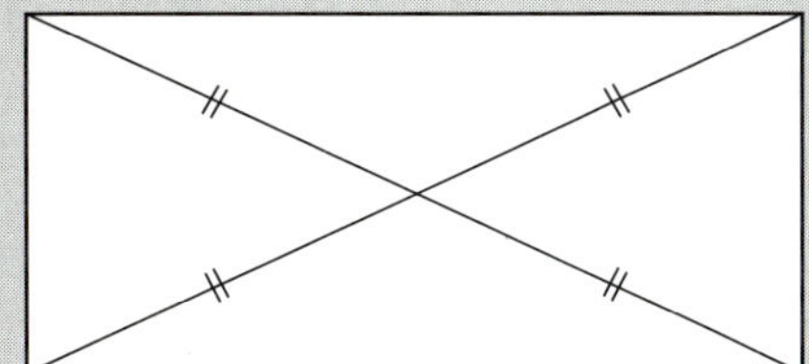

PARALLEL LINES

Introductory activity

Parallel lines

Discuss examples of parallel lines which the children may be familiar with – ruled lines in an exercise book, fence posts, double yellow lines on a road, rail track, etc. Parallel lines can be described as 'always the same distance apart'. Parallel lines do not need to be equal in length.

UA2c/4 SSM3a/5
UA2a/4 SSM3b/5
RS/D
SEa/4→5 SPbe/4

The children should also be asked to point out some parallel lines in the classroom.

UA2c/4 SSM3b/5
UA2a/4 SSM3a/5
PM/D3 RS/D
PCa/5 SEa/4→5 SPbe/4

Problem solving

H60

Textbook page 105   *2D shape: parallel lines*

In question 4, the children draw a new grid for each set of points.

In question 5, the children could use a guess and check approach to find a solution. Possible solutions include placing the sixth point at:

— (6, 3) to make 3 pairs of parallel lines

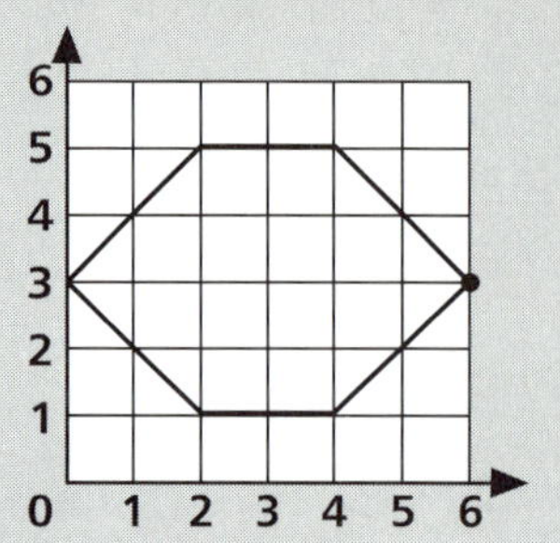

— (5, 4) to make 2 pairs of parallel lines

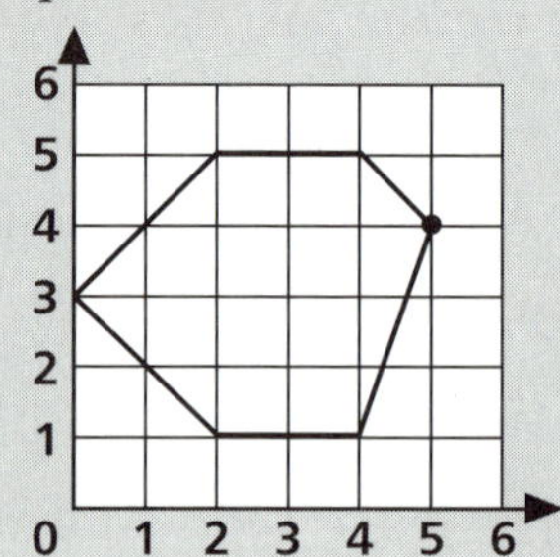

— (6, 4) to have only 1 pair of parallel lines.

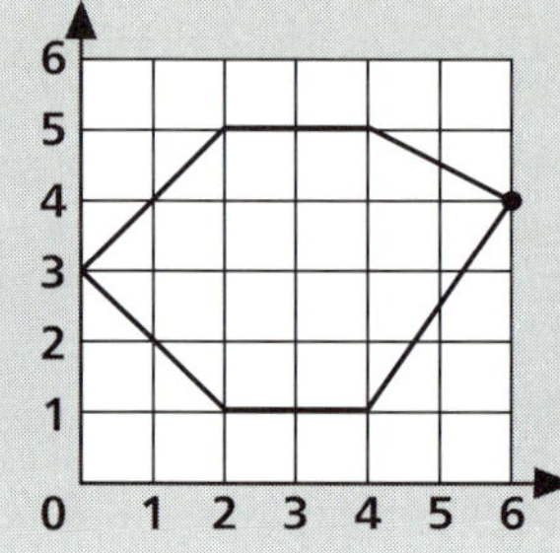

SSM2b/4
SSM2b/4
RS/D4
SEa/5

Textbook page 106   *Other activity: circle patterns*

■ This activity can be attempted at any time.

■ Remind the children how to use a pair of compasses. They should check regularly that the starting radius of 4 cm has not changed.

■ In question 1, this familiar 'flower petal' pattern is produced.

■ In question 2, the children should produce a pattern like this.

■ In question 4, if the children are using blank paper for their own designs, it may be helpful to draw a faint line to keep the centres of the circles aligned:

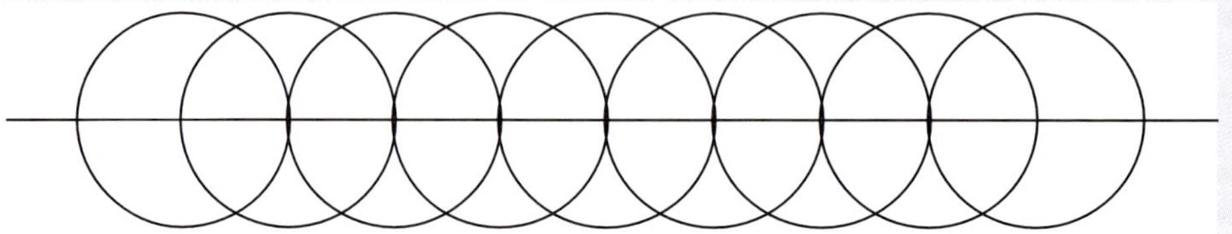

Textbook page 107   *Other activity: 2D shape*

■ The work on this page involves properties of 2D shapes. It is best attempted after Textbook pages 101 and 102 have been completed.

■ The children are required to devise two questions for each illustrated shape: one whose answer is statement A, and the other, statement B. For example, in question 1, suitable questions for statement A (an equilateral triangle) could include:

> What shape is shown here?
>
> What shape has three equal sides?
>
> Which triangle has three equal angles?

and for statement B (2·6 centimetres):

> What is the length of each side of the triangle?
>
> How long is one side of the triangle?

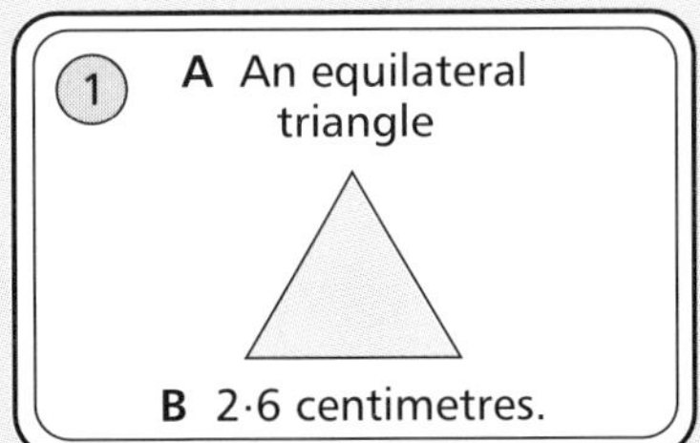

UA3a/5 SSM2a/5
UA3ad/5 SSM2a/5
PSE RS/E1
PRb/5 SEac,Pc/5 Mh/5

Additional activities

1   Circumference and diameter

SSM4c/5→6
SSM4d/5→6
RS/E3
SEd/6

■ Prepare lengths of string to match the diameters of large circular objects such as a lid or a clockface.

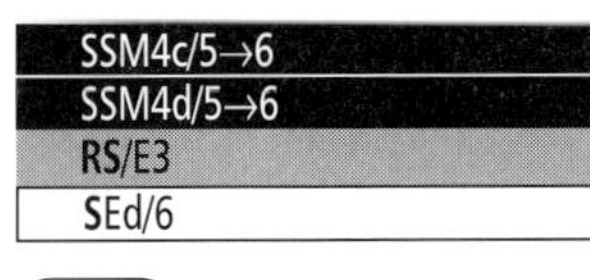

■ Lay each string across the appropriate circle to show the children that its length matches the diameter.

■ For each circle, with the help of the children,
— mark a starting point on the circumference
— fit the string around the circumference, marking each diameter length and counting to see how many times it fits.

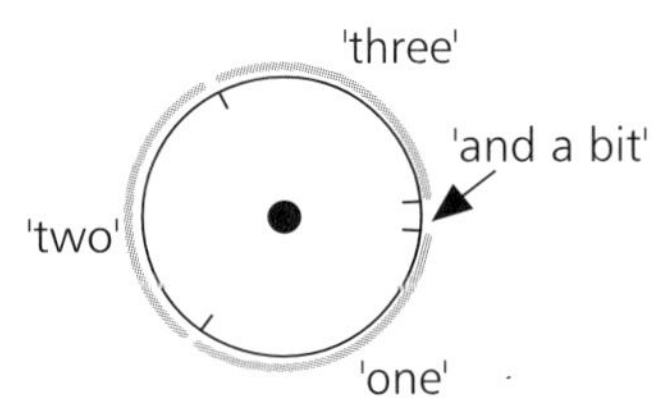

■ Make clear through discussion that **the circumference is 'three and a bit' times the length of the diameter.**

2   Introducing π

■ Ask the children to measure circular objects to find the lengths of
— their circumferences, using a measuring tape
— their diameters, using a ruler or metre stick.

■ Collect the results in a table. Discuss dividing circumference by diameter, using a calculator, to see how many times the diameter fits the circumference. For example,

Circle	Circumference	Diameter	Circumference ÷ Diameter
A	48 cm	15 cm	3·2
B	35 cm	11 cm	3·1818181
C	92 cm	29 cm	3·1724137

Discuss the values in the last column to support the idea that the diameter fits 'three and a bit' times.

■ Tell the children that the circumference of any circle is about 3·14 times the length of its diameter. Introduce the symbol π, pronounced 'pi', and state that, for any circle, **circumference is π times diameter.**

The Handling Data part of Heinemann Mathematics P7 has two sections, Handling Data and Probability. The work associated with the first of these sections is presented in the context of 'Bike Awareness Week', a bicycle care and safety campaign involving children from several schools.

Handling data

There is a final section in Heinemann Mathematics P7: 'Mixed mathematics'. This section integrates a wide range of mathematical topics and is set in the context of a town called Arnley.

Mixed Mathematics

Bike Awareness Week

A context for Handling data

The work on Textbook pages 108–16 and Workbook pages 31–4 is set in the context of 'Bike Awareness Week', during which children from schools in Beckford are involved in a campaign to make them more aware of the need to take care of their bikes and to improve their cycling safety standards. The children also find out about local and national cycling events.

Introducing the context

The context could be introduced by discussing the different types of bike which the children have or know about. Various accessories for bikes and for cyclists could also be discussed.

1 Cycling events

The children could find out from television, newspapers and specialist magazines about local, national and international cycling events such as mountain biking, the Milk Race, the Tour de France and the Olympic Games. The *Guinness Book of Records* contains interesting information about cycling events and records. It may also be possible to access information using a CD-rom encyclopaedia or through the Internet.

The children could use the information they collect to create a database highlighting, for example,

— what the events are

— where they take place

— distances involved

— types of race

— equipment used

— competitors

— record holders.

2 Cycling exhibition

In groups the children could prepare items for display in a 'cycling exhibition'.
For example, they could

— investigate the measurements of a bike and display their results on a poster

— produce a poster about the vocabulary associated with bikes – reference
books, specialist magazines and sales catalogues could be referred to

— find out about past, current and perhaps future developments in bikes and
equipment that cyclists use. Their findings, in pictorial and report forms,
could be displayed under a suitable title, such as 'Cycling Through the 20th
Century'.

3 Road Safety

Discuss with the children how they could become safer cyclists – for example, by

— using cycle ways whenever possible

— taking a cycling proficiency course

— always wearing a helmet

— ensuring their bikes are well maintained.

Make a wall display of the suggestions.

The edges of the display could be surrounded by examples of cycling equipment, such
as a helmet, pair of gloves, jersey, lights, water bottle, pump and toolkit.

4 Helping others

Ask the children to suggest ways in which they could help younger children to
improve their cycling skills. For example, they could

— sketch a plan of a cycle track that could be laid out in the playground and
used to allow the younger children to practise cycling

— devise a simple cycling proficiency programme for the younger children.
This might include information about bike maintenance, appropriate
clothing, road signs and where to cycle.

UA3bc/4	UA3bcd/4
UA3abc/5	UA3abcde/5
HD2abc/4	HD2acdef/4
HD2abcd/5	HD2abcdefg/5

PSE
C/D1
C/E2
O/C1
O/D1
O/E1,2
D/D1,2
I/D1
I/E1,2,3

PUbcd/5
PCd/5
PRbce/5
NUd/5
HCbcf/4
HCbcef/5
HRc/6

Handling data

Overview

This section

- introduces the use of more complex questionnaires for collecting and organizing data

- introduces combined bar graphs in both horizontal and vertical forms

- introduces simple pie charts

- revises trend graphs

- revises median, mode and mean and introduces calculation of the range

- consolidates organizing data in a frequency table and displaying it as a bar graph with and without class intervals

- includes designing questionnaires and carrying out surveys

- consolidates extracting and interpreting data from tables.

	Teacher's Notes	Textbook	Workbook	Reinforcement Sheets
Bike Awareness Week: a context for Handling data	226			
Questionnaires	230	108		
Combined bar graphs	231	109, 110*	31	
Pie charts	235	111*	32*	
Trend graphs	236	112		
Range, median, mode, mean	237	113*		
Frequency tables and bar graphs, including class intervals	238	114*	33, 34*	32
Surveys	240	115, 116		
Other activity	242	117		

Homework provided in Home Link-up.

An extension activity related to the above section of work is as follows:

	Teacher's Notes	Extension Textbook
Handling data: interpretation, money	271	E28, 29

Teaching notes for the Extension Textbook are in a separate section at the end of the Teacher's Notes.

Resources

Useful materials

- squared paper, including 2 mm, $\frac{1}{2}$ cm and 1 cm grids
- calculators
- computer database and spreadsheet packages
- other materials suggested within the introductory activities

Assessment and Resources Pack

Assessment

Handling data Check-up 1
Textbook pages 109–10
Workbook page 31
(Combined bar graphs)

Handling data Check-up 2
Textbook pages 108, 111
Workbook page 32
(Questionnaire, pie charts)

Handling data Check-up 3
Textbook pages 113, 114
Workbook pages 33, 34
(Range, median, mode, mean,
bar graphs, class intervals)

Handling data Check-up 4
Textbook pages 118–20
(Probability)

Round-up 1
Question 7

Round-up 2
Question 6

Round-up 3
Question 5

Resources

Problem Solving Activities
29 Birdwatching
     (Interpreting data, pie chart)
30 Inveralmond league
     (Interpreting data, tables)
31 Daily diet
     (Interpreting data)

Resource Cards
23, 24 Bikes
         (Handling data)

Teaching notes

QUESTIONNAIRES

In Heinemann Mathematics 6, the children collected data by drawing a simple sketch of the survey location and recording the data on the sketch. At an earlier stage, the children used a yes/no questionnaire.

The work is now extended to involve the children in collecting, organizing and interpreting data gathered using a questionnaire, where each question has from three to five possible responses.

The context of Bike Awareness Week is introduced, with children from one of the schools in Beckford completing questionnaires about their bikes.

Introductory activity

1   Out-of-school activities

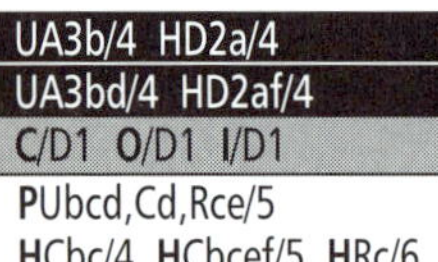

UA3b/4 HD2a/4
UA3bd/4 HD2af/4
C/D1 O/D1 I/D1
PUbcd,Cd,Rce/5
HCbc/4 HCbcef/5 HRc/6

■ Display a questionnaire about the children's leisure pursuits when they are not at school. For example,

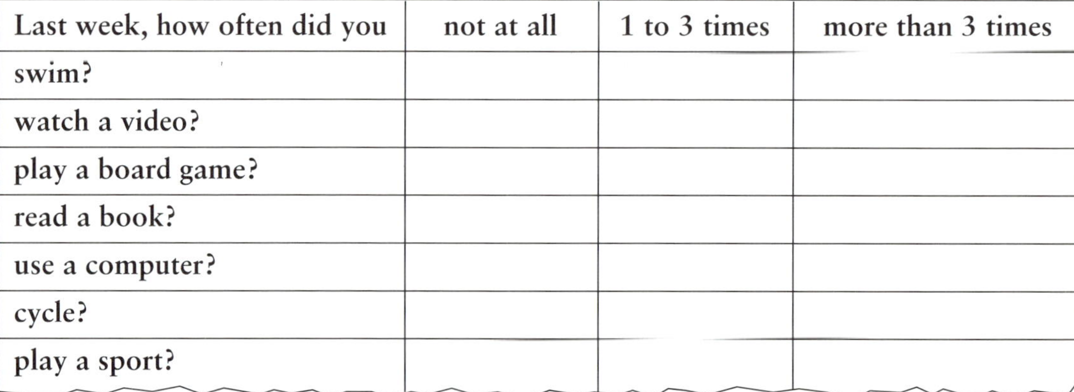

Last week, how often did you	not at all	1 to 3 times	more than 3 times
swim?			
watch a video?			
play a board game?			
read a book?			
use a computer?			
cycle?			
play a sport?			

Discuss the purpose of a questionnaire and who might use one. Ask the children to describe questionnaires they may have seen in magazines or elsewhere.

■ Complete the questionnaire. This could be done by taking each question in turn and asking for a show of hands. Analyse the data collected to see if any general statements can be made about the types of activity. For example,

— the most popular activity was cycling

— none of the children played a board game

— about half watched from 1 to 3 videos

— twice as many children cycled more than 3 times as went swimming more than 3 times.

Discuss ways in which the data could be displayed. Graphs of some of the data could be produced.

■ Using the same set of questions, the children could survey another class in the school to find out whether the statements which are true for their own class are also true for the other class.

Textbook page 108   *Handling data: questionnaires*

Twenty-one blank copies of the questionnaire which appears on this page are required for use in questions 2 and 3. These may be photocopied from page 243 of these notes.

The Bike Awareness Week context should be discussed if this has not already been done as part of the introductory work.

In question 1(c), some children may have difficulty realizing that, to find the number of bikes with more than 5 gears, they have to add together the number with 6–12 gears and the number with more than 12 gears.

In question 1(d), the fraction of the bikes with dropped handlebars is $\frac{6}{30}$ or $\frac{1}{5}$. The fraction of bikes which have water bottles is $\frac{18}{30}$ or $\frac{3}{5}$.

In question 1(e), the children should realize that some bikes in the survey have more than one of the accessories listed.

Before starting question 2, the children should decide how the information is to be collected. Encourage them to discuss

— which people should be given a questionnaire

— how the questionnaires should be distributed

— whether they should complete the questionnaires with the respondents or leave them to be filled in and collected later.

In question 4(b), the children should be encouraged to write facts which are different from those in part (a).

UA3b/4	HD2a/4
UA3bd/4	HD2af/4
C/D1	O/D1	I/D1
HCe/5

COMBINED BAR GRAPHS

In earlier stages of Heinemann Mathematics, work with bar graphs included both vertical and horizontal forms using a wide range of scales. Two more complex forms of bar graphs are now introduced:

— combined bar graphs in which two bar graphs are joined in a single display

— combined bar graphs in which several different responses to the same survey question are displayed.

The Bike Awareness Week context continues, using results from a survey of school cyclists.

Textbook page 109   *Handling data: bar graphs*

As this page revises bar graphs, the children should be able to attempt the questions without the support of any introductory activities. However, some children may need to be reminded of the meaning of 'mode', the item of data which occurs most frequently – in this case, the most common answer.

In question 4, encourage the children to think of different ways of differentiating answers by boys and by girls.

UA3bc/4	HD2abc/4
UA3bcd/4	HD2cdf/4
PSE D/D1	I/D1
HCe/5

Problem solving

Introductory activity

Circus bikes   *(combined bar graphs)*

- Explain that stunt cyclists from a circus visit Fortview
  school during Bike Awareness Week to demonstrate
  their skills and to let the children try out some cycling
  tricks, such as

    — weaving in and out among a row of skittles

    — jumping over an object lying on the ground

    — cycling with the front wheel off the ground

    — cycling without holding the handlebars.

- Display graphs like these, which show the numbers of children who could manage
  the tricks.

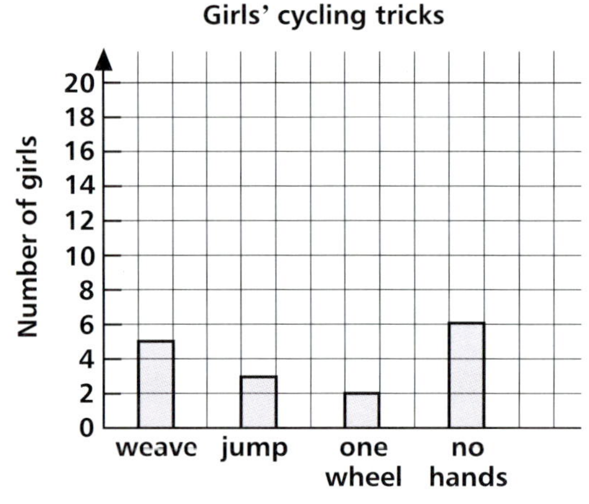

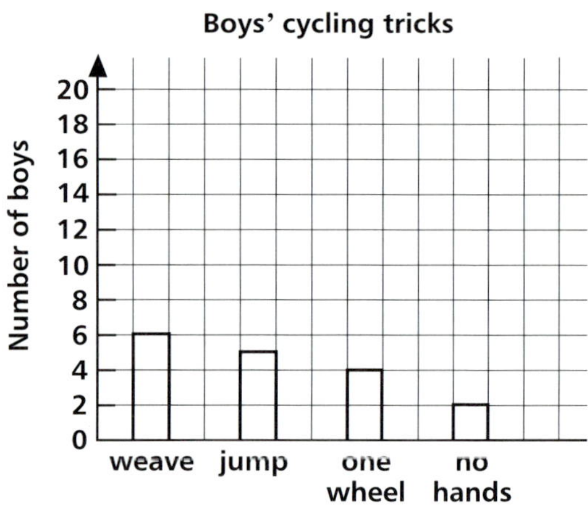

Ask the children to describe how the graphs could be combined into a single
graph.

Modify the graphs by

— drawing bars to represent the boys **above** the existing ones on the girls' graph.	— drawing bars to represent the girls **alongside** the existing ones on the boys' graph.

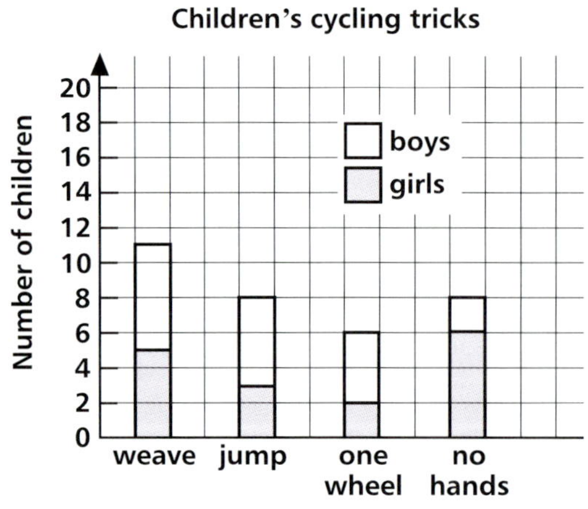

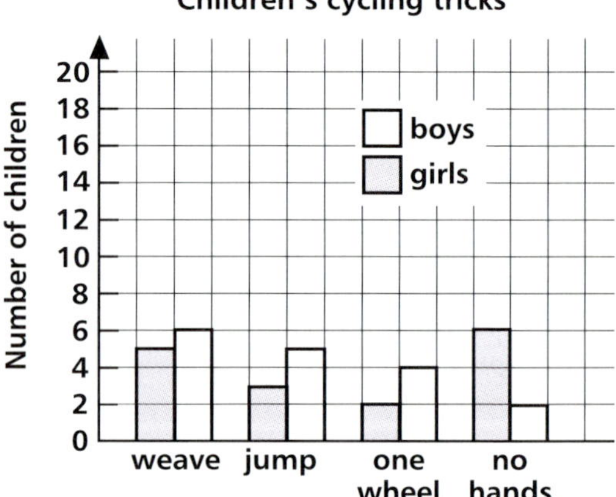

Discuss with the children the need to

— modify the title and the label on the vertical axis

— insert a key to differentiate between bars representing boys and bars representing girls.

Complete the graphs accordingly.

■ Discuss the relative merits of each form of graph:

— the **first graph** shows more clearly the **total number of children** who could manage each trick and is useful for answering a question such as 'Which trick did fewest children manage?'

— the **second graph** shows more clearly the **relative achievement of the boys and the girls** and is useful for answering a question such as 'Which tricks did more boys than girls manage?'

UA3bc/5 HD2ab/5
UA3bcd/5 HD2cf/5
D/D1 I/D1 I/E2
PUc,Cd,Rb/5 HCbc/5

Workbook page 31   *Handling data: combined bar graphs*

The children's answers to question 2 should be discussed to emphasize that some types of question are easier to answer using one form of combined graph rather than the other.

In question 3, some initial help may be required as the bars are shown horizontally.

In question 4, encourage the children to try to make their questions of a different type from those asked in question 2. For example,

— 'Which item was owned by nearly all the children?' (Graph Q)

— 'Did fewer boys than girls own a spanner?' (Graph P)

Introductory activity

Parent bike survey   *(combined bar graphs)*

■ Explain that some children in Fortview school took part in a survey about their families' cycling habits. Display the following table, which shows some of the information collected.

UA3bc/5 HD2ab/5
UA3bc/5 HD2cf/5
D/D1 I/D1 I/E2
PUc,Cd,Rb/5 HCbc/5

Do you have a parent who	Yes	No	Not sure
can cycle?	15	3	2
has a bike?	6	13	1
cycles at least once a week?	4	16	0

Through discussion, build up a combined bar graph as shown which displays **all** the information in the table.

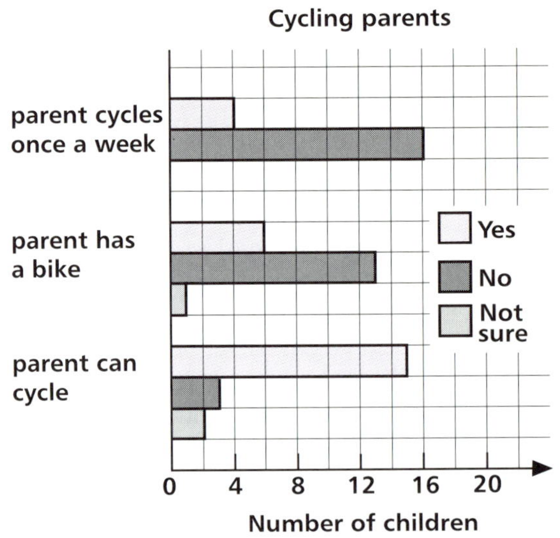

- Ask questions which require the children to interpret the graph. For example,

  — 'How many children answered each question?'

  — 'What fraction of the children have parents who can cycle?'

  — 'Why are there only two bars beside "parent cycles once a week"?'

  — 'Which question resulted in the greatest number of "No" responses?'

Textbook page 110   *Handling data: combined bar graphs*

Discuss the illustrations

  — at the top of the page, which show **questions** about class 7's cycling habits

  — in the middle of the page, which show **answers** given by Class 6 in a survey about safe cycling.

In questions 1 and 2, some children may need help to interpret the keys provided with the graphs.

In question 2(c), there should be some class or group discussion of the 'advice' suggested by individual children.

For question 3, a suitable size of squared grid is $\frac{1}{2}$ cm. The graph can be in vertical or horizontal form.

H61

234

Interpretation and display of data using pie charts is now introduced. The Bike Awareness Week context continues with the scenario of the types of bike owned by children in Denvale school.

Introductory activities

1 Bike magazines *(concept of a pie chart)*

■ Display a pie chart like this to show the bike magazines sold by Denvale newsagents.

Through discussion, establish that the greater the area of the slice of the 'pie', the greater the number of readers it represents. In this example, *Bike Time* is the magazine read by the greatest number of children.

■ Ask a variety of questions which require the children to interpret the pie chart. For example,

— 'Which magazine is read by the fewest number of children?'

— 'Is *Bike Time* read by less than half the children?'

— 'Which magazine is read by more children, *Cycle News* or *Bike Mania*?'

2 Magazine sales *(interpretation of a pie chart)*

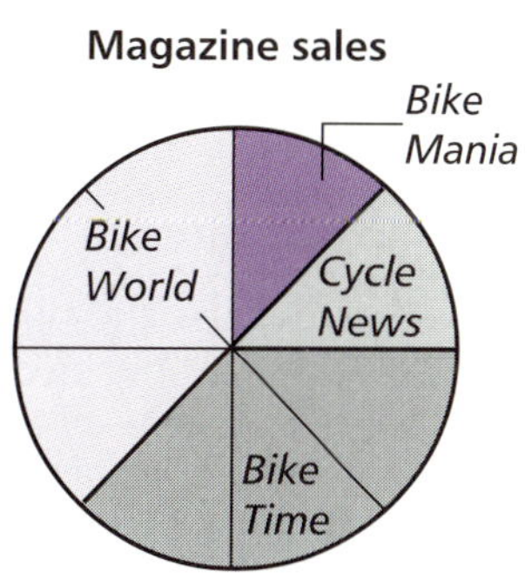
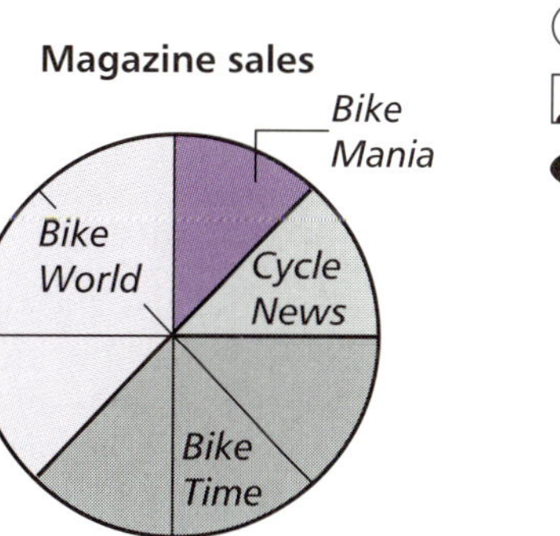

■ Display a pie chart to show the bike magazines bought by eight children in Class 7 at Denvale school.

Through discussion establish that

— there are eight slices or parts in the pie chart

— each part represents one child.

■ Ask a variety of questions about the pie chart. For example,

— 'What magazine was bought by fewest children?'

— 'How many children bought *Bike Time*?'

— What fraction of the children bought *Bike World*?'

3 Bike accessories *(construction of a pie chart)*

■ Explain that ten children in Class 7 were asked which one of four accessories they would choose for their bike. Display their choices as shown.

lights	padlock	bell	water bottle
2	3	4	1

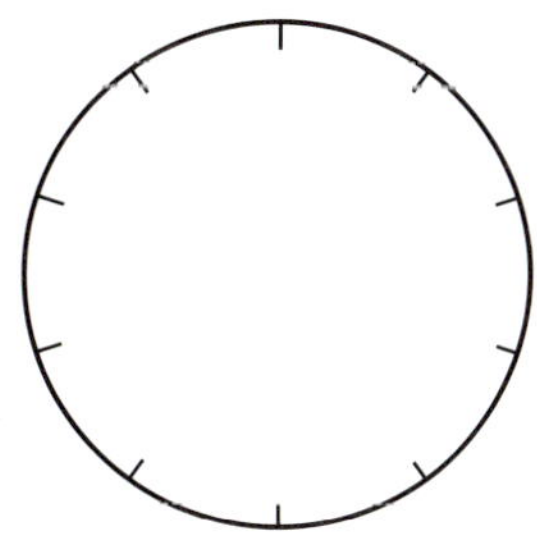

■ Display a circle marked off in ten equal parts and establish that each part represents one child's choice of accessory.

Involve the children in completing a pie chart to represent the given data.

UA3abc/5 HD2ab/5
UA3abcd/5 HD2cf/5
D/D1 I/D1
NUd/5 HCc/5

H62

Textbook page 111   *Handling data: pie charts*
Workbook page 32

On Textbook page 111, in question 2, the children should find their answers by visually comparing the areas of slices on the pie chart.

In questions 5 and 7, the children should simplify the fractions where possible. For example, in question 5(c), $\frac{2}{10}$ simplifies to $\frac{1}{5}$.

On Workbook page 32, in question 2, it may be helpful if the information is collected by a small group of children and then made available for use by others.

TREND GRAPHS

Trend graphs were introduced in Heinemann Mathematics 6 and are now consolidated.

The Bike Awareness Week context continues with an analysis of information about the number of accidents over a period of years in Beckford and Caldwell.

UA3b/5 HD2a/5
UA3bd/5 HD2f/5
I/D1
PRe/5 HCb/5

Introductory activity

Cycling to school   *(revision – trend graphs)*

■ Display this bar-line graph, which shows the number of Class 7 children cycling to Fortview school on the first Monday of the first 6 months of the year.

Ask the children to

— describe the trend (each month the number cycling to school increases)

— suggest a reason for the trend (more children are allowed to cycle to school as this becomes safer with improving weather)

— suggest how to make the trend more obvious (by marking only the top of each line and then joining adjacent tops with a broken line).

■ Display the trend graph alongside the original bar-line graph and confirm the trend – each month the number of children cycling to school increases.

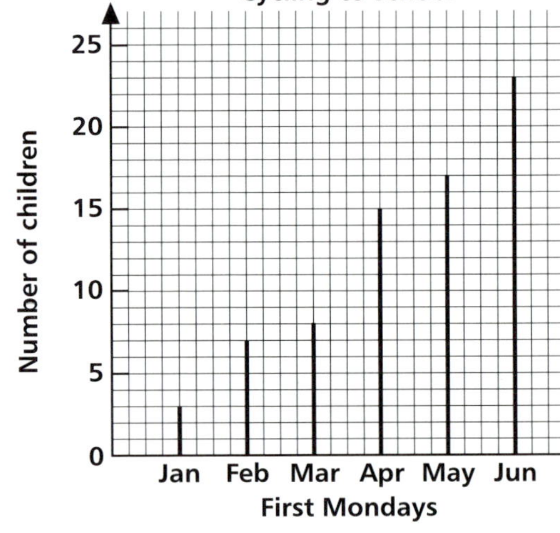

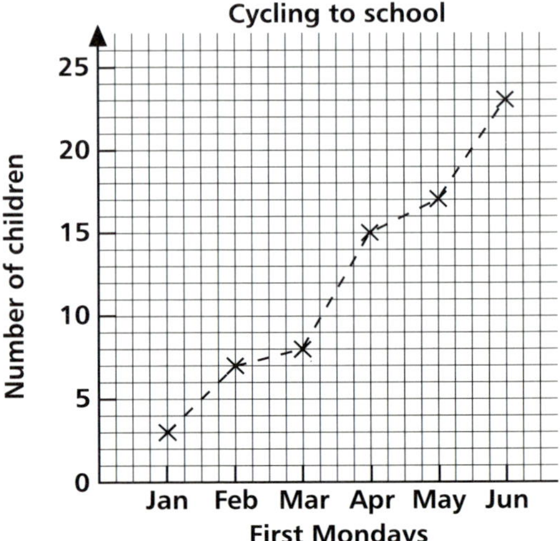

Textbook page 112   *Handling data: trend graphs*

It may be helpful to discuss the first trend graph, its scale and how it has been constructed.

In question 4, the years suggested by the children for the opening of the first cycle way should be discussed. In 1990, the number of accidents reached a peak and, from 1991 onwards, the numbers began to fall. This would suggest that the cycle way opened during 1991 or possibly towards the end of 1990.

In question 7, $\frac{1}{2}$ cm squared paper could be used if 2 mm squared paper is unavailable.

RANGE, MEDIAN, MODE, MEAN

In Heinemann Mathematics 6, finding the mean or average was consolidated and the terms 'mode' and 'median' were introduced. The children also identified the lowest and highest values in a set of data and linked these to the phrase 'the values **range from ____ to ____**'.

The median, mode and mean are now revised and calculation of the actual range (the difference between the highest and lowest values) is introduced.

The scenario for the work is a 'wheelie' competition, one of the special events held during Beckford's Bike Awareness Week.

Introductory activity

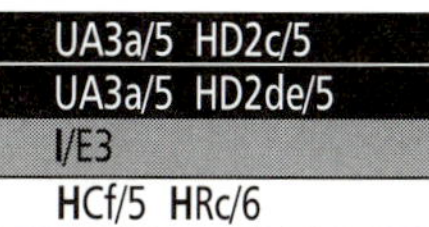

Competitions   *(median, mode, mean, range)*

■ Display the following set of data, which gives the number of entrants in a 'wheelie' competition from eleven different schools.

   6   10   11   5   7   11   12   5   8   11   13

Using the data, revise the meanings of median, mode and mean

— when the data is listed **in order**, the number **in the middle** is called the **median**.

   5   5   6   7   8   10   11   11   11   12   13

               └─ the median is **10**.

— the item which occurs **most frequently** is called the mode. **The mode is 11.**

— the total of all the items divided by the number of items is called the **mean**. The mean is $99 \div 11 = 9$.

■ Use the data to introduce calculation of the range. Ask the children to give the highest (13) and the lowest (5) number of entrants and revise the language 'the number of entrants **ranges from 5 to 13**'.

Explain that the difference between the highest and the lowest numbers is called the **range**. In this example, the range is $13 - 5 = 8$.

■ Repeat for different sets of data. For example,

— the number of entrants from the eleven schools in the 'bike maintenance' competition:

   6   9   11   4   6   7   12   5   6   10   12

— the number of entrants from the eleven schools in the 'best decorated bike' competition:

12   10   8   13   11   9   7   12   12   9   7

Note: The difficulty of finding the median in a set in which the number of items of data is **even** is left until a later stage.

Textbook page 113 *Handling data: range, median, mode, mean*

The questions require the children to calculate the range, median, mode and mean for four sets of data.

Question 2(h) may cause some difficulty as none of the children in the table had the mean score (20) in Round 3. This should be discussed with the group or class.

H63

FREQUENCY TABLES AND BAR GRAPHS, INCLUDING CLASS INTERVALS

In Heinemann Mathematics 6, organizing data in a frequency table using class intervals was introduced.

This work is now consolidated and the term 'frequency' introduced. At this stage the children are not expected to **choose** class intervals when organizing data.

The scenario of special events held during Beckford's Bike Awareness Week continues.

Workbook page 33 *Handling data: frequency tables*

Discuss the scenario. The Highway Code Test and the Cycling Proficiency Test are special events held during Beckford's Bike Awareness Week. The discussion should cover the meanings of the road signs illustrated on the page:

no cycling	Cycle route ahead	No right turn	School bus	National speed limit applies	Double bend first to left	Pedal cycles only

Discuss the use of the heading 'frequency' in place of 'number' in the frequency table.

In questions 1 and 2, some guidance may be required.

In 1(a) and 2(a), the data should be scanned to pick out the lowest and highest scores, and these scores should be circled. A mental calculation will then give the range.

In 1(b) and 2(b), each score should be ticked or scored out as its tally mark is entered in the frequency table. This ensures that each score is used once and once only.

In 2(c), the children can use the same scale for the 'Number of children' as in question 1.

Introductory activity

Sprint scores *(revision – organizing and displaying data using class intervals)*

- Display the scores awarded to 30 children who took part in the sprint event during the Beckford Trials. Build up a frequency table of the scores using class intervals.

Sprint scores					
4	12	8	9	10	21
6	11	15	3	13	16
22	5	13	14	8	7
18	4	18	23	17	13
10	15	13	19	16	12

Scores	Tally marks	Frequency
1–5	IIII	4
6–10	ⵑ II	7
11–15	ⵑ ⵑ	10
16–20	ⵑ I	6
21–25	III	3
	Total	30

In the discussion, emphasize that

— a class interval includes several scores. For example, the class interval 11–15 contains any of the scores 11, 12, 13, 14 and 15

— the class intervals are all of equal size

— the lowest score (3) is within the first class interval (1–5) and the highest score (23) is within the last class interval (21–25).

- Display the data in a bar graph and remind the children that

  — a space can be left between the first bar and the frequency axis

  — adjacent bars can touch.

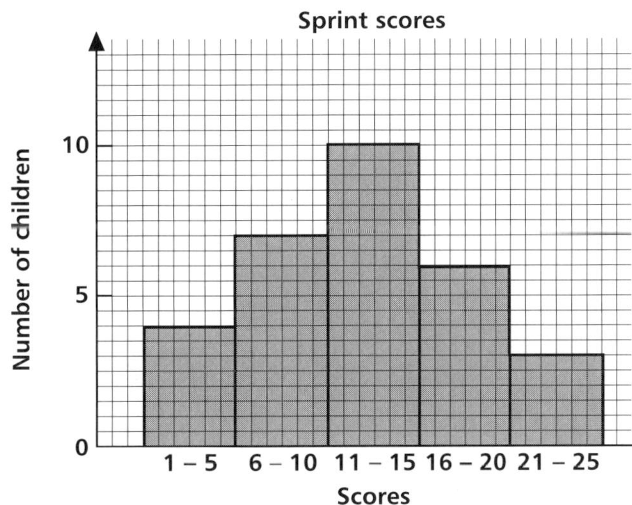

Textbook page 114   *Handling data: class intervals*
Workbook page 34

The cycle-cross context and the idea of Stage points should be discussed. If the introductory activity has not been carried out, the children may need to be reminded of the use of class intervals and the style of bar graph used on the pages.

On Textbook page 114, in question 1(a), it is worth discussing that the number of cyclists (36) can be found using either the table or the bar graph.

On Workbook page 34, in both questions, the children should check that their answer to part (a) and the total frequency in the table in part (c) are the same.

R32 **H**64

SURVEYS

In Heinemann Mathematics 6, the children collected data by drawing a simple sketch of the survey location and recording the data on the sketch. They also worked with database and spreadsheet software packages.

This work is now extended to

— designing and using a questionnaire to collect, organize and interpret data, where each question has more than two possible responses

— collecting data by practical measurement to produce a simple spreadsheet

— designing and carrying out a whole school survey.

The children also have the opportunity to work with a spreadsheet software package. The theme of the questionnaires and surveys is 'safe cycling'.

Textbook pages 115 and 116 *Handling data: surveys*

The work on these two pages requires the children to use and apply, in real situations, the range of handling data skills and techniques which they have acquired. Set the scene through a discussion of Textbook page 115, questions 1(a) and (b).

In question 1(a), encourage the children to

— think about questions which refer to, for example, the cyclists, their bikes and road safety rules

— group their questions using categories such as the above in preparation for designing the questionnaire in part (c).

Some of the questions could be discussed in order to highlight the difference between 'open' questions such as

'What type of bike do you have?'

and 'closed' questions such as

'What type of bike do you have?'   racer ☐   BMX ☐   other ☐

In question 1(b), discuss the advantages and disadvantages of different ways of recording answers – for example, tick boxes, sentence completion and open responses. At this stage a simple tick box system makes it easier to record, collate and analyse the data.

In question 1(c), suggest to the children that they

— discuss the order in which the questions should be asked so that the questionnaire is easier to complete

— sort the questions into groups of related items.

In question 1(d), the task of producing 20 copies of the questionnaire could be shared among the group, or the teacher could arrange for photocopies to be made. Before the children ask 20 cyclists to complete the questionnaire, they should decide

— who is going to collect data and from whom

— when the data is to be collected

— how the responses will be collated.

They could also 'test' the questionnaire with other children before undertaking the real survey.

In question 1(e), encourage the use of tables and charts as well as graphs. The data could be displayed in a booklet or as a wallchart.

In question 1(f), the children are likely to identify the number of respondents giving a particular answer. For suitable fields of data, it might also be possible to calculate a measure such as range, mode, median or mean.

In question 1(g), it may be necessary to emphasize that the suggestions for improving safety should be based **on the data displayed**.

On Textbook page 116, in question 2, enough children may come to school by bike for the data to be collected at school. Alternatively, individual children could make the required measurements at home, bring them to school and share the data. Measurements should be made to the nearest centimetre. The data collected in this activity could be used with suitable software to set up a simple spreadsheet.

In question 3, the children should discuss

— how they intend to tackle the problem

— which tasks each member of the group will be responsible for.

The children should also consider

— how a whole school survey of cyclists could be carried out

— how many cyclists should be surveyed

— the types of question to be asked

— how the responses will be recorded

— how the data will be organized, displayed and analysed.

Encourage the children to be creative and to make their plans and posters as clear and informative as possible.

Additional activity

Using a spreadsheet

UA3b/4 HD2a/4
UA3b/4 HD2a/4
O/E2 I/E1
Hce/5

A spreadsheet is computer software which allows numbers and text to be entered into a table. The user can read totals and means, change data that has been entered, create graphs and explore relationships between different rows or columns. Documentation forming part of the spreadsheet package explains how to set up and use the spreadsheet.

The data collected by the children in question 2 on Textbook page 116 could be used to set up a spreadsheet. Detailed suggestions about how to do this for a similar set of data are provided on pages 266 and 267 of the Teacher's Notes for Heinemann Mathematics 6.

UA3c/5	SSM2ab,3b/5
UA3c/5	SSM2ab,3c/5
RS/D5	S/E2 S/4b
SEa/5	

Textbook page 117   *Other activity: tiling*

■ This activity involves producing tesselations where the basic tile is designed by altering a rectangle. Although the work can be attempted at any time, it would be particularly appropriate after the children have completed the translation work on Textbook page 98.

■ In question 1, discuss the instructions for constructing a basic tile. The card rectangle could be of any size, but suitable dimensions are 5 cm by $2\frac{1}{2}$ cm or 4 cm by 2 cm. Some children might find it easier to use squared grid card. Alternatively, they could draw the basic tile on squared grid or squared dotty paper, before sticking it on card and cutting it out.

■ Emphasize the need to align the card template carefully with any existing tiles before drawing round it to extend the tessellation. It may be worthwhile including the term 'congruent' in the discussion.

■ In question 2, examples of basic tiles are provided. However, the children should be encouraged to design their own tiles and decorate the resulting tessellation.

BAW QUESTIONNAIRE   Name: _______________

Type of bike	Mountain	Racer	BMX	other
Number of gears	less than 6	6 – 12	more than 12	
Style of handlebars		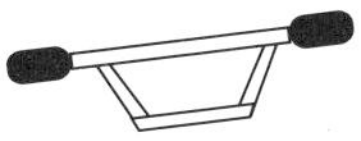	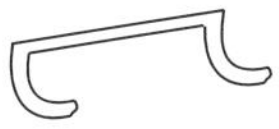	other
Colour of bike	white	silver	red	blue	other
Accessories	mudguards	lights	pump	water bottle	

BAW QUESTIONNAIRE   Name: _______________

Type of bike	Mountain	Racer	BMX	other
Number of gears	less than 6	6 – 12	more than 12	
Style of handlebars		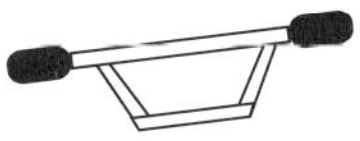	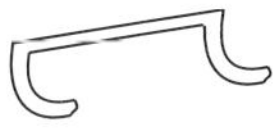	other
Colour of bike	white	silver	red	blue	other
Accessories	mudguards	lights	pump	water bottle	

UA3ac/5	UA3a,4a/5
HD3ab/5	HD3ab/5

PUacdf/5
PCad/5
PRce/5
HPc/5

Probability

Overview

This section

■ revises work on describing the likelihood of events

■ introduces a probability scale with markings 0, $\frac{1}{2}$, 1

■ deals with estimating probabilities as

    0   less than $\frac{1}{2}$ $\frac{1}{2}$ more than $\frac{1}{2}$ 1

■ consolidates and extends work using the language 'fair', 'unfair' and 'equal chance'.

	Teacher's Notes	Textbook	Workbook	Reinforcement Sheets
Estimating probabilities	245	118, 119		
Changing probabilities	248	120*		

Homework provided in Home Link-up.

Resources

Useful materials

■ dice, coins

■ cocktail sticks, triangular paper, Blu-tack

■ other materials suggested within the introductory activities

Assessment and Resources Pack

Assessment

Handling data Check-up 4
Textbook pages 118–20
(Probability)

Teaching notes

In Heinemann Mathematics 6, work on language associated with likelihood was consolidated and extended. Ideas of 'evens' and fairness were introduced and the children listed outcomes of events.

In this section, a probability scale with markings 0, $\frac{1}{2}$, 1 is introduced and descriptions of likelihood are extended to estimating probabilities as 0, less than $\frac{1}{2}$, $\frac{1}{2}$, more than $\frac{1}{2}$ or 1. Ways of changing the probability of an outcome are considered, as are 'fair' and 'unfair' activities.

The context involves activities at a fairground.

ESTIMATING PROBABILITIES

Introductory activities

UA3ac/5 HD3ab/5
UA3a,4a/5 HD3ab/5

PUc,Cad,Rce/5 HPc/5

1   Likelihood   *(revision)*

■ Draw a scale like this on the chalkboard.

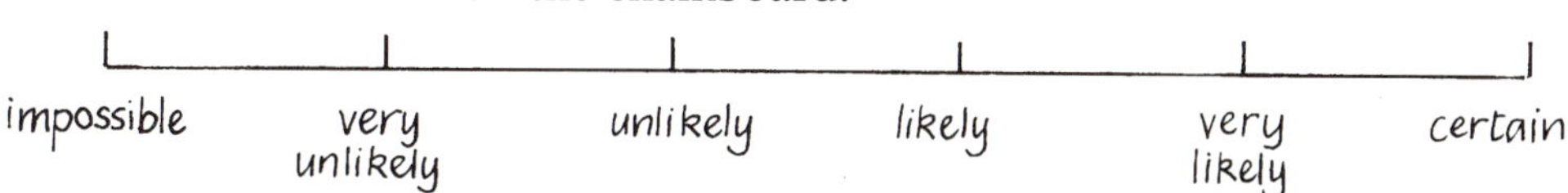

■ Draw four arrows on the scale and tell the children that they show how likely four different events are.

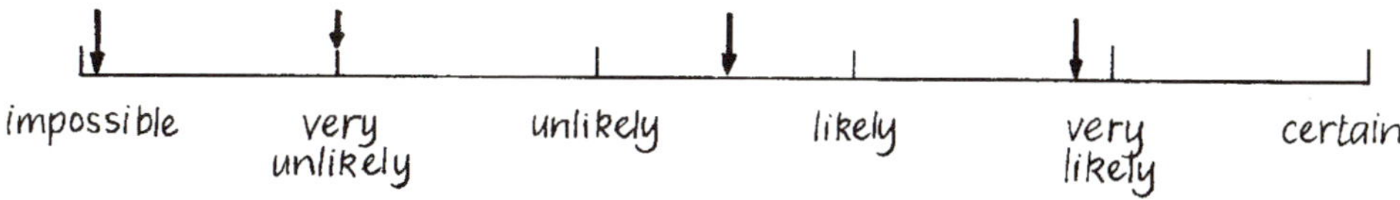

Ask the children which one of these events they think matches each arrow.

- (A) having your picture in the newspaper next year
- (B) receiving something to wear among your Christmas presents
- (C) choosing six correct numbers in the National Lottery
- (D) dropping a slice of bread and jam to land jam side up.

Other events could be used instead of these.

■ After discussion, and with the help of the children, allocate events to arrows.

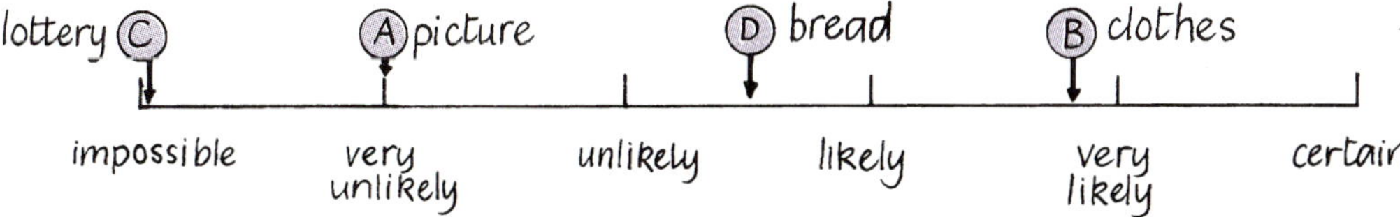

Discuss the likelihood of each event. For example,

— It is **almost impossible** to choose six correct Lottery numbers

— it is **very unlikely** that you will have your picture in the paper

— a slice of bread and jam is neither likely nor unlikely to fall jam side up. There is an **equal chance** of 'jam up' and 'jam down' – the chances are **evens**

— most people find that they are **more than likely** to be given something to wear at Christmas.

2   Probability scale

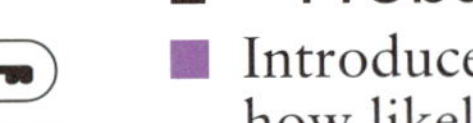

■ Introduce the word 'probability' to describe the chance of something happening – how likely it is. Draw a probability scale with markings 0 ('impossible'), $\frac{1}{2}$ and 1 ('certain') on a chalkboard.

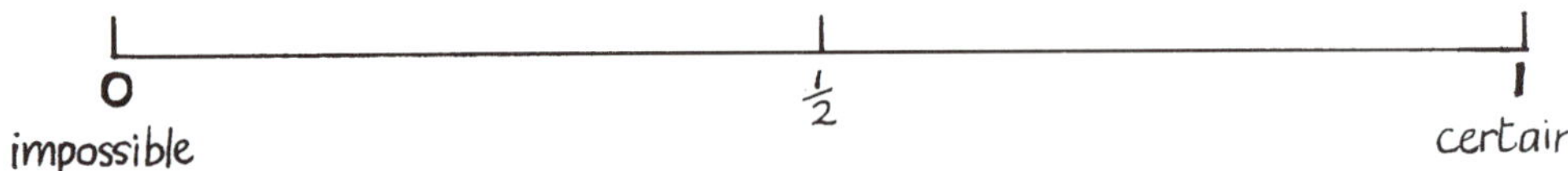

■ Give new descriptions of the likelihood of the four events from activity 1.

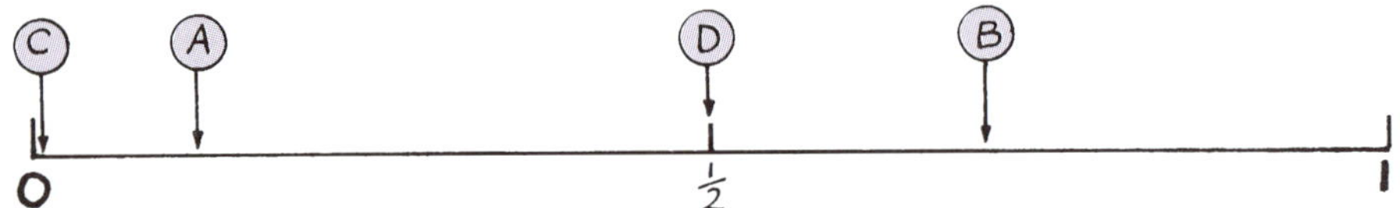

The probabilities of A and C are each **less than** $\frac{1}{2}$.

The probability of D is $\frac{1}{2}$ – **evens**.

The probability of B is **more than** $\frac{1}{2}$.

Ask the children to describe events which would have a probability of **0**: for example, 'being younger tomorrow'.

Repeat for a probability of **1**: for example, 'Guy Fawkes Day will be on November 5th next year'.

3   Pick a number

■ Consider an activity where all the possible outcomes are known: for example, picking one numbered ball from a tub containing this set:

■ There are **20 numbers** altogether, each equally likely to be picked. Ask the children to list all the numbers which could be picked to win if the winning ball had to show

— an odd number: 1, 3, 5, 7, 9, 11, 13, 15, 17, 19 (ten numbers).
Ten out of the twenty numbers are odd.
The probability of an odd number is $\frac{1}{2}$.   (10 out of 20)

— a multiple of 5: 5, 10, 15, 20 (four numbers).
The probability is **less than** $\frac{1}{2}$.   (4 out of 20)

— a number greater than 20: (there are none).
The probability is **0**.

— a number with '1' as a digit:

> 1, 10, 11, 12, 13, 14, 15, 16, 17, 18, 19 (eleven numbers).

> The probability is **more than** $\frac{1}{2}$.   (11 out of 20)

4   Experiments

It is worthwhile asking the children to carry out simple experiments as a rough check on probabilities they have found by thinking about a situation. For example,

— the probability of cutting a pack of playing cards to reveal a red card is $\frac{1}{2}$ (equal numbers of red and black cards).
The children could cut a pack, say, 30 times to see if a red card really turned up **about half** the time.
A larger number of trials will usually give a result closer to the theoretical probability of $\frac{1}{2}$.

— the probability of picking a black cube out of a bag with 1 white, 5 black and 14 red cubes in it is less than $\frac{1}{2}$ (5 out of 20).
The children could pick one cube, record its colour, replace it and shake the bag. If this action is repeated several times, the number of black cubes picked should be **less than half** the number of trials.

UA3ac/5 HD3ab/5
UA3a,4a/5 HD3ab/5

PUc,Cd,Rc/5 HPc/5

Textbook pages 118 and 119   *Probability*

On Textbook page 118, in question 1, the likelihood of some of the events could be described in different ways. For example,

— Debbie ringing the bell: very, very unlikely/almost no chance of happening/nearly impossible

— Elaine eating candy floss: evens/neither likely nor unlikely.

In question 2, there are no green squares with a star on grid R, so the probability of a win is 0.

In question 3 (b), the children may need to be convinced, perhaps by throwing a die, that the probability of a six is **less than** $\frac{1}{2}$. A six is no more likely than a one, two, three, four or five.

In question 3(c), it may be helpful for the children to list outcomes:

— numbers less than 5: 1, 2, 3, 4 (four numbers)

— The probability is **more than** $\frac{1}{2}$ (4 out of 6).

The children could throw a die several times to check that a number less than 5 occurs in **more than half** the throws.

On Textbook page 119, make sure that the children realize the connection between questions 1 and 2 (and between questions 3 and 4). For example, in question 1 (d), they list all the multiples of 7 on the Wheel of Fortune: 14, 21, 35, 49 (four numbers). They should use this in question 2 (d) to find the probability of the pointer stopping at a multiple of 7. There are **four** multiples of 7 and **twelve** numbers altogether on the Wheel of Fortune.

— The probability is **less than** $\frac{1}{2}$ (4 out of 12).

Ways of changing probabilities and situations which are 'unfair' are now considered. The context of fairground activities continues.

Introductory activities

1 Changing probabilities

■ Prepare a cube to act as a die, by writing these numbers on its faces:

1, 2, 2, 2, 4, 4

Ask a child to throw the die several times and record the results. It is best to continue the throws until the results show more twos than fours and more fours than ones.

■ Let the children examine the die so that they see that the numbers are 1, 2, 2, 2, 4, 4. Discuss the probability of throwing

— a one: **less than** $\frac{1}{2}$ (1 out of 6)

— a two: $\frac{1}{2}$ (3 out of 6)

— a four: **less than** $\frac{1}{2}$ (2 out of 6).

■ Ask the children how they would alter the die to give

— **equal probabilities for 1, 2 and 4.** Some might suggest re-numbering – 1, 2, 3, 4, 5, 6. They might suggest changing one of the twos to a one so that the die is numbered 1, 1, 2, 2, 4, 4. A fairly large number of trials should then show that 1, 2 and 4 each occur roughly the same number of times and are now equally likely. The probability of each would be less than $\frac{1}{2}$ (2 out of 6).

— **a probability of more than $\frac{1}{2}$ that the die will show a one.** A possible method is to change the numbers to 1, 1, 1, 1, 2, 4. This gives a probability of more than $\frac{1}{2}$ for throwing a one. Practical experiment should result in a one occurring for **more than half** the throws.

2 Fair and unfair

■ Discuss ideas of fairness with regard to dice. The usual 'fair' die is numbered 1 to 6, with each number **equally likely** to be thrown.

■ The children may be able to suggest a way of making an ordinary 1 to 6 die 'unfair' – by adding weight to a corner or to one face so that the numbers are **not** equally likely to be thrown. For example, a biased die may show a six far more often than it should.

UA3ac/5 HD3ab/5
UA3a,4a/5 HD3ab/5

PUacdf,Cd,Rc/5 HPc/5

Textbook page 120 *Probability*

In question 1 (b), the probability of a red ball could be changed to $\frac{1}{2}$ for machine X by taking out 1 red ball and replacing it by either a green or yellow ball. This would give 4 red balls out of 8 and a probability of $\frac{1}{2}$.

In question 3 (b), the children should find a roughly equal distribution of the six numbers 1, 2, 3, 4, 5, 6 in their results. This should become clearer if more spins are made. In question 3 (c), they should find that 2 occurs far more often than any other number. Transferring the Blu-tack to the back of number 3 (which has 1 and 5 on either side of it) should ensure that the chance of an **odd** number is more than $\frac{1}{2}$ in part (d).

In question 4 (c), there are several ways of changing spinners P, Q and S to give an equal chance of odd and even numbers. For Q, a simple method would be to exchange any one of the odd numbers for an even number so that there are three odds and three evens.

UA3ac/5 HD3ab/5
UA3a,4a/5 HD3ab/5

PUacdf,Cd,Rc/5 HPc/5

H65

Mixed mathematics

Overview

This section presents a wide variety of mathematical content set within the context of a town called Arnley.

The mathematical content includes:

decimals, percentages, rounding, negative numbers, pattern

formulae, length, perimeter, scale, area, weight, volume

rate and speed, 24-hour times, calendar work, bearings

symmetry, graphs and problem solving.

	Teacher's Notes	Textbook	Workbook	Reinforcement Sheets
Mixed mathematics	251	121–5	35, 36	

Resources

Useful materials

- calculator
- ruler, protractor, coloured pencils
- centimetre squared paper
- other materials suggested within the page notes

Teaching notes

The work is set in the context of a town called Arnley. The town is popular with tourists, and a weekly market is held in the square in front of the Town Hall. It has attractive leisure facilities in the form of its 'Water and Ice Palaces' and a shopping street called Stanley Street.

Calculators should be made available for this work.

UA2bc,3a/4 N2c,3g/5
SSM3c,4ac/4
UA2ab,3ad/4 N2b,3c/5
SSM2d,4ad/5 SSM3d/5→6
PSE AS/D3 RN/D1 FPR/E1,2
ME/D1 ME/E5 T/D1,2
PFS/D1 PFS/E3 A/D1,2
PRc/5 NUcd,Ob/5 Mdehk/5
SP/6

Textbook page 121   *Mixed mathematics*

- This page involves rounding, percentages, bearings, weight, scale, 24-hour times and problem solving. The context starts in the town square.

- In question 1(c), ensure that the children realise that this calculation involves the number of tourist visitors (8400) and not the whole population – 40% of 8400 are foreign (3360).

- In question 2, a 360° protractor is required to measure the bearing (300°) of the fountain from the Town Hall. Some children may need to be reminded of the relationship, 1 tonne = 1000 kg, which is required for part (b).

  In 2(c), the scale (1 cm to 20 m) should be used to calculate the perimeter of the town square in metres. The perimeter on the plan is 30 cm, which gives 600 metres when scaled.

- In question 3(b), encourage the children to adopt a systematic approach to the problem. By using the answers to part (a), the children should deduce that a minimum of three buses is required. For example,

Problem solving

Tour starts	Tour finishes		
1220	1340	⟶	Bus 1
1245	1405	⟶	Bus 2
1320	1440	⟶	Bus 3
1345	1505	⟶	Bus 1
1420	1540	⟶	Bus 2
1445	1605	⟶	Bus 3

Textbook page 122   *Mixed mathematics*

UA2bc/5 N2c,3g/5
SSM2c,4c/5 HD2c/5
UA2ab,3d/5 N2b,3c/5
SSM2c,4d/5 HD2d/5
PSE I/E3 RN/D1 FPR/D1
ME/D1 ME/E2,4 S/D1 S/E1
NUd,Ob/5 Mhe/5 SEa/5

- This page involves averages, calendar work, percentages, length, area, symmetry and problem solving. The Arnley context continues in the town's market.

- In question 1(b), some children might find it helpful to use a calendar even though 11 June is not a Tuesday on their current calendar. Counting on and back in 7s from 11 June gives the dates, 28 May, 4 June, 18 June, 25 June, 2 July.

  In part (d), the answer has to be rounded to the appropriate whole number of stalls, 12.

■ In question 3, the children have to appreciate that the 'hundreds' digit gives the floor number and the 'tens' and 'units' digits give the room number. An appropriate way of reading 212 is 'two twelve'. The children should list the rooms for each floor and then count how many of each digit are required.

Ground floor	001	002	003	004	005	
First floor	101	102	103	104	105	106
Second floor	201	202	203	204	205	206
	207	208	209	210	211	212

N2ab,3afg,4a/5 SSM3a,4a/5 HD2c/5
N2ab,3c,4a/5 A2ab,3b/5 SSM4ac/5 HD2d/5
I/E3 RTN/D4 AS/D3 MD/D4 FE/D1 T/D1 PFS/E2
NUd,Ob,Pa/4 NPc/5 AFb/b Mh/5 SMd/6

Textbook page 123   *Mixed mathematics*

■ This page involves decimals, median, mean, volume, rate and speed, pattern and formulae. The context continues at Arnley Water Palace, a modern swimming facility, with flumes, swimming lanes formed by floats and an adjustable floor to alter the depth of the swimming pool.

■ In question 2, it will be worth discussing the scenario of an adjustable floor which can be raised or lowered to change the depth of the water. The children should realize that the surface of the pool stays the same for each calculation and only the depth of the water changes. They may find it helpful to sketch a cuboid to represent the water. For example, in 2(a):

$$\text{Volume} = L \times b \times h$$
$$= 25 \times 16 \times 2$$
$$= 800 \text{ m}^3$$

■ In question 5, the three strings of floats show the same pattern. The children should deduce, from the table, that there are three times as many blue floats as green floats, giving $b = 3 \times g$.

UA2acd/4 N2c,3gh/5 SSM4c/5
UA2acd/4 N2b,3ce/5 SSM3d,4d/5
PSE RTN/D4 AS/D3 MD/D4 FPR/E2,3 ME/E2 PFS/E1,2,3
PRc/5 NUd,Ob/5 Mhi/5

Problem solving

Textbook page 124   *Mixed mathematics*

■ This page involves money, perimeter, area, scale drawing, percentages and problem solving. The context continues at Arnley Ice Palace.

■ Question 1 is a costing activity and for part (c) the children could be encouraged to use the calculator's memory.

■ In question 5, the children should compare the total cost of individual membership for each family with the 'Family Saver' offer of £840 (£70 per month).

Hamiltons	2 adults, 2 children	⟶ £580 + £430 ⟶ £1010
Simpsons	1 adult, 3 children	⟶ £290 + £645 ⟶ £935
Walkers	2 adults, 1 child	⟶ £580 + £215 ⟶ £795

It would not be worthwhile for the Walkers to buy the 'Family Saver'.

Workbook page 35   *Mixed mathematics, problem solving*

- The context continues with shops in Stanley Street.

- In question 1, some children might use a guess and check strategy, but a more reasoned approach would be more appropriate. The first and fourth clues together give the order

  Avid Video ⟵ *Quick Chem* ⟶ *Giftbox*

  The other clues establish the final order

  Post Office, Sweet Tooth, Avid Video, Quick Chem, Giftbox

- In question 2(b), the children should realize that to save most they should buy five *Imps*, the most expensive item.

  In part (c), in order to save 41p, Jill must have bought something worth 140p (99p + 41p): that is, 5 *Yums*.

  In part (d), the two other items must not include *Tofs*. The listing should give:

Dips, Dips	*Dips, Imps*	*Dips, Yums*	*Dips, Fabz*	*Imps, Imps*
Imps, Yums	*Imps, Fabz*	*Yums, Yums*	*Yums, Fabz*	*Fabz, Fabz*

  In part (e), Des's five items must be worth 158p in order to save 59p. His three *Tofs* cost 96p, so his other two items must be worth 62p. The only two items that give a total of 62p are an *Imp* and a *Dip*.

Workbook page 36   *Mixed mathematics*

- This page involves interpretation of a graph and negative numbers. The context continues in Arnley Post Office.

- In question 1, the initial statements have to be interpreted very carefully and the relative lengths of the bars on the graph compared in order to find the correct labelling for the vertical axis. One way of doing this is to find the number of grid 'units' in each bar of the graph.

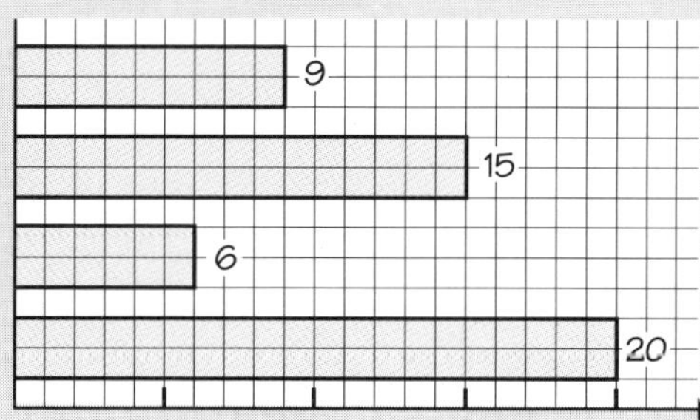

This makes it easier to see that $\frac{15}{20}$ is $\frac{3}{4}$ or 75%, which identifies the first and second class letters. Similarly, $\frac{6}{9}$ simplifies to $\frac{2}{3}$, which identifies the special delivery letters. The bar which represents the 120 special delivery letters is 6 units long and so each grid unit must represent 20 letters. This gives the following:

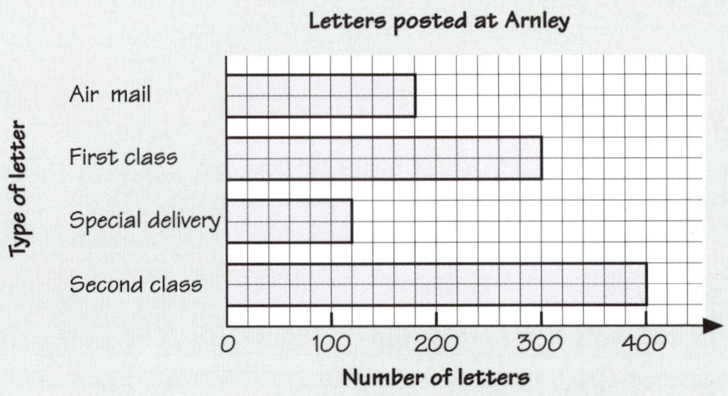

Textbook page 125   *Mixed mathematics*

- This page involves money and interpretation of a graph in the context of the Avid Video shop.

- In question 2(b), the special offer is only worthwhile when three or four *New Releases* are hired.

- In question 4, the maximum amount will be when all 280 *New Releases* are hired at £2·50 each, giving an income of £700. The minimum income will occur when all 280 are hired on the special offer, $70 \times £8 = £560$.

The teaching notes follow for the thirty pages of activities in the Heinemann Mathematics P7 Extension Textbook. The answers are provided separately in the Answer book.

Contents

Extension

Extension Textbook page E1   *Whole numbers: a million*

■ This page contains calculator investigations involving one million. It can be attempted at any time.

■ In question 1, the children may calculate the number of minutes in a day, then in a year, and then in the number of years they have lived. For example,

$$1 \text{ day} \longrightarrow 24 \times 60 = 1440 \text{ minutes}$$

$$1 \text{ year} \longrightarrow 1440 \times 365 = 525\,600 \text{ minutes}$$

$$12 \text{ years} \longrightarrow 525\,600 \times 12 = 6\,307\,200 \text{ minutes}$$

They have lived for far more than 1 million minutes.

■ Questions 2, 3 and 4 involve the diameter, thickness and weight of one-pound coins. The children could be given the measurements they require:

£1 coin   diameter – about 23 mm or 2·3 cm

thickness – about 3 mm

weight – about 9·5 g

However, they could use ten £1 coins to find some of the measurements they need. For example,

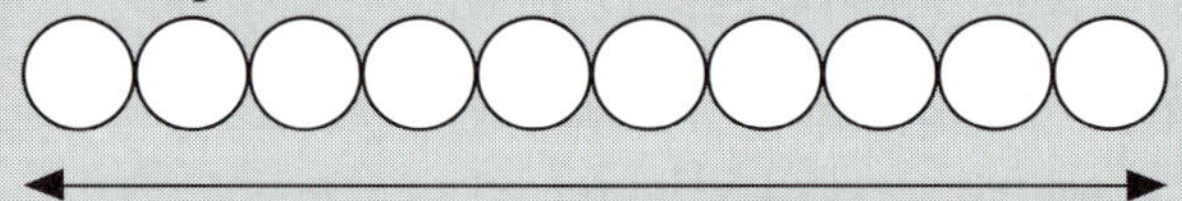

ten £1 pound coins laid in a row stretch for about 22·5 cm.

■ In question 3, the height of Ben Nevis is about 1343 metres.

■ In question 4, a small family saloon typically weighs about 1100 kg.

■ In question 5, encourage the children to think carefully about how they might tackle the problem. Some may think of finding the time taken to count aloud to one hundred and then multiplying this by 10 000. Others may realize that it would take considerably longer to say aloud the many larger numbers involved and so find the time taken to count aloud, say, ten of these. For example,

‘Four hundred and ninety-nine thousand, nine hundred and fifty-one,

four hundred and ninety-nine thousand, nine hundred and fifty-two . . .’

They could then multiply this time by 100 000 to give a total time in seconds, which could then be divided

— by 60 to give minutes

— by 60 again to give hours

— and then by 24 to give the number of days (rounded to the nearest day).

■ In question 6(a), the children must realize that $\boxed{\times}$ and $\boxed{=}$ are to be counted as key presses. A possible solution is

In 6(b), the children should realize that the product of the missing unit digits must end in a zero. A trial and improvement approach can be used to find the missing digits. For example,

$$60 \times 15\,620 = 937\,200 \text{ (too small)}$$
$$65 \times 15\,620 = 1\,015\,300 \text{ (too large)}$$

leading eventually to

$$64 \times 15\,625 = 1\,000\,000.$$

In 6(c), the children should multiply 2 by itself repeatedly using a calculator. Twenty 2s multiplied together give a total greater than a million.

Some children may improve on this by suggesting, for example, 2222×2222, which gives nearly 5 million.

Extension Textbook page E2   *Whole numbers: multiples, factors*

■ This page extends the work on Workbook pages 2 and 3 and Textbook page 6, involving multiples, factors, and triangular and square numbers.

■ In question 1(b) a variety of descriptions is possible. For example, Ledal rods could be described as

— 'multiples of 5'

— 'numbers which divide exactly by 5'

— 'numbers which have 5 as a (common) factor'.

In 1(c), the children have to find a number from those at the top of the page to match each statement. Some of the statements contain more than one condition: for example, a square number which has 10 as a factor.

■ In question 2, the children may list all the factors for each of the six numbers and then find a common factor.

Extension Textbook page E3   *Prime numbers, cubic numbers*

■ The work on this page introduces prime numbers and cubic numbers. It can be attempted at any time after the completion of Textbook page 6, which deals with triangular and square numbers.

■ In question 2, this method of finding prime numbers is known as the 'Sieve of Eratosthenes'.

■ In question 3(c), discuss the children's descriptions to reinforce the meaning of the term 'cubic' and how to find the fifth cubic number, 125, by multiplying 5 by itself three times (i.e. $5 \times 5 \times 5$).
In 3(e), the children should realize that the first row of the table contains the **first** odd number, the second row of the table contains the next **two** odd numbers, the third row contains the next **three** odd numbers and so the fourth row should contain the next **four** odd numbers $(13 + 15 + 17 + 19)$. They should notice that the totals are the first four cubic numbers $(1, 8, 27, 64)$.

Extension Textbook page E4   *Other activity: historic measures*

- The activities on this page can be attempted at any time. They involve units of measure based on parts of the body, as used by the Ancient Egyptians.

- In question 1, the lengths of the children's digits, palms, spans and cubits can be found

    — by measuring directly with a ruler or metre stick or

    — by marking the lengths and then measuring the distance between marks.

- In question 2, the measurements should be rounded to the nearest cubit.

- In question 4, the children can use their measurements from question 1 to calculate the answers, which should be rounded to the nearest whole unit.

- A calculator should be used for question 5.

  In 5(a), the children should find that Goliath's height was about 3 metres 12 centimetres. They may be interested in marking out this length in the corridor or playground and comparing it with their own heights.

  In 5(b), the children could find the side lengths of the Great Pyramid like this:

      Common Cubit 500 × 46 cm = 23 000 cm = 230 m
      Royal Cubit   500 × 52 cm = 26 000 cm = 260 m
      The Common Cubit was used.

- In question 6, the children should find that their heights and their arm spans (fathoms) are roughly equal in length.

Extension Textbook page E5   *Calculator,* M+ M−

- The activities on this page are designed to extend the use of a calculator's memory keys. The work can be attempted at any time after completion of Textbook pages 19 and 20.

- In question 1, the children are **not** expected to use any memory keys when working out the weight of the remaining Zelac.

- In question 4, some children may try a simple guess and check strategy. For example, they could try a combination of **3** crates of Varum plus **2** crates of Boros plus **1** crate of Mignon, leading to the calculation $(3 × 1575) + (2 × 2525) + (1 × 1050)$.

  This gives 10 825 gg, which is too heavy. They could then try other combinations of 6 crates.

- Others may try a more systematic approach, for example, by building up a table like this:

		Number of crates		
Weight of	1	2	3	4
Varum	1575	3150	4725	6300
Boros	2525	5050	7575	10 100
Mignon	1050	2100	3150	4200

The children could then try various combinations until the correct one, 3 crates of Varum + 1 crate of Boros + 2 crates of Mignon, is found.

Extension Textbook page E6   *Other activity: number systems*

- The work on this page deals with numbers expressed in base eight. It can be attempted at any time.

- In question 1, the children should realize that to find the equivalent Earth number they

    — multiply the first digit by 8

    — add the second digit of the Octan number to the product.

For example, in 1 (a),

$$24 \text{ octan} \longrightarrow (2 \times 8) + 4$$
$$\longrightarrow 16 + 4$$
$$\longrightarrow 20$$

- In question 2, the children should divide by 8 to find the number of 'eights' in the Earth number and then note the number of 'ones' left over.

For example, in 2(a),

$$23 \longrightarrow 2 \text{ 'eights' and } 7 \text{ 'ones'}$$
$$\longrightarrow 27 \textbf{ octan}$$

It should be emphasized that this is read as 'two seven, octan' and not as 'twenty-seven'.

- In question 3(a), the children should realize that the missing column heading, 64, is found from eight sets of 'eight'.

In question 3(b), the children should calculate the equivalent Earth number using a similar method to that used in question 1.

For example,

	eights	ones
1	3	5

$$\longrightarrow 135 \text{ octan} \longrightarrow (1 \times 64) + (3 \times 8) + 5$$
$$\longrightarrow 64 + 24 + 5$$
$$\longrightarrow 93$$

UA3a/5
UA3a/5
PSE
PUbd/4→5 NPc/4→5

Extension Textbook page E7   *Other activity: Attic Greek symbols*

UA3c/4 N2a/4
UA3c/4 N2a/4
PSE RTN/D1
PUbdf/4 NPa/4

- The work on this page introduces symbols used by the ancient Greeks of Attica to represent numbers. It can be attempted at any time.

- In question 1, the children should deduce from the illustration that the Attic symbols for 5000 and 50 000 are combinations of the symbols for 5 and 1000 and 5 and 10 000 respectively.

For example,

$$\ulcorner^{\times} \rightarrow 5000 \qquad \ulcorner^{M} \rightarrow 50\,000$$

- In question 2, the children should realize that Attic symbols are written with the highest values on the left and symbols of the same value next to each other.

■ In question 3, the children should place the Attic symbols with the highest values on the left. For example,

33 → △△△||| and **not** |||△△△

■ In question 5, it may be necessary to suggest to the children that they write down the value shown by the symbols on each broken tile, thus:

Row 1		**Row 2**	
A =	7000	E =	72
B =	8000	F =	212
C =	11 100	G =	1606
D =	8000	H =	2016

They can then look for pairs of tiles with totals which match the numbers on the three cards.

Extension Textbook pages E8 and E9   *Decimals: calculator*

■ These pages provide further calculator work on the four operations involving decimals. They can be attempted at any time after the work on Textbook pages 28–41 and Workbook pages 6–8 has been completed.

■ The context

— starts with the children comparing prices quoted by different companies for a day-trip to the ski-slopes by pupils from Denvale School

— continues with pricing of ski-outfits, dry ski-lessons, snacks for petrol for the trip

— concludes with the lengths of the ski-runs.

■ On page E8, in questions 1 and 2, it may be worthwhile discussing with the children the prices quoted by the different companies.

■ In question 3(a), the cheapest outfit consists of all the Plain items, costing £67·06 in total.

In 3(b), the dearest outfit Tom can afford for £75 consists of the 'Plain' suit together with 'Rainbow' items for the rest of the outfit, a total of £73·67.

■ In question 5, the bus hire and ski-equipment prices are **per day**, while the lesson price is the total for **all four days**. The lesson and ski-hire prices are **per child** while the cost of the bus hire is for the **whole party**.

■ On page E9, in question 2, the children could list some of the possible combinations of packs and find the price of each. For example,

3 packs of 10 + 1 pack of 7 → £6·23

1 pack of 10 + 4 packs of 7 → £6·22

2 packs of 10 + 3 packs of 7 → £6·79

The cheapest combination is one pack of 10 and four packs of 7.

■ In question 3(b), the children are expected to work in pence and deduce that the number of litres is 4368 ÷ 56 = 78 litres.

■ In question 4(b), the children should find that the other three blue runs total 7·4 − 2·15 = 5·25 km, and so are each 1·75 km long.

In 4(c), the children could deduce that two of the runs are the same length, with the third being this length **plus or minus** 0·45 km. If one run were 0·45 km **more** than the others, the runs would be 1·65 km, 1·65 km and 2·1 km. This is **not** a solution as one run is longer than 2 km.

One run must be 0·45 km **less** than the others, giving lengths of 1·95 km, 1·95 km and 1·5 km.

Extension Textbook page E10   *Fractions to decimals*

■ This page extends work on fractions and decimals by converting fractions to decimals using a calculator. It can be attempted at any time after the completion of the Decimals section.

■ In question 1, the children might see that some of the decimals 'terminate' after one, two or three decimal places. For example,

$$\tfrac{1}{2} = 0·5 \quad \tfrac{1}{4} = 0·25 \quad \tfrac{1}{5} = 0·2 \quad \tfrac{1}{8} = 0·125$$

Others show repeating digits which would continue if the calculator showed more decimal places, for example,

$$\tfrac{1}{3} = 0·3333333 \quad \tfrac{1}{6} = 0·166666 \quad \tfrac{1}{9} = 0·1111111$$

For $\tfrac{1}{7} = 0·1428571$, the children are unlikely to realize that the block of digits 142857 also repeats.

■ In question 2(c), the children should see $\tfrac{13}{9}$ as $1\tfrac{4}{9}$ (1·4444444) and $\tfrac{14}{9}$ as $1\tfrac{5}{9}$ (1·5555555) to help them predict that, in part (d), $\tfrac{16}{9}$ is $1\tfrac{7}{9}$, i.e. 1·7777777.

■ Answers for question 4(a), using a calculator which shows 8 digits, are:

$$\tfrac{1}{7} = 0·1428571 \qquad \tfrac{4}{7} = 0·5714285$$

$$\tfrac{2}{7} = 0·2857142 \qquad \tfrac{5}{7} = 0·7142857$$

$$\tfrac{3}{7} = 0·4285714 \qquad \tfrac{6}{7} = 0·8571428$$

This may lead the children to notice, in 4(b), that similar digits appear in different decimals. Some may be interested to know that the block of digits '142857' would repeat if the calculator were able to show more decimal places. For example,

$$\tfrac{1}{7} = 0·142857142857142857\ldots$$

$$\tfrac{3}{7} = 0·428571428571428571\ldots$$

■ In question 5, the children are likely to guess and check. In part (a), since both numbers are less than 10, they should discover $\tfrac{7}{8} = 0·875$ without too many trials.

For 5(b), knowing that the denominator is 99 and that the decimal 0·4747474 is less than $\tfrac{1}{2}$, some children may realize that they should try numerators a little less than 50, giving eventually, $\tfrac{47}{99} = 0·4747474$.

Others may simply divide 2-digit numbers by 99 and hopefully see a repeated decimal pattern based on the 2-digit number they entered. For example,

$$\tfrac{17}{99} = 0·1717171 \qquad \tfrac{28}{99} = 0·2828282$$

$$\text{Therefore} \quad \tfrac{47}{99} = 0·4747474.$$

Extension Textbook page E11 — *Decimals: money, mental approximation*

N3d/4
N3b/4
AS/E1
NOab,Mab/4

- This page extends work on mental methods for addition of money, where children are encouraged to look for amounts that add to £1 or nearly £1. It can be attempted at any time after the completion of Textbook page 40, which deals with approximate costs.

- In questions 1 and 2, two of the amounts on each trolley total an **exact** number of pounds. This is then added to the third amount to give the cost as an exact total. For example, in question 2(d),

$$£6·23 + £4·77 = £11$$

$$£11 + £5·75 = £16·75$$

- In questions 3, 4 and 5, two amounts which add **approximately** to give a whole number of pounds should be paired. For example, in question 3(a), when adding £4·37 + £3·61 + £5·24,

    £4·37 + £3·61 is about £8.

    £5·24 is about £5.

    The total is **about £13.**

Extension Textbook page E12 — *Percentages: increase and decrease*

N2c,3g/5
N2b,3c/5
FPR/D1,E2
NUd,Ob/5 HCc/5

- This page extends work on percentages and can be attempted any time after the children have completed Textbook page 46.

- Before the children attempt questions 1 and 2, it may be necessary to discuss the graph and the worked example to emphasize that

    — the graph shows sales for 1995

    — in 1996 the number of kits sold has gone up in some cases and down in others

    — the increase or decrease is given as a percentage and the children have to calculate the **number** of kits this represents. This is then added to or subtracted from the 1995 number read from the graph.

Extension Textbook page E13 — *Fractions as percentages*

UA2bc/5 N2c,4b/5→6
UA2ab/5 N2b,4b/6
PSE RTN/E2 FPR/E2
PUbf/5 NUd/5 NOc/6

- This page involves expressing one quantity as a percentage of another, to the nearest whole number, using a calculator. The work can be attempted after completion of the percentages section on Textbook pages 45–51 and Workbook page 9.

- In questions 1 and 2, the total number of pieces is given, whereas in question 3, the children need to interpret the information in the illustration to find the total (15 + 8 + 7 = 30).

- In question 3(b), the 8 vans comprise 25% of the pack. If the children think of 25% as 'a quarter', they can multiply 8 by 4 to give 32 as the total number of vehicles in the new pack.

- In question 4, different strategies can be used. For example,

    — calculate 15% of 35 (5·25) and 25% of 35 (8·75) and reason that since the number of children must be a whole number, there are 6, 7 or 8 children

    — use a trial and improvement method:
    try 4 children: 4 out of 35 is 11·42857% (too low)
    try 10 children: 10 out of 35 is 28·57142% (too high)
    try 8 children. . . and so on.

UA3b,4b/4 N3a/5
UA3b/4 A2b,3b/5
PS/D1 PS/E2 FE/D1 FE/E4
PUbdef/4→5 PRa/5 NPacd/5
HCf/5 AFb/6

Extension Textbook pages E14 and E15
Pattern: sequences, formulae and graphs

- These pages extend the work on sequences and formulae and can be attempted at any time after Textbook pages 52–6 and Workbook pages 10–12 are completed.

- The context of GRT's Annual Competition might be discussed.

- On page E14, in question 1, the children are likely to find the central number, 24, by seeing a pattern of doubling (or halving) in this sequence.

The other sequences are

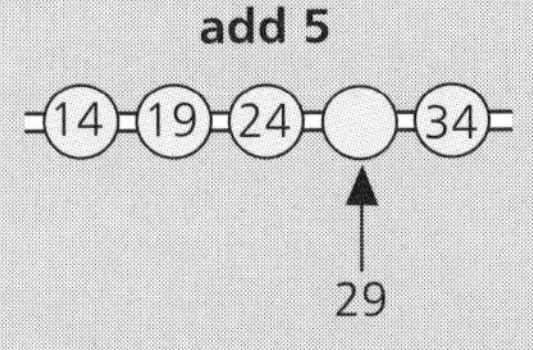

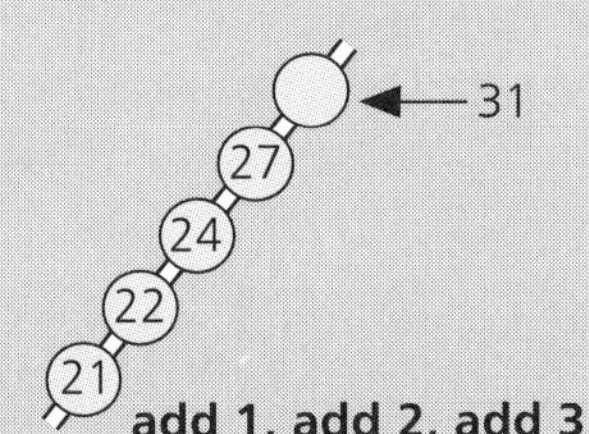

or 'add 1 more each time'.

- In question 2, in this sequence,

the children should **subtract** 14 from 22 to give 8 as the number before 14.

In the last sequence, a guess and check method is appropriate.

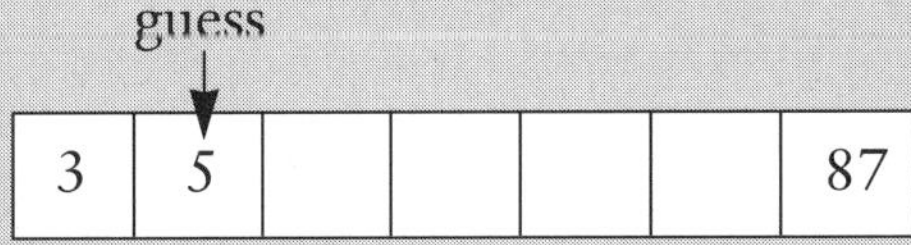

Adding gives   8,   13,   21,   34,   55. But 55 is too small. . .

Guess **more than 5** for the second number.

The correct sequence is

3	9	12	21	33	54	87

- In question 3, each '1' is represented by a coloured square and each '0' by a blank. The two pictures give the formula $F = 7 \times P$.

- On page E15, in question 2, to complete the table in part (a) the children must use the information in the graph **and** the points table.

For Year 3, the points table gives 10 points and the graph gives a prize of £50.

The formula in 2(b) is $S = 5 \times P$.

Number of points (P)	Second prize in pounds (S)
7	→ 35
6	→ 30
10	→ 50

- The table in question 3 leads to the formula $T = 10 + P$. All three formulae

$$F = 7 \times P \qquad S = 5 \times P \qquad T = 10 + P$$

should be used in question 4 to find the total prize money ($£133 + £55 + £19 \rightarrow £207$).

UA3ac/5 N3a/4 SSM3b/4
UA3a,4a/5 A2b/4 SSM3a/4 SSM3d/5
PSE FE/D1 PFS/E1 PM/D3
PUb,Ca,Rabce/5
NPc/5 Mh/5 SPe/4

Extension Textbook pages E16 and E17
Area: enlargement, reduction

- The investigations on these pages deal with the effect on an area of a shape when its sides are enlarged or reduced. They can be attempted at any time after completion of the Area section on Textbook pages 75–8 and Workbook pages 24–7.

- The children

  — draw a starting shape on centimetre squared paper, given the co-ordinates of its vertices

  — multiply or divide these co-ordinates by 2, 3. . . to produce similar shapes

  — investigate the effect on the areas of the shapes. For example,

    — multiplying the side lengths of a shape by 3 has the effect of multiplying the area of the shape by 9 (3×3)

    — dividing the side lengths of a shape by 4 has the effect of dividing the area of the shape by 16 (4×4).

- On page E16, the children are instructed to use a new grid each time so that the enlargements do not overlap. Emphasize that the starting rectangle (in question 1(a)) must be drawn in each new co-ordinate diagram.

- In question 4(a), the children should recognize the first three numbers in their table, 4, 9 and 16, as square numbers and reason that, for side lengths multiplied by 5, the area will be multiplied by 25, the next square number.

- In question 5, the children could draw enlargements, if necessary. However, they are expected to apply the relationship discovered in questions 1–4 and **calculate** the number of flowers directly. For example, in 5(c), the area is multiplied by 4 (2×2), so the number of flowers will be 80 (4×20).

- On page E17, in question 1, in order to avoid overlapping reductions, the children should be told to use a new grid each time.

- In question 4, the illustration may not be sufficient to convey what a patio is and some additional explanation may be needed. The children are expected to apply the relationship discovered in questions 1–3 and calculate the number of slabs directly.

- Similarly, in question 5, the area of the reduction should be calculated directly – as the side lengths are 'one quarter' of those in the original shape. They have been 'divided by 4' and so the area has been divided by 16 (4 × 4).

Extension Textbook page E18 *Other activity: codes*

UA3bc/5
UA3bc/5
PSE
PUbd/5 SEa/4→5

- This page involves finding a code for a picture on an 8 by 8 grid by assigning numbers to the columns of the grid. This work is related to question 3 on page E14, but could be attempted at any time.

- In question 3, the children should realize that corresponding rows on either side of the line of symmetry have the same coloured squares and so must have the same code numbers.

- The two grids in question 4 can be joined to make this picture of an alien.

- When dealing with a code number such as 102, the children may find it useful to set down a series of subtractions like this:

```
    102
  -  64    ← (colour the 64 square)
    ----
     38
  -  32    ← (colour the 32 square)
    ----
      6
  -   4    ← (colour the 4 square)
    ----
      2    ← (colour the 2 square)
```

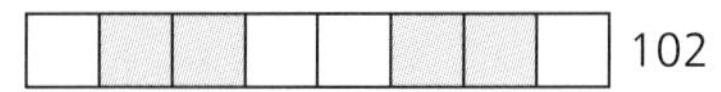

128	64	32	16	8	4	2	1

102

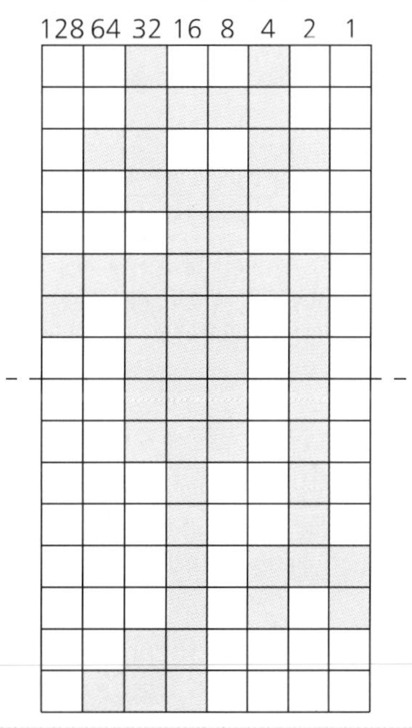

SSM4ab/5
SSM4ab/5
PSE ME/E6,7
PUabcf/5 Mdeh/5

Extension Textbook page E19   *Volume: displacement*

- This page deals with finding the volume of a solid object by displacement. It can be attempted at any time.

- A practical illustration of how the volume of an object can be found by displacing water would be a useful introduction, even though the children are expected to do this for themselves in question 2. They should realize that

  — an initial water level reading is taken

  — the object is then submerged completely

  — the raised water level reading is taken

  — the volume of the object is equal to the difference between the two readings.

- In question 1, the children should record their answers as shown for the volume of the potato at the top of the page.

- In question 2, the children could work with a partner. A measuring jar and a variety of objects should be made available. Objects which will sink in the water – for example, a large key or other metal object – would be ideal.

- In question 3(a), the children should find that the total volume of drink is 360 ml.

  In 3(b), they need to remember that

  — 360 ml is the same as $360 \, cm^3$

  — the volume of a cuboid can be found by multiplying together its length, breadth and height, so they are looking for three numbers which multiply together to give 360.

  Some possible answers are $10 \, cm \times 9 \, cm \times 4 \, cm$, $10 \, cm \times 6 \, cm \times 6 \, cm$, $8 \, cm \times 9 \, cm \times 5 \, cm$.

UA3b/4 SSM4d/5 SSM3a/5→6
UA3b/4 SSM4a/5 SSM4c/5→7
I/D1 T/D4 ME/D9
PRc/5 Mk/5 SMd/6 HCc/5

Extension Textbook page E20   *Speed: mph*

- This page extends the work on speed to miles per hour. It can be attempted at any time after the work on Textbook pages 83–6 has been completed.

- Ensure that the children can interpret the distance table at the top of the page. Explain that lorries are being driven between the cities listed in the table.

- In question 2(d), two answers are expected: Carlisle and Edinburgh; Carlisle and Glasgow.

- For questions 3 and 4, encourage the children to set out their working as shown in the panel.

- In question 5(b), the children should deduce that Donald had 2 hours in which to travel the remaining 128 miles (378 – 250) to deliver his parcel. Driving at 48 mph, Donald would travel only 96 miles in the 2 hours and so could not deliver his parcel in time.

Extension Textbook page E21   *Time: 24-hour clock, durations*

UA2a/5 SSM4a/5
UA2c/5 SSM4a/5
PSE T/D1,2
PUc,Cd/5 Mjk/5

- This page deals with durations involving 24-hour times. The context is a day in an activity holiday organized by the travel agency Eurotravel. The page can be attempted after the children have completed Textbook pages 88–90 and Workbook page 16.

- By using the times on the clocks and the other information in the pictures, the children make up a timetable for the day.

- The first activity is described briefly as 'Cycling' in the table. The children have to invent similar labels for the other activities. Acceptable labels may vary: for example, 'picnicking', 'having a picnic', 'having lunch', and 'eating and resting'.

- For some activities, the starting and finishing times are given and the duration has to be found. For example:

	Started at	Finished at	Time spent
canoeing	14.24	15.48	**1 h 24 min**

For other activities, the starting **or** finishing time and duration are given. For example:

	Started at	Finished at	Time spent
at the café	15.48	**16.33**	45 min

- The most difficult part of the timetable to interpret is the time spent picnicking. The children should calculate that the picnic starts at 12.06. They have no information about the finishing time or the duration. They need to move to the fourth picture and then work backwards. Walking to the river took 20 minutes, so Lisa must have left the picnic site at 14.04. The time spent picnicking was from 12.06 to 14.04: that is, 1 hour 58 minutes.

Extension Textbook page E22   *Angles: position fixing*

UA3b/5 SSM3c/5
UA3b/5 SSM2d,3d/5
A/D2 PFS/E2
PUce,Rc/5 Mahi/5 SPa/5 SPb/6

- This page introduces the idea of using a distance and a bearing to describe the position of a point. It can be attempted after the work on bearings on Textbook pages 94–6 has been completed.

- The context should be discussed with the children. An accident is causing leaked gas to spread from the Ferrox Chemical Plant. The page contains safety advice for the public about what action to take.

- It is worthwhile discussing the diagram. The coloured areas show the spread of gas from the Plant in the centre. The circles are spaced 1 cm apart and give the distance from the Plant in kilometres. Some children may wish to measure distances from the Plant with a ruler.

- In question 2, the farthest spread is towards the South East. The wind must be coming from the opposite direction and can be described as '**from** the North West'. It could also be said to come **from** a direction with bearing 300° from the Ferrox Plant.

In question 4, the actions should be those recommended in the key at the top of the page for the appropriate coloured areas of the map. For example,

Aileen: listen to the radio

Ryan: no action (outside the area of spread)

Samena: use breathing apparatus

Barry: stay indoors.

The red area in question 5 is larger than a 1 cm square, which represents 1 square kilometre on the map. The children could find this by inspection, or by placing a 1 cm square or cube on top, or by rough measurement with a ruler.

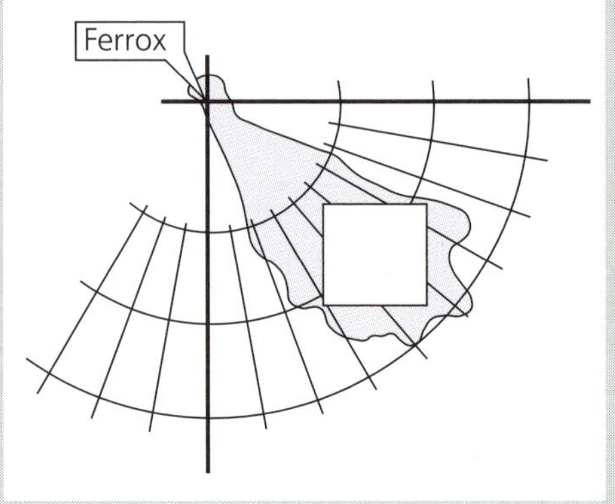

| UA3b,4c/5 SSM2a/5 |
| UA3b,4b/5 SSM3e/5 |
| PSE PM/D4 |
| PUdef,Cd/5 SPf/5 |

Extension Textbook page E23   *Shape: position and movement*

The activities on this page can be attempted at any time. They involve the computer language LOGO, and require a computer with Logotron software.

It is necessary for the children to know how a series of LOGO commands can be saved and used as a single procedure, such as in the given example, SQUARE.

In question 2(a), a sketch based on the given commands should look as follows:

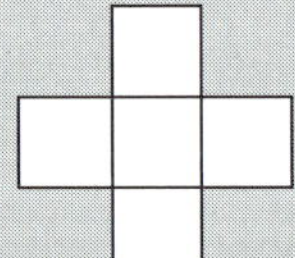

The children could be provided with squared or dotty paper in order to complete their sketches.

In question 3, the children may wish to break the problems down by first trying to draw only a part of each shape, before typing one-line commands using REPEAT.

Possible commands are as follows:

(a) REPEAT 4 [SQUARE RT 9Ø FD 5Ø]

(b) REPEAT 4 [SQUARE FD 5Ø RT 9Ø]

(c) REPEAT 4 [SQUARE RT 9Ø FD 5Ø LT 9Ø BK 5Ø]

(d) REPEAT 8 [SQUARE RT 45]

There are other correct ways of giving commands to draw these patterns.

■ In question 3(b), the children should think of the Turtle drawing this square first.

Extension Textbook page E24   *2D shape: tiling*

UA2d,3c/4 SSM3ab/4
UA2d,3c/4 SSM3bc/4
PSE RS/D5 PM/D4
PUabd,Cad/5 SEa/5

■ The work involves the children in drawing tilings using pentominoes. The activities can be attempted after the work on rotational symmetry, translation and tiling on Textbook pages 97 and 98 and Workbook pages 17, 18 and 20 has been completed.

■ In question 1, it is worth pointing out that two drawings like this show the **same pentomino**.

One can simply be rotated to match the other.

■ In question 2, some children may be able to draw the tiling on squared paper. Others may find it helpful to glue each pentomino on to card, cut it out, then use it as a template.

■ In question 3, the children first have to create a larger tile on squared paper by rotating a pentomino around one of its corners. Again, some children may find it helpful to glue this new, **larger** tile on card, cut it out and use it as a template.

Extension Textbook page E25   *2D shape: curve stitching*

UA2b,3b/4
UA2c,3b/4
PSE
PUabd,Cd/4

■ The activities on this page can be attempted at any time. They involve joining points with straight lines to produce 'curves'.

■ In question 1, it will be worthwhile supervising the children's efforts as this technique is the basis for all of the other designs on the page.

■ In question 3, the children should see that the design on the left involves combining four of the designs from question 2.

The design on the right involves an extended version of the original design.

SSM2b,3c/5
SSM2bd/5
RS/D4 RS/E5 A/D1 A/E4
PUab,Ca,Ra/5 SPd/5

Extension Textbook page E26
2D shape: triangle properties, construction

■ The activities on this page involve

— practical work to show that the angle sum of a triangle is 180° and the use of this fact to calculate angles in triangles

— using compasses to construct an equilateral triangle.

The page can be attempted after the angle work on Textbook page 93 has been completed.

■ In question 1, encourage the children to draw a variety of triangles – some obtuse-angled, some right-angled, some acute-angled – so that the result will be seen to apply to any triangle.

In 1(e), they should find that when the three coloured corners are glued together, they form a straight angle.

■ In question 2, the size of each red angle can be found as follows:

— in 2(a), (b) and (c): by subtracting the total of the two given angles from 180°

— in 2(d) and (e): by subtracting the given angle from 180° and then dividing by 2, as the other two angles are equal in an isosceles triangle

— in 2(f): by dividing 180° by 3, as all three angles are equal in an equilateral triangle.

■ In question 3, the children should be encouraged to give particular attention to

— setting the radius of 7 cm

— drawing arcs of sufficient length to ensure that these cross

— joining the ends of the original line accurately to the point where the arcs cross.

They should realize that, since all three sides are of equal length, the triangle is equilateral and each of its angles will be 60°.

UA2bcd,3bc/5 N3a/5
UA2abd,3bc/5 A2b/5
PSE PS/D1
PUdef,Cd,Ra/5 NPac/5

Extension Textbook page E27   *Other activity: problem solving*

■ This page involves a relationship and can be attempted at any time after the pattern work on Textbook pages 52–6 and Workbook pages 10–12 has been completed.

■ Ensure that the children understand the rules for travelling along the leaves by hopping and jumping.

■ In question 1, the children can **either** draw the three ways **or** describe them, possibly using symbols such as **h** for hop and **j** for jump. For example,

    hhh or **hj** or **jh**

■ In question 3(b), the children should have the following completed table:

Number of ways	1	2	3	5	8

They should notice that each number is the sum of the two previous numbers. The next number in the sequence is found by adding 5 and 8 to give 13.

■ The answers for question 3(c) can be found by continuing the sequence:

1,   2,   3,   5,   8,   ⑬,   ㉑,   34,   ㊽

Extension Textbook pages E28 and E29
Handling data: interpretation, money

■ The activities involve interpreting a wide range of data relating to bicycle costs. They can be attempted at any time after completion of the work on Textbook pages 115 and 116.

■ On page E28, in question 1(b), some children may forget that each bike will require **two** wheels and **two** tyres.

■ In question 2(a), some children may need to be prompted to look for the most expensive item in each category.

Similarly in part (b), the children should look for the cheapest item.

■ In question 3, to find the cost of the frame, the children can subtract the cost of other items, either as a total or one by one, from the cost of the bike. The cost of the frame can then be used to identify the frame size.

■ On page E29, in question 4, the children may use a trial and improvement strategy to select a suitable bike for each customer.

For example, in 4(a),

45 cm frame	£100
2 Super sport tyres	£26
2 spoke wheels	£95
road bars	£10
Lite saddle	£9·95
Completer kit B	£45
Total	**£285·95**

This total is too low, so they can try a more expensive item, such as more expensive handlebars. Racing bars cost £20, giving a total of £295·95, which is within the desired price range. Other combinations are possible.

SSM2c,3a/4
SSM2c,3b/4
S/D1,2 S/E1,2
PUabdef,Ca/5 SEa/5

Extension Textbook page E30   *Other activity: Celtic designs*

■ The work of this page is based on simple Celtic step patterns. It can be attempted at any time after the children have completed the rotational symmetry work on Workbook page 17 and Textbook page 97. The children should use centimetre squared dotty paper.

■ Simple step patterns are based on a square grid of dots. The designs are developed by joining dots with straight lines to make a pattern on a small square. This basic pattern is then repeated by translating or rotating it to give a larger pattern. For example,

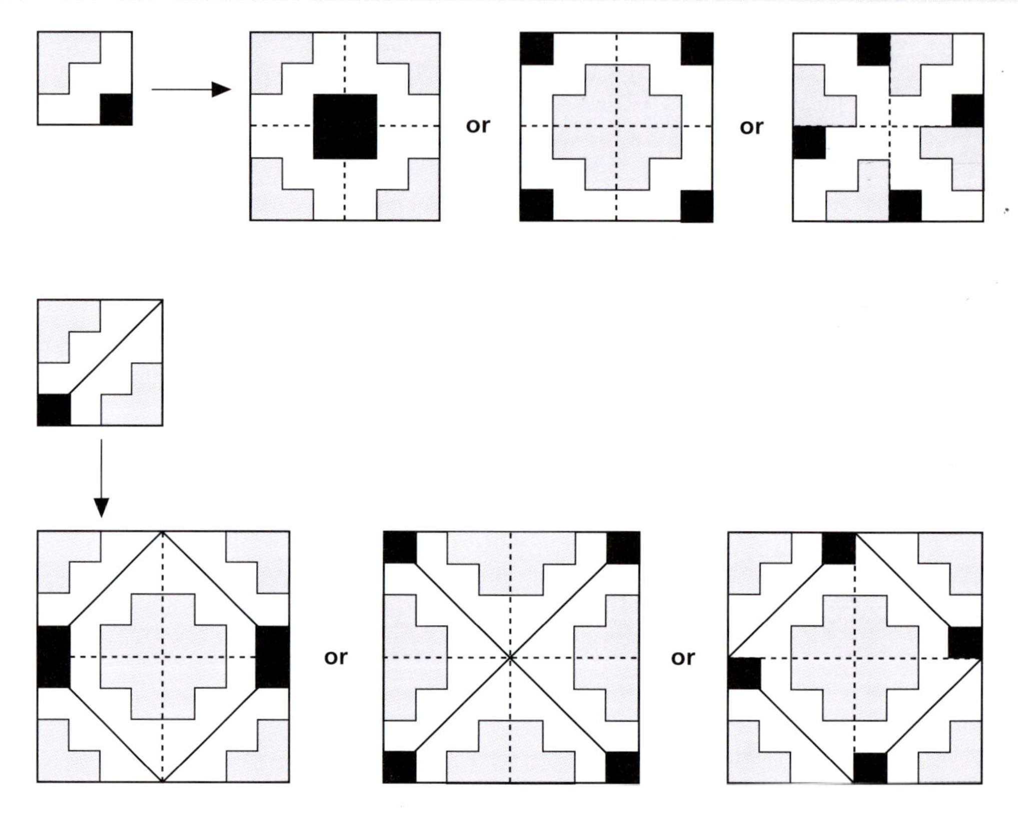

Heinemann Mathematics P7: Comparison Chart for National Curriculum (England and Wales) Programme of Study for Key Stage 2

Key: plain typeface for Level 4; italics for Level 4 to 5 or Level 5; *denotes Level 5 to 6.

USING AND APPLYING MATHEMATICS

Programme of Study	Teacher's Notes	Textbook	Workbook	Reinforcement Sheets	Extension Textbook	Assessment	Problem Solving Activities	Resource Cards
1. Pupils should be given opportunities to:								
a use and apply mathematics in practical tasks, in real-life problems and within mathematics itself								
b take increasing responsibility for organizing and extending tasks								
c devise and refine their own ways of recording								
d ask questions and follow alternative suggestions to support the development of reasoning								
2. Making and monitoring decisions to solve problems	pp. 26–8, *96*, 116–19, 132–6, *160–3, 166–7, 223, 261*	pp. 1–2, *3–4*, 6, 11, 12, 17–18, *20*, 31–2, 40–1, *42–3, 47, 49 50, 52, 53, 60–3, 74–7*, 103, 105, 121, *122*, 124, *125*	pp. 1, 7–8, 10, 11, *24–6, 28*, 35	R1, R7, R12, R15, R16, *R17–R20, R24*	*E1, E2, E5, E8–E10, E13, E21, E24, E25, E27*	**Measure** 2 **Round-ups** 1, 2, 3	1, *3–8, 10, 12–14,* 16, *18, 20, 22, 26–30, 32–5*	**1, 2** (Rockets and meteorites) **3–5** *(Earth cargo)* **9–11** *(Souvenirs)* **21** *(Cube puzzle)* **22** *(Triangles puzzle)*
3. Developing mathematical language and forms of communication	pp. 34, *64–8*, 118–19, 132–6, *160–1, 170–1, 175–7, 225,* 230, *232–8*, 239, 241, *242, 245–8*	pp. 6, 11, 12, *23–5*, 53, *60–3, 74–6, 78–82*, 103, 107, 108, 109, *110–113*, 114, 115–20, 121, *125*	pp. 11, 27, 31, 32, 33, 34, *35*, 36	R10, R24, R32	*E1, E2, E6, E7,* E14–E15, *E16–E18,* E20, *E22, E23,* E24, E25, *E27,* E28–E29	**Handling data** 1, 2, *3,* 4 **Round-up** 2	2, 3, *7–11,* 14, 15, 16, 17, *19, 20, 22, 23, 24–6, 28–31*	**9–11** *(Souvenirs)* **23, 24** (Bikes)
4. Developing mathematical reasoning			p. *35*		E14–E15, *E23*	**Round-ups** 2, 3	9, 15	
1. Pupils should be given opportunities to:								
a develop flexible and effective methods of computation and recording, and use them with understanding								
b use calculators, computers and a range of other resources as tools for exploring number structure and to enable work with realistic data								
c develop the skills needed for accurate and appropriate use of equipment								
2. Developing an understanding of place value and extending the number system								
a read, write and order whole numbers, understanding that the position of a digit signifies its value; use their understanding of place value to develop methods of computation; to approximate numbers to the nearest 10 or 100, and to multiply and divide by powers of 10 when there are whole-number answers	pp. 26–33, *36–40, 44–5*	pp. 5, *7–10, 13–14,* 123	pp. 3–4	R1, *R3–R5*	E7	**Number** 1, *3* **Round-ups** *1,* 3	5, 7	**1, 2** (Rockets and meteorites) **3–5** (Earth cargo) **9–11** *(Souvenirs)*
b extend their understanding of the number system to negative numbers in context, and decimals with no more than two decimal places in the context of measurement and money	pp. 46–9, 78, *79–82,* 83–4, *85–7,* 90–5, *125–9, 148–151*	pp. 15, 28, *29–35,* 39–41, 57, 58, 68–70, 72, 73, 123, 125	pp. 4, *6–8,* 13–15, 36	R11–R16, R22, R23	*E1*	**Number** 7, 8, 9, *10, 12* **Round-up** 3	8	**9–11** *(Souvenirs)* **12, 13** (Matching squares)* **14** *(Oil-rig Heron)*
c understand and use, in context, fractions and percentages to estimate, describe and compare proportions of a whole	pp. 60–3, 69–70, 102–4, *105–11,* 261	pp. 21, 22, 26, 45, 46, 48–51, 121, *122,* 124	pp. 5, 9, *26*	R8, R9, R19, *R20*	E10, *E12,* E13	**Number** 5, 11, *12* **Round-up** 3	11, 12	**6–8** *(Fraction strips)*

NUMBER

The boxed notes on the chart read:

> Although presented as a separate section of the Programme of Study, 'Using and Applying Mathematics' is integral to all sections of work. The philosophy underpinning the whole of Heinemann Mathematics is that mathematical ideas should be developed through activity. By using suggestions for practical work given in the Teacher's Notes, Assessment and Resources Pack and children's materials, teachers will therefore be giving children opportunities to use mathematical equipment and materials. The Teacher's Notes also contain ideas for activities which can play an important role in developing both mathematical language and communication and mathematical reasoning.

> In Heinemann Mathematics children are provided with material in a variety of contexts and formats. Opportunities are provided for them to develop confidence in different aspects of Number work. This includes introducing strategies in mental calculation.
>
> Calculators are built in from Heinemann Mathematics 2 onwards and are an increasingly important tool in the later stages of the course.
>
> Through using the variety of resources provided within the course children have a wide experience of different recording techniques.

3. Understanding relationships between numbers and developing methods of computation

a	explore number sequences, *eg count in different sizes of step, doubling and halving,* using a multiplication square, explaining patterns and using simple relationships; progress to interpreting, generalizing and using simple mappings, *eg c = 15n for the cost of n articles at 15p,* relating to numerical, spatial or practical situations, expressed initially in words and then using letters as symbols	pp. 34, 115–19, 119–23, 152–3, 160–7, 170–1, 261	pp. 6, 52, 53, 54–6, 71, 75–7, 79–80, 123	pp. 10, 11, 12, 24, 25	R21, R24, R25	E3, E10, E14–E15, E16–17, E27	**Number** 13 **Round-up** 3	9, 14, 15	
b	recognize the number relationships between co-ordinates in the first quadrant of related points on a line or shape, *eg vertices of a rectangle, a graph of the multiples of 3*								
c	consolidate knowledge of addition and subtraction facts to 20; know the multiplication facts to 10 x 10; develop a range of mental methods for finding quickly from known facts those that they cannot recall; use some properties of numbers, including multiples, factors and squares, extending to primes, cubes and square roots	pp. 26–8, 34–8, 41–3	pp. 1–2, 6–8, 11, 12, 42–3	pp. 1–3	R1, R3, *R17*	E2, E3	**Number** 1, 2	3,6	
d	develop a variety of mental methods of computation with whole numbers up to 100, and explain patterns used; extend mental methods to develop a range of non-calculator methods of computation that involve addition and subtraction of whole numbers, progressing to methods for multiplication and division up to 3-digit by 2-digit whole numbers	pp. 26–35, 36–43, 86–7, 107–8, 130, 139–42	pp. 1–5, 7–10, 12, 35, 59, 64–7	pp. 1, 7–8	R1–R4, *R13, R16*	E11	**Number** 1, 14 **Measure** 1 **Round-up** 1	1, 4, 6, 17	**3–5** (Earth cargo)
e	understand multiplication as repeated addition, and division as sharing and repeated subtraction; use associated language and recognize situations to which the operations apply								
f	understand and use the relationships between the four operations, including inverses	pp. 46–54, 69–73, 96, 180–5	pp. 3–4, 12, 15–20, 26, 27, 42–3, 83–6, 123	pp. 4, 7–8	R6, R7, R16, R17, R27	E5	**Number** 4 **Measure** 3 **Round-up** 3		
g	extend methods of computation, to include addition and subtraction with negative numbers, all four operations with decimals, and calculating fractions and percentages of quantities, using a calculator where appropriate	pp. 64–73, 83–4, 85–96, 98, 102–6, 109–11, 125–9	pp. 23–7, 31–44, 46–51, 58, 72, 73, 121–5	pp. 7–9, 13, 14, 36	R10, R12–R20	E8–E9, E12	**Number** 6, 8, 9, 11, 12 **Round-ups** 1, 2, 3	10, 13, 31	**1, 2** (Rockets and meteorites)
h	understand and use the features of a basic calculator, interpreting the display in the context of the problem, including rounding and remainders	pp. 46–54, 96, 105–6	pp. 15–20, 42–3, 48, 51, 124, 125	p. 4	R6, R7, R17	E5	**Number** 4, 10 **Round-up** 2	10	

4. Solving numerical problems

a	develop their use of the four operations to solve problems, including those involving money and measures, using a calculator where appropriate	pp. 46–54, 69–73, 96, 180–5	pp. 3–4, 12, 15–20, 26, 27, 42–3, 83–6, 123	pp. 4, 7–8	R6, R7, R16, R17, R27	E5	**Number** 4 **Measure** 3 **Round-up** 3		

Heinemann Mathematics P7: Comparison Chart for National Curriculum (England and Wales) Programme of Study for Key Stage 2 *(cont.)*

*Key: plain typeface for Level 4; italics for Level 4 to 5 or Level 5; *denotes Level 5 to 6.*

	Programme of Study	Teacher's Notes	Textbook	Workbook	Reinforcement Sheets	Extension Textbook	Assessment	Problem Solving Activities	Resource Cards
NUMBER	**b** choose sequences of methods of computation appropriate to a problem, adapt them and apply them accurately	*pp. 46–9, 52–4, 71–3*	pp. *15, 16, 19, 20, 27, 31–2*	*p. 4*	*R6, R12*	*E5, E8–E9, E13*	**Number** *4*		
	c check results by different methods, including repeating the operations in a different order or using inverse operations; gain a sense of the size of a solution, and estimate and approximate solutions to problems	pp. 31–3, *50–1, 92–6*	pp. *5, 17–18, 40–3*	pp. *7–8*	R2, *R7, R15–R17*		**Number** 1, *4, 10*	5	**3–5** *(Earth cargo)*
SHAPE, SPACE AND MEASURES	**1. Pupils should be given opportunities to:**								
	a use geometrical properties and relationships in the solution of problems								
	b extend their practical experience using a wide range of materials								
	c use computers to create and transform shapes								
	d consider a wide range of patterns, including some drawn from different cultural traditions								
	e apply their measuring skills in a range of purposeful contexts								
	2 Understanding and using properties of shape								
	a visualize and describe shapes and movements, developing precision in using related geometrical language	pp. 214–15, *218–21, 225, 242*	pp. 99, 100, *101, 102, 103, 104, 107, 117*	*p. 22*	*R31*	*E23*	**Round-ups** 2, 3	*14, 27*	
	b make 2D and 3D shapes and patterns with increasing accuracy, recognize their geometrical features and properties, and use them to classify shapes and solve problems	pp. 214–15, *218–21, 224, 242*	pp. 97, 99, 100, *101, 102, 103, 104, 106, 117*	pp. 20, *22*	*R31*	*E26*	**Measure** 2* **Shape** *3* **Round-up** 3	24	**21** *(Cube puzzle)*
	c understand the congruence of simple shapes; recognize reflective symmetries of 2D and 3D shapes and rotational symmetries of 2D shapes	pp. 209–10, *218–21*	pp. 97, *101, 102, 122*	pp. 17, 20, 22	*R31*	E30	**Shape** *3* **Round-up** 3	*25, 26*	**21** *(Cube puzzle)*
	3. Understanding and using properties of position and movement								
	a transform 2D shapes by translation, reflection and rotation, and visualize movements and simple transformations to create and describe patterns	pp. *183–5, 212, 223*	pp. *85, 86, 98, 123*	pp. *18, 20*	*R27*	E20*, E24, E30	**Measure** *3* **Round-up** *3*		
	b use co-ordinates to specify location, *eg map references, representation of 2D shapes*	*p. 212, 242*	pp. *98, 101, 102, 105, 117*	pp. *18, 20, 22*	*R31*	E16–E17, E24	**Round-up** 2		
	c use right angles, fractions of a turn and, later, degrees, to measure rotation, and use the associated language	pp. *200–2, 205–6, 218–19*	pp. *92–6, 121*	pp. *29–30*	*R30*	E22, E26	**Shape** 1, *2* **Round-up** *1*	28	**18** (360° protractors) **19, 20** *(Bearings game)*
	4. Understanding and using measures								
	a choose appropriate standard units of length, mass, capacity and time, and make sensible estimates with them in everyday situations	pp. *148–9, 149–51, 155–6, 172–3, 175–7, 190–8*	pp. 68–70, *72–4, 81–2, 87–91, 121, 123*	pp. 15, 16, 28	R22, R23, R28, R29	*E1, E4, E19–E21*	**Number** 7 **Measure** 1, 4 **Round-ups,** 1, 3	17, *21*	**15** *(Eurotravel rally)* **16, 17** *(Space creatures)*

As for all the sections of the Programme of Study, support for a practical teaching approach can be found in the Teacher's Notes. For each maths topic within Measure and Shape there are opportunities for children to gain valuable hands-on experience within a meaningful context.

		c1	c2	c3	c4	c5	c6	c7	c8
	extend their understanding of the relationship between units; convert one metric unit to another, know the rough metric equivalents of Imperial units still in daily use								
b	choose and use appropriate measuring instruments, interpret numbers and read scales to an increasing degree of accuracy	pp. 172–3				E19	Number 7		
c	find perimeters of simple shapes; find practically the circumference of circles, being introduced to the ratio 'π'; find areas and volumes by counting methods, leading to the use of other practical methods, *eg dissection*	pp. 152–3. 160–7*, 170–1*, 225	pp. 71, 77–80*, 121, 122, 124	pp. 24–7*	R25*		Measure 2* Round-up 2*	15, 18*, 22	

1. Pupils should be given opportunities to:

		c1	c2	c3	c4	c5	c6	c7	c8
a	formulate questions about an issue of their choice, and consider them using statistical methods								
b	access and collect data through undertaking purposeful enquiries								
c	use computers as a source of interesting data, and as a tool for representing data								

> As for all the sections of the Programme of Study, support for a practical teaching approach can be found in the Teacher's Notes. There are opportunities for children to gain valuable hands-on experience of gathering, interpreting and presenting data within a context that is relevant to them. Advice is also given in the Teacher's Notes for using software packages currently available.

2. Collecting, representing and interpreting data

		c1	c2	c3	c4	c5	c6	c7	c8
a	interpret tables used in everyday life; interpret and create frequency tables, including those for grouped discrete data	pp. 230, 232–6, 239, 241	pp. 108, 109, 110–12, 114, 115–16, 125	pp. 31, 32, 33, 34, 36	R32	E28–29	Handling data 1, 2, 3 Round-ups 1, 2	29	23, 24 (Bikes)
b	collect and represent discrete data appropriately, using graphs and diagrams, including block graphs, pictograms and line graphs; interpret a wider range of graphs and diagrams that represent data, including pie charts, using a computer where appropriate	pp. 232–4	pp. 109, 110–12, 114, 115–16	pp. 31, 32, 33, 34	R32		Handling data 1, 2, 3 Round-up 1		23, 24 (Bikes)
c	understand and use measures of average, leading towards the mode, the median and the mean in relevant contexts, and the range as a measure of spread	pp. 237–8	pp.109, 113, 115–16, 122, 123				Handling data 3 Round-ups 1, 3		
d	draw conclusions from statistics and graphs, and recognize why some conclusions can be uncertain or misleading		pp.115–16						

3. Understanding and using probability

		c1	c2	c3	c4	c5	c6	c7	c8
a	develop understanding of probability, through experience as well as experiment and theory, and discuss events and simple experiments, using a vocabulary that includes the words 'evens', 'fair', 'unfair', 'certain', 'likely', 'probably' and 'equally likely'	pp. 245–8	pp.118–20			Handling data 4			
b	understand that the probability of any event lies between impossibility and certainty, leading to the use of the scale from 0 to 1	pp. 245–8	pp.118–20			Handling data 4			
c	recognize situations where probabilities can be based on equally likely outcomes, and others where estimates must be based on experimental evidence; make or approximate these estimates								

Heinemann Mathematics P7: Comparison Chart for National Curriculum (England and Wales) Programme of Study for Key Stage 3

Key: plain typeface for Level 4; italics for Level 4 to 5 or Level 5; * denotes Level 5 to 6 or Level 6.

USING AND APPLYING MATHEMATICS

Programme of Study	Teacher's Notes	Textbook	Workbook	Reinforcement Sheets	Extension Textbook	Assessment	Problem Solving Activities	Resource Cards
1. Pupils should be given opportunities to:								
a use and apply mathematics in practical tasks, in real-life problems and within mathematics itself		Although presented as a separate section of the Programme of Study, 'Using and Applying Mathematics' is integral to all sections of work. The philosophy underpinning the whole of Heinemann Mathematics is that mathematical ideas should be developed through activity. By using suggestions for practical work given in the Teacher's Notes, Assessment and Resources Pack and children's materials, teachers will therefore be giving children opportunities to use mathematical equipment and materials. The Teacher's Notes also contain ideas for activities which can play an important role in developing both mathematical language and communication and mathematical reasoning.						
b work on problems that pose a challenge								
c encounter and consider different lines of mathematical argument								
2. Making and monitoring decisions to solve problems								
a find ways of overcoming difficulties that arise; develop and use their own strategies	pp. 26–8, 132–6, 223 *162–3,*	pp. 1–2, 6, 17–18, *20,* 31–2, 60–3, *74,* 103, *105,* 121, 123, *125*	pp. 1, 7–8, 24, 28, 35	R1, R7, R12, R16	*E1, E5, E10, E13, E27*	**Round–ups** 1, *3*	*3–6, 18, 33, 34*	**3–5** *(Earth cargo)* **9–11** *(Souvenirs)* **21** *(Cube puzzle)* **22** *(Triangles puzzle)*
b select, trial and evaluate a variety of possible approaches; identify what further information may be required in order to pursue a particular line of enquiry; break complex problems into a series of tasks	pp. 26–8, 132–6, *162–3*	pp. 3–4, 11, *20,* 31–2, 60–3, *75–6,* 103, 121	pp. 7–8, 24, 35	R1, R12, R16, *R24*	*E1, E2, E5, E10, E13, E27*	**Measure** 2 **Round–up** *2*	*1, 4–6, 8, 10, 12, 18, 22, 30, 32–4*	**1, 2** *(Rockets and meteorites)* **12** *(Cube puzzle)* **22** *(Triangles puzzle)*
c select and organize mathematics and resources; extend their work to related tasks; select, follow and reflect on alternative approaches of their own	pp. 96, 135–6, *160–1*	pp. 11, *20,* 42–3, 62, 63, 123		*R17*	*E5, E8–E9, E21, E25*	**Round–up** 1		**1, 2** *(Rockets and meteorites)*
d review progress while engaging in work, and check and evaluate solutions.	pp. *96,* 116–19, 135–6, *166–7*	pp. 17–18, 40–1, *42–3,* 47, 49, 50, 52, 53, 62, 63, 77, 123, *125*	pp. 7–8, 10, 11, 25, 26, 28, 35	R7, R15, R16, *R17, R18,* R19, *R20, R25*	*E5, E8–E9, E24, E27*	**Round–up** *2*	*3–5, 7, 10, 12–14, 16, 20, 26–30, 32, 34, 35*	
3. Communicating mathematically								
a understand and use mathematical language and notation	pp. 34–6, 64–8, 160–1, 170–1, 175–7, 225, 235, 237–8, 245–8	pp. 11, *23–5,* 75–6, 79–82, 103, 111, 113, 118–20, 121	p. *32*	R10, R24	*E2, E6, E16–E17*	**Handling data** 3, *4*	*8, 9, 11, 15*	**9–11** *(Souvenirs)*
b use mathematical forms of communication, including diagrams, tables, graphs and computer print-outs	pp. 118–19, 230, *232–6,* 239, 241	pp. 53, 108, 109, 110–12, 114, *115–16*	pp. *11, 31, 32,* 33, 34, 35, 36	R32	E14–E15, *E18,* E20, *E22, E23,* E25, *E27,* E28–E29	**Handling data** 1, *2,* 3	*14, 15, 17, 20, 29–31*	**23, 24** *(Bikes)*
c present work clearly using diagrams, graphs and symbols appropriately, to convey meaning	pp. 118–19, *232–4,* 242	pp. 53, 78, *103,* 109, 110–12, 114, *115–17*	pp. 11, 27, *31, 32,* 33, 34, 35	R32	E7, *E18,* E24, *E27*	**Handling data** 1, *2,* 3 **Round–up** *2*	*2, 3, 14, 15, 16, 22, 23, 24, 25, 26, 28, 34*	
d interpret mathematics presented in a variety of forms; evaluate forms of presentation	pp. 183–5, 225, 230, *232–3,* 235, 236, 239	pp. 42–3, 85, 86, 108, 109, 111, *112,* 114, *115–16,* 121	pp. *31, 32,* 34	*R17, R27,* R32	*E4, E8–E9,* E28–E29	**Handling data** 1, *2,* **Round–up** *2*	*17, 18, 21, 30, 31*	**9–11** *(Souvenirs)* **23, 24** *(Bikes)*
e examine critically, improve and justify their choice of mathematical presentation		pp. *115–16*						
4. Developing skills of mathematical reasoning								
a explain and justify how they arrived at a conclusion or solution to a problem	pp. 132–8, 156	pp. 60–62, 74						

NUMBER

Programme of Study								
1. Pupils should be given opportunities to:								
a use calculators and computer software, *eg spreadsheets*		In Heinemann Mathematics children are provided with material in a variety of contexts and formats. Opportunities are provided for them to develop confidence in different aspects of Number work. This includes introducing strategies in mental calculation. Calculators are built in from Heinemann Mathematics 2 onwards and are an increasingly important tool in the later stages of the course. Through using the variety of resources provided within the course children have a wide experience of different recording techniques.						
b develop and use flexibly a range of methods of computation, and apply these to a range								

2. Understanding place value and extending the number system

a	understand and use the concept of place value in whole numbers and decimals, relating this to computation and the metric system of measurement	pp. 26–33, 36–40, 44–9, 78, 79–82, 83–4, 85–7, 90–5, 148–51	pp. 1–5, 7–10, 13–15, 28, 29, 30, 31–2, 33–5, 39–41, 68–70, 72, 73, 123	pp. 1, 4, 6–8, 15	R1, R2, R3–R5, R11, R12, R13–R16, R22, R23	E1, E7	**Number** 1, 3, 7, 10 **Round–up** 1	5, 7, 8	**1, 2** (Rockets and meteorites) **3–5** (Earth cargo) **9–11** (Souvenirs)
b	understand and use decimals, ratios, fractions and percentages, and the interrelationships between them; understand and use negative numbers	pp. 60–3, 69–71, 78, 79–82, 83–4, 85–7, 102–4, 105–11, 125–9	pp. 21, 22, 26, 28, 29, 30, 31–2, 33–5, 45, 46, 48–51, 57, 58, 121, 123, 125	pp. 5, 6, 9, 13, 14, 36	R8, R9, R11, R12, R13, R15, R19, R20	E10, E12, E13*	**Number** 5, 7, 8, 9, 11, 12 **Round–up** 3	8, 11, 12	**6–8** (Fraction strips) **9–11** (Souvenirs) **12, 13** (Matching squares) **14** (Oil-rig Heron)
c	understand and use index notation, leading to standard form				R20				**9–11** (Souvenirs)

3. Understanding and using relationships between numbers and developing methods of computation

a	consolidate knowledge of number facts, including multiplication to 10 x 10, developing use of methods for finding quickly from known facts those that they cannot recall; use some common properties of numbers, including multiples, factors and primes, leading to powers and roots	pp. 26–8, 34, 36–8, 41–3	pp. 1–2, 6–8, 11	pp. 1–3	R1, R3	E2, E3	**Number** 2	3, 6	
b	extend mental methods of computation, to consolidate a range of non-calculator methods of addition and subtraction of whole numbers, and multiplication and division of whole numbers by whole numbers, understanding and using accurately the methods that they choose	pp. 26–33, 36–43, 86–7, 107–8, 130, 139–42	pp. 1–5, 7–11, 35, 59, 64–7	pp. 1, 7–8	R1–R, R13, R16	E11	**Number** 1, 2, 14 **Round–up** 1	1, 4, 6, 7, 17	**3–5** (Earth cargo)
c	calculate with negative numbers, decimals, fractions, percentages and ratio, understanding the effects of operations, eg squaring, multiplying and dividing by numbers between 0 and 1, and selecting an appropriate non-calculator or calculator method	pp. 64–73, 83–4, 85–96, 98, 102–6, 109–11, 125–9	pp. 23–6, 27, 31–2, 33–44, 46–8, 50, 51, 58, 72, 73, 121, 123, 125	pp. 7–9, 13, 14, 36	R10, R12, R13–R18, R20,	E8–E9, E12	**Number** 4, 6, 9, 11, 12 **Round–ups** 1, 2, 3	10, 12, 13, 31	**1, 2** (Rockets and Meteorites)
d	understand when and how to use fractions and percentages to make proportional comparisons	pp. 60–3	pp. 22, 49		R9, R19		**Round–up** 1		**1, 2** (Rockets and Meteorites) **6–8** (Fraction strips)
e	understand and use the facilities of a calculator, including the use of the constant function, memory and brackets, to plan a calculation and evaluate expressions	pp. 46–54, 71–3, 96, 105–6	pp. 15–20, 27, 42–3, 48, 51, 125	p. 4	R6, R7, R17	E5	**Number** 10 **Round–up** 2	10	
f	mentally estimate and approximate solutions to numerical calculations, leading to multiplication and division with numbers of any size rounded to one significant figure	pp. 31–3, 92–5	pp. 5, 40–3	pp. 7–8	R2, R15–R17		**Number** 1, 10	5	**3–5** (Earth cargo)

4. Solving numerical problems

a	develop an understanding of the four operations and the relationship between them, and apply them to solving problems, including those that involve ratios, proportions and compound measures, using metric or common Imperial units where appropriate	pp. 46–54, 69–73, 96, 180–5,	pp. 3–4, 15–20, 26, 27, 42–3, 83–6, 123	pp. 4, 7–8	R6, R7, R16, R17, R27	E5	**Number** 4 **Measure** 3 **Round–up** 3		

Heinemann Mathematics P7: Comparison Chart for National Curriculum (England and Wales) Programme of Study for Key Stage 3 *(cont.)*

*Key: plain typeface for Level 4; italics for Level 4 to 5 or Level 5; * denotes Level 5 to 6 or Level 6.*

	Programme of Study	Teacher's Notes	Textbook	Workbook	Reinforcement Sheets	Extension Textbook	Assessment	Problem Solving Activities	Resource Cards
NUMBER	**b** select suitable sequences of operations and methods of computation, including trial-and-improvement methods, to solve problems involving integers, decimals, fractions, ratios and percentages, *eg using a spreadsheet to consider sets of numbers that have a given sum and find the set that has the maximum product*	pp. *46–9, 52–4, 71–3*	*pp. 15, 16, 19, 20, 27,* 31–2	p. *4*	*R6,* R12	*E5,* E8, *E9,* E13*	**Number** *4* **Round–up** *2*		
	c use a variety of checking strategies and apply them appropriately to calculations; use estimation and inverse operations, and confirm that results are of the right order of magnitude	pp. *50–1, 92–6*	pp. *17–18, 40–3*	pp. *7–8*	*R7, R15–R17*		**Number** *4, 10*		
	d give solutions in the context of the problem, selecting an appropriate degree of accuracy, interpreting the display on a calculator, and recognizing limitations on the accuracy of data and measurements	pp. *98,* 140–2	pp. 31–2, *42–4,* 65–7		R12, *R17*				
ALGEBRA	**1. Pupils should be given opportunities to:** **a** explore a variety of situations that lead to the expression of relationships								
	b consider how relationships between number operations underpin the techniques for manipulating algebraic expressions								
	c consider how algebra can be used to model real-life situations and solve problems								
	2. Understanding and using functional relationships **a** appreciate the use of letters to represent variables	pp. *160–1*	pp. *75–6, 123*		*R24*				
	b explore number patterns arising from a variety of situations, using computers where appropriate; interpret, generalize and use simple relationships, and generate rules for number sequences; express simple functions initially in words and then symbolically, representing them in graphical or tabular form	pp. 34, 116–19, *119–23*	pp. 6, 52, 53, *54–6, 123*	pp. 10, 11, *12*	*R21*	*E3, E10, E14–E15* E16–E17, *E27*	**Number** 13 **Round–up** *3*	*9, 14, 15*	
	c interpret graphs that describe real-life situations								
	d explore the properties of standard mathematical functions, including linear and square, reciprocal and other polynomial functions; make and interpret tables and graphs of functions, sketch their graphs, and use graphical calculators and computers to								

3. Understanding and using equations and formulae

Ref	Description								
a	appreciate the use of letters to represent unknowns	pp. 152–3, 170–1	pp. 71, 79–80					9	
b	construct, interpret and evaluate formulae and expressions, given in words or symbols, related to mathematics or other subjects, or real-life situations, using computers and calculators where appropriate	pp. 118–19, 119–23, 160–7, 170–1	pp. 53, 54–6, 75–7, 123	pp. 11, 12, 24, 25, 26	R21, R24, R25	E14–E15	**Number** 13 **Measure** 1 **Round–up** 3		
c	manipulate algebraic expressions; form and manipulate equations or inequalities in order to solve problems								
d	solve a range of linear equations, simple linear simultaneous equations, inequalities, and quadratic and higher-order polynomial equations, selecting the most appropriate method for the problem concerned, including trial-and-improvement methods								

1. Pupils should be given opportunities to:

Ref	Description								
a	use a variety of different representations								
b	explore shape and space through drawing and practical work using a wide range of materials								
c	use computers to generate and transform graphic images and to solve problems								

> As for all the sections of the Programme of Study, support for a practical teaching approach can be found in the Teacher's Notes. For each maths topic within Measure and Shape there are opportunities for children to gain valuable hands-on experience within a meaningful context.

2. Understanding and using properties of shape

Ref	Description								
a	visualize, describe and represent shapes, including 2D representations of 3D objects, using geometrical language with increasing precision	pp. 214–15, 218–219, 225, 242	pp. 99, 100, 101, 102, 103, 104, 117	p. 22	R31		**Round–ups** 2, 3	14	
b	construct 2D and 3D shapes from given information; understand the congruence of simple shapes, and classify triangles, quadrilaterals, polygons and other shapes, knowing and using their properties	pp. 214–15 218–21, 224, 242	pp. 97, 99, 100, 101, 102, 103, 104, 106, 117	pp. 20, 22	R31	E26	**Measure** 2* **Shape** 3 **Round–up** 3	24	**21** (Cube puzzle)
c	understand the symmetry properties of 2D and 3D shapes and use these to solve problems in 2 and 3 dimensions	pp. 209–10, 218–21	pp. 97, 101, 102	pp. 17, 20, 22	R31	E30	**Shape** 3 **Round–up** 3	25, 26	**21** (Cube puzzle)
d	measure angles, and use the language associated with them; explain and use the angle properties of polygons and other 2D configurations, including those associated with parallel and intersecting lines	pp. 200–6, 218–21	pp. 92–6, 101, 102, 121	pp. 22, 29–30	R30, R31	E22, E26	**Shape** 1, 2 **Round–up** 1	28	**18** (360° protractors) **19, 20** (Bearings game)
e	understand and use Pythagoras' theorem								
f	understand the trigonometrical relationships in right-angled triangles, and use these to solve problems including those involving bearings								

3. Understanding and using properties of position, movement and transformation

Ref	Description								
a	use co-ordinate systems to specify location, initially using rectangular Cartesian co-ordinates in the first quadrant		p. 105			E16–E17			

Heinemann Mathematics P7: Comparison Chart for National Curriculum (England and Wales) Programme of Study for Key Stage 3 *(cont.)*

*Key: plain typeface for Level 4; italics for Level 4 to 5 or Level 5; * denotes Level 5 to 6 or Level 6.*

SHAPE, SPACE AND MEASURES

Programme of Study	Teacher's Notes	Textbook	Workbook	Reinforcement Sheets	Extension Textbook	Assessment	Problem Solving Activities	Resource Cards
b recognize and visualize the transformations of translation, reflection, rotation and enlargement, and their combination in two dimensions; understand the notations used to describe them	pp. *212, 223*	*p. 98*	pp. *18, 20*		E24, E30	**Shape** *3*		
c understand and use the properties of transformations to create and analyse patterns, to investigate the properties of shapes, and to derive results, including congruence	pp. *212, 218–19, 242*	pp. *98, 101, 102, 117*	pp. *18, 20, 22*	*R31*	E24	**Round–up** *2*		
d develop an understanding of scale, including using and interpreting maps and drawings, and enlarging shapes by different scale factors; develop an understanding of and use mathematical similarity	pp. *149–51*	pp. *69, 70, 96*	*p. 15*	*R23*	*E16–E17, E22*	**Measure** *1, 2* **Round–up** *1*	*18*, 28*	
e determine the locus of an object moving according to a given rule, including, where appropriate, using practical methods and the devising of instructions for a computer to produce desired shapes and paths					*E23*		*27*	
4. Understanding and using measures **a** choose appropriate instruments and standard units of length, mass, capacity and time, and make sensible estimates in everyday situations, extending to less familiar contexts; develop an understanding of the relationship between units, converting one metric unit to another; know Imperial units in daily use and their approximate metric equivalents	pp. *148–51, 155–6, 172–3, 175–7, 190–8*	pp. *68–70, 72–4, 81–2, 87–91, 121, 123*	pp. *15, 16, 28*	R22, R23, R28, R29	*E1, E19–E21*	**Number** *7* **Measure** *1, 4* **Round–ups** *1, 3*	*17, 21*	**15** *(Eurotravel rally)* **16, 17** *(Space creatures)*
b develop an understanding of the difference between discrete and continuous measures; read and interpret scales, including decimal scales, and understand the degree of accuracy that is possible, or appropriate, for a given purpose	pp. 172–3		p. 28		*E19*	**Number** *7*		
c understand and use compound measures, including speed and density	pp. *182–5*	pp. *85, 86, 123*		*R27*	*E20**	**Measure** *3* **Round–up** *3**		
d find perimeters, areas and volumes of common shapes, including circles and cylinders, by counting and dissection methods, progressing to the derivation and use of standard formulae; distinguish between formulae by considering dimensions, *eg recognize that $\frac{4}{3}\pi r^2$ cannot represent the volume of a sphere*	pp. *152–3, 160–7*, 170–1*, 225**	pp. *71, 75–80*, 121*	pp. *24–7**			**Measure** *1, 2** **Round–up** *2**	*15, 18*, 22*	

HANDLING DATA

1. Pupils should be given opportunities to:

a formulate questions that can be considered using statistical methods

b undertake purposeful enquiries based on data analysis

c use computers as a source of large samples, a tool for exploring graphical representations, and a means to simulate events

d engage in practical and experimental work in order to appreciate some of the principles which govern random events

As for all the sections of the Programme of Study, support for a practical teaching approach can be found in the Teacher's Notes. There are opportunities for children to gain valuable hands-on experience of gathering, interpreting and presenting data within a context that is relevant to them. Advice is also given in the Teacher's Notes for using software packages currently available.

	Strand	Statement of Attainment	Teacher's Notes	Textbook	Workbook
INFORMATION HANDLING	**PROBLEM SOLVING AND ENQUIRY**		pp. 132–6, 166–7, 184–5, 251, 252, 253	pp. 3–4, 6, 11, 12, 20, 31–2, 42–3, 47, 49, 50, 60–3, 74, 77, 78, 85, 86, 103, 107, 109, 121–5	pp. 7–8, 25–8, 35, 36
	COLLECT	By selecting sources of information for tasks including a questionnaire which allows several responses to each question	p. 230	p. 108	
	ORGANIZE	By using diagrams or tables	pp. 230, *239*	pp. 108, *114*	p. *34*
	DISPLAY	By using a database or spreadsheet table with up to 3 fields defined by pupils			
		By constructing graphs (bar, line, frequency polygon) and pie charts involving simple fractions or decimals	pp. 232–4	pp. 109–11, 114–16	pp. 31, 32, *33*, 34
		By constructing graphs (bar, line, frequency polygon) and pie charts involving continuous data which has been grouped			p. 33
	INTERPRET	From a range of displays and databases by retrieving information subject to one condition	pp. 230, 232–6, 239	pp. 108–12, 114–16, 125	pp. 31–4
NUMBER, MONEY AND MEASUREMENT	**RANGE AND TYPE OF NUMBERS**	Work with whole numbers up to 100 000 (count, order, read/write)			
		Work with whole numbers up to a million (read/write only)	pp. 44, 46 *(further work)*	pp. 13, 14	
		Work with fractions (all previous plus twentieths, fiftieths, hundredths) and equivalences among these and decimals (in applications)	p. 78	p. 28	
		Percentages, decimals to 2 places and equivalences among these in applications in money and measurement	pp. 78, 102–6, 136, 252	pp. 28, 45–8, 123, 124	p. 9
	MONEY	Use all UK coins/notes to £20 worth or more, including exchange			
	ADD AND SUBTRACT	Add and subtract mentally for 2-digit whole numbers, beyond in some cases, involving multiples of 10 or 100	pp. 26–8, 31–3, 92–6	pp. 1–2, 5, 40–3	pp. 1, 7–8
		Add and subtract, without a calculator, for 4 digits with at most 2 decimal places (easy examples only)	pp. 29–30, 83–4	pp. 3–4, 31–2	
		Add and subtract, with a calculator, for 4 digits with at most 2 decimal places	pp. 50–1, 92–6, 252	pp. 40–3, 72, 73, 121–5	pp. 7–8
	MULTIPLY AND DIVIDE	Multiply and divide mentally for whole numbers by single digits (easy examples only)	pp. 34, 36–40, 92–6, 130	pp. 7–8, 40–3, 59	pp. 2, 3, 7–8
		Multiply and divide mentally for 4-digit numbers including decimals by 10 or 100	pp. 86–7, 90–1	pp. 35, 39	
		Multiply and divide, without a calculator, for 4 digits with at most 2 decimal places by a whole digit	pp. 41–3, 85–6, 88–90	pp. 11, 12, 33, 34, 36–8	
		Multiply and divide, with a calculator, for 4 digits with at most 2 decimal places by a whole number with 2 digits	pp. 46–9, 52–4, 92–6, 180–5, 252	pp. 15, 16, 19, 20, 40–3, 72, 73, 83, 84, 121, 123–5	pp. 4, 7–8
	ROUND NUMBERS	Round any number to the nearest appropriate whole number, 10 or 100	pp. 31–3, 36–8, 46–9, 92–5, 98, 182–5, 252	pp. 5, 7–8, 15, 16, 40–4, 84–6, 122	pp. 4, 7–8
	FRACTIONS, PERCENTAGES AND RATIO	Find simple fractions (1/7, 3/4, 3/5, 60/100) of quantities involving at most 4 digits (easy examples only)	pp. 107–8, 252	pp. 27, 49, 122	
	PATTERNS AND SEQUENCES	Continue and describe more complex sequences	pp. 34, 116–17	p. 52	p. 10
	FUNCTIONS AND EQUATIONS	Recognize and explain simple relationships between two sets of numbers or objects	pp. 118–23	pp. 53–6, 123,	pp. 11, 12
	MEASURE AND ESTIMATE	Measure in standard units length: small lengths in millimetres; large lengths like buildings in metres	pp. 148–53, 251–2	pp. 68–7, 121–2	p. 15
		Measure in standard units weight: extended range of articles, for example own weight		pp. 72, 74	
		Measure in standard units volume: accuracy extended to small containers in millilitres; 1l = 1000 ml	pp. *160–3*, 172–3	pp. *75–6*	pp. *24*, 28

Reinforcement Sheets	Extension Textbook	Assessment	Problem Solving Activities	Resource Cards
R16–R20, R25	E1, E2, E4–E10, E13, E16–E19, E21, E23–E25, E27–E29	**Measure** 2 **Shape** 3 **Round-ups** 1–3	All	**21** (Cube puzzle) **22** (Triangles puzzle)
R32				
R32		**Handling data** 1, 2 **Round-up** 1	31	
	E20, E28–E29	**Handling data** 1, 2 **Round-up** 1		
	E7		5	**3–5** (Earth cargo)
	E1	*Further work* in **Number** 3 and **Round-up** 1		
			11, 12	
R18		**Number** 11 **Round-up** 3		**12, 13** (Matching squares)
R1, R2, R15–R17		**Number** 1, 10	1, 4, 7, 17	**1, 2** (Rockets and meteorites)
		Number 8 **Round-up** 2	13	
R15–R17	E8–E9	**Number** 10 **Round-up** 2	31	
R3, R15–R17		**Number** 1, 10		
R13, R14		**Number** 9		
		Number 9 **Round-ups** 1, 2 *Further work* in **Number** 14		
R6, R15–R17	E8–E9	**Number** 4, 10 **Measure** 3		
				Round-ups 1, 2
R2, R3, R6, R15–R17		**Number** 1, 4, 10 **Measure** 3 **Round-up** 3	5	**3–5** (Earth cargo) **9–11** (Souvenirs)
R19	E12		12	
	E14, E15, E27	**Number** 13	14	
R21	E14–E17	**Number** 13 **Round-up** 3	9	
R22, R23		**Measure** 1 **Round-up** 1		
				16, 17 (Space creatures)
			15	**16, 17** (Space creatures)

Strand		Statement of Attainment	Teacher's Notes	Textbook	Workbook
NUMBER, MONEY AND MEASUREMENT	**MEASURE AND ESTIMATE**	Measure in standards units area: right-angled triangles on cm squared grids	pp. 163–7	p. 77	pp. 25, 26
		Measure in standard units temperature			
		Estimate small weights, small areas, small volumes in easily handled standard units		p. 74	
		Recognize when kilometres are appropriate			
		Select appropriate measuring devices and units for weight		p. 74	
		Be aware of common Imperial units in appropriate practical applications	pp. 175–7	pp. 81–2	
	TIME	Use 24-hour times and equate with 12-hour times	pp. 192–8, 252	pp. 89–91, 121, 123	p.16
		Calculate duration in hours/minutes, mentally if possible	pp. 190–1, 193–8, 252	pp. 87–91, 121	p.16
		Time activities in seconds with a stopwatch	pp. 183–5	pp. 85, 86	
		Calculate speeds (practical activities only)	pp. 183–5	pp. 85, 86	
	PERIMETER, FORMULAE, SCALES	Calculate perimeter of simple straight-sided shapes by adding lengths	pp. 152–3, 252	pp. 71, 121	
SHAPE, POSITION AND MOVEMENT	**RANGE OF SHAPES**	Discuss 3D and 2D shapes referring to faces, edges, vertices, diagonals, sides, angles	pp. 214–15, 220–1 *Further work* on p. 223	pp. 99, 100, 103, 104, *Further work* on p. 105	
		Recognize pentagon, hexagon	pp. 214–15	pp. 17, 99, 100	
		Identify and name equilateral and isosceles triangles	pp. 209–10		p. 17
		Extend shape vocabulary to radius, diameter, circumference		p. 106	
		Create or copy a tiling using a shape template	p. 212, 242	pp. 98, 117	pp. 18, 20
		Make 3D models, solid or skeletal, including using nets: cube and cuboid only			
		Use the rigidity property of triangles in model making		p. 103	
	POSITION AND MOVEMENT	Give directions for a route or journey			
		Use an 8-point compass rose	pp. 205–6	p. 94	
		Use a co-ordinate system to locate a point on a grid		p. 105	
		Create patterns by rotating a shape			
	SYMMETRY	Identify and draw lines of symmetry, generally up to 4	pp. 209–10, 218–21, 252	pp. 101, 102, 122	pp. 17, 22
		Create symmetrical shapes			
	ANGLE	Draw, copy and measure angles accurately within 5 degrees	pp. 200–2, 252	pp. 92, 96, 121	pp. 29–30
		Use standard notation, 060°, 150°, 300°, to express bearings	pp. 205–6, 252	pp. 94, 96, 121	

Reinforcement Sheets	Extension Textbook	Assessment	Problem Solving Activities	Resource Cards
R25				
				16, 17 (Space creatures)
		Round-up 1		
			17	
	E20			
R29	E21	**Measure** 4 **Round-up** 3		**15** (Eurotravel rally)
R28, R29	E21	**Measure** 4 **Round-up** 3		**15** (Eurotravel rally)
	E1	**Measure** 3		
	E20	**Measure** 3 **Round-up** 3	*21*	
		Round-ups 2, 3	24	
		Shape 3	24	
	E26			
	E24			
		Round-up 2		
		Shape 3		
				19, 20 (Bearings game)
	E16–E17	**Shape** 3		
	E23, E24			
R31	E30	**Shape** 3 **Round-up** 3	25, 26	
	E30			
R30	E26	**Shape** 1, 2 **Round-up** 1	27, 28	**18** (360° protractors)
	E22	**Shape** 2	28	**19, 20** (Bearings game)

Strand	Statement of Attainment	Teacher's Notes	Textbook	Workbook
INFORMATION HANDLING				
COLLECT	By selecting sources of information for tasks, including practical experiments.			
	By selecting sources of information for tasks, including surveys using questionnaires.		pp. 115–16	
	By selecting sources of information for tasks, including sampling using a simple strategy.			
ORGANIZE	By designing and using diagrams and tables.		pp. 115–16	
	By designing and using a database or spreadsheet with fields defined by pupils.	p. 241		
DISPLAY	By constructing straight line and curved graphs for continuous data where there is a relationship such as direct proportion – travel, temperature, growth graphs.			
	By constructing pie charts of data expressed in percentages.			
INTERPRET	From an extended range of displays (diagrams, tables, graphs, pie charts) and databases, retrieving information subject to more than one condition.	p. 241		p. 36
	By describing the main features of a graph so as to show an awareness of the significance of the information.	pp. 232–4	p. 110	pp. 31, 36
	By calculating the average (mean) to compare sets of data.	pp. 237–8, 252	pp. 113, 115–16, 123	
NUMBER, MONEY AND MEASUREMENT				
RANGE AND TYPE OF NUMBERS	Work with negative numbers (eg temperature).	pp. 125–9	pp. 57, 58	pp. 13, 14, 36
	Work with all widely used fractions and equivalence among these and decimals (in applications).	pp. 60–3, 79–82	pp. 21, 22, 29, 30	pp. 5, 6
	Work with decimals to 3 places (practical applications in measurement).	pp. 79–82	pp. 29, 30	p. 6
MONEY	Use relationships between currencies to do simple calculations.			
ADD AND SUBTRACT	Add and subtract mentally for 2-digit numbers including decimals.	p. 130	pp. 59	
	Add and subtract without a calculator for 4 digits with at most 2 decimal places.			
	Add and subtract with a calculator for any number of digits with at most 3 decimal places.	pp. 79–82	pp. 17–18, 30	
	Add and subtract positive and negative numbers in applications such as rise in temperature.	pp. 128–9	p. 58	p. 14
MULTIPLY AND DIVIDE	Multiply and divide mentally for any whole number by a multiple of 10 or 100 (such as 20 or 200).	pp. 36–40	pp. 7–10	
	Multiply and divide mentally for any numbers including decimals by 10, 100, 1000.	pp. 36–40, 86–7, 90–1	pp. 7–10, 35, 39	
	Multiply and divide without a calculator for 4 digits with at most 2 decimal places by a single digit.	pp. 50–1, 89–90 *Further work* on pp. 139–43	pp. 17–18, 36–8 *Further work* on pp. 64–6	
	Multiply and divide with a calculator for any pair of numbers but at most 3 decimal places in the answer.	p. 98	p. 44	
ROUND NUMBERS	Round any number to one decimal place.			
FRACTIONS, PERCENTAGES AND RATIO	Find widely used fractions and percentages of whole number quantities.	pp. 102–4, 252 *Further work* on pp. 64–73	pp. 46, 121 *Further work* on p. 23–7	pp. 9, 36
	With a calculator find a fraction or percentage of a quantity.	pp. 71–3, 105–6, 109–11, 252	pp. 48, 50, 51, 122, 124	
	Without a calculator as previously defined.	pp. 104–5, 107–8, 252	pp. 47, 49, 124	p. 36
	Find ratios between quantities.	pp. 180–5	pp. 83, 84	
	Use simple unitary ratio.			

Reinforcement Sheets	Extension Textbook	Assessment	Problem Solving Activities	Resource Cards
			29	**23, 24** (Bikes)
		Round–up 2		
		Round–up 3		
		Round–up 3		**14** (Oil-rig *Heron*)
R8, R9, R11	E10, E13	**Number** 5, 12		**6–8** (Fraction strips) **12, 13** (Matching squares)
R11		**Number** 7		**9–11** (Souvenirs)
	E11			
			8	
R7, R11		**Number** 4		
		Round–up 3		
R3, R4	E1	**Number** 2		
R3, R4, R13, R14		**Number** 2		**9–11** (Souvenirs)
R7				**9–11** (Souvenirs)
	E5		6, 8	**9–11** (Souvenirs)
		Number 11 **Round–up** 3	10, 31	
R20	E12, E13	**Number** 12 *Further work* in **Number** 6		
R18, R19		**Number** 11 **Round–up** 3 *Further work* in **Number** 6		

	Strand	Statement of Attainment	Teacher's Notes	Textbook	Workbook
NUMBER, MONEY AND MEASUREMENT	**PATTERNS AND SEQUENCES**	Continue and describe sequences involving square and triangular numbers.	pp. 35, 36	p. 6	
		Find specified items in sequences.	pp. 116-17	p. 52	p. 10
		Prime numbers.			
	FUNCTIONS AND EQUATIONS	Use a 'function machine' in reverse for inverse operations.			
		Solve simple equations and inequations.			
		Use notation to describe general relationship between 2 sets of numbers.			
		Use and devise simple rules.	pp. 118-23	pp. 53-6	pp. 11, 12
	MEASURE AND ESTIMATE	Measure and draw using standard units.			
		Estimate areas in square metres.	p. 252	pp. 78, 122	p. 27
		Estimate small lengths in millimetres.			
		Estimate larger lengths in metres.	p. 251	pp. 122, 124	
		Work with square kilometre, hectare, tonne when appropriate.	pp. 155-6, 251	pp. 73, 74, 78, 121	p. 27
		Read scales on measuring devices, including estimating between graduations.			
		Realize that volume can be conserved when shape changes.			
	TIME	Time activities with a digital stopwatch in seconds, tenths, hundredths.			
	PERIMETER, FORMULAE, SCALES	Calculate, using rules, areas of rectangles and squares.	pp. 160-7, 252	pp. 75-7, 121, 124	pp. 24-6
		Calculate, using rules, volumes of cuboids and cubes.	pp. 170-1, 252	pp. 74-80, 123, 124	
		Use scales such as 1 cm to 1, 2, 5 or 10 m, or represented by a ratio such as 1 : 100, to interpret or draw maps, plans, diagrams; or to make models.	pp. 149-51, 251, 252	pp. 69, 70, 96, 121, 124	p. 15
SHAPE, POSITION AND MOVEMENT	**RANGE OF SHAPES**	Discuss the side, angle, diagonal properties of quadrilaterals: square, rectangle, rhombus, parallelogram, kite, trapezium.	pp. 218-19, 225	pp. 101, 102, 104, 107	p. 22
		Define and classify quadrilaterals.			
		Relate diameter and circumference (practical work only).	p. 225		
		Make 3D models, solid or skeletal, including using nets: triangular prism, pyramid, tetrahedron.	pp. 214-15	pp. 99, 100	
		Draw triangles given 3 sides, 2 sides and included angle, 2 angles and one side.			
		Draw triangles to scale in applications involving heights and distances.			
	POSITION AND MOVEMENT	Use bearings and distances to produce accurate scale drawings of routes.			
		Use co-ordinates in all four quadrants to plot position.			
		Calculate distances along grid lines.			
	SYMMETRY	Determine whether or not shapes have rotational symmetry.	pp. 209-10, 252	pp. 97, 122	pp. 17, 20
		Move a tile of a shape on a squared grid in order to translate, reflect or rotate the shape.	p. 242	p. 117	
	ANGLE	Use 'reflex' to describe angles.	pp. 200-1	p. 92	pp. 29-30
		Use the fact that vertically opposite angles are equal.			
		Use the properties of angles formed by a line crossing parallel lines.			
		Know the sum of the angles of a triangle is two right angles.			

Chart for Mathematics 5–14, Level E *(Cont.)*

Reinforcement Sheets	Extension Textbook	Assessment	Problem Solving Activities	Resource Cards
	E2	**Number** 13	3	
	E14-E15		14	
	E3			
		Number 13 **Round-up** 3	9	
R21	E14-E15		15	
		Measure 2 **Round-up** 1		**16, 17** (Space creatures)
	E19			
	E19			
R25	E16-E17	**Measure** 2 **Round-up** 2	18, 22	
	E22	**Round-up** 2	22	
	E23	**Measure** 1 **Shape** 2 **Round-up** 1 *Further work* in **Round-up** 1	18, 28	
R31		**Shape** 3		
				21 (Cube puzzle)
	E26			
	E30		26	
	E30	**Round-up** 2		
R30		**Shape** 1 **Round-up** 1		
	E26			

Heinemann Mathematics P7: Comparison Chart for Common Curriculum (NI) Programme of Study for Key Stage 2

*Key: plain typeface for Level 4; italics denotes Level 4–5 and Level 5; * denotes Level 5–6 and Level 6.*

PROCESSES IN MATHEMATICS

Programme of Study	Teacher's Notes	Textbook	Workbook	Reinforcement Sheets	Extension Textbook	Assessment	Problem Solving Activities	Resource Cards
Using mathematics								
The entire course is designed to enable children to use mathematical equipment and materials, to work systematically, and to develop strategies for solving problems. Some examples are referenced below.								
Pupils should have opportunities to:								
a appreciate the special characteristics of the materials and equipment they handle and so take increasing responsibility for selecting and using the materials and equipment required for their work	pp. *160–3, 248*	pp. *20, 77, 78, 104, 120*	pp. *25, 27, 28*	*R25*	*E4, E19, E24,* E25, *E26, E30*	**Measure** *2*	*28*	**21** (Cube puzzle) **22** (Triangles puzzle)
b select and use the mathematics appropriate to the current work, for example, *counting squares to find the shape with the greatest area*	pp. *160–3, 183–4, 230*	pp. 3–4, *20,* 31–2, *42–3, 47, 49, 50, 63, 77, 78, 84, 86, 115–16, 125*	pp. 7–8, *25, 27, 28, 36*	R12, *R16–R20, R25, R27*	*E1, E4, E6,* E7, *E8–E9, E14–E19, E24,* E25, *E26, E28–E30*	**Measure** *2*	*6, 10, 15, 17, 18,* 19, *21, 22, 28, 29, 33*	**3–5** *(Earth cargo)* **9–11** (Souvenirs) **22** (Triangles puzzle)
c gather information for an activity, initially with help from the teacher; progress to identifying and obtaining the information needed to carry out their work, for example, *measure the dimensions of the classroom in order to draw a simple scale plan*	pp. *132–3, 230, 232–3, 245–8*	pp. *42–3, 78, 101–2, 110, 115–16, 118–20, 125*	pp. *22, 27, 31, 35*	*R17, R31*	*E1, E4, E19, E21, E22*	**Handling Data** *1, 2,* 4	7, 9, *10,* 17, *18, 21, 22, 28–30, 32, 33, 35*	**23, 24** *(Bikes)*
d plan and organize their work, learning to work systematically, for example, *draw all the possible arrangements of six squares in order to find which ones are nets of a cube*	pp. *35, 132–5, 230, 232–3, 248*	pp. 3–4, *6,* 12, 31–2, 60, *62–3, 78, 115–16, 120*	pp. *7–8, 27, 35*	R12, *R16*	*E1, E6,* E7, E14–E15, *E18, E23, E24,* E25, *E27–E30*	**Round-ups** 1, *2, 3*	1–5, 6, *7, 8, 10–15,* 16, 17, *18,* 19, 20, *21, 22,* 23, *24,* 25, *26–35*	**21** (Cube puzzle)
e try different mathematical approaches to problems and look for ways to overcome difficulties	pp. *35,132–5*	pp. *6,* 12, *60, 62, 63*	pp. *7–8, 35*	*R16*	*E1, E22, E23, E27, E30*	**Round-ups** 1, *2, 3,*	1, 5, 6, *7, 8, 10, 12–14,* 16, 23, 25, *26–30, 32–5*	**21** (Cube puzzle)
f develop their own mathematical strategies for solving problems, initially through discussion with the teacher, for example, *use trial and improvement methods; work backwards; make organized lists; simplify the task; look for patterns;* review progress, making changes where necessary	pp. *35,132–5, 248*	pp. 3–4, *6,* 12, 31–2, 60, *62, 63, 101–2, 120*	pp. 7–8, 22, 35	R12, *R16, R31*	*E1,* E7, *E13–15, E19, E23, E27–E30*	**Round-ups** 1, *2, 3,*	1–3, 5, 6, *7, 8, 10–15,* 16, *17,* 19, 20, *21, 22,* 23, *24,* 25, *26–35*	**21** (Cube puzzle)
Communicating mathematically								
Pupils should have opportunities to:								
a understand and use the language of: – number; – shape; – measures; – simple probability; – relationships, for example, *'multiple of', 'factor of'* and *'parallel to'*	pp. 34, *36, 245–7*	pp. *101–3, 105*	p. *22*	*R31*	*E2, E16–E17, E24, E26, E30*			
b interpret situations mathematically using appropriate symbols or diagrams, for example, *% (percentage), > (greater than), < (less than)*								
c discuss their work; compare their ideas and methods with others, for example, *when finding ways to measure the capacity of your lungs or the thickness of a magazine; when investigating the number of children crossing the road to school in order to establish the need for a crossing patrol*	pp. *132–3,*	pp. *62, 74, 103,*				*32*		

d record results, initially in given format; choose the most appropriate format and use it to present information and results clearly; explain the reasons for their choice of presentation	pp. 132–3, 230, 232–3, 245–8	pp. 60, 62, 63, 78, 103, 104, 115–16, 118–20	p. 27, 31		E21, E23, E24, E25, E27		9, 12, 19, 20, 24, 25, 30, 32, 35	
Mathematical reasoning								
Pupils should have opportunities to:								
a recognize general patterns and relationships and make predictions about them	pp. 35, 116–19, 119–21	pp. 6, 52, 53	pp. 10, 11		E3, E14–E17, E26, E27		9, 14, 15	
b ask and respond to open-ended questions; follow alternative suggestions		p. 107		R31	E16–E17	**Handling data** 4		
c explain their thinking	pp. 230, 245–8	pp. 78, 118–21, 124	p. 27		E16–E17, E20, E22	**Handling data** 4	6, 15, 32	
d understand general statements and investigate whether particular cases match them, for example; *odd number + even number = odd number; the taller people are, the more they 'weigh'*	p. 35	p. 6			E3			
e make a general statement based on evidence, for example, *from a road safety survey, most pupils are injured on the road between 3.00 and 4.00 in the afternoon; all triangles will tessellate*	pp. 35, 230, 236, 245–7	pp. 6, 104, 110, 112, 113			E3, E16–E17			
f check their results and consider whether they are reasonable, for example, *using inverse operations and estimating to find the approximate answer*		pp. 17–18, 42–3	pp. 7–8	R16, R17		**Number** 4		
Understanding number and number notation								
Pupils should have opportunities to:								
a read, write and order whole numbers, initially to 100 and progressing to using any whole number, understanding that the position of a digit signifies its value; use their understanding of place value to develop computational methods		pp. 13–14		R5	E1	**Number** 3 **Round-up** 1	5, 7	**6–8** (Fraction strips)
b extend understanding of place value to include decimals, initially to 1 decimal place and then up to 2 decimal places; use this to multiply and divide numbers by 10, 100 and 1000	pp. 36–8, 39–40, 78, 79–82*, 90–1	pp. 9–10, 28, 29, 35, 39	p. 6	R4, R13, R14		**Number** 2, 7*		**6–8** (Fraction strips)
c estimate within calculations, initially with numbers within 100 and extending to all whole numbers, approximate numbers to the nearest 10 or 100; estimate and approximate to gain a feeling for the size of a solution to a problem, for example, *understand that 32 x 9 is approximately 30 x 10*	pp. 31–3, 46–51, 92–5	pp. 5, 7–8, 15, 17–18, 40–1, 121	p. 3, 4, 7–8	R2, R3, R7, R15, R16		**Number** 1, 4, 10, 12*		**3–5** (Earth cargo)
d understand and use, in context, vulgar fractions, decimal fractions and percentages; understand the equivalence of simple fractions; explore the relationships between fractions and percentages, for example, *understand that half price is the same as 50% off*	pp. 60–5, 67–72, 79–82*, 102–3, 104–11	pp. 21–3, 25, 27, 29, 30, 45, 46–51, 110, 111, 122, 123, 124	pp. 5, 6, 9, 32, 36	R8–R11, R18–R20	E8–E10, E12, E13	**Number** 5, 6, 11, 12 **Handling data** 1, 2	10–12, 31	**6–8** (Fraction strips) **12–13** (Matching squares) **Round-ups** 1, 3

*Key: plain typeface for Level 4; italics denotes Level 4–5 and Level 5; * denotes Level 5–6 and Level 6.*

NUMBER

Programme of Study	Teacher's Notes	Textbook	Workbook	Reinforcement Sheets	Extension Textbook	Assessment	Problem Solving Activities	Resource Cards
Patterns, relationships and sequences								
Pupils should have opportunities to:								
a explore and predict patterns and sequences of whole numbers initially within 100 and extending to larger numbers, including counting in different sizes of step, doubling and halving numbers, finding multiplication patterns in the hundred square, predicting subsequent numbers in a sequence; follow simple sets of instructions to generate a sequence; devise rules for determining sequences	pp. 116–17	pp. 52, 123	pp. 10, 11		*E3, E7, E14–E15, E27*	**Number** 13		
b understand and use multiples and factors and terms, including prime, square and cube; appreciate that multiplication and division are inverse operations	pp. 34, *36, 96*	pp. 15, *42–3*	pp. 2–4	*R17*	*E2, E3*	**Number** *2, 10*	*3*	
c interpret, generalize and use simple relationships expressed in numerical, spatial and practical situations, for example, *finding equivalent forms of 2-digit numbers; understanding square and triangular numbers;* understand and use simple function machines	pp. 35, *118–19, 119–21*	pp. 54–6, *123*	pp. 6, 11, *12*	*R21*	*E2, E3, E6, E14–E17, E27*	**Number** *2, 13* **Round-up** *3*	*9, 14, 15*	
d understand that a letter can stand for an unknown number, for example, 6 + a = 24		pp. *54–5*		*R21*	*E14–E15*	**Number** *13* **Round-up** *3*	*9*	
Operations and their application								
Pupils should have opportunities to:								
a consolidate knowledge of addition and subtraction facts to 20; understand and use this knowledge to calculate quickly facts that they cannot recall; add mentally two 2-digit numbers up to 100 and subtract mentally one 2-digit number from another; know the multiplication facts to 10 x 10; use these facts when solving problems	pp. 26–30	pp. 1–4	pp. 1–3	R1	E11	**Number** *1, 2*	1, 4, 17	**1, 2** (Rockets and meteorites)
b engage in a range of activities to develop understanding of the four operations of number and their interrelationships; appreciate the use of brackets; develop a range of non-calculator methods of computation to include addition and subtraction with up to 2 decimal places and multiplication and division of decimals by whole numbers; use these operations to solve problems, using a calculator where necessary	pp. 41, *42–3, 46–54, 62–3, 69–71, 83–4, 85–6, 88–90, 92–6, 107–8, 139–40, 140–3, 182–4*	pp. *9–12, 15–20, 22, 23, 27, 30, 31–2, 33, 34, 37–8, 40–3, 47–9, 64–7, 72–4, 81–4, 86, 121, 122, 123, 124, 125*	pp. 4, *7–8, 35,* 36	*R6, R7, R9, R11, R12, R15–19, R27*	*E1, E4, E5, E8–E10, E11, E12, E28–E29*	**Number** *4, 8, 9, 10, 11, 14* **Measure** *3* **Round-ups** *1, 2, 3*	6, 8, 10, 13, 18, 22, 31	**3–5** (Earth Cargo) **6–8** (Fraction strips)
Money								
Pupils should have opportunities to:								
a understand and use the conventional way of recording money; use the four operations to solve problems			p. 35		E28–E29	**Round-up** *2*		
b estimate and approximate to gain a feeling for the size of a solution to a problem before carrying out a calculation			pp. 7–8	R16		**Number** 10		
c interpret a calculator display in relation to money								

	Pupils should have opportunities to:								
a	develop skills in estimation of length, 'weight', volume/capacity, time, area and temperature through practical activities, using metric units where appropriate		p. 74			E8–E9, E11, E22	Round-up 1		
b	develop the language associated with a wider range of metric units and be confident with the terms metre, gram and litre, and their relevant prefixes of kilo, centi, milli					E11			
c	appreciate important ideas about measurement; including the continuous nature of measurement and the need for appropriate accuracy					E4	Round-up 1		
d	choose and use appropriate metric units and measuring instruments in a variety of situations, interpreting numbers on a range of measuring instruments, for example, measure the perimeter of the playground to the nearest metre using a trundle wheel	pp. 148–9, 172–3	pp. 68, 74, 121		R22	E1, E4, E19	Measure 1 Round-up 1	28	
e	understand the relationship between units, for example, know that kilograms and grams are used to weigh food; convert from one metric unit to another, for example, know that 175 centimetres is 1.75 metres; use the four operations to solve problems, working with up to 3 decimal places, where appropriate	pp. 148–9, 172–3	pp. 39, 68, 69, 72, 73, 121	p.28	R14, R22	E1, E4, E19	Number 7 Measure 1 Round-ups 1, 3	22	16, 17 (Space creatures)
f	know the Imperial units still in common use, including foot, yard, mile, pound and pint	pp. 175–7	pp. 81–2						
g	understand and use negative numbers in context, for example, know that if the temperature rises during the day from –3°C to 4°C, the temperature has risen by 7 degrees	pp. 125–9	pp. 57–8	pp. 13, 14, 36			Round-up 3		14 (Oil-rig Heron)
h	understand the concept of perimeter and calculate the perimeter of simple shapes; find areas by counting squares and volumes by counting cubes; calculate areas and volumes of simple shapes in two and three dimensions	pp. 160–6, 170–3,	pp. 71, 75–80, 107, 121–4	pp. 24, 25, 27, 28	R24, R25	E16–E17, E19, E22	Measure 2 Round-up 2*	15, 18, 22	
i	understand and use scale in the context of simple maps and drawings, for example, draw a simple plan of the classroom and know that a 1 centimetre square represents 1 square metre; calculate the actual distance as the crow flies between two places on a map using the scale of 1 cm to 1 km	pp. 143–5	pp. 69, 70, 78, 96, 124	p. 27		E22	Shape 2 Round-up 1	18, 28	
j	know the units of measurement in time and the relationship between them	pp. 182–4, 190–4	pp. 83, 84, 86, 87, 88, 91	p.16	R27, R29	E1, E21	Measure 4 Round-up 3		15 (Eurotravel rally)
k	recognize time on the analogue clock, including the hour, half and quarter hours, five-minute intervals and one-minute intervals; understand the relationship between the 12 and 24-hour clocks, including am and pm; read analogue and digital displays and understand the relationship between them; use timetables involving the 24-hour clock and perform simple calculations related to the timetables	pp. 190–1, 193–8	pp. 87–91, 121	p.16	R28, R29	E20, E21	Measure 4 Round-up 3		15 (Eurotravel rally)
l	know the months of the year; explore calendar patterns		p.122						

Heinemann Mathematics P7: Comparison Chart for Common Curriculum (NI) Programme of Study for Key Stage 2 *(Cont.)*

*Key: plain typeface for Level 4; italics denotes Level 4–5 and Level 5; * denotes Level 5–6 and Level 6.*

SHAPE AND SPACE

Programme of Study	Teacher's Notes	Textbook	Workbook	Reinforcement Sheets	Extension Textbook	Assessment	Problem Solving Activities	Resource Cards
Exploration of shape								
Pupils should have opportunities to:								
a use materials, for example, *geoboards, construction sets and paper* to construct and handle a wide range of regular and irregular 2D shapes; classify these through examination of angles and sides; look for line and rotational symmetries in practical situations; reflect shapes, for example, *by using a mirror;* use shapes to explore and create tessellations; name and describe common 2D shapes, including squares, rectangles, circles, triangles, hexagons and pentagons; begin to understand the meaning of congruence in 2D shapes	pp. *209–10, 212, 218–21, 223*	pp. *97, 98, 101–7, 117, 122*	pp. *17, 18, 20, 22*		*E18, E24, E30*	**Shape** *3* **Round-ups** 2*, 3	24, 25, *26*	**22** (Triangles puzzle)
b use materials, for example, *blocks, construction sets and cereal packets* to construct various 3D shapes; investigate the number of faces, edges and vertices on these shapes; name and describe common 3D shapes, including cubes, cuboids, cones, cylinders, spheres, triangular prisms and pyramids; use nets to explore the relationship between 2D and 3D shapes	pp. *214–15*	pp. *99–100*				**Round-up** 2		**21** *(Cube puzzle)*
c recognize geometrical properties and use these to solve problems	*see p. 225 for work at SEd/6)*	p. *107*				**Round-up** 3		
Position, movement and direction								
Pupils should have opportunities to:								
a investigate practically, 1/4 turns, 1/2 turns and whole turns to understand the notion of angle in the context of turning; find right angles in 2D and 3D shapes in the environment; understand clockwise and anticlockwise; know the 8 points of the compass; use a programmable device, for example, *a Roamer,* to extend understanding of movement and turning	pp. 205–6	p. 94			*E22*	**Shape** 2		***19, 20*** *(Bearings game)*
b develop the language associated with line and angle including vertical, horizontal, perpendicular, parallel, acute, obtuse and reflex	pp. 200–2, *203–4,* 223	pp. 92, *105*	pp. 29–30	R30	E22*	**Shape** 1, 3 **Round-up** 1		
c recongnize properties of acute, obtuse and reflex angles, for example, *know that an acute angle is less than a right angle and that a reflex angle is greater than two right angles*	pp. 200–2, *203–4*	pp. 92, *93, 107*	pp. 29–30	R30		**Shape** 1, 3* **Round-up** 1		
d investigate angles in triangles, including scalene, right angle, equilateral and isosceles, and quadrilaterals, including square, rectangle, rhombus, kite, parallelogram, trapezium; measure and draw angles to the nearest degree up to 360° with reasonable accuracy	pp. *200–2, 218–19*	pp. *92, 93, 95*	pp. *29–30*	R30	*E26*	**Shape** *1, 2* **Round-up** *1*	*28*	**18** *(360° protractor)*
e use co-ordinates to plot points and draw shapes in the first quadrant	p. 223	pp. 56, *105*	p. 12		*E16–E17*	**Shape** 3		
f be introduced to a programming language, for example, *LOGO,* and use it to create pictures and patterns and to generate mathematical shapes					*E23*		*27*	

Collect, represent and interpret data

Pupils should have opportunities to:

a use data drawn from a range of meaningful situations, for example, *situations arising in other subjects*								
b collect, classify, record, represent and interpret discrete numerical data, using graphs, tables and diagrams, including Venn, Decision tree and Carroll diagrams, pictograms, block graphs, bar charts, bar-line graphs and line graphs with the axis starting at zero (initially with given intervals); explain their work orally or through writing and draw conclusions	*pp. 230, 232–3, 236, 239*	*pp. 110, 112, 114, 125*	*pp. 31, 33, 34, 36*	R32		**Handling data** *1, 3* **Round-up** *1*		**23, 24** *(Bikes)*
c interpret tables and lists used in everyday life, for example, *those found in a catalogue or road safety accident report*; interpret a wide range of graphs and diagrams, including a pie chart; create and interpret frequency tables, including those for grouped discrete data, for example, *birthdays*; use tallying methods, including the 5-bar gate	*pp. 230, 232–3, 235, 239, 114, 125*	*pp. 110, 111, 33, 34*	*pp. 31, 32,*	R32	E12, *E28–E29* **Round-ups** *1, 2*	**Handling data** *1–3*	*29–31*	
d design an observation sheet and use it to record a set of data leading to a frequency table; collate and analyse the results; progress to designing and using a data collection sheet, interpreting the results		pp. 115–16						
e enter information in a database and using at least 2 criteria; use an appropriate interrogate it, computer package to produce a variety of graphical representations of data	*pp. 230, 241*	*pp. 108, 115–16*			E20, *E28–E29*			**23, 24** *(Bikes)*
f understand, calculate and use the mean and range of a set of discrete data, for example, *calculating the mean score of two teams that have played different numbers of games in order to compare their performance*	*pp. 230, 232–3, 237–8*	*pp. 113, 115–16*	p.33		*E14–E15*	**Handling data** *3* **Round-up** *3*	*9*	

Introduction to probability

Pupils should have opportunities to:

a become familiar with and use the language of probability, including certain, uncertain, likely, unlikely, impossible and fair, by participating in games and other practical activities;								
b understand possible outcomes of simple random events, for example, *that buttered toast will fall with either the buttered side up or the buttered side down*; understand that there is a degree of uncertainty about the outcome of some events, while others are certain or impossible, for example, *it is certain to get dark tonight; impossible for a person to turn into a fish; uncertain whether or not it will rain tomorrow*								
c place events in order of 'likelihood'; understand and use the idea of 'fifty-fifty' or 'evens', and know whether events are more or less likely than this, for example, *know that if a die is thrown there is an equal chance of an odd or even number but the chance of getting a 5 is less than an even chance*	*pp. 245–8*	*pp. 118–20*				**Handling data** *4*		

Checklist of materials needed in HMP7

analogue clockfaces		
bathroom scales		
box of paper clips		
calculators		
card/sticky tape/scissors		
centimetre-squared paper		
cocktail sticks or tooth picks		
colouring pens/pencils		
computer database and spreadsheet packages		
construction kits (e.g., 'Clixi')		
counters		
cylinders, such as kitchen roll centres, washing up liquid bottles, etc		
dice/coins (for probability work)		
graph paper		
kitchen scales		
large sheets of paper (newspaper size)		
long metric tape		
metre stick or tape		
number cards		
paper, card or plastic shapes		
plastic strips and fastener		
protractors (360°)		
ream of paper in a packet		
ruler or tape showing feet and inches		
rulers showing cm and mm		
stopwatch or wristwatch for timing in seconds		
string and metal nut or key (for use as a pendulum)		
tins of food showing weight in grams		
tracing paper		

Index